OXFORD
UNIVERSITY PRESS

Oxford University Press, Inc., publishes works that
further Oxford University's objective of excellence
in research, scholarship, and education.

Oxford   New York
Auckland   Cape Town   Dar es Salaam   Hong Kong   Karachi
Kuala Lumpur   Madrid   Melbourne   Mexico City   Nairobi
New Delhi   Shanghai   Taipei   Toronto

With offices in
Argentina   Austria   Brazil   Chile   Czech Republic   France   Greece
Guatemala   Hungary   Italy   Japan   Poland   Portugal   Singapore
South Korea   Switzerland   Thailand   Turkey   Ukraine   Vietnam

Copyright © 2003 by Oxford University Press, Inc.

First published by Oxford University Press, Inc., 2003
198 Madison Avenue, New York, New York 10016
www.oup.com

First issued as an Oxford University Press paperback, 2005
ISBN-13: 978-0-19-518249-1

The Library of Congress has catalogued the cloth edition as follows:
Ehrman, Bart D.
   Lost Christianities : the battles for scripture and
the faiths we never knew / Bart D. Ehrman
      p. cm.   Includes bibliographical references and index.
   ISBN-13: 978-0-19-514183-2
1. Apocryphal books (New Testament)—Criticism, interpretation, etc.
2. Heresies, Christian—History—Early church, ca. 30–600.
3. Church history—Primitive and early church, ca. 30–600.
I. Title.
BS2840.E4 2003   229'.9206—dc21   2003053097

Illustration credits
Pages 25: Caire (Le), Insitut français d'archéologie orientale. 34: Erich Lessing/Art Resource,
NY. 43: Scala/Art Resource, NY. 50: Rylands Library, University of Manchester. 62: Institute
for Antiquity and Christianity, Claremont, CA. 75: SuperStock, Inc. 125: Institute for Antiquity
and Christianity, Claremont, CA. 166: Courtesy of Robert M. Grant. 208: Cameraphoto/Art
Resource, NY. 218: Photo courtesy of Bruce Metzger: Manuscripts of the Greek Bible, Oxford
University Press. 245: British Library, London.

3

Printed in Canada

Lost Christianities

LOST CHRISTIANI

THE BATTLES FOR SCRIPTURE A
THE FAITHS WE NEVER KNEY

Bart D. Ehrman

OXFORD
UNIVERSITY PRESS

To Sarah

Contents

Preface

This is a book about the wide diversity of early Christianity and its sacred texts. Some of these texts came to be included in the New Testament. Others came to be rejected, attacked, suppressed, and destroyed. My goals are to examine some of these noncanonical writings, see what they can tell us about the various forms of Christian faith and practice in the second and third centuries, and consider how one early Christian group established itself as dominant in the religion, determining for ages to come what Christians would believe, practice, and read as sacred Scripture.

Unless otherwise indicated, translations of texts are my own.

I would like to thank a number of people who have provided their generous support, without whom the book could not have been written. First is Bruce Nichols, who suggested the book and helped me refine its character at the preliminary stages. Robert Miller, senior executive editor at Oxford University Press, and Laura Brown, president of Oxford University Press, USA, convinced me that Oxford was the best venue for publication; I am grateful for their support all along the way, and especially for the extensive help Robert has given over the years.

In the early stages of my research, I was helped by my reliable and insightful graduate students, Stephanie Cobb, now teaching at Hofstra University, and Diane Wudel, now teaching at Wake Forest Divinity School. An inordinate amount of the research assistantship fell on the shoulders of my current graduate student, Carl Cosaert, who bore the burden with remarkable ease.

I have been given unusually helpful advice by those who read the book in manuscript, Robert Miller and Peter Ginna at Oxford University Press, and scholars and friends who went well above and beyond the call of collegial duty in lending a hand to another scholar in the field: Elizabeth Clark at Duke, Michael

Holmes at Bethel College, Andrew Jacobs at the University of California Riverside, Dale Martin at Yale, and Elaine Pagels at Princeton. The world would be a happier place if all authors had such careful, knowledgeable, interested, and generous friends and readers.

Finally I would like to thank my wife, Sarah Beckwith, a medievalist in the Department of English at Duke, whose scintillating intelligence, uncanny intellectual range, and broad generosity make her not only a dialogue partner extraordinaire but also a woman I plan to be around the rest of my life. I have dedicated the book to her.

Major Christian Apocrypha Discussed

Date and Contents

(Arranged alphabetically, by genre)

GOSPELS

Title	Probable Date	Content
Epistle of the Apostles	Mid 2nd c.	Anti-Gnostic dialogue between Jesus and the disciples after the resurrection, emphasizing the reality of the flesh and of Jesus' own fleshly resurrection
Gospel according to the Hebrews	Early 2nd c.	A Gospel recording events of Jesus' life, possibly embodying Gnostic ideas, used by Jewish-Christians in Egypt
Gospel of the Ebionites	Early 2nd c.	A Gospel used by Jewish-Christian Ebionites, embodying their antisacrificial concerns; possibly a conflation of canonical accounts
Gospel of the Egyptians	Early 2nd c.	A Gospel in which the woman Salome figures prominently, used by non-Jewish Christians in Egypt and stressing ascetic ideals
Gospel of Mary	2nd c.	Dialogue of Mary Magdalene with the apostles in which she reveals a vision granted to her conveying Jesus' secret teachings
Gospel of the Nazareans	Early 2nd c.	An Aramaic version of Matthew's Gospel, possibly lacking the first two chapters, used by Jewish Christians
Gospel of Nicodemus	5th c.	Legendary account of Jesus' trial before Pilate, his crucifixion, and descent into Hades (may incorporate a later form of the Acts of Pilate)
Gospel of Peter	Early 2nd c.	Fragmentary narrative of Jesus' trial, death, and resurrection, with an account of Jesus' emergence from the tomb; probably the Gospel proscribed by the second-century bishop Serapion
Gospel of Philip	3rd c.	Collection of disparate Gnostic mystical reflections recorded by his disciple Philip; discovered at Nag Hammadi
Gospel of the Savior	Late 2nd c.	Fragmentary Coptic Gospel recounting Jesus' last hours, including his prayer before his arrest and a final address to the cross

GOSPELS (*continued*)

Title	Probable Date	Content
(Coptic) Gospel of Thomas	Early 2nd c.	Collection of 114 sayings of Jesus, some possibly authentic, others embodying Gnostic concerns; discovered at Nag Hammadi
(Infancy) Gospel of Thomas	Early 2nd c.	Entertaining account of the miraculous deeds of Jesus between the ages of five and twelve
Gospel of Truth	Mid 2nd c.	Gnostic celebration of the joys of salvation brought by Christ's revelation of true knowledge; discovered at Nag Hammadi
Papyrus Egerton 2	Early 2nd c.	Fragmentary account from an otherwise unknown Gospel of four episodes from the life of Jesus, three with parallels in the New Testament Gospels
Proto-Gospel of James	Mid 2nd c.	Influential narrative of the birth, young life, and betrothal of Mary, the mother of Jesus, and of Jesus' own miraculous birth
Secret Gospel of Mark	58? 1758? 1958?	Discovered by Morton Smith in 1958, allegedly a longer version of Mark's Gospel written for the spiritually elite, with possible homoerotic overtones

ACTS

Title	Probable Date	Content
Acts of John	Late 2nd c.	An episodic account of the missionary activities and miraculous deeds of Jesus' disciple John the son of Zebedee, missionary to Ephesus
Acts of Paul	End 2nd c.	A composite text of the missionary activities and miraculous deeds of the apostle Paul, which includes the Acts of Thecla and 3 Corinthians
Acts of Peter	End 2nd c.	An account of the missionary activities of the apostle Peter, especially his miraculous overpowering of his heretical adversary, Simon Magus
Acts of Pilate	Mid 2nd c.	Account of Jesus' trial, which exonerates Pilate for his involvement and shows Jesus' superiority to the pagan gods
Acts of Thecla	End 2nd c.	An account of the conversion, persecutions, and miraculous escapes of Paul's most famous female convert

ACTS (continued)

Title	Probable Date	Content
Acts of Thomas	3rd c.	An account of the missionary activities and miraculous deeds of Jesus' brother Thomas, missionary to India

EPISTLES AND RELATED LITERATURE

Title	Probable Date	Content
1 Clement	ca. 96	Sent from the Christians of Rome to the Christians of Corinth to urge the restoration of unity by reinstating their deposed presbyters
2 Clement	Mid 2nd c.	Proto-orthodox Christian homily celebrating the salvation provided by God, based on an interpretation of Isa. 54:1
3 Corinthians	Late 2nd c.	Written by "Paul" to the Corinthians to counter the claims of two Gnostic teachers and emphasize proto-orthodox doctrines of God, creation, and the flesh
Correspondence of Paul and Seneca	4th c.	Fourteen letters between Paul and the Roman philosopher Seneca, forged to show Paul's high standing in philosophical circles of his day
The Didache	ca. 100	Proto-orthodox church manual that discusses Christian ethics (the "two-paths"), rituals such as baptism and Eucharist, and community life
Epistle of Barnabas	ca. 135	Proto-orthodox letter allegedly by Paul's companion Barnabas, which argues that the Judaism is a false religion and the Old Testmant is a Christian book
Letter to the Laodiceans	Late 2nd c.	Containing a pastiche of Pauline phrases, evidently inspired by a reference in Col. 4:16 to a letter to the Laodiceans, possibly made to counter a Marcionite forgery
Letter of Peter to James and its Reception	Early 3rd c.	Letter allegedly by Peter urging the acceptance of the Jewish Law as essential for salvation, and attacking his "enemy" (apparently Paul); includes the positive reply of James, Jesus' brother

EPISTLES AND RELATED LITERATURE

(continued)

Title	Probable Date	Content
Letter of Ptolemy to Flora	Mid 2nd c.	Letter by the famous Gnostic Ptolemy to a proto-orthodox enquirer, in which he details a distinctively Gnostic understanding of the Old Testament
The Preaching of Peter	Early 2nd c.	Known only from quotations by later authors, a defense ("apology") for Christian belief against pagan attacks
Pseudo-Clementine Literature	3rd c.	A set of *Homilies* and biographical acounts (*Recognitions*) about and allegedly by Clement of Rome that describe his journeys and association with Peter and that embrace a Jewish-Christian, anti-Pauline perspective
Pseudo-Titus	5th c.	Letter allegedly written by Paul's companion Titus which argues for a strictly ascetic life and opposes all forms of sexual activity
Treatise on the Resurrection	Late 2nd c.	In the form of a letter to a proto-orthodox Christian, Rheginus, a Gnostic explanation of death and the spiritual resurrection

APOCALYPSES AND RELATED LITERATURE

Title	Probable Date	Content
Apocalypse of Paul	4th c.	A description of Paul's ascent into heaven, where he is shown the fate of individual souls; based in part on the Apocalypse of Peter
Apocalypse of Peter	Mid 2nd c	A proto-orthodox vision of the abodes of the blessed and the damned, narrated by the apostle Peter
(Coptic) Apocalypse of Peter	3rd c.	A Gnostic revelation given to Peter, which shows the error of the proto-orthodox belief that salvation comes through the real physical death of Jesus
First Thought in Three Forms	Late 2nd c.	Gnostic mythological document in which the "First Thought," the first emanation from the true God, describes her three descents to the world to reveal saving knowledge to humans

APOCALYPSES AND
RELATED LITERATURE
(continued)

Title	Probable Date	Content
Hymn of the Pearl	Late 2nd c.	Tale of a youth from the East who is sent to rescue a great pearl from a dragon in Egypt; sometimes taken as a figurative Gnostic depiction of the descent of the soul into the world of matter
Origin of the World	3rd c.	A detailed description of a Gnostic myth explaining how the divine realm, the material world, and humans came into existence, based on an interpretation of early chapters of Genesis
Second Treatise of the Great Seth	3rd c.	A Gnostic revelation that gives a docetic interpretation of Christ's death, in explicit opposition to proto-orthodox views
Secret Book of John	Mid 2nd c.	Nag Hammadi treatise that provides a full Gnostic myth of creation and redemption, showing how the divine realm, the material world, and humans came into existence
Shepherd of Hermas	Mid 2nd c.	Proto-orthodox book that records visions given to the author, Hermas, as interpreted by angelic figures, including one in the form of a shepherd

Lost Christianities

Introduction:
Recouping Our Losses

It may be difficult to imagine a religious phenomenon more diverse than modern-day Christianity. There are Roman Catholic missionaries in developing countries who devote themselves to voluntary poverty for the sake of others, and evangelical televangelists who run twelve-step programs to ensure financial success. There are New England Presbyterians and Appalachian snake handlers. There are Greek Orthodox priests committed to the liturgical service of God, replete with set prayers, incantations, and incense, and fundamentalist preachers who view high-church liturgy as a demonic invention. There are liberal Methodist political activists intent on transforming society, and Pentecostals who think that society will soon come to a crashing halt with the return of Jesus. And there are the followers of David Koresh—still today—who think the world has already started to end, beginning with the events at Waco, a fulfillment of prophecies from Revelation. Many of these Christian groups, of course, refuse to consider other such groups Christian.

All this diversity of belief and practice, and the intolerance that occasionally results, makes it difficult to know whether we should think of Christianity as one thing or lots of things, whether we should speak of Christianity or Christianities.

What could be more diverse than this variegated phenomenon, Christianity in the modern world? In fact, there may be an answer: Christianity in the ancient world. As historians have come to realize, during the first three Christian centuries, the practices and beliefs found among people who called themselves Christian were so varied that the differences between Roman Catholics, Primitive Baptists, and Seventh-Day Adventists pale by comparison.

Most of these ancient forms of Christianity are unknown to people in the world today, since they eventually came to be reformed or stamped out. As a result, the sacred texts that some ancient Christians used to support their religious perspectives came to be proscribed, destroyed, or forgotten—in one way or another lost. Many of these texts claimed to be written by Jesus' closest followers. Opponents of these texts claimed they had been forged.

This book is about these texts and the lost forms of Christianity they tried to authorize.

The Varieties of Ancient Christianity

The wide diversity of early Christianity may be seen above all in the theological beliefs embraced by people who understood themselves to be followers of Jesus. In the second and third centuries there were, of course, Christians who believed in one God. But there were others who insisted that there were two. Some said there were thirty. Others claimed there were 365.

In the second and third centuries there were Christians who believed that God had created the world. But others believed that this world had been created by a subordinate, ignorant divinity. (Why *else* would the world be filled with such misery and hardship?) Yet other Christians thought it was worse than that, that this world was a cosmic mistake created by a malevolent divinity as a place of imprisonment, to trap humans and subject them to pain and suffering.

In the second and third centuries there were Christians who believed that the Jewish Scripture (the Christian "Old Testament") was inspired by the one true God. Others believed it was inspired by the God of the Jews, who was not the one true God. Others believed it was inspired by an evil deity. Others believed it was not inspired.

In the second and third centuries there were Christians who believed that Jesus was both divine and human, God and man. There were other Christians who argued that he was completely divine and not human at all. (For them, divinity and humanity were incommensurate entities: God can no more be a man than a man can be a rock.) There were others who insisted that Jesus was a full flesh-and-blood human, adopted by God to be his son but not himself divine. There were yet other Christians who claimed that Jesus Christ was two things: a full flesh-and-blood human, Jesus, and a fully divine being, Christ, who had temporarily inhabited Jesus' body during his ministry and left him prior to his death, inspiring his teachings and miracles but avoiding the suffering in its aftermath.

In the second and third centuries there were Christians who believed that Jesus' death brought about the salvation of the world. There were other Christians who thought that Jesus' death had nothing to do with the salvation of the world. There were yet other Christians who said that Jesus never died.

How could some of these views even be considered Christian? Or to put the question differently, how could people who considered themselves Christian hold such views? Why did they not consult their Scriptures to see that there were not 365 gods, or that the true God had created the world, or that Jesus had died? Why didn't they just read the New Testament?

It is because there was no New Testament. To be sure, the books that were eventually collected into the New Testament had been written by the second century. But they had not yet been gathered into a widely recognized and authoritative canon of Scripture.[1] And there were other books written as well, with equally impressive pedigrees—other Gospels, Acts, Epistles, and Apocalypses claiming to be written by the earthly apostles of Jesus.

The Lost Scriptures

The Gospels that came to be included in the New Testament were all written anonymously; only at a later time were they called by the names of their reputed authors, Matthew, Mark, Luke, and John. But at about the time these names were being associated with the Gospels, other Gospel books were becoming available, sacred texts that were read and revered by different Christian groups throughout the world: a Gospel, for example, claiming to be written by Jesus' closest disciple, Simon Peter; another by his apostle Philip; a Gospel allegedly written by Jesus' female disciple Mary Magdalene; another by his own twin brother, Didymus Judas Thomas.[2]

Someone decided that four of these early Gospels, and no others, should be accepted as part of the canon—the collection of sacred books of Scripture. But how did they make their decisions? When? How can we be sure they were right? And whatever happened to the other books?

When the New Testament was finally gathered together, it included Acts, an account of the activities of the disciples after Jesus' death. But there were other Acts written in the early years of the church: the Acts of Peter and of John, the Acts of Paul, the Acts of Paul's female companion Thecla, and others. Why were these not included as parts of Scripture?

Our New Testament today contains a number of epistles, that is, letters written by Christian leaders to other Christians, thirteen of them allegedly by Paul. Scholars debate whether Paul actually wrote all of these letters. And there are other letters *not* in the New Testament that also claim to be written by Paul, for example, several letters sent by "Paul" to the Roman philosopher Seneca, and a letter written to the church of Laodicea, and Paul's *Third* Corinthians (the New Testament has First and Second Corinthians). Moreover, there were letters written in the names of other apostles as well, including one allegedly written by Simon Peter to Jesus' brother James, and another by Paul's companion Barnabas. Why were these excluded?

The New Testament concludes with an apocalypse, a revelation concerning the end of the world in a cataclysmic act of God, written by someone named John and brought into the New Testament only after Christian leaders became convinced that the author was none other than John the son of Zebedee, Jesus' own disciple (even though the author never claims to be *that* John). But why were other apocalypses not admitted into the canon, such as the apocalypse allegedly written by Simon Peter, in which he is given a guided tour of heaven and hell to see the glorious ecstasies of the saints and, described in yet more graphic detail, the horrendous torments of the damned? Or the book popular among Christian readers of the second century, the *Shepherd* of Hermas, which, like the book of Revelation, is filled with apocalyptic visions of a prophet?

We now know that at one time or another, in one place or another, all of these noncanonical books and many others were revered as sacred, inspired, scriptural. Some of them we now have; others we know only by name. Only twenty-seven of the early Christian books were finally included in the canon, copied by scribes through the ages, eventually translated into English, and now on bookshelves in virtually every home in America. Other books came to be rejected, scorned, maligned, attacked, burned, all but forgotten—lost.[3]

Losses and Gains

It may be worth reflecting on what was both lost and gained when these books, and the Christian perspectives they represented, disappeared from sight. One thing that was lost, of course, was the great diversity of the early centuries of Christianity. As I have already pointed out, modern Christianity is not lacking in a diversity of its own, with its wide-ranging theologies, liturgies, practices, interpretations of Scripture, political views, social stands, organizations, institutions, and so on. But virtually all forms of modern Christianity, whether they acknowledge it or not, go back to *one* form of Christianity that emerged as victorious from the conflicts of the second and third centuries. This one form of Christianity decided what was the "correct" Christian perspective; it decided who could exercise authority over Christian belief and practice; and it determined what forms of Christianity would be marginalized, set aside, destroyed. It also decided which books to canonize into Scripture and which books to set aside as "heretical," teaching false ideas.

And then, as a coup de grâce, this victorious party rewrote the history of the controversy, making it appear that there had not been much of a conflict at all, claiming that its own views had always been those of the majority of Christians at all times, back to the time of Jesus and his apostles, that its perspective, in effect, had always been "orthodox" (i.e., the "right belief") and that its opponents in the conflict, with their other scriptural texts, had always represented small splinter groups invested in deceiving people into "heresy" (literally meaning "choice"; a heretic is someone who willfully chooses not to believe the right things).

What Christianity *gained* at the end of these early conflicts was a sense of confidence that it was and always had been "right." It also gained a creed, which is still recited by Christians today, that affirmed the right beliefs, as opposed to the heretical wrong ones. Relatedly, it gained a theology, including a view that Christ is both fully divine and fully human, and a doctrine of the Trinity which maintained that the Godhead consists of three persons—Father, Son, and Holy Spirit—distinct in number but equal in substance. Moreover, it gained a hierarchy of church leaders who could run the church and guarantee its adherence to proper belief and practice. And it gained a canon of Scripture—the New Testament—comprising twenty-seven books that supported these leaders' vision of the church and their understanding of doctrine, ethics, and worship.

These gains are obviously significant and relatively well known. Less familiar are the losses incurred when these particular conflicts came to an end. It is these losses which we will be exploring throughout this book. It is striking that, for centuries, virtually everyone who studied the history of early Christianity simply accepted the version of the early conflicts written by the orthodox victors. This all began to change in a significant way in the nineteenth century as some scholars began to question the "objectivity" of such early Christian writers as the fourth-century orthodox author Eusebius, the so-called Father of Church History, who reproduced for us the earliest account of the conflict. This initial query into Eusebius's accuracy eventually became, in some circles, a virtual onslaught on his character, as twentieth-century scholars began to subject his work to an ideological critique that exposed his biases and their role in his presentation. The reevaluation of Eusebius was prompted, in part, by the discovery of additional ancient books, uncovered both by trained archaeologists looking for them and by bedouin who came across them by chance, other Gospels, for example, that also claimed to be written in the names of apostles.

In this book we will examine these lost books that have now been found, along with other books that were marginalized by the victorious party but have been known by scholars for centuries. We will also consider how the twenty-seven books of the New Testament came to be accepted as canonical Scripture, discussing who made this collection, on what grounds, and when. And we will explore the nature of these early conflicts themselves, to see what was at stake, what the opposing views were, how the parties involved conducted themselves, what strategies they used, and what literature they revered, copied, and collected on the one hand and despised, rejected, and destroyed on the other. Through it all, we will be focusing our attention on the diversity of early Christianity, or rather the diversity of early Christianities, a diversity that came to be lost, only to be rediscovered, in part, in modern times.

The Stakes of the Conflict

Before launching into the investigation, I should perhaps say a word about what is, or at least what was, at stake. Throughout the course of our study I will be asking the question: What if it had been otherwise? What if some other form of Christianity had become dominant, instead of the one that did?[4]

In anticipation of these discussions, I can point out that if some other form of Christianity had won the early struggles for dominance, the familiar doctrines of Christianity might never have become the "standard" belief of millions of people, including the belief that there is only one God, that he is the creator, that Christ his son is both human and divine. The doctrine of the Trinity might never have developed. The creeds still spoken in churches today might never have been devised. The New Testament as a collection of sacred books might never have come into being. Or it might have come into being with an entirely different set of books, including, for example, the Gospel of Thomas instead of the Gospel of Matthew, or the Epistle of Barnabas instead of the Epistle of James, or the Apocalypse of Peter instead of the Apocalypse of John. If some other group had won these struggles, Christians might never have had an Old Testament; if yet a different group had won, Christians might have had *only* the Old Testament (which would not have been called the "Old" Testament, since there would have been no "New" Testament).

Moreover, we will see that as vital as the outcome of these early Christian struggles was for the internal character of the religion, it was even more significant for the effect and impact that this religion had externally, on the history of civilization itself. It is conceivable that if the form of Christianity that established itself as dominant had not done so, Christianity would never have become a major world religion within the Roman Empire. Had that happened, the empire might never have adopted Christianity as its official religion. In that case, Christianity would never have become the dominant religion of the European Middle Ages, down to the Renaissance, the Reformation, and on to today. Had the conflicts been resolved differently, as odd is this may seem, people in the West—we ourselves—might have remained polytheists to this day, worshiping the ancient gods of Greece and Rome. On the other hand, the empire might have converted to a different form of Christianity and the development of Western society and culture might have developed in ways that we cannot imagine.

However one plays such games of imagination, it is clear that the victory of one form of Christianity was a significant event both for the internal workings of the religion and for the history of civilization, especially in the West. But it was also a victory that came with a price. In this study, as I have indicated, we will be exploring both what was gained and what was lost once the conflicts of the early Christian centuries had been resolved.

The Shape of Our Study

For those who like to have a road map for their journey, I can explain how the book has been structured. It contains three major parts. The first, "Forgeries and Discoveries," looks at several intriguing literary texts: (a) a Gospel allegedly written by Jesus' disciple Peter, (b) a legendary account of Thecla, a female companion of the apostle Paul, (c) a Gospel claiming to be written by

Judas Thomas, supposedly Jesus' twin brother, and (d) a longer, but until recently lost, version of the Gospel of Mark.

Although differing from one another in significant ways, these texts all appear to represent forgeries, three of them ancient, one of them (possibly) modern; moreover, they all advocate understandings of Jesus and/or forms of Christianity that were not destined to come into the mainstream. To this extent, they may be taken as representative of a larger number of fabricated accounts known from the early Christian centuries, some recognized as forgeries already in antiquity, others not discovered (or rediscovered) until relatively recent times.

As we will see, it is principally through such literary texts—many of them lost, and only some now found—that we know about alternative forms of Christianity, as there are very few archaeological discoveries (for example, of buildings, coins, or artwork) that can contribute to our knowledge.

After examining these four instances of forgery at some length, we will move to the second part of the book, "Heresies and Orthodoxies," to consider broader social phenomena, based on information drawn from such forgeries and from a wide array of other surviving sources. In particular, we will discuss the widely disparate beliefs of several important Christian groups: the Jewish-Christian Ebionites, the anti-Jewish Marcionites, and a variety of groups called "Gnostic." Standing over and against each of these groups was a form of Christianity that endorsed the beliefs and practices that eventually came to dominate the religion toward the middle of the third century. Since, from the distance of a later perspective, this group (or groups) may be considered the forebears of Christian orthodoxy, we will call them the "proto-orthodox."

This will take us to the third part, "Winners and Losers," where we move beyond the diverse texts, beliefs, and practices of these various groups to consider the conflicts that raged between them, as each of them contended for converts, insisting that its views were right while those of the others were wrong. In particular, we will consider how proto-orthodox Christians engaged in these internecine battles which eventually led to their victory. As we will see, these confrontations were waged largely on literary grounds, as members of the proto-orthodox group produced polemical tractates in opposition to other Christian perspectives, forged sacred texts to provide authorization for their own perspectives (forgeries, that is, claiming to be written by Jesus' own apostles), and collected other early writings into a sacred canon of Scripture to advance their views and counteract the views of others. It is out of these conflicts that the New Testament came into being, a collection of twenty-seven books taken to be sacred, inspired, and authoritative.

The study will conclude then with some thoughts on the significance of the victory of this one form of Christianity over the others, as we reflect on what was achieved and what was sacrificed when so many alternative forms of Christianity and the texts they espoused came to be lost to posterity, only to be found again, in part, in modern times.

Part One

FORGERIES AND DISCOVERIES

Almost all of the "lost" Scriptures of the early Christians were forgeries. On this, scholars of every stripe agree, liberal and conservative, fundamentalist and atheist. The book now known as the Proto-Gospel of James claims to have been written by none other than James, the brother of Jesus (see Mark 6:3; Gal. 1:19). It is an intriguing text in which, among other things, Jesus' mother, Mary, is said to have remained a virgin even after giving birth, as proved by a post-partum inspection by an overly zealous midwife who finds her "intact." But whoever actually wrote the book, it was not James. So, too, with a book now called Pseudo-Titus, allegedly written by the Titus known from the New Testament as a companion of the apostle Paul. It also is an interesting book, arguing page after page against sexual love, even within the confines of marriage, on the grounds that physical intimacy leads to damnation: "Why," it asks, "do you strive against your own salvation to find death in love?" But whoever actually wrote the book, it was not Titus. The same holds true for nearly all of the Gospels, Acts, Epistles, and Apocalypses that came to be excluded from the canon: forgeries in the names of famous apostles and their companions.

That Christians in the early centuries would forge such books should come as no surprise. Scholars have long recognized that even some of the books accepted into the canon are probably forgeries. Christian scholars, of course, have been loathe to call them that and so more commonly refer to them as "pseudonymous" writings. Possibly this is a more antiseptic term. But it does little to solve the problem of a potential deceit, for an author who attempts to pass off his own writing as that of some other well-known person has written a forgery.[1] That is no less true of the book allegedly written to Titus that made it into the New Testament (Paul's Letter to Titus) than of the book allegedly written by Titus that did not (Pseudo-Titus), both claiming to be written by apostles (Paul and Titus), both evidently written by someone else.[2]

9

Forgery, of course, is not the only kind of pseudonymous writing there is. In the modern world, at least, pseudonymity occurs in two forms. On the one hand, there are simple pen names, usually considered innocent enough. When Samuel Clemens wrote *Huckleberry Finn* and signed off as Mark Twain, no one much objected. When Maryann Evans published *Middlemarch* and *Silas Marner* under the name George Eliot, there was no public outrage (although in her case it did raise, at first, a good deal of public curiosity).

On the other hand, there are works written under a false name with the intent to deceive. In 1983 when the Hitler Diaries appeared, the world was fooled for a time. A now (in)famous German forger had done credible work, and for several days even experts and newspaper magnates were fooled into thinking that these were authentic handwritten diaries kept by the Führer himself up to the last days of World War II. The forgery was soon exposed, however, and people were not amused—especially the experts and media moguls who had been duped.[3]

People in the ancient world did not appreciate forgeries any more than people do today. There are numerous discussions of forgery in ancient Greek and Latin sources. In virtually every case the practice is denounced as deceitful and ill-spirited, sometimes even in documents that are themselves forged. An interesting example occurs in a fourth-century Christian text, the so-called *Apostolic Constitutions*, a book giving instructions about Christian belief and practice, written in the names of the twelve disciples. The book warns its readers not to read books that *claim* to be written in the names of the twelve disciples but are not. But why would a forger condemn forgery? Possibly to throw a reader off the scent of his or her own deception.

An interesting parallel case may occur even within the pages of the New Testament. A book written in Paul's name, 2 Thessalonians, warns against a letter, allegedly written by Paul, that had disturbed some of its readers (2:2). In an interesting twist, scholars today are not altogether confident that 2 Thessalonians itself was written by Paul.[4] And so we have a neat irony: Either 2 Thessalonians was written by Paul and someone else was producing forgeries in Paul's name, or 2 Thessalonians itself is a forgery that condemns the production of forgeries in Paul's name. Either way, someone was forging books in Paul's name.

Second Thessalonians aside, scholars are reasonably sure that forgeries have found their way into the New Testament. This does not apply to any of the Gospels, whose authors chose to remain anonymous and only decades later were reputed to be either followers of Jesus (Matthew the tax collector and John the son of Zebedee) or companions of the apostles (Mark the secretary of Peter and Luke the traveling companion of Paul). Nor can the Book of James or the Apocalypse of John be labeled forgeries. The former was written by someone named James, but he does not claim to be Jesus' brother; and the name was quite common among first-century Jews (as many as seven people are called James just in the New Testament). So too the Apocalypse: It was written by someone named John, but nowhere does he claim to be any particular John.

Other books, however, are widely regarded as forged. The author of 2 Peter explicitly claims to be Simon Peter, the disciple of Jesus, who beheld the transfiguration (1:16–18). But critical scholars are virtually unanimous that it was not written by him. So too the Pastoral epistles of 1 and 2 Timothy and Titus: They claim to be written by Paul, but appear to have been written long after his death.[5]

How could forgeries make it into the New Testament? Possibly it is better to reverse the question: Why shouldn't forgeries have made it into the New Testament? Who was collecting the books? When did they do so? And how would *they* have known whether a book that claims to be written by Peter was actually written by Peter or that a book allegedly written by Paul was actually by Paul? So far as we know, none of these letters was included in a canon of sacred texts until decades after they were written, and the New Testament canon as a whole still had not reached final form for another two centuries after that. How would someone hundreds of years later know who had written these books?

The debates over which books to include in the canon were central to the formation of orthodox Christianity. We will observe some of these debates in the following chapters. First, however, I should say a word about terms. As I pointed out, scholars sometimes refer to forged documents as pseudonymous writings, or they use the technical term *pseudepigrapha,* meaning "false writings" but taken to mean "writings written under a false name." This is not an altogether helpful term, however, since it is typically taken to refer only to the *noncanonical* books that claimed, and sometimes received, scriptural standing (e.g., the Gospel of Peter, which we will be exploring in the next chapter). But by rights it should cover some of the New Testament books as well, including the letter of 2 Peter.

And so sometimes these noncanonical books are called *apocrypha.* That term, too, may be a bit misleading, as it technically refers to "secret" writings that have been uncovered (the Greek word literally means "covered over" or "hidden"), and there was nothing particularly secretive about a number of these writings: They were used, and written to be used, in communal settings as authoritative texts. Still, the latter term has taken on a broader sense of "noncanonical document of the same kind as found in the canon (i.e., Gospels, epistles, etc.)." I will use the term *Christian apocrypha* in that sense throughout the discussion.

In the four chapters that follow, we will consider several of these apocryphal texts, forged documents that disclose alternative forms of Christianity that came to be lost. These chapters will serve to set the stage for our broader consideration, in part 2, of the social groups that embodied some of these understandings of the faith. Most of these groups were eventually reformed or repressed, their traces covered over, until scholars in the modern period began to rediscover them and to recognize anew the rich diversity and importance of these lost Christianities.

Chapter One

The Ancient Discovery of a Forgery: Serapion and the Gospel of Peter

Ancient Christians knew of far more Gospels than the four that eventually came to be included in the New Testament. Most of them have been lost to us in all but name. Some are quoted sporadically by early church writers who opposed them. A few have been discovered in modern times.

We can assume, and in many cases we know, that the Christians who read, preserved, and cherished these other Gospels understood them to be sacred texts. The Christians who rejected them argued that they were heretical (promoting false teachings) and, in many instances, forged.

The Christians who won the early conflicts and established their views as dominant by the fourth century not only gave us the creeds that have been handed down from antiquity,[1] they also decided which books would belong to the Scriptures. Once their battles had been won, they succeeded in labeling themselves "orthodox" (i.e., those who hold to the "right beliefs") and marginalized their opponents as "heretics." But what should we call Christians who held the views of the victorious party prior to their ultimate victory? It may be best to call them the forerunners of orthodoxy, the "proto-orthodox."

Proto-orthodox Christians accepted the four Gospels that eventually became part of the New Testament and viewed other Gospels as heretical forgeries. As the famous theologian of the early and mid-third century, Origen of Alexandria, claimed, "The Church has four Gospels, but the heretics have many" (*Homily on Luke 1*).[2] He goes on to list several of the heretical Gospels he himself has read: the Gospel according to the Egyptians, the Gospel according to the Twelve Apostles, the Gospel of Basilides, the Gospel according to Thomas, and the Gospel according to Matthias.

We know almost nothing of the Gospels of the Twelve Apostles and of Basilides, a famous second-century Gnostic heretic.[3] The Gospels of the Egyptians and of Matthias are known only through a few quotations by Origen's older contemporary, Clement of Alexandria. These quotations give a sense of what we lost when these texts disappeared. The Gospel of the Egyptians apparently opposed the notion of procreative sex. In one passage, a female follower of Jesus, Salome, known slightly from the New Testament Gospels (see Mark 16:1), says to Jesus, "Then I have done well in not giving birth," to which Jesus is said to reply, "Eat of every herb, but do not eat of the one that is bitter" (Clement of Alexandria, *Miscellanies* 3.9.66). At an earlier point he is said to have declared, "I have come to undo the works of the female" (*Miscellanies* 3.9.63). The Gospel according to Matthias may have been an even more mystical affair. At one point Clement quotes the intriguing words, "Wonder at the things that are before you, making this the first step to further knowledge" (*Miscellanies* 2.9.45).[4]

The other Gospel that Origen mentions, the Gospel of Thomas, has been discovered in its entirety in modern times and is arguably the single most important Christian archaeological discovery of the twentieth century. It is a fascinating document, the subject of an extensive modern literature; we will look at it at length in a later chapter.[5]

Clement and Origen were not alone in acknowledging the existence of other Gospels and assigning them to heretical forgers. The early fourth-century church father Eusebius also mentions the Gospels of Thomas and Matthias, along with the Gospel according to the Hebrews and the Gospel of Peter (*Church History* 3.25). The last named is of particular interest, because Eusebius gives an extended account of how it was used, questioned, and eventually condemned as heretical by a proto-orthodox leader, to be relegated to the trash heaps of discarded Gospels. But then it turned up again, not in a trash heap but in the tomb of an Egyptian monk, discovered over a hundred years ago.

Eusebius, Serapion,
and the Gospel of Peter

Prior to its discovery, virtually everything we knew about the Gospel of Peter came from Eusebius's account. In his ten-volume *Church History*, Eusebius narrates the history of the Christian Church from the days of Jesus down to his own time, in the early fourth century. This writing is our best source for the history of Christianity after the period of the New Testament to the time of the emperor Constantine, the first Roman emperor to convert to Christianity. The work is filled with anecdotes and, of yet greater use to historians, extensive quotations of earlier Christian writings. In many instances, Eusebius's quotations are our only source of knowledge of Christian texts from the second and third centuries. The account we are particularly interested in here concerns Serapion, a proto-orthodox bishop of the city of Antioch, Syria, one of the hubs of Christian activity in the early centuries, and his encounter with the Gospel of Peter.[6]

Serapion had become bishop in 199 CE. Under his jurisdiction were not just the churches of Antioch but also the Christian communities in the surrounding area, including one in the town of Rhossus. Serapion had made a visit to the Christians of Rhossus, trying, in good proto-orthodox fashion, to correct their misperceptions about the true gospel message. While there he learned that the church in Rhossus used as its sacred text a Gospel allegedly written by Simon Peter. Not knowing the character of the book, but assuming that it must be acceptable if Peter himself had written it, Serapion allowed its use, prior to returning home to Antioch.

But some "informers" came forward to cast doubts on the authenticity of the book, inducing him to read it for himself. When he did so, he realized that this Gospel was susceptible to heretical misconstrual, specifically that some of the passages found in it could be used in support of a docetic Christology.

Docetism was an ancient belief that very early came to be proscribed as heretical by proto-orthodox Christians because it denied the reality of Christ's suffering and death. Two forms of the belief were widely known. According to some docetists, Christ was so completely divine that he could not be human. As God he could not have a material body like the rest of us; as divine he could not actually suffer and die. This, then, was the view that Jesus was not really a flesh-and-blood human but only "appeared" to be so (the Greek word for "appear" or "seem" is *doceo,* hence the terms *docetic/docetism*). For these docetists, Jesus' body was a phantasm.

There were other Christians charged with being docetic who took a slightly different tack. For them, Jesus was a real flesh-and-blood human. But Christ was a separate person, a divine being who, as God, could not experience pain and death. In this view, the divine Christ descended from heaven in the form of a dove at Jesus' baptism and entered into him;[7] the divine Christ then empowered Jesus to perform miracles and deliver spectacular teachings, until the end when, before Jesus died (since the divine cannot die), the Christ left him once more. That is why Jesus cried out, "My God, my God, why have you forsaken me?" (see Mark 15:34). Or as it can be more literally translated, "Why have you left me behind?" For these Christians, God *had* left Jesus behind, by reascending to heaven, leaving the man Jesus to die alone on the cross.[8]

For proto-orthodox Christians, both forms of docetism were strictly off-limits. With regard to the first—Jesus the phantasm—they asked: If Jesus did not have a real body, how could he really die? And if he did not die, how could his death bring salvation? If he did not have real blood, how could he shed his blood for the sins of the world? With regard to the second view—Jesus and Christ as separate beings—they asked: If the divine element in Jesus did not suffer and die, how was his death different from that of any other crucified man? How could his death be redemptive? It might be a miscarriage of justice, perhaps, or a bad end to a good man. But it would be of no real relevance to the plan of God for salvation. And so proto-orthodox Christians denounced both kinds of docetism as heresy and fought them with all their might. It was not just their lives at stake but their eternal lives, the salvation of their souls.

When Serapion read the Gospel of Peter for himself, he realized that it could be used in support of a docetic Christology. And so he wrote a little pamphlet, "The So-Called Gospel of Peter," in which he explained the problems of the text, pointing out that whereas most of the Gospel was theologically acceptable, there were "additions" to the Gospel story that could be used in support of a docetic view. Serapion concluded that because the book was potentially heretical, it must not have been written by Peter—operating on the dubious assumption that if a text disagreed with the truth as he and his fellow proto-orthodox Christians saw it, then it could not possibly be apostolic.

Serapion then penned a letter to the Christians of Rhossus in which he forbade further use of the Gospel and appended his pamphlet detailing the problem passages. Eusebius narrates the tale and quotes the letter. But he does not cite the passages.

That is unfortunate, since now it is impossible to know for certain whether the Gospel of Peter discovered in the nineteenth century is the book condemned by Serapion and known to Eusebius. Most scholars, however, assume that it is, for this book, too, would have been acceptable in the main to proto-orthodox thinkers. Yet there are several passages that could well lend themselves to a docetic construal. And this is a book written in the first person by someone who calls himself Simon Peter.

No one today thinks that Jesus' disciple Peter wrote the book. To that extent, Serapion was right. He had discovered a forgery.

The Discovery of the Gospel of Peter

The text was forgotten for centuries, known only from Eusebius's brief account. That changed dramatically during an archaeological excavation conducted by a French team operating out of Cairo, digging in upper Egypt in the town of Akhmim during the winter season of 1886–87.[9] Under the direction of M. Grébant, the team uncovered the tomb of a monk in the Christian section of the town's cemetery. The tomb could date anywhere from the eighth to the twelfth centuries. What was of greatest significance, however, was not the tomb itself but what was in it, along with the monk. The monk had been buried with a manuscript.

The manuscript probably dates to the seventh or eighth century, and it is reasonable to assume that it was the cherished property of the monk. It is an intriguing document. Sixty-six pages in length, written on parchment, it contains fragmentary remains of several apocryphal texts, not all of them Christian but all of them significant. The first text, on pp. 2–10 (p. 1 contains only the drawing of a cross), is a portion of the Gospel of Peter, about which I will be speaking momentarily. Next, on pp. 13–19, sewn into the book upside down (accidentally, one would suppose), is a fragmentary copy of the Apocalypse of Peter, an intriguing account, now known more fully from an ancient Ethiopic translation, in which Peter is shown the glorious afterlives of the saints and the eternal torments of the sinners. Then there are two passages taken from the Jewish apocryphal book known as 1 Enoch, which is an account, known more fully from other sources, of a revelation supposedly delivered to Enoch, the famous figure from the Hebrew Bible who did not die but was taken alive up to heaven (Gen. 5:21–24). Finally there is a fragmentary text of the Acts of Saint Julian.

This was a remarkable find, not least for its silent and completely unexpected testimony in microcosm of Christian unity and diversity, tolerance and intolerance. Tolerance: Here was a medieval monk buried with proscribed books, an array of texts, both Jewish and Christian, both orthodox and heretical. And yet intolerance: The manuscript contains the Apocalypse of Peter, whose author condemns to the fires of hell everyone who disagrees with his view of how to behave (including women who braid their hair to make themselves attractive, anyone who disobeys their parents, and bankers who lend money out at interest); and the Gospel of Peter, which is intolerant of Jews—who are portrayed as ignominious and responsible for the death of Jesus—and was itself condemned to oblivion by intolerant Christian leaders who objected to its theological views.

The Gospel of Peter

It is regrettable that the manuscript presents only a fragment of the Gospel of Peter. Not that the document in the monk's tomb is itself fragmentary: It is complete. But the first line of the Gospel text begins (after the opening decorative) in midsentence and also ends, prior to two blank pages, in midsentence. Whoever copied this Gospel in the seventh or eighth century, then, had before him only a fragment, which he transcribed into this small anthology along with other fragmentary texts available to him.

The surviving fragment of the Gospel contains an account of Jesus' trial, crucifixion, and resurrection.[10] It is impossible to know whether the book originally contained more than that—whether, for example, it was a "complete" Gospel like those of the New Testament, which begin with either Jesus' baptism (Mark and John) or his birth (Matthew and Luke), and contain accounts of his sayings and deeds, along with a narrative of his passion and resurrection. Scholars typically assume that the Gospel of Peter originally contained more than the passion and resurrection narratives that survive in the Akhmim fragment, that it was a fuller account like the New Testament Gospels—that is, that it contained stories from Jesus' public ministry as well. This is because several tiny fragments of Jesus' sayings have been discovered elsewhere in Egypt which may also have derived from the Gospel. These other fragments contain conversations between Jesus and Peter recorded in the first person—conversations not found in the fragment of the Gospel discovered in the monk's tomb.[11]

In any event, the Gospel fragment as we have it begins with the following words:

> . . . but none of the Jews washed his hands, nor did Herod or any of his judges.
> Since they did not wish to wash, Pilate stood up.

It is a significant beginning for two reasons. It shows that, just before the fragment begins, the Gospel contained an account of Pilate washing his hands—a story found, among our New Testament Gospels, only in Matthew 27:24. Yet it displays a marked difference from the account in Matthew, which says not a word about anyone *refusing* to wash their hands. Thus in the Gospel of Peter, Herod, the "king of the Jews," and his Jewish judges, unlike the Roman governor Pilate, refuse to declare themselves innocent of Jesus' blood. This intimates an important aspect of the rest of the account. For here it is not the Romans who are responsible for Jesus' death. It is the Jews. This fragmentary Gospel is far more virulently anti-Jewish than any of those that made it into the New Testament.

The intimation of an anti-Jewish slant is confirmed in the very next verse:

> Then King Herod ordered the Lord to be taken away and said to them, "Do everything that I ordered you to do to him."

Here it is the Jewish king, not the Roman governor, who orders Jesus' death.

The narrative continues with the request of Joseph (of Arimathea) for Jesus' body, the mockery of Jesus, and his crucifixion. These accounts are both like and unlike what we read in the canonical Gospels. For example, in v. 10, Jesus is said to be crucified between two criminals, as in the other Gospels, but here we find the unusual statement that "he was silent, as if he had no pain." This last statement could well be taken in a docetic way: Perhaps Jesus appeared to have no pain because he did *not* have any (whether the author *meant* it to be taken that way or not is another matter). Some scholars have seen this as supporting evidence that this fragment is from the "heretical" Gospel known to Serapion. Further confirmation may come several verses later. When Jesus is about to die, he utters his "cry of dereliction" in words similar to, but not identical with, those found in Mark's account. Here he says, "My power, O power, you have left me" (v. 19; cf. Mark 15:34); he is then said to be "taken up," even though his body remains on the cross. Is Jesus here bemoaning the departure of the divine Christ from him prior to his death, the view, as we have seen, of some docetic Christians?

There is another interesting feature in this Gospel's account of Jesus' crucifixion. As in the Gospel of Luke, only one of the two criminals has something disparaging to say.[12] He says it, however, not to Jesus but to the soldiers crucifying him. He tells them that he and the other criminal have deserved their punishment. But he asks, "This one, the Savior of the people, what wrong has he done you?" (v. 14). Angered by the rebuke, the soldiers order that "his legs not be broken, so that he would die in torment."[13]

After Jesus dies, the account continues by describing his burial and then, in the first person, the distress of the disciples: "We fasted and sat mourning and weeping, night and day, until the Sabbath" (v. 27). As in Matthew's Gospel, the Jewish leaders ask Pilate for soldiers to guard the tomb (see Matt. 27:62–66). This Gospel, however, provides more elaborate detail. The centurion in charge is named Petronius, who along with a number of soldiers rolls a huge stone in front of the tomb and seals it with seven seals. They then pitch their tent and stand guard (vv. 29–33).

Then comes perhaps the most striking passage of the narrative, an actual account of Jesus' resurrection and emergence from the tomb, found in none of our other early Gospels. A crowd has come from Jerusalem and the surrounding area to see the tomb. During the night hours, they hear a great noise and see the heavens open up; two men descend in great splendor. The stone before the tomb rolls away of its own accord, and the two men enter. The soldiers standing guard awaken the centurion, who comes out to see the incredible spectacle. From the tomb there emerge three men; the heads of two of them reach up to the sky. They are supporting the third, whose head reaches up beyond the skies. Behind them emerges a cross. A voice then speaks from heaven: "Have you preached to those who are asleep?" The cross replies, "Yes" (vv. 41–42).

The soldiers run to Pilate and tell him all that has happened. The Jewish leaders beg him to keep the story quiet, for fear that they will be stoned, once the Jewish people realize what they have done in putting Jesus to death. Pilate commands the soldiers to silence, but only after reminding the Jewish leaders that Jesus' crucifixion was indeed their fault, not his (vv. 45–49). The next day at dawn, not knowing what has happened, Mary Magdalene goes with several women companions to the tomb to provide a more adequate burial for Jesus' body. But the tomb is empty, save for a heavenly visitor who tells her that the Lord has risen and gone. The manuscript then ends in the middle of a story that apparently described Jesus' appearance to some of his disciples (perhaps similar to that found in John 21:1–14): "But I, Simon Peter, and Andrew, my brother, took our nets and went off to the sea; and with us was Levi, the son of Alphaeus, whom the Lord . . ." (v. 60). Here the manuscript breaks off.

It is this ending which shows that the author is trying to pass himself off as Jesus' own disciple. The good Christians of Rhossus notwithstanding, modern scholars have not been much fooled. This account was probably written after the canonical Gospels, long after Peter had died.

Before giving reasons for thinking so, I should give a brief word of background. Most scholars think that Mark is our earliest surviving account of Jesus' life, written somewhere around 65 or 70 CE; that Matthew and Luke were produced ten or fifteen years later, possibly 80–85 CE; and that John was the last of the canonical accounts, written near the end of the first century, around 90 or 95 CE. The earliest traditions of Peter's death, however, indicate that he was executed during the persecution of Christians under the emperor Nero, around 64 CE.

The author of the Gospel of Peter may have utilized the Gospels of the New Testament for his own accounts, but it is rather difficult to know for certain. There are not, for example, extensive word-for-word agreements between his account and any of the canonical four, and apart from evidence of this sort, it is difficult to establish that one author used another for a source. It may just as well be that this author, like our New Testament authors, had heard numerous stories about Jesus' life and death and recorded them in his own fashion, adding his own touches. In this case, the touches involve some intriguing legendary accretions—especially about the giant resurrected Jesus and the walking cross that speaks to the skies.

The Gospel of Peter and
Traditions about Pontius Pilate

One of the reasons for thinking that the Gospel of Peter was written after our canonical accounts (and therefore long after Peter's death) involves the treatment of "the Jews" in his narrative. The kind of heightened anti-Judaism here corresponds with views that were developing in Christian circles in the second century, a period in which Christian anti-Judaism began to assert itself with particular vigor. One by-product of this increased animosity is that Christians began to exonerate Pilate for Jesus' death and to blame Jews—all Jews—more and more.

It is an illuminating exercise to trace the treatment of Pilate through our surviving Gospels. The more he is excused, the more the Jews are blamed. Our earliest account, Mark, shows Pilate and the Jewish people reaching a kind of agreement to have Jesus crucified. Pilate then orders it, and Jesus is taken off immediately to his death (Mark 15:1–15). In Matthew's Gospel, written somewhat later, Pilate is warned by his wife, who has had a bad dream, not to be involved in the affair; Pilate then shows that he wants nothing to do with Jesus' death by washing his hands of the business. "I am innocent of this man's blood. See to it yourselves," he declares. The Jewish crowd then responds, "His blood be on us and our children" (Matt. 27:25), a response doomed to wreak havoc in the hands of Christian persecutors of Jews throughout the Middle Ages. But it is also completely consonant with views developing in early Christianity: If Pilate is innocent, then the Jews are themselves responsible for killing their own messiah (Matt. 27:11–26).

In Luke's Gospel, written about the same time as Matthew, Pilate declares Jesus innocent three times, to no avail, and tries to arrange for King Herod, in town for the Passover Feast, to do the dirty work for him. But again it is to no avail. With little way out, Pilate yields to the demands of the Jewish leaders and orders Jesus crucified (Luke 23:1–15). In John's Gospel, the final canonical account to be written, Pilate again declares Jesus innocent three times, and then finally, when his hand is forced, turns Jesus over—not, however, to the Roman soldiers but to the Jewish people. Jesus is then crucified (John 18:28–19:16).

So too in the somewhat later Gospel of Peter, where the Jewish culpability is heightened even further and Pilate takes a back seat both to the Jewish king Herod and to the Jewish people. It is Herod who orders the execution and the Jewish people who take full responsibility for what they have done: "Then the Jews, the elders, and the priests realized how much evil they had done to themselves and began beating their breasts, saying, 'Woe to us because of our sins. The judgment and the end of Jerusalem are near'" (v. 25). It is worth noting that it was in the second and third centuries that Christians began blaming the destruction of Jerusalem by the Roman armies in 70 CE on the Jews themselves, not for a foolish uprising against the power of Rome but for killing Christ, whose death was avenged by the destruction of the city and the slaughter of its inhabitants.[14]

The traditions about Pilate's innocence did not stop there. Some years later, around 200 CE, the proto-orthodox Christian apologist (i.e., intellectual defender of the faith), heresiologist (i.e., exposer of heresies), and moralist Tertullian mentions a legendary report that Pontius Pilate had sent a letter to the Roman emperor Tiberius, indicating that this one who had been crucified was shown by his miraculous deeds to have been divine. Tiberius, Tertullian indicates, was completely convinced, and brought a motion to the Roman Senate to have Jesus declared a god. The Senate proved recalcitrant, however, so that even though the emperor acknowledged Christ's divinity, he was not allotted a place in the Roman pantheon (Tertullian, *Apology* 5). Pilate, however, was said to have converted after Jesus' resurrection and become a Christian. This is all stuff of legend, of course, borne out by no non-Christian source.

An entire literature surrounding Pilate eventually emerged within Christian circles, including other versions of the letter that he reportedly sent to the emperor,[15] and several later, lengthier accounts of how the emperor reacted when he learned that one of his governors had executed the Son of God. According to a medieval legend, called the "Surrender of Pilate" (*Paradosis Pilati*), the emperor recalled Pilate to Rome and put him on trial: "By daring to do an evil deed you have destroyed the whole world!" Pilate responds, as one might expect: "Almighty King, I am innocent of these things; it is the multitude of the Jews who are reckless and guilty."[16] Even so, the emperor orders Pilate's execution. Before placing his head on the chopping block, however, Pilate, now a devout Christian, prays that Christ not blame him for yielding in ignorance to the machinations of the Jews. A voice then comes from heaven: "All generations and families of the Gentiles shall call you blessed . . . and you yourself shall appear as my witness at my second coming" (v. 10).

In some parts of the church the exoneration of Pilate went even further. In the Coptic (Egyptian) church, his death came to be seen as that of a Christian martyr; in one of history's most remarkable metamorphoses, he eventually came to be regarded there as a Christian saint.

All this has brought us a long way from the Gospel of Peter. But already we can see the trajectory: Pilate is exonerated to implicate the Jews, as those who killed their own Messiah.

The Popularity of the Gospel of Peter

We have seen a number of intriguing features of the Gospel of Peter: its similarity to the New Testament Gospel accounts of Jesus' death, its legendary accretions, its virulent anti-Judaism, its potentially docetic character, its suppression by the proto-orthodox bishop Serapion, its importance for the Christians of Rhossus. But was it used only in Rhossus? Was the Gospel of Peter merely a local production, forged on the site, with limited impact on the rest of Christendom? It was virtually unknown, after all, down through the ages until French archaeologists happened to find it in a monk's tomb.

Nevertheless, there are indications that the Gospel of Peter was widely popular in the early church, arguably at least as popular as one of the Gospels that did make it into the New Testament, the Gospel of Mark.[17] It is worth observing that the Gospel of Mark itself is hardly ever cited in the early centuries of Christianity, even within the writings of the proto-orthodox. Possibly this is because as the shortest of the four Gospels that came to be included in the New Testament it was not read as much as the others. As readers have long noticed, nearly all the stories found in Mark are found also in Matthew and/or Luke. For this reason Mark eventually came to be seen as a condensed edition of Matthew, a kind of *Reader's Digest* version. Possibly it was not read as much as the others, since their fuller accounts could give its story and much more.

The archaeological finds of early Christian manuscripts bear out the conclusion that the Gospel of Mark was not widely read. Over the past hundred years or so, numerous fragmentary copies of ancient Christian writings have turned up, principally in the sands of Egypt, where the consistently dry climate makes preservation possible over the centuries. The earliest manuscripts of the early Christian literature were written, as was most literature, pagan, Jewish, and Christian, on writing material manufactured from papyrus, a reed that grows on the banks of the Nile and that can be made into a very nice writing surface resembling coarse paper. Since the 1880s, thirty manuscripts of the New Testament Gospels have been discovered that date from the second and third centuries. Most of them contain only one or the other of the Gospels, as these books were originally circulated separately, not as a collection. Of these thirty (fragmentary) Gospel manuscripts, only one contains the Gospel of Mark.

In contrast, from the same period, five (partial) unidentified Gospels have been discovered; these are texts that provide accounts of Jesus' words and deeds but that are too fragmentary to establish which Gospel they belonged to, except to say that they did not belong to any Gospel we know about by name. In addition, there are three fragmentary copies of the Gospel of Thomas, allegedly written by Jesus' twin brother, Didymus Judas Thomas (the subject of chapter 3). And there are two fragmentary copies of a Gospel allegedly written by Mary Magdalene, in which she reveals the secrets that Jesus had given her as his closest companion. From the same period we also have three fragmentary copies of the Gospel of Peter (this is not counting the later copy found in the monk's tomb in Akhmim).

And so it is an interesting question to ask: Which Gospel was more popular in early Christianity, Mark or Peter? It is rather hard to say. But if the material remains are any gauge, one would have to give the palm to Peter, with three times as many surviving manuscript remains as Mark.

These three fragments of the Gospel of Peter are small. One of them consists of just seven partial lines. But the fragments, taken as a whole, have a significance that transcends their size. One of them appears to have come from a second-century (or early third-century) copy that contained the same account of Joseph of Arimathea asking for Jesus' body that is found in the larger copy discovered in the monk's tomb in Akhmim. That is significant because it shows that the later seventh- or eighth-century copy may faithfully represent the text as found already in Serapion's day.

The other two fragments come from other portions of the Gospel, and there are debates about whether they stem from the *same* Gospel of Peter or a different one. It is hard to know, because the credit card-sized fragments contain so little text, making their reconstruction complicated. But both of them appear to represent a conversation between Jesus and Peter, in which Peter speaks in the first person. The first (the one with only seven partial lines) has Jesus predicting that all the disciples, even Peter, will betray him. This would be, then, the familiar account of the Last Supper, but told by Peter himself.

The second contains a saying not found in the canonical Gospels but known to scholars of Christian antiquity from another surviving document called 2 Clement, a proto-orthodox document of the mid-second century, which nonetheless records a rather peculiar interchange between Jesus and Peter.[18] According to 2 Clement, the conversation went like this:

> For the Lord said, "You will be like sheep in the midst of wolves."
> But Peter replied to him, "What if the wolves rip apart the sheep?"
> Jesus said to Peter, "After they are dead, the sheep should fear the wolves no longer. So too you: Do not fear those who kill you and then can do nothing more to you; but fear the one who, after you die, has the power to cast your body and soul into the hell of fire." (2 Clement 5:2–4)

The fragment of the Gospel of Peter we are concerned with here, published just in 1994, contains a similar account, with two main differences. For one thing, here the words of Jesus are given a broader context. It begins with Jesus telling his disciples that they are to be "as innocent as doves but wise as serpents" and that they will be like "sheep among the wolves." They respond, quite sensibly, one might think: "But what if we are ripped apart?" Then comes the second difference: "And Jesus replied to me. . . ." What follows is the saying that dead sheep have nothing to fear from wolves, and so on.

Since in the version of 2 Clement this is a response to Peter, but in this fragment it is a response to someone speaking in the first person, it seems likely that the fragment comes from a Gospel in which the author is speaking in the name of Peter himself, as in the longer text discovered in the monk's tomb in Akhmim. It is not completely clear where the anonymous author of 2 Clement derived his knowledge of this conversation. Since it is not in any of the other Gospels. Possibly he too had read the Gospel of Peter and accepted it as an authoritative account of Jesus' words.[19]

One other interesting archaeological find relates to the Gospel of Peter and shows that the book continued to be read and revered as Scripture for centuries. There was published in 1904 an edition of a small ostracon, a piece of earthenware pottery, broken off and used for writing/drawing. It has not received much critical attention from scholars but is one of the oddest pieces to survive from Christian antiquity. It appears to date from the sixth or seventh century. On one side of the triangular piece (roughly 3? × 4? × 5½?) is a crude drawing of a man with wide eyes, long nose, hair at the top of his head, a beard (or a collar?) on his chin, shoulders, and stick arms with stick hands, one open in a gesture of prayer, the other holding a stick or staff (with a cross at the top) raised up over his head. The ostracon contains several pieces of writing, all in Greek. Over the stick figure's head is written "Peter"; to the left is written "The Saint"; and to the right is written "The Evangelist." That is noteworthy: Peter is identified not merely as an apostle or a disciple of Jesus but as an author of one of the Gospels, an Evangelist. More striking still is the Greek writing on the reverse side: "Let us venerate him, let us receive his Gospel."

Somebody revered Peter and his Gospel, somebody living in Egypt, some four or five hundred years after Serapion had forbidden the Gospel's use. And this Egyptian was not alone. She or he must have been part of a community, which must have had a contemporary copy of the Gospel and accepted it as a sacred text. Nor was the community of the ostracon's inscriber alone: A fragment of the Gospel was buried, presumably as a cherished text, in the tomb of a monk a century or so later. The Gospel of Peter may have become lost to us, but it was widely used in the early centuries of Christianity, and it continued to be used down to the early Middle Ages in some parts of the church.

The Accompanying Apocalypse of Peter

The community or communities that used the Gospel of Peter may have used other noncanonical texts as well. As I have noted, the Gospel of Peter is bound

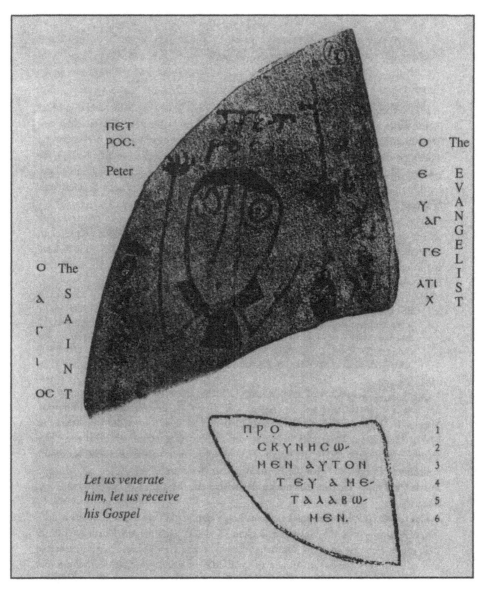

ΠΕΤ
ΡΟC.

Peter

Ο   The
Α
Γ   S
ι   A
     I
ΟC N
     T

ΠΡΟ   1
CΚΥΝΗCѠ   2
ΜΕΝ ΑΥΤΟΝ   3
ΤΕΥ Α ΜΕ   4
ΤΑ ΛΑΒѠ   5
ΜΕΝ.   6

Ο   The
Ε
Υ   E
Αρ V
     A
ΓΕ N
     G
ΑΤΙ E
Χ   L
     I
     S
     T

*Let us venerate
him, let us receive
his Gospel*

Ostrakon (pottery sherd) from the sixth or seventh century depicting the "evangelist
Peter" and urging (on the back side) its readers to revere his Gospel.

up in a manuscript that contains other documents, including one we will meet with again in our discussion, since it stood on the fringes of the New Testament canon for centuries. Like the Gospel, it, too, is attributed to Peter. This, however, is an "apocalypse," a revelation of the heavenly realities that can make sense of life here on earth. In this case, the realities are not so much future catastrophes that God will bring against this planet, as one finds in the book of Revelation, the one apocalypse that made it into the New Testament. Instead, the Apocalypse of Peter shows the fates of those who have died, both those who have done the will of God and those who have opposed him. These fates are described in remarkably concrete and authoritative terms, for Jesus himself takes his disciple Peter on a guided tour of the abodes of the blessed and damned, of heaven and hell. Dante did not invent the idea of such a tour; *The Divine Comedy* was already standing in a long Christian tradition, going back at least to the once-lost but now-found Apocalypse of Peter.[20]

The account begins with Jesus teaching his disciples on the Mount of Olives and the disciples asking when the end will come (cf. Matthew 24). Jesus responds by telling them the parable of the fig tree: ". . . as soon as its shoots have come forth and the twigs grown, the end of the world shall come" (ch. 1). Peter and the others are understandably confused: "And I, Peter, answered and said to him, 'Interpret the fig tree to me: How can we understand it? For throughout all its days the fig tree sends forth shoots and every year it brings forth its fruit" (ch. 2).

Jesus goes on to explain that the fig tree refers to Israel and that in the future there will come forth from it false Christs and prophets. This is then the beginning of the end, which Jesus describes not so much in terms of earthly disasters—there are some of these, to be sure—as in terms of the fates of individuals in the afterlife.

It is the fate of the damned and their various eternal tortures that have sparked the greatest interest in this text. The torments are particularly lurid, with the punishments matching the sinners' crimes. Blasphemers are hanged by their tongues, forever, over unquenchable fire; women who braided their hair to make themselves attractive to lustful men are hanged by their hair; the men who committed fornication with these women are hanged by their genitals. Those who trusted in riches are eternally cast onto a razor-sharp pillar of fire; bankers who made money on interest spend eternity up to their knees in filth; children who disobeyed their parents are incessantly eaten by savage birds; slaves who disobeyed their masters are forced to gnaw their own tongues without ceasing.

The blessings of the saved are understandably less graphic. Anyone with sufficient imagination can devise numerous creative torments, but there are only so many ways to describe eternal bliss. Still, for this text, the rewards of the blessed make any temporary hardship here on earth clearly worth the price. This is an eternal ecstasy reserved for the few.

The author of this firsthand narrative, allegedly Peter himself, clearly produced his account not merely to entertain his Christian readers but also to advance several major theological views. In particular, of course, he shows that anyone who sides with God will reap a reward whereas anyone who opposes God will pay an everlasting and horrific price. Just as important, however, the author stresses that God is in control of all that happens in this world, appearances notwithstanding. In other words, this account, like other early Christian "apocalypses," is not meant simply to scare people into avoiding certain kinds of behavior—lying, committing adultery, blaspheming, relying on wealth, etc.—but also to explain that the evil and suffering of this age will be resolved in the next, that what happens here will be overturned there, that those who succeed by being wicked now will pay an eternal price later, whereas those who suffer for doing what is right now will be vindicated forever, as God shows once and for all that he and he alone is sovereign over this world.

The Gospel of Peter and
Other Early Christian Literature

This initial foray into the Christian apocrypha of the second century shows that Christians were reading far more sacred literature than one might think. They were not reading only the books that eventually made it into the New Testament. There is no way of knowing whether during the time of Serapion of Antioch (end of the second century) the Christians of Rhossus ever had heard of Matthew, Mark, Luke, and John. Their Gospel was the Gospel of Peter, until the bishop asserted his authority and banned its use. Whether he was successful in doing so, in the short run, is something we will never know. What we can know is that the Gospel was being read not just in Syria but also in Egypt, possibly at an early stage, since the papyri that contain it are roughly contemporary with Serapion. And it is more widely attested than even some of our canonical books, including the Gospel of Mark.

Christians were reading other texts as well. Some were reading the Acts of Pilate, a book I have not yet mentioned. This is an account which describes the trial of Jesus in a much fuller fashion than in the surviving fragment of the Gospel of Peter, showing the guilt of the Jews and the superiority of Jesus over everything pagan. In this account, which is referred to by the second-century author Justin Martyr, the images of the Roman gods bow down to Jesus when he enters the room. At a later date this account was combined with a detailed description of Christ's descent into Hades, which took place between his death and resurrection to form what is now known as the Gospel of Nicodemus. Had Tertullian read early versions of any of this material? He certainly had read some version of the letter Pilate had sent back to the Roman emperor, proclaiming Jesus' innocence and divinity. As we saw at the outset, his contemporary Origen had read yet other Gospels—those according to the Egyptians, the

Twelve Apostles, Matthias, Basilides, and Thomas. And we know of apocalypses being read as well, including the one allegedly written by Peter and lost until discovered in a monk's tomb along with Peter's Gospel.

What else might early Christians have been reading as Scripture? Lots of texts, most of them proscribed, burned, lost. Some of them have been recently found, if only in tantalizing fragments. What we would give for a complete copy of Peter's Gospel, or of the stories of Pilate, or of the Gospels or apocalypses that we know only by name. But only a few of these early Christian writings managed to survive the proscriptions of their proto-orthodox enemies, sometimes circulating in clandestine copies in the Middle Ages, occasionally being quoted by this or that church father for reasons of his own, and in those rare moments of genuine discovery, sometimes turning up in the sands of Egypt, uncovered by trained archaeologists digging through ancient garbage heaps of ancient cities or stumbled upon by bedouin, going about their business and serendipitously unearthing finds that can tell us something about the lost Christianities of antiquity.

Chapter Two

The Ancient Forgery of a Discovery: The Acts of Paul and Thecla

Most texts revered as sacred by ancient Christians have been lost. Some of these have been discovered in modern times, but the majority are still relegated to oblivion, known only by name and, when we are fortunate, by a general sense of what they must have been like. Several, however, have been long available, even if almost entirely forgotten.

Forgotten, that is, to the world at large, not so much to scholars of antiquity, who spend their lives learning ancient and obscure languages, poring over ancient manuscripts and massive printed tomes, studying the records of the past. One of the ancient texts known well to scholars of Christian antiquity but virtually unknown to others is a fascinating document of the second century called the Acts of Thecla, an account of the exploits of a woman disciple of the apostle Paul.

There was a time—a millennium and a half ago—when Thecla was a household name, at least in Christian households. Her following was huge. Pilgrims flocked to her shrines in Asia Minor, Syria, and Egypt. Devotees committed their lives to her adoration. Revered as a model martyr and worshiped as a saint, in some parts of the Christian world Thecla vied for centuries with Mary, the Mother of Jesus herself, as most important person outside the Trinity.[1]

The stories of Thecla's miraculous life, much like the stories of Jesus, originally circulated in oral traditions, possibly from the early second century onwards. But they are best known from a written account, the Acts of Thecla, eventually included in part of a larger corpus of writings known as the Acts of Paul, which narrates tales of Paul's journeys and miraculous adventures. One of the striking features of the accounts of Paul and Thecla is that we know it was forged. Of course, we know that the Gospel of Peter was forged as well, along with other books we have already mentioned—the Gospel of Thomas, the Gospel of Philip, and the Apocalypse of Peter—and scores of other books from the ancient world. But in this case there is a difference. The author who forged the Acts of Paul and Thecla was caught and confessed to the deed.

The Practice of Forgery in Antiquity

Ancient people not only suspected forgery on occasion; they also had the means to detect it.[2] It is wrong to say—as it sometimes is said, even by scholars who ought to know better—that forgery in antiquity was so common that no one took it seriously and that few people were swayed by it. The ancient sources that discuss the practice attack it; and if no one was swayed by the ruse, there would have been scant reason to employ it. Many forgers were so good that they succeeded completely; even today scholars debate the authorship of numerous works from antiquity, including some that came to be included in the sacred canon of Scripture.

The means of detection in the ancient world were much the same as those used today, although they are used much more efficiently now, of course, given our advanced technologies and data retrieval systems. If a work refers to an event that transpired centuries after its reputed author died, that would be a good indication that something is not right. If it uses words or ideas or philosophical notions that had not come into existence during the alleged author's lifetime, that might be a key. If it uses a writing style completely at variance with what can be found in the author's undisputed works, that would be a clue.

An amusing anecdote from the period of our concern, the second and third Christian centuries, illustrates the point. The famous Roman physician Galen (129–99 CE) was a prolific author whose books found a wide market. One day, walking along a street in Rome, he passed a book stall that was selling a book by "Galen" and he overheard an argument between two potential buyers, one of whom declared the book a fraud, on the grounds that it was not written in Galen's distinctive style. That both pleased the famous writer himself and sparked an idea: Galen dashed off a booklet called *On His Own Books*, a work describing how one could distinguish the genuine books of Galen from the forgeries. The booklet still survives today.

Why did forgers in the ancient world perpetrate their frauds? Ancient sources discuss the problem and suggest several motivations.[3] As may have been the case of Galen's forgery, sometimes there was a profit motive. This was especially true when new libraries were starting up in major cities and kings were competing with one another for the best holdings. In an age before texts could be flawlessly reproduced by mechanical means, it was thought that original documents were superior to later copies that could, and almost always did, contain scribal errors. A remarkable number of "original" texts of Aristotle might appear when they could fetch a good price.

In some instances, forgers were driven by animosity and sheer spite. We know of one instance in which a Greek author of the fourth century BCE,

Anaximenes, forged letters in the name and style of his archenemy, the historian Theopompus, letters filled with invective against the major cities of Greece. He then sent the letters to the ruling councils of each of the cities, making Theopompus a persona non grata wherever he wanted to go.[4]

At just the opposite end of the motivational spectrum, documents were occasionally forged in someone else's name out of admiration and humility. We know of this best from a school of philosophers from the second century CE who were self-conscious devotees of the classical Greek philosopher Pythagoras. These neo-Pythagoreans, highly educated and skilled themselves, produced significant philosophical treatises, but wrote them in the name of Pythagoras. Why? Because, they claimed, their own ideas were simply elaborations of the system devised by the greatest mind the world had ever seen. To sign their own names would have been an act of hubris and, in a somewhat ironic sense, a false attribution.

Probably the most common reason for forging a document in someone else's name in the ancient world, however, was in order to receive a hearing for one's views. Suppose you were a completely unknown but aspiring young philosopher, who believed that you had something to say to the world and that the world ought to hear it. It would do little good to publish your ideas under your own name, a name no one knew or cared about. If you wanted the work to be read, it would be much better to sign the treatise "Plato." Or to transpose the matter onto Christian territory: If there were problems in your church that you needed to address, problems of church organization or of false teaching, you could produce a letter but circulate it not in your own name but in the name of someone who would be taken seriously, such as the apostle Paul.

And so we have a letter called 3 Corinthians, allegedly written by Paul, but from the second century, opposing a docetic view.[5] We have three other letters allegedly written by Paul, but evidently from the late first century, dealing largely with problems of church organization, called 1 and 2 Timothy and Titus. And there are other letters allegedly from Paul, several to the Roman philosopher Seneca, in which Paul is shown to be one of the greatest philosophical minds of his age, and one to the church of Laodicea—all from later times.[6] Other letters that were forged in Paul's name no longer exist, including one to the Christians of Alexandria, Egypt. Some of these "Pauline" letters were thought by one Christian group or another to belong to sacred Scripture.

The Forging of the Acts of Paul

We also have the Acts of Paul, which includes the tales of Thecla. In this particular case we know that the book was forged because, in one of the rare instances of the kind to come down to us from antiquity, the forger was caught in the act.

The story is told by the proto-orthodox church father Tertullian, who, on this score at least, is probably to be trusted as providing reliable information.[7] Among the many surviving works of Tertullian is a treatise that discusses in detail the practice of baptism, explicating its biblical and theological rationale and meaning. At one point in the treatise ("On Baptism," chap. 17), Tertullian deals with the issue of who is allowed to administer baptism, in a passage that has helped sully Tertullian's reputation over the years as one of Christian history's worst misogynists. For among other things, Tertullian strictly forbids the practice of allowing women, who are seen as inferior to men, to baptize. He points out that some Christians have appealed to the example of Thecla as a woman who was authorized both to teach (men) and to baptize, but he undercuts the example by indicating that the tales of Thecla had been forged by a presbyter (i.e., a church elder) in Asia (meaning Asia Minor, modern Turkey). Moreover, Tertullian indicates that this Christian forger had been convicted by a church tribunal and that during his trial he had confessed to doing it "for the love of Paul." That is to say, in his own eyes, the forger's motives were pure as the driven snow. He had evidently wanted to celebrate the apostle Paul's life, and he did so by fabricating miraculous tales that transpired during the course of his missionary journeys, including the tales of Thecla, his famous female convert. The church court that tried the case did not find the defense compelling; they reprimanded the presbyter and removed him from office.

We can assume that the story of Thecla known to us today is the same story fabricated by this presbyter of Asia Minor. We should not think, however, that he made the story up out of whole cloth. Indeed, there are reasons for thinking that he compiled stories he had heard, oral traditions that had been in circulation for years, and used them to compose a literary account.[8] The full text of the Acts of Paul included not only stories of Paul's adventures as a miracle-working apostle and the narrative of Thecla, but also the letter of 3 Corinthians mentioned above, actually composed in Paul's name as if he had written it. A clear deceit was in play here.

But how did the presbyter pass his work off as genuine, an authentic account of Paul and a faithful reproduction of at least one of his writings, 3 Corinthians?[9] We can never know for certain. One common ploy used by ancient forgers was to claim that they had "found" an older writing which they were reproducing for the world to see for the first time. Such claims were almost impossible to substantiate, and so were quite reasonable as a way to present one's own work as someone else's. If this *is* how the infamous presbyter of Asia Minor proceeded, then he not only forged an account; he also forged a discovery. For that matter, even if he used some other means of presenting his work to the world, he forged a discovery. With the appearance of this work, the world could see for the first time new episodes from the life of Paul and, of yet more importance to our discussion here, episodes from the life of his most famous female convert, Thecla.[10]

The Story of Thecla

The tale of Thecla is full of intrigue. One can see how, even after its exposure as a forgery, it continued to grip the imagination and inspire the awe of readers down to the Middle Ages. Here Paul is not portrayed as he is in the New Testament, as a Christian missionary who preaches to the Gentiles a message of the death and resurrection of Jesus for the salvation of the world; here he proclaims a message of sexual renunciation, in which those who choose the life of chastity will be saved. Thecla is his main convert, who commits herself to Paul's gospel of abstinence, much to the chagrin of her fiancé and at least one other man in her life.

The narrative proceeds through four major scenes of action. The first takes place in the Asia Minor city of Iconium, where Paul arrives to preach his message from the home of a Christian, Onesiphorus. Day by day he proclaims:

> Blessed are the pure in heart, for they will see God. Blessed are those who have kept the flesh chaste, for they will become a temple of God. Blessed are those who are self-controlled, for God will speak to them. Blessed are those who have wives as if they did not have them, for they will be the heirs of God. . . . Blessed are the bodies of the virgins, for these will be pleasing to God and will not lose the reward for their chastity. (Acts of Thecla 5–6)

The message attracts a large number of fascinated listeners, including Thecla, Onesiphorus's next-door neighbor. For three days and nights she sits in a window listening to Paul, enraptured by his words, not stirring an inch. Her mother becomes distressed at her behavior and calls for help from Thecla's fiancé, Thamyris. They both, of course, have something to lose if Paul's message sinks home: the man a wife and the mother, one might suppose, social and financial security through a marital connection. But Thamyris's attempts to make Thecla see reason are to no avail. Now she has eyes only for Paul and his message of sexual renunciation.

The next scene involves the prosecution of Paul and Thecla. Thamyris is incensed at his loss and drags Paul off to the governor of Iconium to stand trial for creating a disturbance. The other married men in town, as might be expected, lend their wholehearted support. Thecla, however, manages to bribe her way into Paul's jail cell and spends the night sitting at his feet, listening to his eloquent words, and "kissing his bonds" (Acts of Thecla 18). The story, as interpreters have long noted, is as much about the displacement of sexual desire as its renunciation.

When Thamyris learns where his beloved is, he comes and finds her with Paul "bound together with him in affection" (Acts of Thecla 19). They take Paul off to trial, while Thecla stays behind, rolling around in the place where Paul had been sitting. She is also then brought, and both stand trial. Because he is an outsider, Paul is flogged and exiled from the city as a troublemaker. But the

Portrayal of Paul preaching his gospel, seated by a tower, from which his soon-to-be disciple Thecla listens with rapt attention, from an ivory panel of the fifth century.

evil not from outside but resident within requires more drastic expulsion: Thecla's own mother pleads for her execution. The governor orders Thecla burned at the stake. But as the execution begins, as one would expect for such a saint devoted to God, a divine intervention occurs. The blaze around Thecla does not touch her body, and God sends a preternatural thunderstorm that douses the fire, allowing Thecla to escape.

She tracks down Paul and begs him to allow her to join him on his journeys, offering to cut off her hair (to look like a male traveling companion?) and "follow you wherever you go." But Paul refuses to baptize Thecla, for fear she might change her mind and prove herself unworthy.

The next scene takes Paul and Thecla to Antioch, where another test awaits. Walking along the streets, they encounter an influential citizen of the city, Alexander, who is immediately inflamed with passion for Thecla and decides to have her then and there. He tries to bribe Paul for her, but Paul—not putting himself in the best light—replies, "I do not know the woman you are speaking of, nor is she mine." Alexander then takes matters, and Thecla, into his own hands and tries to force himself on her. She publicly humiliates him, however, repulsing his advance, tearing his cloak, and pulling off his crown. The crowd that has gathered finds it all amusing (Acts of Thecla 26).

Alexander, however, does not. He takes her to the local magistrate, who condemns her to be thrown to the wild beasts for assaulting one of the city's leading citizens. What follows is a series of adventures in the arena, in which

Thecla is repeatedly protected from all harm and female onlookers show their true character as proponents of truth and enemies of injustice. One woman in particular, an aristocrat named Tryphaena, houses Thecla before the exhibition with the wild beasts, taking her under her wing as a "second daughter" in place of one she had earlier lost to illness. Other women in the city gather at the spectacle and cry out against the outrageous death sentence. A lioness loosed upon Thecla comes up to her and, rather than mauling her, licks her feet. The exhibition closes with Thecla still alive and well.

And so more festivities are planned for the following day. When it arrives, Thecla is set down in the arena and wild beasts are loosed upon her. For a while she is protected by a fierce lioness, who kills a bear in her defense but then is killed in a fight with a lion. More beasts are sent in. Recognizing that she may have no other chance for redemption, Thecla notices a large vat filled with water and human-eating seals. To the dismay of the crowds, she throws herself into the vat, crying out, "In the name of Jesus Christ, on this final day I am baptized" (Acts of Thecla 34).

It is an act of desperation, but it works. God once again intervenes, sending a lightning bolt down into the vat to kill all the seals and allowing Thecla to emerge unscathed, covered with a cloud to conceal her nakedness from curious bystanders. More miraculous interventions occur in the arena, until finally the governor gives up and releases her.

The final scene comes as a bit of an anticlimax. Now that her trials are over and she has been baptized, Thecla "longs for Paul" and begins to search for him. She dresses as a man[11] and finally tracks Paul down in another town. Informing him of her adventures, including her baptism, she announces that she is returning to Iconium. Paul not only lets her go but commissions her: "Go and teach the word of God" (Acts of Thecla 41).

At home, Thecla finds (somewhat conveniently for the plot) that her ex-fiancé, Thamyris, has died. She comforts her mother and then leaves for Seleucia, near the south coast of Asia Minor, where she spends a long life preaching the Christian gospel so as to "enlighten many."

Apocryphal Acts and Christian Ideology

As I have indicated, even though the story of Thecla is not widely known today outside of circles of early Christian scholars and their students, at one time it was extremely popular, with Thecla becoming a cult hero in widespread and often remote regions of Christendom from the third century down to the Middle Ages. Already at the beginning of the third century, soon after it was written, the text was having a large impact, enough for Tertullian to show real concern that it was being used to authorize women to teach and baptize in the Christian churches—activities restricted to men throughout proto-orthodox Christianity. Somewhat later, the Thecla narrative was expanded to include tales of the many miracles she wrought once she arrived in Seleucia; tales of her "death," in which she never actually died but sank, living, into the ground; tales of her reappearing, out of the ground, in other places that had sacred cultic sites devoted to her; and yet other tales of her life of renunciation and her miraculous deeds. In the mid-fifth century, the Roman emperor Zeno, who had been temporarily removed from office, had a dream of Thecla indicating that he would soon be restored to office. Out of gratitude to her for her supernatural assistance, he built a large church in her honor in Seleucia. Other buildings followed, so that by the sixth century there were two other churches on the site, along with a public bath and a number of cisterns. It became a major place of international pilgrimage. Nor was it alone: Devotion to Thecla was widespread in Egypt, Syria, and even Rome.[12]

But to return where we began: Why did the presbyter of Asia Minor forge the text in the first place? Why claim to discover a series of adventures of Paul's companion Thecla? Given the quality of the tales, one might suspect that he wrote his narrative for the purpose of entertainment, as a kind of early Christian novel. Scholars have long noted that the various Apocryphal Acts, that is, the surviving accounts of the activities of individual apostles, such as Paul, Peter, Thomas, John, and Andrew (all of which we have), appear to be modeled on the ancient pagan "romances," or novels, that have come down to us from Greek and Roman late antiquity.[13] Five Greek (pagan) novels, and two Roman, have survived, which, like the Apocryphal Acts, deal with individuals in relation to civic life and portray their travels, catastrophes, near-death experiences, miraculous escapes, encounters with ruthless tyrants, painful separations, and joyful reunions.

The overarching themes of these ancient novels, however, are quite different from what one finds in the Christian Apocryphal Acts. The Greek novels, such as *Chareas and Callirhoe* and *Leucippe and Cleitophon,* are almost always highly episodic accounts of two star-crossed lovers who are tragically separated before they can consummate their love and who experience heart-wrenching trials and painful tribulations (shipwrecks, attacks by pirates, imprisonments, kidnappings, and near-death experiences) before finally overcoming the capricious whims of the gods or fate to be reunited so as to enjoy the sexual embrace of their long lost partner, in socially sanctioned marriage. The stories thus celebrate heterosexual love as the glue that binds together society, that unites families, that provides social unity for the city, that keeps society healthy, prosperous, and civilized.[14]

The Christian Apocryphal Acts are also about sexual love and the relationship of the individual to larger society. And they employ many of the same subplots as the novels. But the Christian agenda of these books stands in stark contrast to the pagan, for here sexual love is not the goal to be achieved but the pitfall to be avoided. The ultimate good here is not the welfare of the state but the abandonment of the state. Families in these tales are not to be united in social harmony but torn apart in social disruption. It is not life in this world that matters but life in the world above. The pleasures of life are not to be achieved but forsaken. The Christians who wrote and cherished these works were not interested in making the traditional social order a happy place in which people could enjoy life to its fullest; they were interested in escaping this social world and all its trappings, to enjoy a spiritual union with God and to form their own distinctively Christian societies, rooted in a different set of values from those of the world at large. Using the form of the ancient novel, they transformed its message.

Thus, even if the Acts of Thecla was meant to entertain, it was also meant to instruct and encourage. But in addition to reversing the seemingly wholesome pagan agenda of the ancient novels, what other specific lessons are meant to be conveyed?

Tertullian, of course, read the account as authorizing women to exercise leadership roles in the church, and he maintained that it was beginning to be used to that end in his day. One can certainly see how the account would function that way. To be sure, the gender relations in the text are not completely flat and stereotyped. It is not the case that all men are bad here and all women good, as is sometimes maintained. It is Thecla's mother, Theoclia, after all, who first demands her execution, and Paul is portrayed as the apostle of God. But even Paul does not come off well in places, such as when he lies about not knowing Thecla, leading to her near rape in Antioch. And most of the other men—Thamyris, Alexander, the local magistrates—are far from models of up-right behavior. Women, on the other hand, take center stage and are generally worth emulating: Thecla, the inspired devotee of sexual renunciation, protected by God from all harm at every point; her protectress in Antioch, Tryphaena, who shelters and defends her before an almost implacable male force; the women of Antioch who scream for justice and finally get their way with the male administrators. Even among the wild beasts, it is the lioness who sides with God and his beloved; the male animals are like the men, fierce and hungry to take what they think is theirs, the pure virgin of God.

One other ideological point of the narrative relates to Thecla's acts of baptizing (herself) and of teaching (others), roles that Tertullian insisted belong to men. Interestingly enough, in his treatise on baptism, Tertullian cites Paul's own writings in support of his own views. The irony is that Paul himself—the historical Paul—may have lined up on the other side of the issue.

Women in Paul and the Apocryphal Acts

Scholars of Paul have debated his view of women in the church. For a long time, it was seen as an uncomplicated matter. Tertullian himself quotes 1 Cor. 14:34–35 to show that women were to be silent in church and exercise no authority over men. As the text says,

> Let the women be silent in the churches, for they are not permitted to speak; but let them be in subjection, just as the law says; but if they want to learn anything, let them ask their husbands at home. For it is shameful for a woman to speak in church.

The passage coincides rather well with Paul's (in)famous instructions to Timothy:

> I do not allow a woman to teach, nor to exercise authority over a man; they are to be quiet. For Adam was formed first, and then Eve. And Adam was not deceived, but the woman was deceived and fell into a transgression. But she will be saved through bearing children—if they remain in faith, love, and holiness, with moderation (1 Tim. 2:12–15).

In other words, women earn salvation by keeping quiet and pregnant; it is men who have the authority to teach. So says Paul.

Or does he? Scholars today are not so convinced. As I have already pointed out, most critical scholars think that 1 Timothy is pseudonymous: its vocabulary, writing style, theological modes of expression, and presupposed historical situation[15] all differ significantly from what can be found in Paul's authentic letters.[16] But what about the passage in 1 Corinthians? No one doubts that Paul wrote *that* letter. Even so, there are good reasons for thinking Paul did not write the passage about women being silent in chapter 14.[17] For one thing, just three chapters earlier Paul condoned the practice of women speaking in church. They are to have their heads covered, he insists, when they pray and prophecy—activities done out loud in antiquity. How could Paul condone a practice (women speaking in church) in chapter 11 that he condemns in chapter 14?

It has often been noted that the passage in chapter 14 also appears intrusive in its own literary context: Both before and after his instructions for women to keep silent, Paul is speaking not about women in church but about prophets in church. When the verses on women are removed, the passage flows neatly without a break. This too suggests that these verses were inserted into the passage later. Moreover, it is striking that the verses in question appear in different locations in some of our surviving manuscripts of Paul's letter as if they had originally appeared as a marginal note (drawn from the teaching of the forged letter of 1 Timothy?) and inserted as judged appropriate in different parts of the chapter. On these grounds, a number of scholars have concluded that Paul's instructions for women to be silent in 1 Corinthians may not be from Paul, just as the letter to Timothy is not from Paul.

What, then, was Paul's attitude toward women in the church? In his undisputed letters, Paul indicates that "in Christ there is no male and female" (Gal. 3:28), that is, that men and women were completely equal in Christ. Moreover, as scholars of the late twentieth century began to emphasize, churches connected in some way with Paul appear to have had women leaders. Just in the greetings to the church of Rome, for example, Paul mentions several women who worked with him as Christian missionaries (Rom. 16:3, 6, 12), another who was the patron of the church meeting in her home (16:3), one other, a woman named Phoebe, who was a deacon in the church of Cenchrea (16:1), and most striking of all, yet another woman, Junia, whom Paul describes as "foremost among the apostles" (16:7).[18]

Paul, and his churches, may have been more open to women and their leadership roles than people have traditionally thought and far more than Tertullian thought. No wonder that members of Paul's churches (primarily women members?) told stories about the adventures of his female companions like Thecla. And no wonder that men in the churches eventually decided to clamp down, forging documents in Paul's name condemning the practice of having women speak in church (1 Timothy), inserting passages into Paul's authentic letters urging women to be silent (1 Cor. 14:34–35), calling church councils to condemn an elder of a Pauline church who had dared collect narratives of Paul's woman disciple Thecla and pass them off as authentically Pauline.

Some scholars have wondered whether the stories of Thecla were causing problems in the Pauline churches years before this accused forger did his work, wondered whether the existence of such stories is what led the author of 1 Timothy, whoever he was, to compose his letter in Paul's name. It is indeed striking that the letter predicts that in "later times" there will be people who condemn the practice of marriage (4:1–4): "Paul" himself speaks against the practice in the Acts of Thecla. Moreover, the canonical letter of 1 Timothy explicitly urges its readers not to listen to "the profane tales of old women" and condemns younger women who are "idlers, going about from door to door . . . as gossips and busybodies, saying things they should not" (4:8, 5:13). The younger women who have lost husbands are to "marry, bear children, rule their households, and give the enemy no grounds to reproach us" (5:14).

This is certainly not the view advanced in the Acts of Thecla, which urges women not to marry, not to bear children, and to leave their households. For *that* "Paul," the Paul of the Acts of Thecla, "blessed are the continent, for God shall speak with them" and "blessed are the bodies of the virgins, for they will be well pleasing to God and will not lose the reward of their chastity." Possibly the stories of Thecla and others like them are what motivated the author of 1 Timothy to write his letter in Paul's name.

Some of the Other Apocryphal Acts

The view of sexual renunciation found in the Acts of Thecla recurs in other Apocryphal Acts as well. One of the most intriguing is the Acts of Thomas, an account of the exploits of the apostle Thomas, probably written in Syria some time in the third century.[19] It is a famous account, in that it is the first to present the well-known legend that the apostle Thomas became a missionary to India. One of the most striking features of the text is that it assumes that this apostle Thomas was Jesus' brother. The name *Thomas* is an Aramaic equivalent of the

Greek word *Didymus,* which means "twin." Thomas was allegedly Jesus' identical twin, otherwise known as Jude (Mark 6:3), or Didymus Judas Thomas.

One might wonder how some early Christians could have thought that Jesus had a twin brother. If, after all, his mother was a virgin, and, presumably, Jesus was the unique Son of God that she bore, how could she at the same time bear a mortal brother, his twin, his identical twin? Unfortunately, none of the texts that present or presuppose the tradition gives us any hint.

We do know of a parallel situation in ancient Greek and Roman mythology, however, instances of a son of a god who is born to a mortal and who has a twin brother whose father was human. The best known example is the Greek god Heracles (Roman Hercules), whose mortal twin was Iphicles. The story of their conception intrigued ancient storytellers. A woman named Alcmena had conceived a child with her husband, Amphitryon, but then she became irresistibly attractive to the god Zeus, who came down and made love with her in human form—in the form of Amphitryon. She never knew the difference. Two children developed in her womb and then came forth at birth, one the son of a mortal, the other the son of a god.[20]

Did the Syrians who considered Thomas to be Jesus' twin brother imagine something roughly similar in his case? That Joseph and Mary had conceived a child through sexual intercourse and that subsequently (or perhaps before) she conceived through the Holy Spirit? One cannot very well object that this is not taught in the New Testament. Remember, these people did not yet *have* the New Testament.

In any event, the Acts of Thomas narrates the adventures of Thomas, Jesus' brother, in his missionary work on the way to and in India. The plot is fairly basic. The apostles draw lots to decide who will go to which region to spread the gospel. The lot for India falls to Thomas, who tells his companions that it is the last place on earth he wants to go: "Wherever you wish to send me, send me, but elsewhere. For I am not going to the Indians!" (Acts of Thomas 1).[21]

The ascended Jesus, however, has other plans for his mortal twin. An Indian merchant arrives in Jerusalem, looking for a skilled carpenter to build a castle for the king of India. Jesus descends from heaven in bodily form, appears to the merchant, and tells him that he has a slave who would be ideal for the job (he was, after all, apprenticed for years to his father, Joseph the carpenter). Jesus writes out a bill of sale to the merchant, who then approaches Thomas and asks if he is the slave of Jesus. He has no choice but to reply truthfully, "Yes, he is my Lord." The deal is done: Thomas is taken off to India.

The narrative is designed to show that Thomas, like the other apostles, is supernaturally empowered to do miracles. He can predict the future, cast out demons, heal the sick, raise the dead. It is also designed to show that a source for supernatural power, and in fact for all right relationship with God, comes from living the life of renunciation, free from sexual activity of any kind, even within the context of marriage. In one of the more intriguing accounts early in the narrative, Thomas and his merchant-owner arrive in the city of Andrapolis in time for a large wedding feast. The king of the city has an only daughter who is that day being given in marriage, and everyone is invited to attend. Thomas is dragged along to the proceedings, somewhat unwillingly, and asked to pray over the blissfully married couple, as they are about to consummate their marriage in the bridal chamber, bringing health and a bright future to the life of the community.

After his rather noncommittal prayer, in which he asks the Lord Jesus to "do to them what helps, benefits, and is profitable for them," he leaves with the other guests, so the bride and groom can begin the private festivities. The bridegroom then lifts the curtain of the bridal chamber to gather his beloved in his arms, only to find her speaking with Thomas—or at least with someone who looks exactly like Thomas. This, needless to say, causes a bit of consternation, not just because the groom has been eagerly awaiting the moment but also because he has just seen Thomas leave and cannot understand how he managed to creep back in.

As it turns out, it is not Thomas at all but his identical twin, Jesus, who has come down from heaven to persuade the bride and groom to refrain from consummating their marriage: "If you refrain from this filthy intercourse you become temples holy and pure, released from afflictions and troubles, known and unknown, and you will not be involved in the cares of life and of children, whose end is destruction" (Acts of Thomas 12).[22] Jesus goes on to show that children are an enormous burden, that they either become demon-possessed, diseased, or lazy burdens, destined for heinous sins and ultimate condemnation. It is better, Jesus insists, to refrain from sex altogether and live the life of purity, bringing no more sinners into the world and being wedded, ultimately, to God.

As one might expect from such a Christian account, Jesus is entirely persuasive and convinces the couple on the spot. For the entire night they "refrained from filthy lust," much to the chagrin of the king, who arrives the next morning to find his daughter cheerful and unspoiled. As she herself tells her father: "I have set at naught this husband and these nuptials . . . because I have joined in a different marriage. I have had no conjugal intercourse with a temporary husband, whose end is repentance and bitterness of soul, because I have been united to my true husband" (Acts of Thomas 14). Incensed, the king sends off to have Thomas, "that sorcerer," arrested, but too late. He has already set sail.

Clearly, as with the Acts of Thecla, this book stands in direct opposition to the Greek Romances' celebration of marital love as the glue that holds together society. Here sex of any kind, even within marriage, is portrayed as foul and to be avoided at all costs. For these Christian Acts, the good of society is not of ultimate interest. There is a greater world that cannot be seen, far superior to this one, and life in this world should be directed entirely toward life in that other one, lest we be entrapped in the bodily desires of this age and suffer dire consequences in the age to come.

A comparable message appears in another of the Apocryphal Acts, the last we will consider in this chapter. The Acts of John narrates the legendary adventures of John, the son of Zebedee, one of Jesus' closest disciples in the New

Testament Gospels. He continues to be an important figure after Jesus' death, according to the early chapters of the canonical Acts of the Apostles, but he quickly drops out of sight in that narrative as the book turns its entire attention to the missionary activities of Paul. Later Christians, not content with the silence shrouding John's later life, filled the gap with numerous stories, some of which have made it into this second-century Apocryphal Acts of John.[23]

Once again we are handicapped by not having the complete text. It was, of course, a noncanonical book, and parts of it were theologically dubious to the proto-orthodox. It was eventually condemned as heretical at the Second Council of Nicaea in the eighth century, so that most manuscripts of it were either destroyed or lost.[24] One of the offensive passages occurs in John's description of Jesus, which has a decidedly docetic flavor, for John indicates that Jesus appeared to different people in different guises at the same time (e.g., as an old man and as a youth, simultaneously to different people), that he never blinked his eyes, that sometimes his chest felt smooth and tender but sometimes hard as stone. As John later says, "Sometimes when I meant to touch him, I met a material and solid body; at other times again I felt him, the substance was immaterial and bodiless and as if it were not existing at all" (chap. 93). One time, John indicates, he noticed that Jesus never left any footprints—literally a God striding on the earth.

This docetically inclined Christology is played out in a way disturbing to the orthodox understanding of Jesus' death as an atonement as well. Here Jesus tells his disciples:

> You hear that I suffered, yet I suffered not; that I suffered not, yet I did suffer; that I was pierced, yet was I not wounded; hanged, and I was not hanged; that blood flowed from me, yet it did not flow; and in a word, those things that they say of me I did not endure, and the things that they do not say, those I suffered. (chap. 101)

Such views may well be acceptable for Christians reflecting on the mysteries of Christ's divinity. But for the orthodox, they created enormous problems for the doctrine of redemption, since if Jesus did not really suffer, bleed, and die, then he could scarcely have purchased redemption through his blood.

Not all of the Acts of John, however—in fact, very little of it—is concerned with delving into theological niceties. Most of it is filled with entertaining accounts of John's own adventures. Among the most famous is the tale of John and the bedbugs. Arriving at an inn late at night and tumbling onto the bed for some much needed sleep, John is dismayed to find the mattress infested with bedbugs. Desperately needing his rest, and to the amusement of his companions, John orders the bedbugs out. Amusement turns to amazement, however, when the next morning John's companions wake to find the bugs obediently gathered together in the doorway, awaiting permission to return to their home in the straw. John awakens and grants his permission; they return, and he goes on his way (chaps. 60–61).

Saint John the Evangelist raises Drusiana from the dead, as depicted by Giotto di Bondone (1266–1336). Peruzzi Chapel, S. Croce, Florence, Italy.

John's supernatural powers are also shown in more massive demonstrations, including his destruction of pagan temples, through a word alone, and especially in his ability to raise the dead. A particularly intriguing episode comes in an account that continued to inspire storytellers and artists down through the Middle Ages, with a brilliant portrayal by Giotto, still on view in the Peruzzi chapel of the Church of Santa Croce in Florence. It is the bizarre story of the raising of Drusiana, the chaste and beautiful wife of Andronicus, a story that involves almost unheard-of chastity and crass immorality, a tale of attempted necrophilia, supernatural intervention, miraculous resurrection, and conversion to the life of purity.

It is a long and somewhat involved story. Andronicus is an important citizen of Ephesus. Both he and Drusiana have converted to Christianity through the missionary preaching of the apostle John, and as part of their commitment to Christ, they remain celibate with one another. But as so often happens in these accounts, another prominent citizen of Ephesus, Callimachus, falls in love with Drusiana and wants to commit adultery with her. As a recent convert to the life of chastity, she feels incredible guilt in stirring up such a wicked desire in him. The guilt causes her to become ill, and she dies.

They bury her in a family tomb. But not even her death assuages the passions of the wicked Callimachus, who bribes the family steward to let him into the crypt so that he can have sex with Drusiana's corpse. Before he can perform the evil deed, however, an enormous serpent appears, bites the steward (killing him), and entwines itself around Callimachus.

Soon thereafter, the apostle John and Andronicus come to the crypt to pay their respects. Discovering the doors open, they enter to find an angel, who informs them of what has happened. Along with the dead Drusiana they find the dead steward and Callimachus, dead beneath the serpent. What follows is a scene of seriatim resuscitation: First John raises Callimachus from the dead, who confesses to everything he did and wanted to do, and who converts to the true faith. John then raises Drusiana from the dead. She in turn wishes the steward raised and is empowered to do the deed herself. Once raised, however, rather than converting to faith in Christ, the steward curses them all, wishes himself still dead, and runs from the tomb. They find him later, wish fulfilled, felled by another poisonous serpent bite.

And so, in the end, chastity is preserved, in life and in death. Those who remain chaste have power far beyond what humans can possibly attain otherwise. Those who oppose the chaste and refuse to adopt their ways, on the other hand, not only fail to live well; they are also killed off as opponents of God and his representatives on earth.

Lost Views of Renunciation

We have seen that, as enjoyable as they are to read, the Christian Apocryphal Acts were about more than entertainment. They were about a new way of life, a new way of observing and living in the world, a new way of human existence, not rooted in what the modern press has labeled "family values" of community, children, and life in the home. These texts were meant to be disruptive of traditional society; they were designed to tear apart the fabric of communal existence and split up the home. The values they embodied are not those of this world: the warm protection of benevolent social forces, the satisfying enjoyment of the pleasures of life. Those who wrote these texts and those who embodied their perspectives looked not to the enjoyment of life in this world but to the world above, the world of God, which required the renunciation of this world and its pleasures and the establishment of alternative communities of like-minded Christians. To be sure, these texts focused on community, family, and sex. But it was precisely in order to *disrupt* the values of everyday life and its enjoyments.

This stress on the ascetic life—the life apart from the pleasures of the flesh—may have been a leading factor in the creation of these texts. But where did this doctrine of renunciation itself begin?[25] For the early Christians, it may have started with Jesus himself, who anticipated that this world and life as we know it would all come to an abrupt end when God appeared in judgment to overthrow the forces of evil in control of this earth and set up his own Kingdom, the Kingdom of God, in which there would be no more oppression, injustice, poverty, disease, famine, natural disaster, suffering, or evil.[26] If this world is soon to disappear, why be attached to its pleasures? It is better to prepare for the coming Kingdom, living simply and humbly in expectation of that final day. "Seek first the Kingdom of God . . . and all these other things will be added to you" (Matt. 6:3). When would that be? "Truly I tell you, some of you standing here will not taste death before the Kingdom of God has come in power" (Mark 9:1). There is no point becoming attached to this world if it is soon to be overhauled and remade.

Certainly Jesus' early followers were no hedonists. Paul appears to have expected that he, too, was living at the end of the age and that God would soon intervene in a cataclysmic act of judgment, to be brought by Jesus himself (1 Thess. 4:14–18; 1 Cor. 15:51–55). How should one live, then, in light of that coming reality?

> Concerning the matters about which you wrote, it is good for a man not to touch a woman; but because of sexual immorality, let each man have his own wife and let each woman have her own husband. . . . To those who are not married, and to the widows, I say that it is good for them to remain even as I am; but if they cannot keep themselves under control, let them marry. . . . In view of the present distress, I think that it is good for a person to remain as he is. Are you bound to a wife? Do not get separated. Are you separated from a wife? Do not get married. . . . Those who marry will suffer an affliction to their flesh, and I would spare you of that. This is what I mean, brothers: The time has grown short. From now on, those who have wives should be as those who do not. . . . For the outward form of this world is passing away (1 Cor. 7:1, 8, 26–31).

Even though the apocalyptic vision of Jesus, and then of Paul, faded, becoming lost to most of Christianity, the ascetic lifestyle it promoted lived on. A shift occurred in early Christian thinking, away from the sense that this world would be destroyed in a future act of divine wrath, toward the notion that this world was only a transient testing ground, a reflection of a greater reality, a mere shadow of the world that *really* mattered, the "real" world, the world of God. Christians for the most part stopped thinking in chronological terms about the present evil age and the future age to come, and started thinking in spatial terms about the present evil world (down here) and the good world of God (up there). Life lived for the real world, the upper world, could not be tied to life in this plastic or shadowy existence down here. The pleasures of this life were snares to be avoided if one were to experience a spiritual existence with God above. Anything that tied one too closely to this world must, as a result, be avoided at all costs. This was especially true of the pleasures of the body and, in particular, sex.

This, then, becomes one strand of Pauline Christianity. It is tied closely to the kind of Pauline Christianity known through the ages as the Christianity of Tertullian, and after him of the monastic communities that celebrated abstinence, and of the desert monks who worked to discipline the flesh in order to attain the salvation of the soul. But, in one of history's ironies, this ascetic strand of Christianity is also tied closely to the forms of lost Christianity opposed by Tertullian and his like.

The ascetic ideal went hand in glove with what we, in hindsight, might think of as the "liberated" form of ancient Christianity, which stressed the equality of women in Christ. For apocalypticists like Jesus, Paul, and their immediate followers, this age and the social conventions it embraces are passing away. That includes the distinctions between the sexes. And so it is no wonder that Jesus was reputed to have women followers who associated with him in public, ate with him, touched him, supported him. And no wonder, either, that Paul had women leaders in his churches and insisted that in Christ "there is not male and female."[27]

But neither Jesus nor Paul urged a social revolution. Why revolt against the present system in order to make society better in the long haul? For these people, there was never going to *be* a long haul. The end was coming soon, and the best one could do was prepare for it.

Even so, one can see how the message of Jesus and his followers would be attractive to women. In the coming kingdom there would be no oppression or injustice or inequality. Women and men would be equal. Some of Jesus' followers started implementing the ideals of that kingdom in the present, working to alleviate poverty and suffering, working for justice, striving for equality. This implementation of the ideals of the kingdom was clearly evident in the early churches, where slave and free, Greek and barbarian, man and woman were all given an equal standing.

That is why the tales of Thecla and other ascetic women were not an anomaly in the early Christian movement. They were a significant statement of an important stream of early Christianity. Here were women who refused to participate in the constraints of patriarchal society. They remained unmarried, not under the control of a husband. And they were travelers, not staying at home under the authority of a paterfamilias, a father, a male head of household. The ascetic life went hand in hand with freedom to decide what to do with their own bodies, how to treat them, how to live in them; it went hand in hand with freedom of movement, not restricted to the household and household chores and the care and education of children, which occupied most women's time.

Thus the asceticism advocated in the texts of the Apocryphal Acts both manifested and helped bring about a kind of liberation for Christian women. It is no surprise that women feature so prominently in the tales and no surprise that some scholars suspect that women were principally responsible for telling the tales, spreading the tales, embracing the tales, making the tales their own. Nor is it any surprise that other Christians hated the tales, outlawed the tales, burned the tales. It was these other Christians who, at the end of the day, proved the more powerful, for it was through the machinations of these other Christians—powerful proto-orthodox leaders and writers like Tertullian—that this stream of early Christianity was lost, only to be rediscovered in modern times.

Chapter Three

The Discovery of an Ancient Forgery: The Coptic Gospel of Thomas

As with political and broad cultural conflicts, the winners in battles for religious supremacy rarely publicize their opponent's true views. What if they were found to be persuasive? It is far better to put a spin on things oneself, to show how absurd the opposition's ideas are, how problematic, how dangerous. All is fair in love and war, and religious domination is nothing if not love and war.

And so, in early Christianity, as we have seen, most of the writings of the losing sides in the battles for dominance were destroyed, forgotten, or simply not reproduced for posterity—in one way or another lost. So much lost, so many texts. Some scholars would give anything to recoup them. But comparatively little has been found.

The little that has been found, of course, is spectacular. Discoveries began to be made in a significant way well back in the seventeenth century. And they escalated over time, as monastic libraries in Greece, Egypt, and other places were diligently searched, as archaeological expeditions turned up unhoped-for treasure, and as bedouin inadvertently stumbled across findings valued beyond our wildest dreams.

Some Spectacular Discoveries

There can be legitimate debates over what is the most significant manuscript discovery of modern times. Probably few would dispute the importance of the Dead Sea Scrolls, the first lot of which was found by pure serendipity in 1947 in a cave west of the Dead Sea, just thirteen miles east of Jerusalem, as a shepherd boy was looking for a lost goat. Other caves were searched; eleven yielded manuscript treasures.[1] And what treasures they were: manuscripts possessed and/or produced by a sectarian group of Jews living at roughly the same time and place as John the Baptist and Jesus; copies of the Hebrew Scriptures a thousand years older than anything previously in existence, allowing scholars to check the accuracy of scribes who copied the text in the intervening centuries; documents that describe and legislate on the daily life of this ascetic sect of Jewish monastics, known to history as the Essenes; books that expound their apocalyptic views of the world and its approaching end; texts that reveal their worship and liturgical life. This is a cache of manuscripts that will occupy scholars for decades still to come, possibly centuries.[2]

The importance of the Dead Sea Scrolls for early Christianity cannot be minimized. But the importance is indirect. Despite what one reads in sensationalist media guides and in dramatic theories sometimes advanced by otherwise competent scholars, the scrolls never mention John the Baptist or Jesus or any of Jesus' followers; they contain nothing Christian. They are important for early Christian studies (as opposed to early Jewish studies, for which they are directly relevant) because they give us a rare firsthand glimpse of society, culture, and religion in the birthplace of Christianity at just the time Christianity was born.

What about finds of direct significance for the early Christian movement? For a long time, the most significant discovery was one which has, again, ceased being a household term or even an object of study by laypeople interested in early Christianity. But it continues to retain its unique importance. The book known as the *Didache* (Greek for "teaching"; the full title is "The Teaching of the Twelve Apostles to the Nations") was discovered in the Patriarchal Library of Constantinople in 1873.[3] Published a decade later, its impact was huge, for this was a very ancient Christian writing, probably as ancient as some of the writings that became part of the New Testament, known to have been considered canonical by some Christian groups in the early centuries, a document that was totally unlike any of the books that did become canonical. This was a "church order," a book that gives instructions about the ethical life to be striven after by Christians and, yet more significant, directions concerning their liturgical life, indicating how Christians are to baptize (outdoors in cold running water, whenever possible), fast (on Wednesdays and Fridays, not Mondays and Thursdays like the Jews), pray (saying the Lord's Prayer three times a day), and celebrate the Eucharist (with prayers provided by the author, first over the cup and then the bread—the reverse order of the liturgy as it developed down to today). Moreover, the document gives extended instructions about what to do with itinerant apostles, teachers, and prophets, who are assumed to be in abundant supply, some of whom are living at the (considerable) expense of the communities they visit. The document tries to bring such prophetic freeloaders under some kind of control. The *Didache* thus gives significant insight into church life at the time of its composition, probably around 100 CE.

Other discoveries might be touted as even more revolutionary for our knowledge of early Christianity and its Scriptures. Some would point to the discovery, throughout the course of the twentieth century, of ancient manuscripts of the New Testament, hundreds of years older than manuscripts available to early Bible translators, such as those responsible for the King James Bible.[4] Among other things, these early manuscripts are significant for showing that the books of the New Testament were not copied with the assiduous care you might think or hope for. In fact, the earliest copyists appear to have been untrained and relatively unsuited to the tasks; they made lots of mistakes, and these mistakes were themselves then copied by subsequent copyists (who had only the mistake-ridden copies to reproduce) down into the Middle Ages. The more recently discovered earlier manuscripts, however, are closer to the originals of the New Testament books and so more likely to give us a sense of the original wording of each book.

Unfortunately, none of the original copies of any of the books of the New Testament survives, nor do any of the first copies nor any of the copies of the copies. By the end of the nineteenth century, prior to more recent discoveries, our earliest complete texts of the New Testament were from about the fourth century—that is, three hundred years after the writings themselves had been produced, three hundred years in which scribes of varying temperament and ability copied, and often miscopied, their Scriptures. Papyrus discoveries of the twentieth century improved matters significantly, however, so that now we have fragmentary copies of some New Testament writings that date from the late third century and earlier. The earliest surviving copy of any New Testament book is a little fragment called P^{52} (since it was the fifty-second papyrus cataloged). It is the size of a credit card, broken off from a larger page that originally formed part of an entire manuscript of the Gospel of John. It was discovered in a trash heap in Upper Egypt, probably in the city of Oxyrhynchus, and is housed now in the John Rylands Library in Manchester, England. Written on both sides,[5] it contains several verses from John's account of Jesus' trial before Pilate (John 18). Paleographers—experts in ancient handwriting—can date the fragment; it appears to have been written sometime in the first half of the second century, 125 CE ± twenty-five years, possibly just twenty-five or thirty years after John itself was first published.[6] This and other early papyri finds have helped us reconstruct the original words of the New Testament books, an important task, one must admit, since it is impossible to know what the New Testament means if you don't know what it says.

Other scholars would consider the discovery of noncanonical texts to be at least as important for understanding the history of earliest Christianity, including the Gospel of Peter already discussed, discovered in fragments about as old as our earliest New Testament texts (except for the remarkable but tiny P^{52}). Some would place at the top of this list of noncanonical discoveries a curious fragmentary manuscript of an "Unknown Gospel" that scholars designate Papyrus Egerton 2. We do not have enough of this text to determine which Gospel it came from or what it was called (hence the title *Unknown Gospel*). It was discovered among some papyri housed in the British Museum and published

A fragment of the Gospel of John (18:31–33, 37–38) discovered in a trash heap in the sands of Egypt. This credit-card sized scrap is the earliest surviving manuscript of the New Testament, dating from around 125–150 CE. Both front and back pictured here.

first in 1935; the manuscript itself appears to date to 150 CE ± twenty-five years, and it contains four fragments that narrate words and deeds of Jesus: a controversy with Jewish leaders, a healing of a leper (in which the poor fellow laments that he had been traveling with a group of lepers and inadvertently became infected), a controversy over whether to pay tribute to the state authorities, and the story of some kind of miracle that Jesus performs on the banks of the Jordan River, a story that, unlike the other three, has no parallel in the Gospels of the New Testament.[7] But even the other three are told quite differently from the more familiar canonical versions. This has led some scholars to think that this Unknown Gospel was produced earlier than Matthew, Mark, Luke, and John. Others think that it was written later by someone familiar with these other Gospels but who had also been influenced by oral traditions of Jesus that continued to be in circulation long after the Gospels of the New Testament were written. We need always to remember that these canonical Gospels were not seen as sacrosanct or inviolable for many long years after they were first put into circulation; no one, except possibly their own authors, considered them to be the "last word" on Jesus' teachings and deeds.

This is clear as well from the most recent noncanonical Gospel discovery, published in 1999 and called by its editors the *Gospel of the Savior*.[8] Discovered among papyri purchased and more or less buried away in the Berlin Egyptian Museum in 1967, this text was not recognized as a lost Gospel until the early 1990s. The text is written in Coptic, an ancient Egyptian language. Most of its thirty surviving pages are highly fragmentary, containing just a few broken-off lines with several surviving words. But there are several nearly complete pages, enough to provide some clues concerning what this lost Gospel contained. At the least, it gave an account of Jesus' final hours. The surviving portion of the text recounts the final instructions of Jesus to his disciples, his prayer to God that the "cup" might be taken from him, and then a final address to the cross itself.

These passages differ from the parallel accounts of the New Testament in some remarkable ways. For example, when Jesus asks his Father to "remove this cup from me," he does so not in the Garden of Gethsemane (as in the canonical accounts) but in a vision in which he has been transported to the throne room of God himself. In addition, this account records God's replies to Jesus' requests. But probably the most intriguing portion of this hitherto lost Gospel is its ending, where Jesus (who is called "the Savior" throughout the narrative) speaks several times directly to the cross. At one point, for example, he cries out, "O cross, do not be afraid! I am rich. I will fill you with my wealth. I will mount you, O cross. I will be hung upon you" (fragment 5H). We have no way of knowing what, if anything, the cross said in reply. Even so, this is obviously like the Gospel of Peter, where, at Jesus' resurrection, God speaks to the cross from heaven, and the cross responds. Whether the *Gospel of the Savior* originally contained much more than these final events and sayings of Jesus' life—for example, an entire account of his ministry—cannot be determined.

In other cases, however, complete texts of previously lost Gospels have been uncovered. And in the opinion of probably the majority of scholars of early Christianity, these are the most significant manuscript discoveries of modern times. In particular, it is the discovery of a library of texts in Upper Egypt, near the village of Nag Hammadi, that has generated the greatest scholarly interest and media attention. This was a discovery of inestimable value, as significant for early Christian studies as the Dead Sea Scrolls were for early Jewish studies. Had the Dead Sea Scrolls not been found, scholars would consider the Nag Hammadi library the greatest manuscript discovery of modern times. And among the books of the Nag Hammadi library, none has provoked such attention and created such intellectual fervor and excitement as the Gospel of Thomas, the single most important noncanonical book yet to be uncovered, a collection of the sayings of Jesus, some of which may be authentic, many of which were previously unknown.

The Discovery of the Nag Hammadi Library

It is an intriguing story, this chance discovery of a cache of ancient Christian documents in 1945, in a remote part of Upper Egypt, a story of serendipity, ineptitude, secrecy, ignorance, scholarly brilliance, murder, and blood revenge. Even now, after scholars have spent years trying to piece it all together, details of the find remain sketchy.[9]

We do know that it occurred in December 1945—about a year and a half before the discovery of the Dead Sea Scrolls hundreds of miles away in the Judean desert—when seven bedouin fieldhands were digging for *sabakh,* a nitrate-rich fertilizer, near a cliff called Jabal al-Tarif along the Nile in Upper Egypt. The fertilizer was used for the crops they grew near their small hamlet of al-Qasr, across the river from the largest village of the area, Nag Hammadi, some three hundred miles south of Cairo and forty miles north of Luxor and the Valley of the Kings. The leader of the group, the one responsible for the find once it was made and the one who later divulged the details of the discovery, was named, memorably enough, Mohammed Ali. It was Ali's younger brother, however, who actually made the find, accidentally striking something hard below the dirt with his mattock. It turns out to have been a human skeleton.[10] Digging around a bit, they uncovered, next to the skeleton, a large earthenware jar, about two feet high, with a bowl over the top, sealed with bitumen.

Mohammed Ali and his companions were reluctant to open the jar, for fear that it might contain an evil genie. On further consideration, they realized it might also contain gold, and so without further ado they smashed into it with their mattocks. But there was no genie and no gold—just a bunch of old leatherbound books, of little use to this group of illiterate bedouin.

Ali divided up the find, ripping the books apart so everyone would get a fair share. His companions evidently wanted no part of them, however, and so he wrapped the lot in his turban, returned home, and deposited them in the outbuilding where they kept the animals. That night, his mother evidently used some of the brittle leaves to start the fire for the evening meal.

The story gets a bit complicated at this point, as real life intrudes, but in an almost unreal way. Mohammed Ali and his family had for a long time been involved in a blood feud with a tribe in a neighboring village. It had started some six months earlier, when Ali's father, while serving as a night watchman over some imported German irrigation machinery, had shot and killed an intruder. By the next day, Ali's father had been murdered by the intruder's family. About a month after they discovered the old books in the jar, Mohammed Ali and his brothers were told that their father's murderer was asleep by the side of the road, next to a jar of sugarcane molasses. They grabbed their mattocks, found the fellow still asleep, and hacked him to death. They then ripped open his chest, pulled out his still warm heart, and ate it—the extreme act of blood vengeance.

As it turns out, the man they had murdered was the son of a local sheriff. By this time, Mohammed Ali had come to think that perhaps these old books he had found might be worth something. Moreover, he was afraid that since he and his brothers would be prime suspects in this cold-blooded murder, his house would be searched for clues. He gave one of the books over to the local Coptic priest for safekeeping until the storm blew over.

This local priest had a brother-in-law who was an itinerant teacher of English and history, who stayed in his home once a week while making his rounds in the parochial schools in the area. The history teacher realized that the books might be significant enough to fetch a good price, and he went to Cairo to try to sell the volume in his possession. It was not an altogether successful attempt, as the book was confiscated by the authorities. Eventually, however, he was allowed to sell it to the Coptic Museum.

The director of the museum had a good idea what the book was, and to make a long story short, in conjunction with a young visiting French scholar of antiquity, Jean Doresse, whom he had known in Paris—known fairly well, in fact, as the director had proposed marriage to Mrs. Doresse before she became Mrs. Doresse—managed to track down most of the remaining volumes and acquire them for the museum. Doresse had the first chance to look them over as a scholar. Eventually an international team was assembled by UNESCO to photograph, study, translate, and publish them. The international team was headed by an American scholar of the New Testament and early Christianity, James Robinson. The work was finally accomplished, we now have editions of the collection available in quality English translations, and you can purchase them online or in almost any really decent used bookstore.[11]

What is this ancient collection of books? The short answer is that it is the most significant collection of lost Christian writings to turn up in modern times.[12] It includes several Gospels about Jesus that had never before been seen by any western scholar, books known to have existed in antiquity but lost for nearly 1,500 years. The cache contained twelve leather-bound volumes, with pages of a thirteenth volume removed from its own, now lost, binding and tucked inside the cover of one of the others. The pages are made of papyrus. The books themselves are anthologies, collections of texts compiled and then bound together. Altogether there are fifty-two treatises preserved among these volumes. But six of the treatises are duplicates, making a total of forty-six documents in the collection. They include Gospels by such persons as Jesus' disciple Philip and secret revelations delivered to his disciple John and another to James; they include mystical speculations about the beginning of the divine realm and the creation of the world, metaphysical reflections on the meaning of existence and the glories of salvation; they include expositions of important religious doctrines and polemical attacks on other Christians for their wrongheaded and heretical views—especially Christians we would call proto-orthodox.

The documents are written in ancient Coptic. But there are solid reasons for thinking that they were each originally composed in Greek. For some of the books there is no question about it: Among the texts, for example, is a small extract taken from Plato's *Republic*. For other works, including the Gospel of Thomas, we have Greek fragments that date from a much earlier period.[13] For some works, linguists are able to determine that the Coptic is "translation" rather than "original composition" Coptic.

The leather-bound books themselves were manufactured in the second half of the fourth century. We know this because the spines of the leather bindings were strengthened with scrap paper, and some of the scrap paper came from receipts that are dated 341, 346, and 348 CE. The books thus must have been manufactured sometime after 348 CE.

The date of the books, of course, is not the same as the date of the documents found within the books—just as the Bible (another anthology) lying on my desk was manufactured in 1998, but the documents it contains were written some 1,900 years earlier. So, too, with the Nag Hammadi texts: They were originally written long before the end of the fourth century when these particular books were made. The Greek fragments of the Gospel of Thomas I just mentioned date from the second century, and as I've pointed out in an earlier chapter, this Gospel along with others in the collection was known to church fathers of the second and third centuries. When were the texts of these books written? Obviously they were produced at different times and places (Plato's *Republic,* e.g., in the fourth century BCE); but most of them appear to have been in existence by the second Christian century at the latest. Scholars have engaged in hard fought debates over the dates of some of these books, especially over whether they were composed as early as the first century, before the books of the New Testament. Among these particular debates, those over the Gospel of Thomas are probably the most heated.

We do not know exactly who wrote these books or why they came to be hidden under the cliff of Jabal al-Tarif, just above the bend of the Nile, north of Luxor. It is probably significant that a Christian monastery, founded by the famous Christian monk Saint Pachomius in the fourth century, is located just three miles away. Scholars have been inclined to think that these books may have come from the library of the monastery, a view supported by the contents of the scrap paper in their bindings. But why would monks have disposed of the books?

As we will see more fully in a later chapter, a significant moment occurred in the history of the formation of the New Testament canon in the late fourth century. It was in the year 367 CE that the powerful bishop of Alexandria, Athanasius, wrote a letter to the churches throughout Egypt under his jurisdiction, in which he laid out in strict terms the contours of the canon of Scripture. This was the first time anyone of record had indicated that the twenty-seven books that we now have in our New Testament canon, and only those twenty-seven books, should be considered as Scripture. Moreover, Athanasius insisted that other "heretical" books not be read. Is it possible that monks of the Pachomian monastery near Nag Hammadi felt the pressure from on high and cleaned out their library to conform with the dictates of the powerful bishop of Alexandria? If so, why did they choose to hide the books instead of burn them? Is it possible that they, the ones who hid the books in an earthenware jar off in the wilderness, were actually fond of these books, and decided to hide them away for safekeeping until the tides of scriptural preference shifted, and they could be retrieved for their library of sacred texts? We will never know.

We will be discussing others of these books in the so-called Nag Hammadi library later, when we come to examine one form of early Christian Gnosticism, arguably the most significant and certainly one of the most fascinating forms of Christianity that came to be "lost." For now, we will look at just one of the books, the one that has proved most intriguing and significant for historians of early Christianity, a forgery known by name from ancient times, which came to be lost, only now to be discovered. It is a forgery of the teachings of Jesus written in the name of one who should know them better than anyone: his twin brother, Didymus Judas Thomas.

The Sayings of Thomas

The Gospel of Thomas is a complete text: we have its beginning, its end, and everything in between.[14] It consists of 114 sayings of Jesus, and apart from the introductory verse by the author, almost nothing else. There are no stories told about Jesus here: no birth, no baptism, no miracles, no travels, no trials, no death, no resurrection, no narrative of any kind. Most of the sayings are simply introduced by the words, "Jesus said. . ." followed by another verse that begins, "Jesus said. . . ." In some instances there is dialogue between Jesus and the disciples, in which they say or ask something and Jesus responds, or he says something and they respond. These are the closest thing to a narrative in the book. There is no obvious organizing pattern to the collection of sayings. A few of them are connected by topic or by "catchwords," but for the most part the sequence appears to be completely random.

Over half of the sayings found in the Gospel of Thomas are similar to sayings found in the New Testament Gospels (79 of the 114, by one count). In some instances, these similarities are quite close. Here, for example, you can find the well-known parable of the mustard seed

> The disciples said to Jesus, "Tell us what the kingdom of heaven is like." He said to them, "It is like a mustard seed. It is the smallest of all seeds. But when it falls on tilled soil, it produces a great plant and becomes a shelter for birds of the sky." (Saying 20, cf. Mark 4:30–31)[15]

And, in a somewhat more terse form than in the New Testament, the comment about the blind leading the blind:

> Jesus said, "If a blind man leads a blind man, they will both fall into a pit." (Saying 34; cf. Matt. 15:14)

And one of the beatitudes:

> Jesus said, "Blessed are the poor, for yours is the kingdom of heaven." (Saying 54; cf. Luke 6:20)

Many of these sayings are pithier and more succinct than their canonical counterparts. Is it possible that Thomas presents a more accurate version of the sayings than, say, Matthew, Mark, and Luke (there are fewer parallels to John)—that is, a closer approximation to the way Jesus actually said them?

Other sayings begin in a familiar way, similar to something in the New Testament Gospels, but then shift into a different, somewhat odd sounding key. For example, Saying 2:

> Jesus said, "Let him who seeks continue seeking until he finds. When he finds, he will become troubled. When he becomes troubled, he will be astonished, and he will rule over the all."

The saying begins like Matt. 7:7–8, "Seek and you shall find." But what does it mean when it speaks of being troubled, becoming astonished, and ruling over "the all"? Or consider Saying 72:

> A man said to him, "Tell my brothers to divide my father's possessions with me." He said to him, "O man, who has made me a divider?" He turned to his disciples and said to them, "I am not a divider, am I?" (cf. Luke 12:13–14)

Or take an example near the end, Saying 113:

> His disciples said to him, "When will the kingdom come?" Jesus said, "It will not come by waiting for it. It will not be a matter of saying, 'Here it is' or 'There it is.' Rather, the kingdom of the father is spread out upon the earth, and people do not see it."

Again, the passage starts in a familiar way (cf. Mark 13:4 or esp. Luke 17:20–21), but ends somewhere else.

Then there are a large number of sayings that sound even more remote from what one finds on the lips of Jesus in the canonical Gospels (except for in a few set phrases). Just to take three rather striking instances:

> Jesus said, "This heaven will pass away, and the one above it will pass away. The dead are not alive and the living will not die. In the days when you consumed what is dead, you made it what is alive. When you come to dwell in the light, what will you do? On the day when you were one you became two. But when you become two, what will you do?" (Saying 11)
> His disciples said, "When will you become revealed to us and when shall we see you?" Jesus said, "When you disrobe without being ashamed and take up your garments and place them under your feet like little children and tread on them, then will you see the son of the living one, and you will not be afraid." (Saying 37)
> Jesus said, "That which you have will save you if you bring it forth from yourselves. That which you do not have within you will kill you if you do not have it within you." (Saying 70)

What is one to make of these peculiar sayings? What do they mean? And where did they come from?

First, on the matter of where they came from. Since so many of the sayings are similar to those of the New Testament Gospels, there have always been scholars who have claimed that "Thomas" (no one thinks this was really Thomas, the brother of Jesus, but for the sake of convenience, we will grant him his pseudonym) used the New Testament Gospels as a source, modifying their sayings and adding some of his own.[16]

To explain this position more fully, I need to digress for a moment. The closest parallels with the sayings of Thomas are those found in Matthew, Mark, and Luke. These three are commonly known as the Synoptic Gospels (literally meaning: "seen together"), since they have so many stories and sayings in common that they can be put in parallel columns and compared carefully with one another. Long before the Gospel of Thomas was discovered, scholars were intrigued by the question of why the Synoptics were so similar to one another, why they often tell exactly the same stories, in the same sequence, sometimes word for word the same, and yet at other times they differ in stories told, sequence, and wording. The solution that was eventually devised for this "Synoptic Problem," a solution that is still held by the majority of researchers today, is that Matthew and Luke both used Mark as a source for a number of their stories. But Matthew and Luke have a number of additional passages almost entirely made up of sayings that are not found in Mark. Mark could not therefore be the source for these passages. Where then did Matthew and Luke acquire them? The theory developed that Matthew and Luke took these passages, principally sayings, from another source that has since been lost. The German scholars who devised this theory decided to call this other source *Quelle,* the German word, conveniently enough, for "source." It is frequently called Q for short.

Q then provided the material found in Matthew and Luke but not in Mark. It is widely assumed that Q was an actual document, written in Greek, in circulation in the early church, a document that recorded at least two deeds of Jesus (the story of Jesus' temptations is in Q, as is an account of his healing the son of a centurion) and a number of his teachings, including the Lord's Prayer, the Beatitudes, and other familiar sayings.[17]

In the nineteenth century, one of the principal objections to the existence of this hypothetical lost Gospel, Q, was that it was hard to imagine—impossible for some scholars—that any Christian would have written a Gospel containing almost exclusively Jesus' teachings. Most striking was the circumstance that in none of the Q materials (that is, in none of the passages found in Matthew and Luke, but not in Mark) is there an account of Jesus' death and resurrection. How, asked skeptical scholars, could any early Christian write a Gospel that focused on Jesus' sayings without emphasizing his death and resurrection? Surely *that* is what Gospels are all about: the death of Jesus for the sins of the world and his resurrection as God's vindication of him and his mission.

This was a common argument against the existence of Q, until the Gospel of Thomas was discovered. For here was a Gospel consisting of 114 sayings of Jesus, with no account of Jesus' death and resurrection. Even more than that, this was a Gospel that was concerned about salvation but that did not consider Jesus' death and resurrection to be significant for it, a Gospel that understood salvation to come through some other means.

Salvation through some other means? What other means? Through correctly interpreting the secret sayings of Jesus.

The very beginning of the Gospel of Thomas is quite striking, in that it reveals the author's purpose and his understanding of the importance of his collection of sayings and, relatedly, of how one can acquire eternal life:

> These are the secret sayings which the living Jesus spoke and which Didymus Judas Thomas wrote down. And he said, "Whoever finds the interpretation of these sayings will not experience death." (Saying 1)

The sayings recorded here are said to be secret; they are not obvious, self-explanatory, or commonsensical. They are hidden, mysterious, puzzling, secret. Jesus spoke them, and Didymus Judas Thomas, his twin brother—wrote them down. And the way to have eternal life is to discover their true interpretation. Rarely has an author applied so much pressure on his readers. If you want to live forever, you need to figure out what he means.

Before proceeding to an interpretation of the Gospel, an interpretation that has suddenly assumed an eternal importance, I should say a final word about Thomas in relation to the Synoptics.

No one thinks that Thomas represents the long-lost Q source. A large number of the sayings in Q are not in Thomas, and a number of the sayings in Thomas are not in Q. But they may have been similar documents with comparable theological views. The author of Q, too, may have thought that it was the sayings of Jesus that were the key to a right relationship with God. If so, in losing Q we have lost a significant alternative voice in the very earliest period of early Christianity. Most scholars date Q to the 50s of the Common Era, prior to the writing of the Synoptic Gospels (Mark was some ten or fifteen years later; Matthew and Luke some ten or fifteen years after that) and contemporary with Paul. Paul, of course, stressed the death and resurrection of Jesus as the way of salvation. Did the author of Q stress the sayings of Jesus as the way? Many people still today have trouble accepting a literal belief in Jesus' resurrection or traditional understandings of his death as an atonement, but call themselves Christian because they try to follow Jesus' teachings. Maybe there were early Christians who agreed with them, and maybe the author of Q was one of them. If so, the view lost out, and the document was buried. In part, it was buried in the later Gospels of Matthew and Luke, which transformed and thereby negated Q's message by incorporating it into an account of Jesus' death and resurrection. One more form of Christianity lost to view until rediscovered in modern times.

We are still left with the question of where the pseudonymous author of the Gospel of Thomas, posing as Jesus' twin, Didymus Judas Thomas, derived his sayings. While the matter continues to be debated among scholars, most think that he did not use the Synoptic Gospels as a source: There are not enough word-for-word agreements to think he did (unlike the extensive agreements among the Synoptics themselves). Most think, instead, that he had heard the sayings of Jesus as they had been transmitted orally, by word of mouth (just as Mark, for example, heard his stories), and then collected a number of them together, some similar to those found in the Synoptics, some like the Synoptic sayings but with a twist, some not at all like the Synoptic sayings.

Interpreting the Gospel of Thomas

If understanding these sayings correctly is the prerequisite for eternal life, how are we to interpret them? Few matters have been more hotly debated by scholars of early Christianity over the past several years.[18] As we will see in a later chapter, a majority of the documents discovered at Nag Hammadi are closely tied into one or another of the various forms of religious belief and identity that scholars have identified under the umbrella term *Gnosticism*. On those grounds, from the beginning, a majority of interpreters have understood the Gospel of Thomas itself as some kind of Gnostic Gospel. More recently, this view has come under attack, principally by scholars who fear that interpreting Thomas from a Gnostic perspective requires one to *import* Gnosticism into a text that does not itself show signs of Gnostic perspectives. The debates have therefore centered on whether or not there *are* Gnostic perspectives evident in the text itself. I will be arguing below that there are and that these can help us explain some of the more difficult sayings of the Gospel.[19]

I will be giving a fuller explanation of that system later. For now it is enough to give it in broad outline and show how it can unpack some of the more peculiar sayings of this fascinating book, which was lost and now is found.

Gnostic Christians varied widely among themselves in basic and fundamental issues.[20] But many appear to have believed that the material world we live in is awful at best and evil at worst, that it came about as part of a cosmic catastrophe, and that the spiritual beings who inhabit it (i.e., human spirits) are in fact entrapped or imprisoned here. Most of the people imprisoned in the material world of the body, however, do not realize the true state of things; they are like a drunk person who needs to become sober or like someone sound asleep who needs to be awakened. In fact, the human spirit does not come from this world; it comes from the world above, from the divine realm. It is only when it realizes its true nature and origin that it can escape this world and return to the blessed existence of its eternal home. Salvation, in other words, comes through saving *knowledge*. The Greek term for knowledge is *gnosis*. And so these people are called Gnostics, "the ones who know." But how do they acquire the knowledge they need for salvation? In Christian Gnostic texts, it is Jesus himself who comes down from the heavenly realm to reveal the necessary knowledge for salvation to those who have the spark of the divine spirit within.

Let me stress that I do not think the Gospel of Thomas attempts to describe such a Gnostic view for its readers or to explicate its mythological undergirding. I think that it *presupposes* some such viewpoint and that if readers read the text with these presuppositions in mind, they can make sense of almost all the difficult sayings of the book.

For example: Saying One claims that the one who finds the interpretation of Jesus' secret sayings will not experience death. The sayings are thus secret; they are not open to the public but only for those in the know. Moreover, their interpretation—*knowing* what they mean—is what brings an escape from the death of this world. Saying Two, quoted above, is about seeking and finding. Knowledge is to be sought after, and when you realize that everything you thought you knew about this world is wrong, you become troubled. But then you realize the truth about this world, and you become amazed. And when that happens, you return, ultimately, to the divine realm from which you came and rule with the other divine beings over all there is. Or as expressed in another saying, "Whoever has come to *understand* the world has found only a corpse, and whoever has found a corpse is superior to the world" (Saying 56). This material world is dead; there is no life in it. Life is a matter of the spirit. Once you realize what the world really is—death—you are superior to the world and you rise above it. That is why the one who comes to this realization "will not experience death" (Saying 1).

Coming to this realization of the worthlessness of this material world, and then escaping it, is like taking off the clothing of matter (the body) and being liberated from its constraints. Thus an effective image of salvation: "When you disrobe without being ashamed and take up your garments and place them under your feet like little children and tread on them, then will you see the son of the living one and you will not be afraid" (Saying 37). Salvation means escaping the constraints of the body.

According to this Gospel, human spirits did not originate in this material world but in the world above:

> Jesus said, "If they say to you, 'Where did you come from?' say to them, 'We came from the light, the place where the light came into being of its own accord.' If they say to you, 'Is it you?' say, 'We are its children, and we are the elect of the living father.'" (Saying 50)

Thus we came from the world above, the world of light, where there is no enmity, no division, no darkness; we ourselves came from the one God and are his elect, and he is our ultimate destination: "Jesus said, 'Blessed are the solitary and elect, for you will find the kingdom. For you are from it, and to it you will return'" (Saying 49).

It is indeed amazing that this material world came into being as a place of confinement for divine spirits. But as amazing as it is, it would have been completely impossible for it to be the other way around, that human spirits came into being as a result of the creation of matter:

> If the flesh came into being because of spirit, it is a wonder. But if spirit came into being because of the body, it is a wonder of wonders. Indeed, I am amazed at how this great wealth [i.e., the spirit] made its home in this poverty [i.e., the material world/body]. (Saying 29)

For spirits trapped in this material world it is like being drunk and not being able to think straight, or being blind and unable to see. Jesus came from above, according to this Gospel, to provide the sobering knowledge or the brilliant insight necessary for salvation, and those who were trapped here were in desperate need of it:

> Jesus said, "I took my place in the midst of the world and I appeared to them in flesh. I found all of them intoxicated; I found none of them thirsty. And my soul became afflicted for the sons of men, because they are blind in their hearts and do not have sight. . . . But for the moment they are intoxicated. When they shake off their wine, then they will repent." (Saying 28)

Why then is it that the "dead are not living and the living will not die" (Saying 11)? Because the dead are merely matter; and what is not matter but spirit can never die. How is it that "on the day you were one you became two" (Saying 11)? Because you were once a unified spirit, but becoming entrapped in a body, you became two things—a body and a spirit—not one. The spirit must escape, and then it will be one again.

This salvation will not, therefore, be salvation that comes *to* this world; it will be salvation *from* this world. The world itself, this material existence, is not something that was created good (contrary to the doctrines of the proto-orthodox). It is a cosmic catastrophe, and salvation means escaping it. For that reason, the Kingdom of God is not something coming to this world as a physical entity that can actually be said to *be* here in this world of matter. The Kingdom is something spiritual, within:

> If those who lead you say to you, "See the kingdom is in the sky," then the birds of the sky will precede you. If they say to you, "It is in the sea," then the fish will precede you. Rather the kingdom is inside of you, and it is outside of you. . . . When you come to know yourselves . . . you will realize it is you who are the sons of the living Father. (Saying 3)

Notice once again the key: *knowing* yourself, who you really are.

Since this world is a place to escape, no one should be tied to material things: "Do not be concerned from morning until evening and from evening until morning about what you will wear" (Saying 36). Instead, all that the world

The opening of the Coptic Gospel of Thomas, which begins (in the middle of the page) with the words "These are the secret words which the living Jesus spoke, and Didymus Judas Thomas wrote them down."

has to offer, all the riches it can provide, should be rejected in order to escape this world: "Whoever finds the world and becomes rich, let him renounce the world" (Saying 110). And so, one should not be attached to anything in this world; as indicated in the pithiest of the sayings of the Gospel, "Become passers-by" (Saying 42).

The key to the salvation brought by Jesus is having the proper knowledge, gnosis—knowledge of your true identity:

When you come to know yourselves, then you will become known, and you will realize that it is you who are the sons of the living father. But if you will not know yourselves, you dwell in poverty [i.e., the material world/the body] and you are that poverty. (Saying 3b)

Jesus himself is the one who can provide this knowledge, knowledge that the human spirit is divine, as divine as Jesus himself and one with Jesus: "He who will drink from my mouth will become like me. I myself shall become he, and the things that are hidden will be revealed to him" (Saying 108). And so Jesus brings the knowledge necessary for the divine spirits to be reunited with the realm whence they came. That is why Jesus is not a "divider" (Saying 72). He is not a divider but a unifier.

This stress on becoming "one," reunified with the divine realm in which there is no conflict and no division, is why the text emphasizes so strongly oneness, singleness, solidarity: "For many who are first will become last, and they will become one and the same" (Saying 4); "Blessed are the solitary and elect, for you will find the Kingdom" (Saying 22). Or as Jesus indicates when the disciples ask, "Shall we then as children enter the Kingdom?":

> When you make the two one, and when you make the inside like the outside and the outside like the inside, and the above like the below, and when you make the male and the female one and the same, so that the male not be male nor the female female; and when you fashion eyes in place of an eye, and a hand in place of a hand, and a foot in place of a foot, and a likeness in place of a likeness, then you will enter the kingdom. (Saying 22)

Restore all things to their original unity, where there are not parts but only a whole, no above and below, no outside and inside, no male and female. That is where there is salvation to those who have been separated off, divided from the divine realm. Perhaps it is this idea which can make sense of what is possibly the most peculiar and certainly the most controversial saying of the Gospel of Thomas, Saying 114:

> Simon Peter said to them, "Let Mary leave us, for women are not worthy of life." Jesus said, "I myself shall lead her in order to make her male, so that she too may become a living spirit resembling you males. For every woman who will make herself male will enter the kingdom of heaven."

The saying has caused a good bit of consternation, especially among feminist historians of early Christianity who are inclined to see, for good reason, that many Gnostic groups were more open to women and their leadership roles in the church than were the proto-orthodox. But how does one understand this verse, that women must become male in order to enter the Kingdom?

It is virtually impossible to understand what the verse can mean without recognizing that in the ancient world, the world of this text, people generally understood gender relations differently than we do. Today we tend to think of men and women as two kinds of the same thing. There are humans, and they are either male or female. In the ancient world, genders were not imagined like that. For ancient people, male and female were not two kinds of human; they were two *degrees* of human.

As we know from medical writers, philosophers, poets, and others, women in the Greek and Roman worlds were widely understood to be imperfect men. They were men who had not developed fully. In the womb they did not grow penises. When born, they did not develop fully, did not grow muscular, did not develop facial hair, did not acquire deep voices. Women were quite literally the weaker sex. And in a world permeated with an ideology of power and dominance, that made women subservient and, necessarily, subordinate to men.

All the world, it was believed, operates along a continuum of perfection. Lifeless things are less perfect than living; plants less perfect than animals; animals less perfect than humans; women less perfect than men; men less perfect than gods. To have salvation, to be united with God, required men to be perfected. For some thinkers in the ancient world, the implications were clear: For a woman to be perfected, she must first pass through the next stage along the continuum and become a man.[21]

And so, salvation for this Gospel of Thomas, which presupposes a unification of all things so that there is no up and down, in and out, male and female, requires that all divine spirits return to their place of origin. But for women to achieve this salvation, they obviously must first become male. The knowledge that Jesus reveals allows for that transformation, so that every woman who makes herself male, through understanding his teaching, will enter then into the Kingdom.

As I have pointed out, for this Gospel, it is Jesus himself who brings that knowledge. "When you see one who was not born of a woman [i.e., Jesus, who only "appeared" to be human], prostrate yourselves on your faces and worship him. That one is your father" (Saying 15). Or as he says later in the Gospel, "It is I who am the light which is above them all. It is I who am the all. From me did the all come forth, and unto me did the all extend. Split a piece of wood, and I am there. Lift up the stone, and you will find me there" (Saying 77). Jesus, the all in all, permeates the world and yet comes to the world as the light of the world that can bring the human spirit out of darkness so as to return to its heavenly home by acquiring the self-knowledge necessary for salvation.

This then is the Gospel of Thomas, a valuable collection of 114 sayings of Jesus, many of which may reflect the historical teachings of Jesus, but all of which appear to be framed within the context of later Gnostic reflections on the salvation that Jesus has brought. Unlike the Gospels of the New Testament, in this Gospel Jesus does not talk about the God of Israel, about sin against God and the need for repentance. In this Gospel it is not Jesus' death and resurrection that bring salvation. In this Gospel there is no anticipation of a coming Kingdom of God on earth.

Instead, this Gospel assumes that some humans contain the divine spark that has been separated from the realm of God and entrapped in this impoverished world of matter, and that it needs to be delivered by learning the secret teachings from above, which Jesus himself brings. It is by learning the truth of this world and, especially, of one's one divine character, that one can escape this bodily prison and return to the realm of light whence one came, the Kingdom of God that transcends this material world and all that is in it.

A remarkable document, an ancient forgery condemned as heretical by early proto-orthodox Christians and lost or destroyed, until the remarkable discovery of the Gnostic library in Upper Egypt, near Nag Hammadi, preserved now for us as the secret sayings of Jesus, which, if rightly understood, can bring eternal life.

Chapter Four

The Forgery of an Ancient Discovery? Morton Smith and the Secret Gospel of Mark

Undoubtedly the best known forgeries of recent memory are the infamous Hitler Diaries.[1] Headline news in April 1983, both before and after their exposure as fabrications, the Hitler Diaries were significant for showing that the art of forgery is still alive and well among us, that some people will go to extraordinary lengths to perpetrate a fraud, and that even experts can be fooled. In this case there is little doubt about the motivation. The West German swindler who wrote the diaries, Konrad Kujau, was paid $4.8 million for his sixty volumes of work, which he produced over the course of three years. Eventually convicted of the fraud and sentenced to prison, he emerged penniless but not broken; he went into the business of producing "genuine forgeries" of great masterpiece painters Monet, Rembrandt, and van Gogh, signing them with both his and their names, and selling them as curiosities for tidy sums. Eventually, in what appeared for a time to be a never-ending story, a counterfeit submarket was established in which Kujau imitators sold fakes of his forged paintings. To cap it all off, Kujau wrote an autobiographical account of his exploits which was to appear in 1998; instead, a different book was published in his name, entitled *Die Originalität der Fälschung* ("The Originality of Forgery"). Somewhat appropriately, he claimed, evidently truthfully, not to have written a word of it.

Kujau was most famous, however, for the fraud he perpetrated on the public in the Hitler Diaries, sold to the German magazine *Stern* for serial publication. English publication rights were sold to the *Sunday Times* and *Newsweek* magazine. There was, naturally, some concern over the authenticity of these amazing documents, which allegedly were Adolf Hitler's own handwritten diaries kept from June 1932 all the way up to the end of his life, April 1945. Kujau claimed that the diaries had been pulled from a downed German plane trying to escape Berlin in 1945 and had remained in East Germany until smuggled out by his brother, an officer in the East German army. In the early days of the "discovery," some suspected an East German or neo-Nazi plot, since the diaries appeared to put a human face on the Führer and to exonerate him of any direct involvement with the Final Solution. But on the face of it, the diaries looked authentic. They were, in fact, verified by a famous British historian, Hugh Trevor-Roper, author of *The Last Days of Hitler*. It was on Trevor-Roper's recommendation that the *Times* had agreed to pay out an enormous sum for publication rights.

But the day before the first installment was to appear, Trevor-Roper expressed some second thoughts. He had seen the diaries only briefly under tight security, and believed, a bit late in the day, that further corroboration was needed. Experts were called in. And the diaries were shown beyond any doubt to be forged. Kujau later explained how he had done them: pouring tea on the pages and striking them on his table to make them look old and worn, using a Gothic style script for authenticity, borrowing heavily from published biographies for the nuts and bolts of Hitler's daily life, and adding mundane and at times insipid details of his thoughts and feelings to round it all out. As it turns out, the political agenda is not what drove the deceit. Kujau just wanted the money.

Other forgeries have been perpetrated in modern times, of direct relevance to our current study of early Christian apocrypha. One might think that in our day and age, no one would be so deceitful as to pawn off any firsthand accounts of Jesus as authentic. But nothing could be further from the truth. Strange Gospels appear regularly, if you know where to look for them.[2] Often these record incidents from the "lost years" of Jesus, for example, accounts of Jesus as a child or a young man prior to his public ministry, a genre that goes all the way back to the second century. These accounts sometimes describe Jesus' trips to India to learn the wisdom of the Brahmins (how *else* would he be so wise?) or his exploits in the wilderness, joining up with Jewish monks to learn the ways of holiness.

These new Gospels do not need to concern us overly much here; most of them are as artificial as one can imagine and are useful chiefly in revealing the gullibility even of modern readers. They tend to be the stuff of supermarket tabloids and are valuable in showing that there are still forgers in our midst who have no qualms about fabricating complete lies, even about their own religion, in order to make a splash and possibly get across their point of view. Or, at least, to earn some royalties.

But what about serious forgery by trained academics, experts in ancient languages and history? Does such a thing ever occur in the modern world? Do scholars ever forge documents for their own ends, whatever those ends may be?

The answer here again is quite unambiguous, for it occasionally does happen and the forgers themselves are occasionally detected. It tends to be harder to pin forgery on a real scholar than on a creative but unskilled layperson: No one attempts the deed without feeling reasonably good about his or her chances of pulling it off, and given sufficient scholarly ingenuity, it is indeed sometimes possible to stay a step ahead of the skeptics. But not always.

An amusing instance involves an article published in a highly respected scholarly journal in 1950.[3] The article was entitled, somewhat ironically, "An Amusing Agraphon." The term *agraphon* literally means "unwritten," but it is a technical term used by New Testament scholars to refer to a saying of Jesus that is recorded in some ancient source other than the canonical Gospels. There are a large number of such sayings, for example, in the noncanonical Gospels (as we are seeing) and other places.[4] In Acts, Paul quotes Jesus as saying, "It is more blessed to give than to receive" (Acts 20:35). Jesus may well have said so, but the saying is not found in the canonical Gospel accounts of his teachings, and so it is an agraphon.

The "amusing agraphon" was allegedly found in a manuscript that contained a set of sermons on the Gospel of Matthew. The author of the article was a respected professor of classics at Princeton University, Paul Coleman-Norton, who indicated that in 1943, while with the U.S. armed forces in the town of Fédhala, in French Morocco, he was visiting a Muslim mosque and was shown there a peculiar thick tome filled, as one might expect in that setting, with Arabic writings. But inserted among its leaves was a single parchment page containing a Greek text, a fragmentary copy of a Greek translation of a set of originally Latin homilies on Matthew chapters 1–13 and 19–25. Given the situation—war time in French Morocco—and the exigencies of the moment, he was not able to photograph the page, but he was allowed to make a careful transcription of it. Later, when Coleman-Norton was able to study the text at greater leisure, he found that it contained a striking and previously unknown agraphon.

In Matt. 24:51, after Jesus' famous warning about the one who will be "cast into the outer darkness where there will be weeping and gnashing of teeth," the manuscript indicated that Jesus' conversation continued. One of the disciples, puzzled by Jesus' statement, asked a question that may have occurred to others over the years: "But Rabbi, how can this happen for those who have no teeth?" Whereupon Jesus is said to have replied: "Oh you of little faith! Do not be troubled. If some have no teeth, then teeth will be provided."

It is a terrific little agraphon, almost too good to be true. And in fact, it was too good to be true. My own professor in graduate school, Bruce Metzger, had been a student of Coleman-Norton in the classics department at Princeton *before* the war. As Metzger himself tells it, his revered Latin professor used to regale his class (in the 1930s) with the witticism that dentures would be provided in the afterlife for all those who were toothless, enabling them to weep and gnash their teeth.

No one else has ever seen the ancient page of Greek text in French Morocco that allegedly contained the verse. Metzger concludes—and everyone appears to agree with him—that Coleman-Norton simply made the story up and published it, with an erudite philological analysis, in the respected *Catholic Biblical Quarterly*.

Why? Possibly because he thought it would be a good joke to play on his fellow scholars and possibly to see if he could get away with it. And he nearly did.[5]

I have begun this chapter with these accounts of modern forgery not because I think that the text I want to discuss here is the same thing—a forgery by a modern scholar intent on deceiving the academic world—but because scholars in increasing numbers have begun to suspect that it is. As far as I can tell, the jury is still out. The person at the center of the controversy is no longer living to answer the charges—one of the reasons, no doubt, they have started to proliferate. This was one of the truly brilliant scholars of ancient Christianity in the late twentieth century: massively erudite, enormously well-read, and, to put it bluntly, an intellectual cut above most of the academics he had to contend with. And he knew it. Known for his rapier wit, his general unwillingness to suffer fools gladly, and an occasional mean streak, Morton Smith was not someone to cross swords with.

Morton Smith spent the bulk of his career as professor of ancient history at Columbia University. His learned scholarly contributions covered many fields: Greek and Latin classics, New Testament, Patristics, second-temple Judaism, rabbinics. Few could match his range or depth. But he is probably best known for a remarkable discovery made relatively early in his distinguished career: the discovery of a previously unknown letter by Clement of Alexandria, a famous proto-orthodox church father of the early third century, many of whose other writings we still possess. In this newly discovered letter, Clement indicates that the church in Alexandria had *several* versions of the Gospel according to Mark. One was for regular Christians, and another was for the spiritually advanced. But this one for the spiritually advanced had been pilfered by a group of heretics, who corrupted its teachings to make it conform with their own lawless and licentious religious practices. Clement writes this letter to explain the situation and to indicate what the second version of Mark's Gospel (for the spiritually elite) contained. In doing so, he quotes two of the passages from this other version, passages not known from the New Testament. If authentic, this letter would raise significant questions for the study of the New Testament and the history of early Christianity. It would make us rethink our interpretations of the earliest surviving accounts of Jesus. It would drive us to reconsider our reconstruction of the historical Jesus. It would be one of the most significant discoveries of the twentieth century. If it were authentic.

The Discovery

We need to begin with the tale of the discovery, as recounted by Morton Smith in his sundry publications on the Secret Gospel of Mark, especially the two books published fifteen years after the discovery—one for a general audience, a beautifully written piece that reads like a detective novel, and one for scholars, a detailed linguistic and philological analysis of the text and its significance.[6]

In 1941, as a twenty-six-year-old graduate student, Smith had gone to the Holy Land on a traveling fellowship from Harvard Divinity School. Unfortunately, the Mediterranean was closed by the war, and he was stuck in Jerusalem. While there he became acquainted with a leader of the Greek Orthodox Church, who invited him to services at the famous Church of the Holy Sepulchre and, eventually, to visit the famous Orthodox monastery of Mar Saba, some twelve miles southeast of Jerusalem. Mar Saba was established in the fifth century of the Christian era and had been the scene of ongoing monastic activity virtually nonstop ever since.

While Smith was there on his visit, he absorbed the fascinating worship life of the monks, who devoted their lives to the adoration of God, beginning their communal daily services of worship six hours before sunrise. During the day he was shown around the place. He saw, among other things, the monastery libraries, not much used by the monks, who had matters other than study on their minds. After two months, Smith returned to Jerusalem and his work, writing a doctoral dissertation in modern Hebrew, later translated into English as *Tannaitic Parallels to the Gospels,* a work of real erudition.[7]

When the war ended, Smith returned to Harvard, and there did a *second* Ph.D. on ancient Palestine. During that time, he became interested in Greek manuscripts, their discovery and decipherment, working under a well-known scholar of classics. Eventually he landed a teaching position, then another, and eventually became professor of ancient history at Columbia.

In 1958, Smith was awarded a sabbatical and decided to return to Mar Saba, now not as a young graduate student but as an established scholar. His interests had evolved over the years; now he was far less intrigued by the monastic patterns of worship and far more interested in the monastic library. Everyone connected with the monastery knew that its literary treasures had been removed long ago to the library of the Greek Patriarchate in Jerusalem. But Smith recalled that the monastic library was a disordered shambles and that its collection had never even been cataloged. He decided to spend his sabbatical making a catalog, partially in hopes of finding something of significance among either the ancient printed editions or the few manuscripts (i.e., handwritten documents) still there.

He worked daily, going through a few volumes at a time. It is not easy producing a catalog like this; the books are in Greek and Latin, some are missing their covers and title pages, and it is only by reading around in them a bit that one can learn what they are. But Smith was unusually gifted in languages and was able to make progress, one volume at a time, determining what each book was and preparing cards for a full catalog. And he found some interesting and valuable items, for example, fragments of a fifteenth-century manuscript of an otherwise lost work of the ancient Greek playwright Sophocles, fragments that had been used to strengthen the binding of an eighteenth-century prayer book.[8] Nothing that he found, however, prepared him for what was to become the major discovery of his life and arguably one of the most significant finds of the twentieth century.

Leafing through a volume that was missing its cover and title page, but which he recognized as an early edition of the writings of Ignatius of Antioch, a proto-orthodox bishop of the early second century, Smith found, scrawled on the blank pages at the end, a handwritten copy of a letter. It was in Greek, in what appeared to be an eighteenth-century style of handwriting.[9] The handwritten text began with the words, "From the letters of the most holy Clement, the author of the Stromateis. To Theodore . . ."

After deciphering that much, Smith realized he was on to something. Scholars of ancient Christianity know a great deal about "Clement, author of the Stromateis." This is Clement of Alexandria, a famous theologian and ethicist who lived and wrote around 200 CE. A number of his writings still survive, including a book of ethical instructions concerning how Christians should live their daily lives and a book that is called the Stromateis, which means something like "the miscellanies," a collection of somewhat random theological and moral reflections. Smith already knew that among all the writings of Clement that survive, none is a personal correspondence, a letter. This, then, was a new discovery of a lost document from early Christianity. How often does *that* happen? For most scholars, never.

On the spot, Smith decided to photograph the three pages that contained the handwritten copy of Clement's letter, but chose to hold off translating the entire text until later, reasoning that if some such treasure had turned up, there might be more where that came from; given his limited time, he did not want to miss a thing. Using a handheld camera, he took three sets of photos, just to be sure. And then he went about his business hunting for other significant finds and cataloging the results.

Nothing else of comparable significance turned up. And Smith did not realize the full significance of this handwritten letter until later, when he translated it and saw what it actually contained. The letter is addressed to an otherwise unknown person named Theodore, written in response to some of his queries about a particularly notorious sect of early Christians known as the Carpocratians, named after the founder of their sect, Carpocrates.

We know about Carpocrates and his followers from the other writings of Clement and from those of his older contemporary, Irenaeus, bishop of Lyons, and some years later, Hippolytus of Rome.[10] The Carpocratians were particularly vilified by such proto-orthodox authors because they were believed to engage in wild licentious activities as part of their liturgical services of worship, which were reputed to be nothing short of sexual orgies conducted under the guise of religion. In one place Clement indicates that the Carpocratians had invented a theology to justify their lecherous activities, proclaiming that since God had made all things, all things were to be held in common among God's people. Thus no one was to own any property or to keep anything to himself or herself. This included one's spouse. To celebrate the sovereignty of God over all things, therefore, the Carpocratians urged a kind of liturgical spouse-swapping, in which each person would have sex with someone else's spouse as part of the worship service (*Miscellanies* 3.2).

Irenaeus also indicates that the Carpocratians taught a peculiar doctrine of reincarnation, which said that the soul must be progressively trapped in human bodies until it had experienced everything that a body could experience, after which it could be released. The way to ensure a quick release, then, was to allow the body to engage in every kind of profligate activity. And so, on religious grounds, claims Irenaeus, the Carpocratians urged every bodily experience imaginable, including every sexual experience imaginable, all as part of their plan of salvation (see *Against Heresies* 1.25). The Carpocratians, in short, were not looked upon as a moral lot.

And that is the Christian sect Clement takes on in this letter. He begins by congratulating Theodore, who was evidently some kind of church leader, for "silencing the unspeakable teachings of the Carpocratians." He goes on to indicate that they are the heretics prophesied in Scripture, dwellers in darkness, filled with falsity, slaves of their own servile desires. He then notes that the Carpocratians claim sacred authority for their teachings in the Gospel of Mark, but that they have falsified some of what Mark said and misinterpreted other things. Clement proceeds, then, to clarify some important aspects of Mark's Gospel and to show how the Carpocratians had falsified it.

Clement indicates that Mark wrote an account of Jesus' public ministry based on his acquaintance with the apostle Peter in Rome; in his Gospel, however, Mark did not divulge the secret teachings of Jesus to his disciples. But after Peter was martyred, Mark moved to Alexandria and there composed a second "more spiritual Gospel" for those who were more spiritually advanced. Even though he still did not divulge the greatest secrets of Jesus' teachings, he did add stories to his Gospel to assist the Christian elite in progressing in their knowledge of the truth.

After Mark died, Carpocrates managed to persuade an elder of the church in Alexandria to provide him with a copy of this Secret Gospel, which he interpreted according to his own nefarious doctrines and, what is worse, modified by adding some of his own teachings to it. According to this letter, in other words, there were three versions of Mark's Gospel available in Alexandria: the original Mark (presumably the Mark we are familiar with in the canon); a Secret Mark, which he issued for the spiritually elite; and a Carpocratian Mark, filled with the false teachings of the licentious heretic.

And now comes the most significant part. Clement goes on to quote two passages from Mark's second, secret edition. Here, presumably, we have access to two very ancient accounts of Jesus, known from no other source, until this lost letter reappeared. The first passage, Clement indicates, occurs immediately after what is now Mark 10:34, and reads as follows:

They came to Bethany, and a woman was there whose brother had died. She came and prostrated herself before Jesus, saying to him, "Son of David, have mercy on me." But his disciples rebuked her. Jesus became angry and went off with her to the garden where the tomb was.

Immediately a loud voice was heard from the tomb. Jesus approached and rolled the stone away from the entrance to the tomb. Immediately he went in where the young man was, stretched out his hand, and raised him by seizing his hand.

The young man looked at him intently and loved him; and he began pleading with him that he might be with him. When they came out of the tomb they went to the young man's house, for he was wealthy.

And after six days Jesus gave him a command. And when it was evening the young man came to him, wearing a linen cloth over his naked body. He stayed with him that night, for Jesus was teaching him the mystery of the Kingdom of God. When he got up from there, he returned to the other side of the Jordan.

It is this newly recovered story which has caused the greatest stir in connection with Smith's discovery. For even though it is similar to stories in the canonical Gospels, such as the raising of Lazarus in John 11 and the story of the rich young man in Mark 10, there are significant differences. And some of the differences, especially near the end, have appeared to some interpreters, notably Smith himself, to have clear homoerotic overtones. Jesus becomes acquainted with a young man who loves him and who comes to him wearing nothing but a linen cloth over his naked body. Jesus then spends the night with him, teaching him about the mystery of the Kingdom. What is *that* all about?

Before discussing Smith's own interpretation, which is what led to the initial furor over the discovery, we should consider what else Clement says about the text. He next quotes several words that Theodore had asked about, words that clearly advance the homoerotic hints already noticed. But Clement insists strongly these were not to be found in the Secret Gospel itself but were, therefore, a Carpocratian corruption. The words were: "Naked man with naked man."

After all that, the final passage quoted from the Secret Gospel comes as a bit of an anticlimax. Clement indicates that after Mark 10:46 came another addition, which simply said, "And the sister of the young man Jesus loved was there, along with his mother and Salome. And Jesus did not receive them."

The letter goes on to say that the other passages Theodore had asked about (but which are not cited) are falsifications of the text. It concludes, "Now the true interpretation and that which is in accordance with the true philosophy. . . ." And here the text breaks off. We do not know what Clement said next.

Authenticating and Interpreting the Letter

Morton Smith devoted much of his research for the next fifteen years to studying this find. Roughly speaking, the work involved establishing the authenticity of the letter and determining the meaning of the passages quoted from the

The Monastery of Mar Saba, where Morton Smith made his remarkable find.

Secret Gospel. In 1973, Smith published the results of his labors in two books, one a popular account for general audiences, full of interesting anecdotes and still worth reading, *The Secret Gospel: The Discovery and Interpretation of the Secret Gospel According to Mark,* the other an erudite report on his investigations for scholars in the field, *Clement of Alexandria and a Secret Gospel of Mark,* an amazing book of scholarship but inaccessible for the most part to those who do not have the requisite ancient languages and extensive expertise in the field of Christian antiquity.

With respect to the authentication of the letter, there were, and still are, significant questions to be addressed: Was the letter actually written into the blank pages of this book by a scribe in the eighteenth century? If so, did he have a fragmentary copy of a letter of Clement at his disposal? Was this letter written by Clement, or could it have been forged? If it was written by Clement, did Clement actually know of two, or three, versions of Mark in his Alexandrian community? If he did, was he correct in thinking that both canonical Mark and Secret Mark came from the same author? And if he was correct that they did, did he get the sequence correct? That is to say, was Clement right that Secret Mark was an expansion of canonical Mark? Or is it possible that what Clement thought of as Secret Mark was in fact the original version of Mark, and that the stories in question came to be edited *out* by scribes who did not like their implications (possibly their homoerotic overtones?), thereby creating the Mark that we have in the New Testament?

Such questions had to be answered even before Smith could move on to interpret the passages of Secret Mark that Clement quotes. The first thing to establish was that an eighteenth-century scribe had written the letter on the blank pages of the book. The book itself, Smith later discovered, was itself a rare volume. Some additional research showed that this was the edition of the letters of Ignatius produced by the seventeenth-century Amsterdam printer Isaac Voss. Ignatius was a famous proto-orthodox bishop of Antioch, Syria, who died soon after most of the books of the New Testament had been written. He is an intriguing person himself: The writings we have from his hand are all letters that he dashed off in haste as he was being taken under armed guard to Rome, where he was to be martyred by being thrown to the wild beasts in the arena. Voss produced this particular edition of Ignatius's letters in 1646, and a significant edition it is. Throughout the Middle Ages there were *thirteen* or more letters circulating in the name of Ignatius, including one allegedly written to none other than Jesus' mother, the Virgin Mary. In the early seventeenth century, scholars had come to suspect that some, or all, of these letters were in fact forgeries. The debates were heated because the letters advocated the practice of having one bishop over each church, and as Puritans and Anglicans in England were thrashing over the question of the theological legitimacy of the office of bishop in the Church of England, Ignatius's correspondence was brought into play, by Anglicans, in order to show that there had *always* been bishops in the churches, from the beginning. One of the most significant participants in these exchanges was the young John Milton, years before he began work on *Paradise Lost*. An ardent Puritan, Milton insisted that the Ignatian letters were in fact forged. The world of scholarship turned against him, as it was eventually shown beyond reasonable doubt that whereas some of the letters written in Ignatius's name were forged, not all of them were. Some were authentic.[11]

The 1646 edition by Isaac Voss was the first to print just the authentic letters in their original Greek, none of the forgeries.[12] It was in a copy of this book that Smith found the letter from Clement. Obviously the letter could not have been copied into the back of the book before the book itself was produced; as a result, this copy of the letter could date to no earlier than the end of the seventeenth century. But how could a more precise date be determined?

Smith could not show palaeographers—experts in ancient handwriting— the book itself: It was still in the library of Mar Saba. But he did have the photographs. And so he showed them to a number of experts, most of whom agreed that the handwriting style did in fact appear to be that of an eighteenth-century hand. There was some disagreement—some thought the hand was late seventeenth century; some thought early nineteenth; some thought there were some strange letter formations, as if the scribe had been influenced by western styles of writing. But for the most part there was fair agreement: It was a Greek handwriting style of around 1750, plus or minus fifty years. The scribe of the letter, it was widely thought, was a scholar who produced his text in a hurry.

The next question was whether this copyist actually reproduced a genuine letter of Clement of Alexandria. There is no difficulty believing that a scribe of the eighteenth century might have had a fragmentary copy of an ancient letter at his disposal—possibly a loose sheet in the ancient library, known for its famous ancient texts—and that rather than simply discard it, he decided to preserve its contents by copying it onto the only spare pages to be found, those in the blank pages at the back of a book at hand. But how could one establish that the letter was from Clement rather than, say, from a forger pretending to be Clement hundreds of years later (who fooled, then, the eighteenth-century scribe who copied the letter)? The first step Smith took in answering the question was to show the letter to scholars who were experts in Clement, who had spent their lives studying Clement, who would recognize a new work by Clement simply on the basis of its subject matter and writing style. When he did so, the majority of the experts agreed, this looked very much like something Clement would write. If someone had forged it, she or he had done highly credible work.

But how could one know for sure? The only way to decide is by making a careful point-by-point comparison of the vocabulary, writing style, modes of expression, and ideas found in the letter with the vocabulary, writing style, modes of expression, and ideas found in the writings known to have been produced by Clement. This, needless to say, is not a simple task, not the sort of thing most people would care to undertake. But Smith did it. One word at a time. It was slow, arduous, painstaking work of many years. The results are published in his scholarly volume, and they are impressive.

It is possible to verify the Clementine vocabulary and style of the letter because previous scholars have devoted so much work to such things for many of the significant early Christian writers. In particular, in the early twentieth century, a German scholar named Otto Stählin published a four-volume critical edition of the works of Clement, based on a careful analysis of all the surviving manuscripts of his writings. The final volume of *Clemens Alexandrinus* appeared in 1936 and included detailed indexes of all the Clementine materials, including a complete vocabulary list, with indications of how frequently each and every word occurs in Clement's writings. This was not an easy kind of work to produce in the days before computers. But Smith was able to use this and similar resources to determine whether his discovery followed Clement's writing style and used his distinctive vocabulary and whether it ever used a style or words uncharacteristic of Clement.

The end result was that this letter looks *very* much like something Clement would have written. In fact, it is so much like Clement that it would be well nigh impossible to imagine someone other than Clement being able to write it, before tools like those produced by modern Clement scholars such as Stählin were available. Smith's verdict was that the letter actually was written by Clement of Alexandria.

But what about the quotations of Secret Mark? Is it really plausible that these come from an edition of Mark's Gospel different from the edition that made it into the canon?

The first thing to point out is that on the face of it, there is nothing at all implausible about the idea that Mark's Gospel circulated in different versions. In fact, we *know* that it did, since we have numerous manuscripts of Mark's Gospel, as well as of all the other books of the New Testament, and no two of these manuscripts are exactly alike in all their particulars. In all of them, this, that, or the other verse is worded differently. And some of the differences are significant. For example, when Jesus is approached by a leper who wants to be healed (Mark 1:41), rather than indicating that Jesus felt compassion (as found in most manuscripts), some of our earliest manuscripts instead say that he became angry. This clearly makes for a rather different version of the story.

Of even greater significance are the last twelve verses of Mark, in which Jesus appears to his disciples after the resurrection, telling them to preach the gospel to all the nations and indicating that those who believe in him will speak in strange tongues, handle snakes, and drink poison without feeling its effects. But this amazing and startling ending is not found in the oldest and best manuscripts of Mark. Instead, these manuscripts end at Mark 16:8, where the women at Jesus' tomb are told that he has been raised, are instructed to inform Peter, but then flee the tomb and say nothing to anyone, "for they were afraid." And that is the end of the story. For many readers this ending is even more amazing and strange than the other one, for in these manuscripts there is no account of Jesus appearing to his disciples after the resurrection.

In any event, there were different versions of Mark available in the early church, read by different people in different places. As a result, there is nothing at all implausible about there being two versions of Mark's Gospel in a big city like Alexandria.

But were the quotations of Secret Mark in this letter of Clement actually written by the author of the Gospel of Mark? Here again, it is a question of vocabulary, writing style, modes of expression, and theology. A careful analysis of the quotations of Clement indicates that these passages, while not in the style of Clement himself, are very much in the style of Mark as found in the New Testament.

Which version then came first: Secret Mark or canonical Mark? Here Smith pulls a switch, but it is a switch that has proved convincing to several other scholars as well. The quotations that Clement thought of as a second edition, Secret Mark, were in fact, Smith argued, part of the original Gospel of Mark, but were taken out by later scribes. And so the two versions of Mark were not, technically speaking, both produced by him. He wrote the longer version, and it came to be shortened by subsequent scribes who copied his text.[13] Clement misunderstood the true relationship of these two versions.

There are some interesting features of the shorter version—the one found in the New Testament—that can be explained if the longer version were the original, and this is some of the evidence that Smith and others have adduced for their view. To take the second quotation first. Clement indicates that it appeared after the first part of Mark 10:46: "And they came to Jericho; and as he was leaving Jericho with his disciples. . . ." This is a strange verse for several reasons. Why does it say "they came to Jericho" but then not indicate what happened there? In other words, why would Mark mention their arrival in town if they left without doing anything? And why does the text say that "they" came but that "he and his disciples" left? Why not just say "they" came and "they" left? These may seem like minor issues, but they are the kind of small details that should give one pause.

Notice what happens when the second passage cited by Clement is inserted into the account. They come to Jericho. Jesus encounters three women there but refuses to see them (this is not the first time in Mark's Gospel that Jesus might seem a bit rude; see Mark 3:31–35). Then he and his disciples leave. The passage seems to make better sense and the tiny problems with the details disappear.

Or consider the other of Clement's two quotations of the Secret Gospel. One passage that has always perplexed students of the canonical version of Mark's Gospel occurs near the end, when Jesus is arrested in the Garden of Gethsemane. When the soldiers seize him, all his disciples flee. But there is someone else there, "a young man" who is "clothed with a linen cloth over his naked body." The soldiers grab this unnamed man, but he escapes, nude, leaving them with the linen cloth in their hands (Mark 14:51–52). Who *is* this person, this follower of Jesus who has never been mentioned before? What is he doing in Gethsemane? And why is he wearing only a linen garment? Interpreters have propounded a host of possible solutions to these questions over the centuries, but there has never been any consensus.[14]

Once the longer passage of the so-called Secret Gospel is inserted, however, suddenly it makes sense, for in that story, too, there is a young man who comes to Jesus wearing nothing over his naked body but a linen cloth. This is a person Jesus has raised from the dead. He became Jesus' follower. He is the one grabbed in the garden. Maybe this *was* originally part of Mark's Gospel.

Smith, however, went even further. Not only was this passage originally in Mark. It is a key to understanding the ministry of the historical Jesus. Smith spins out an interpretation of the text which, at the end of the day, left most scholars breathless and many incensed. According to Smith, this passage reflects an actual practice of the historical Jesus. We know from other ancient sources that Jesus was widely considered to be a "magician." In an ancient context, that did not mean someone who, like David Copperfield today, can perform illusionist tricks with mirrors and sophisticated contraptions. A magician was someone who could, in reality, manipulate the workings of nature through mystical powers connecting him to the divine realm.

For Smith, Jesus really was a magician. In fact, Smith wrote another book devoted to the subject, called, appropriately enough, *Jesus the Magician*. And this identification of Jesus has a lot to do with this text. Smith is struck, quite understandably, by the fact that the young man comes to Jesus wearing nothing but a linen cloth over his nakedness. That sounds like someone coming forward for baptism, since in the early church, people were baptized, as adults, in the nude (after taking off a simple robe worn to the ceremony). Now the Synoptic Gospels of Matthew, Mark, and Luke do not indicate that Jesus baptized people. But the Gospel of John indicates that he *may* have done so (John 3:22; 4:1–2).[15] Moreover, the apostle Paul talks about baptism and indicates that at baptism a person is somehow "united" with Christ (Rom. 6:1–6). Did Paul, after Jesus' death, make up such a view himself? No, argues Smith, it was a view known to Jesus' followers before his death, because it was Jesus' own view. Jesus himself baptized people, and in that baptism they came to be united with him.

This being united with Jesus is somehow connected with the Kingdom of God because the text from the Secret Gospel indicates that this young man spent the entire night with Jesus being taught about the Kingdom. Smith thinks this conveys a historical datum about Jesus: Whomever Jesus baptized experienced a spiritual unity with him that involved a magical, visionary journey with him into the Kingdom of God. Moreover, this was not simply some kind of spiritual ecstasy. No, this mystical experience of the kingdom allowed the person, says Smith, to be "set free from the laws ordained for and in the lower world." Indeed, "freedom from the law may have resulted in completion of the spiritual union by physical union." In other words, when Jesus baptized a man, their spiritual union culminated in a physical coupling. Smith expresses some uncertainty concerning the ceremonies involved in this unification of Jesus and the man he was baptizing, but he does indicate in one of his footnotes that physical "manipulation, too, was probably involved; the stories of Jesus' miracles give a very large place to the use of his hands."[16]

The hands of a healer here take on a whole new meaning. In this fragment from Clement, Smith discovered that Jesus was a magician who engaged in sex with the men that he baptized.

I do not want to go into a prolonged discussion of every aspect of Morton Smith's interpretation of the Secret Gospel. Most scholars found his explication unconvincing at best; some were predictably outraged. Smith appeared to love it.

It has been pointed out, with some justice, that the text says nothing about Jesus using magic. It does not mention baptism. There is no word about an ecstatic vision or a spiritual unity with Jesus, let alone about anyone having sex with the Son of God. Some reviewers concluded that Smith found in the text what he brought to the text, and noted that he had been interested in ecstatic visions, heavenly journeys, law-free morality, and Jesus the magician years before he published his books on the Secret Gospel.[17] And, predictably, other scholars have interpreted the text in other ways. Some, for example, have seen it as a simple pastiche from other Gospel accounts, for example, borrowing phrases from the Gospels of Mark and John (rich young man; raising of Lazarus) and interpreted it as a later story wrongly thought to belong to Mark, a story that simply gave another account of Jesus raising someone from the dead and then giving him instructions in the mysteries of the Kingdom (cf. Mark 4:10–12).[18]

And yet one does need to take into account some of the peculiar details. Why *would* the text stress that this fellow was completely naked under his linen garment and that Jesus spent the night with him?

The Question of Forgery

Rather than pursue that question, I want to deal with the prior one. Is this an authentic letter of Clement, or was it forged? And if it was forged, forged by whom?

I am sorry to say that I will not be able to give a definitive answer, for reasons that will soon be apparent. At the outset, however, I should emphasize that the majority of scholars Smith consulted while doing his research were convinced that the letter was authentic, and probably a somewhat smaller majority agreed that the quotations of Secret Mark actually derived from a version of Mark. Even today, these are the majority opinions. But they have never been the full consensus. Some scholars have thought the letter was forged, either in antiquity or in the Middle Ages or in the modern period. Some have suspected from the beginning that Smith forged it. Those who think so appear to be increasing in number—or at least they are speaking out more, now that Smith is not around to respond.[19]

Among the earliest doubters was one of the greatest scholars of Christian antiquity of the twentieth century, Smith's own teacher at Harvard, Arthur Darby Nock, one of the few people in the field who could probably claim intellectual superiority to Smith in several of his own areas of expertise. Nock was one of the first scholars to whom Smith showed the photographs. And Nock was suitably impressed, even amazed by what he read. But to the end of his life his instincts—he was famous for his instincts—told him no, this was not genuinely Clementine. In his view, it was a "mystification for the sake of mystification," that is to say, a forgery by someone to see if she or he could get away with it. But Nock evidently did not think that it would have been a modern forger, let alone Smith. Others have thought otherwise.

There are a number of factors to consider. The first is nearly as amazing as the discovery itself, and it has been the source of heated contention ever since its announcement. From the moment Smith took his photographs, no other scholar has been able to subject the book to a careful and controlled examination.

There is no doubt that the book existed. There is no doubt that Smith photographed the relevant pages. There is no doubt that the letter is written is an eighteenth-century style of Greek hand. There is no doubt that the writing style of the letter is like Clement's. And there is no doubt that the quotations of Secret Mark are very much like Mark. But no one has carefully examined the book.

Why does that matter? After all, we have the photographs! It matters because the only way to see if a modern person has forged the text is to have the manuscript available for analysis. On the most basic level, until there is a chemical analysis of the ink, we cannot really know if the scribe was writing in the late 1750s—or the late 1950s.

It is true that a modern forgery would be an amazing feat. For this to be forged, someone would have had to imitate an eighteenth-century Greek style of handwriting and to produce a document that is so much like Clement that it fools experts who spend their lives analyzing Clement, which quotes a previously lost passage from Mark that is so much like Mark that it fools experts who spend their lives analyzing Mark. If this is forged, it is one of the greatest works of scholarship of the twentieth century, by someone who put an uncanny amount of work into it.

But it would not have been impossible. What seems most incredible to most of us is that someone could imitate an eighteenth-century style of handwriting in Greek! In fact, this is not at all impossible. We know of numerous forgers since the Renaissance who taught themselves different Greek and Latin writing styles and produced documents that fooled experts for years. Some documents are still probably unsuspected. In the 1850s and 1860s, a Greek scholar named Constantine Simonides passed off dozens of forgeries of ancient texts (including some in hieroglyphics) and made a small fortune doing it. For a long while, he managed to convince a good number of people that he in fact had forged the famous manuscript of the Bible, Codex Sinaiticus, discovered by the great manuscript hunter Constantine Tischendorf in the Monastery of St. Catherine's at Mount Sinai. This was the most significant New Testament manuscript discovered in the nineteenth century, and Simonides claimed that he himself had fabricated it. And he was so good at his craft, as everyone knew, that learned societies throughout England debated the merits of his claims for months.[20]

Someone with skill and patience can learn how to imitate a style of writing.[21] Moreover, it should be pointed out that in the case of the letter of Clement, there was not a *particular* scribe's hand that had to be imitated, simply a hand that looked like other hands of the eighteenth century. We cannot know if this eighteenth-century hand was actually writing in the eighteenth century until we can examine the ink. And the manuscript is unavailable.

I do not mean to say that it has *always* been unavailable, even though that is what scholars in the field invariably claim. Whether in serious publications or in popular accounts on the internet, nearly everyone who discusses the authenticity of this letter of Clement points out that no western scholar except Smith has ever laid eyes on the book. As it turns out, that is not true. In one of those quirky coincidences of history, the very evening I completed my first draft of this chapter, I met the last western scholar on earth to see the book.

I was at my colleague Elizabeth Clark's house for a social event. Also there was a scholar named Guy Stroumsa, a professor of comparative religions at Hebrew University in Jerusalem and a respected expert in early Christianity. Stroumsa happened to be in town to visit his daughter, who was just starting her Ph.D. program in classics at Duke University. The event was organized around Stroumsa's visit. He gave a brief talk—about Clement of Alexandria, as it turned out—and then we had a light dinner and social, academic conversation. He and I had never met before, but we knew each other's work. I told him I was writing a book on lost Christianities, and told him I had just completed a draft of my chapter on the Secret Gospel of Mark. To my astonishment—and everyone else's—Stroumsa told me that years ago he had tracked down the book and seen it with his own eyes. He could confirm that the letter was in the final pages (which, of course, no one doubted). But he suspects that no one will ever see the letter again.

I immediately stopped drinking and started listening. As a graduate student in 1976, Stroumsa found himself discussing the Secret Gospel with his teacher in Jerusalem, David Flusser, a highly erudite scholar of the New Testament and early Judaism. Flusser had claimed that the letter was probably forged. Stroumsa suggested they try to find it. It was, after all, only a forty-five-minute drive to the monastery. And so they called up another scholar at the university and a Greek Orthodox monk connected with the monastery, who happened to be doing a Ph.D. there at the time (and who could open the doors for them once they were there, so to speak). They all piled into Stroumsa's car and drove out to the monastery.

The dust was heavy over the library in the upper room of the tower, where Smith had done his work of cataloging nearly eighteen years earlier. Stroumsa suspected that no one had been in the library since. The monks were not taken to reading the complicated tomes stored in this out-of-the-way place. The foursome began their hunt, opening one book after the other, looking for an edition of Ignatius with a handwritten text on the final pages. After about fifteen minutes, one of the monks found it. It was right there on a shelf, where Smith had left it.

The scholars persuaded the monks to allow them to take the book back to the library of the Greek Patriarchate in Jerusalem, where they could find someone to do a chemical analysis of the ink. But once they had conveyed the book back with them, things turned out to be more complicated than they had expected. No one at the National Library was able to perform the necessary testing; Stroumsa was told that the only agency that could do it was the police department. When he informed the librarian who was keeping the book, he was told, "No thanks." The Greek Orthodox Christians were not eager to hand over one of their prized possessions—whether they read the book or not, it was still one of the sacred tomes of their library—to the Israeli (Jewish) authorities. That brought the matter to a close.

Some years later, someone told Stroumsa of a rumor that the letter of Clement had been cut out of the book for "safe-keeping." Stroumsa called the librarian at the Greek Patriarchate and was told that it was true. He himself had done just that. And he now did not know where the pages were.

And that's the end of the story. Did the librarian hide the pages, to keep scholars from rifling through the monks' treasured possessions looking for lost Gospels? Did he burn the pages simply to get them off his hands? Where are they now? Do they still exist? I'm afraid that as of this moment, no one appears to know. Maybe that will change. What is certain is that no one has carefully examined the book itself, and it may be that no one ever will.

Issues to Be Addressed

There are several matters to consider when reflecting on the question of whether the letter of Clement could be a modern forgery. When Smith was first maligned for not preserving the book, he quite rightly pointed out that it was not his to preserve. He assumed that it was still in the library, where he had found it. Fair enough. But one still must wonder. Smith was a brilliant scholar who spent fifteen years verifying the Clementine style of the writing. He knew full well about forgeries. And he knew that the only way to certify the authenticity of a document was to examine the document itself. Even if one is not allowed to apply chemical tests, one can look carefully at what cannot show up on photographs, especially those taken by a handheld camera of 1950s vintage— tiny marks on the page, indentations that indicate where the pen started and stopped, tiny flows of ink over lines, and the like. Many a forgery has been uncovered by a careful analysis of the actual physical specimen. But no one can verify this particular document. And one wonders why Smith himself did not go back to take a look. He was an expert in manuscripts. He knew what he would have to look for. He knew that he had not actually examined the pages themselves, say, under a magnifying glass, but had simply photographed them and moved on. Why spend so many years of one's life verifying a text without making the most important step?

In order to say for certain whether the text was actually written in the eighteenth century, we would need to examine the manuscript. Given the fact that we don't have it, I should point out several important questions raised by scholars who are skeptical of Smith's claims (not just his interpretation), and add a few of my own.

If this is a genuine letter of Clement, why does no other ancient source refer to it? To be sure, numerous ancient writings are never referred to. But one might think that such an important document would be known to *someone* among all the Christian heresy hunters of antiquity.

Why is it that Clement himself never mentions the letter, or the Secret Gospel, or the Carpocratians' corruption of it, in all his other writings? He certainly discussed the Carpocratians a good deal, attacking their views and detailing their heinous activities. Why does he not mention the Secret Gospel they have falsified?

Why does this text take a different stand on the spiritually elite than Clement does elsewhere in his writings? Elsewhere he maintains that those who are advanced in "knowledge," that is, those who are above the run-of-the-mill Christian, have more spiritual interpretations of the texts read in the church. Nowhere does he indicate that they actually have different versions of the same text. But here it turns out, as he says quite openly, they actually have a spiritual gospel written just for them. To some prominent scholars of Clement, this does not sound like Clement.[22]

And why does Clement here contradict what he says elsewhere about taking oaths? In his other writings, he is quite explicit that one must not swear falsely.[23] In this text, he advises that when confronting the Carpocratians about the existence of a Secret Gospel of Mark, one should "even deny it on oath," that is, tell a bald-faced lie under oath in order to win the argument. As Clement elsewhere is quite clear that one does not need to lie in order to uncover the truth, doesn't this letter contradict what he taught otherwise?

Moreover, if the contents of the letter seem somewhat unlike Clement in a couple of places, why is it that, on the other hand, the vocabulary and writing style of this document are *so* much like Clement? One impressive study, in fact, has shown that this letter of Clement is more like Clement than Clement ever is.[24] That may sound odd at first, so I should explain how it works. Suppose you have a friend who uses the word *awesome* a lot, and you want to impersonate her. It may turn out that if you were actually to count, she uses the term *awesome,* say, once every three hundred words. But when you imitate her, you use it once every fifty words so that anyone accustomed to hearing her speak will recognize this as one of her characteristic words and think, "Yes, sounds just like her." What we have here is a similar phenomenon: There is too much that is like Clement in this short letter, more than could be expected in any passage of comparable length elsewhere in Clement.

But how could someone imitate Clement so closely, using rare words that he uses, for example, but more frequently than he himself does? One should not forget the modern scholarship on Clement, especially the volumes by Stählin that provided indexes to all of Clement's vocabulary. As others have pointed out, if Smith could check to see if this vocabulary is like Clement's by using Stählin, then someone just as easily could have used Stählin to *make* this vocabulary like Clement's.[25]

Another intriguing issue involves the way the fragment of the letter ends. After discussing the nefarious ways of the heretical Carpocratioans, the author indicates, "Now the true explanation and that which accords with the true philosophy—" And that's where the text breaks off. Some readers have considered this a perfect place to end a forged piece right as the reader's hopes are raised but before they can be met.

On a different matter: What is one to make of the dedication of Smith's two books? The learned volume is dedicated to Arthur Darby Nock, the brilliant scholar who thought that the letter was a "mystification for the sake of mystification." The other volume, strikingly enough, is dedicated to "The One Who Knows." As one reviewer has asked, "Who is 'the one who knows'? And what does he know?"[26]

One other more technical matter. As I have pointed out several times in this study, when early Christian texts were copied by hand over the years, their copyists naturally made mistakes, which were then copied by still later copyists who copied these mistaken copies, and so forth. If this letter of Clement is authentic, it was written in the early third century and copied over the years until the copy was made that was reproduced by the eighteenth-century scribe who wrote it on the blank pages of the book that Smith discovered. But as it turns out, this letter as Smith found it does not have any major copying mistakes. How could this be? One classical scholar, Charles Murgia, an expert in copying practices of scribes and of forged texts, concluded that what we have in this letter is not a *copy* of a text but an *original edition.* That is to say, whoever put it in the back of this book was not copying a text but composing one, so that the letter is a forgery, of either the eighteenth century or later, say, the twentieth.[27]

There are two final issues to consider. Although not noted by other skeptics, these, in my view, are either signs of forgery or terrific ironies.

First, it is very peculiar that the letter appears in the particular book that it does: Voss's 1646 edition of the letters of Ignatius. If the letter is authentic, the placement in this volume is a brilliant irony; Voss's edition was the first to remove from the Greek manuscript tradition of Ignatius the forged Ignatian documents and the interpolations made into Ignatius's text by theologically motivated scribes. And what is the newly discovered text of Clement? A letter that describes forged documents and interpolations made into Mark's text by theologically motivated scribes. And it is a letter that itself may have been forged! Is this a craftily placed fingerprint or an intriguing coincidence?

Second, the letter begins on the first blank page at the end of the book. Surprisingly, scholars have not taken any notice of what is on the facing page, the final printed page of Voss's volume. Possibly they haven't noticed because the facing page is not found in the photographs of Smith's scholarly edition, the one that scholars engage with, but only in the popular edition, where the intended readers obviously cannot make heads or tails of it, since it is a commentary written in Latin about texts written in Greek. But the content of the page is striking. In his discussion here, the author, Voss, is noting a set of falsifications of manuscripts of the Epistle of Barnabas, another early Christian text. Voss lambastes scribes who have altered the text by making an addition to it. He points out that Ignatius was not the only one whose text was falsified by someone who wanted to make additions to it; so was Barnabas. And so he says: "Just as Ignatius had his own interpolators, who adulterated his text, so there have been others who believed that the same thing was permitted for the letter of Barnabas." He goes on to quote a bit of these falsified additions in one of the available manuscripts, and concludes by saying that he has given enough to give his readers an idea of what he means. He concludes by saying, in reference to the scribe who interpolated the falsified material, "That very impudent fellow filled more pages with these trifles." He then discusses one other textual falsification, which he indicates has misled previous scholars in their interpretation of the text. And that is the end of his discussion.

But then, on the opposite side, begins the letter of Clement, of several pages, which most scholars have taken as authentic, but which others consider to be a textual falsification and which goes at some length to discuss textual falsification, alleged "additions" (interpolations) of another ancient Christian text, the Gospel of Mark. Was there an "impudent fellow" involved in these interpolations as well, either in ancient or modern times?

Considering the Possibilities

Many scholars who simply are not sure whether Smith, or someone else, forged this letter of Clement have proceeded on the assumption that it is original and then given their own interpretation and assessment of its historical significance. What if we reverse the procedure and assume, for the sake of an argument, that it was forged? It would almost certainly have to have been forged after Stählin's 1936 edition of Clement was published. It would have to have been forged by someone who had access to the library of Mar Saba (not everyone is admitted). If the ironies of its placement in this particular book are not simply intriguing circumstances but fingerprints, then it would have to have been perpetrated by someone who knew the book was there in the library, who realized that this was the perfect place to copy the letter—for example, from an earlier visit to the library. Whoever perpetrated the fraud would have had to spend many years thinking it over and working out the wording of the letter, to make it sound like Clement, and the wording of the quotations of Secret Mark, to make them sound like Mark. This person would have had to become skilled in Greek manuscripts and to have learned to write in an eighteenth-century Greek hand. He or she would have had to have time, after long hours of practice, to write the letter in the back of the book. And he or she would have to invent a plausible account of its discovery.

What fun it would be to photograph the text and try it out, then, on a few scholars to see if it appeared convincing. If the first ones to see the photos were not convinced, well enough! Simply let it die there. But if they *were* convinced, maybe show the photos to a few more people. And then more. And then, yet more intriguing, decide to analyze what you yourself had written and make all sorts of discoveries about it, recognizing a few places where you missed the mark, where the forgery wasn't quite like Clement's style, point them out, and indicate that this is a sure sign that the letter wasn't forged, since no one would make such a gaff.

Is it conceivable that a scholar would forge this letter, just to see if it could be done? To create a "mystification for the sake of mystification?"

In the annals of forgery, it has been done before. One of the earliest known instances is another rather humorous account. In the fourth century before the Christian era, a philosopher known to history as Dionysius the Renegade[28] forged and published a play in the name of the fifth-century tragedian Sophocles. The play was cited as an authentic text by Dionysius's personal rival, the philosopher Heraclides. When Dionysius mocked Heraclides for not knowing a forged text when he saw it, Heraclides insisted that it was authentic. Dionysius claimed that he himself had forged it, and pointed out to Heraclides that the first letters of several of the lines were an acrostic, which spelled out the name Pankalos, who happened to be Dionysius's lover. Heraclides persisted, claiming that this was an accident. He was told, though, that if he would read on he would find yet more hidden messages, including the lines: "An old monkey is not caught by a trap. Oh yes, he's caught at last, but it takes time." This was probably convincing enough, but a final acrostic hidden in the text dealt the death blow. It said, "Heraclides is ignorant of letters and is not ashamed of his ignorance."[29]

I am not willing to say that Smith was a latter-day Dionysius the Renegade, that he forged the letter of Clement which he claimed to discover. My reasons should be obvious. As soon as I say that I am certain he did so, those pages cut from the back of the book will turn up, someone will test the ink, and it will be from the eighteenth century!

But maybe Smith forged it. Few others in the late twentieth century had the skill to pull it off. Few others had enough disdain of other scholars to want to bamboozle them. Few others would have enjoyed so immensely the sheer pleasure of having pulled the wool over the eyes of so many "experts," demonstrating once and for all one's own superiority. Maybe Smith did it.

Or maybe this is a genuine letter by Clement of Alexandria, and there really were different versions of the Gospel of Mark available in ancient Alexandria, one of which was lost until modern times, when it was uncovered, in part, in an ancient letter in an ancient library of an ancient monastery. If so, then the letter provides us with a glimpse of yet another lost form of Christianity, a group of Carpocratians who utilized an expanded version of the Gospel of Mark that they modified for their own purposes, possibly in order to justify their morally dubious communal activities.

Either way, whether forged or authentic, Morton Smith's letter of Clement provides us with one of the most interesting documents relating to early Christianity to be discovered in the twentieth century.

Part Two

HERESIES AND ORTHODOXIES

There is more to the question of Lost Christianities than the few texts we have already considered—more even than the dozens of others we have not—texts lost from sight, forgotten, thought to have been destroyed, only to reappear in modern times, the result of the archaeologist's diligent search or, more commonly, the fortunes of serendipity. For lost Christianities also involves the social groups that utilized these texts, groups of Christians who, like all groups of Christians at all times and in all places, understood themselves to be the fortunate heirs of the truth, handed down to them by their faithful predecessors, who received their understandings about God, Christ, the world, and our place in it from people who should know—ultimately from the apostles of Jesus, and through them from Jesus himself, the one sent by God.

Not everyone could be right, of course, in this understanding, for different groups of Christians in the ancient world held varying, even contradictory, points of view. Unless Jesus provided an entire panoply of self-contradictory teachings, then some, most, or all of these groups represented perspectives that were not his. Groups that insisted there was only one God (and that Jesus had taught so) could not be right if groups insisting there were two Gods (and that Jesus had taught so) were right.

In some ways, this matter of being "right" was a concern unique to Christianity. The Roman Empire was populated with religions of all kinds: family religions, local religions, city religions, state religions. Virtually everyone in this mind-boggling complexity, except the Jews, worshiped numerous gods in numerous ways.[1] So far as we can tell, this was almost never recognized as a problem. No one, that is, thought it was contradictory, or even problematic, to worship Jupiter and Venus and Mars and others of the "great" gods, along with local gods of your city and the lesser divine beings who looked over your crops, your daily affairs, your wife in childbirth, your daughter in sickness, and your son in his love life. Multiplicity bred respect and, for the most part, plurality bred tolerance. No one had the sense that if they were right to worship their gods by the means appropriate to them, you were therefore wrong to worship your gods by the means appropriate to them.

Moreover, one significant feature of these ancient religions—with the partial exception, again, of Judaism—is that worship never involved accepting or making doctrinally acceptable claims about a god. There were no creeds devised to proclaim the true nature of the gods and their interaction with the world, no doctrinally precise professions of faith to be recited during services of worship, no such thing as "orthodoxy" (right beliefs) or "heresy" (false beliefs). What mattered were traditionally sanctioned acts of worship, not beliefs.

But then came Christianity. As soon as some of Jesus' followers pronounced their belief that he had been raised from the dead, Christians began to understand that Jesus himself was, in some way, the only means of a right standing before God, the only way of salvation.[2] But once that happened, a new factor entered the religion scene of antiquity. Christians by their very nature became exclusivists, claiming to be right in such a way that everyone else was necessarily wrong. As some of the early Christian writings exclaimed, "There is salvation in no one else, for there is no other name under heaven given among humans by which we must be saved" (Acts 4:12) and "The one who believes in his name has eternal life; the one who does not obey the son will not see life, but the wrath of God remains on him" (John 3:36). Or, as Jesus himself was recorded as saying, "I am the way, the truth, and the life: No one comes to the Father except through me" (John 14:6).

Moreover, since Christians maintained that (a) what ultimately mattered was a right relationship with God, (b) a right relationship with God required belief, and (c) belief had to be in *something*, rather than some kind of vague, abstract faith that things were right (or wrong) with the world, then Christians, with their exclusive claims, had to decide what the content of faith was to be. What exactly does one have to believe about God in order to be right with him? That he is the supreme God above all other gods? That he is the only God and that no others exist? That he created the world? That before now he never had any involvement with the world? That he created the evil in the world? That he is completely removed from evil? That he inspired the Jewish Scriptures? That a lesser deity inspired those Scriptures?

What does one need to believe about Jesus? That he was a man? An angel? A divine being? Was he a god? Was he God? If Jesus is God and God is God, how can we be monotheists who believe in one God? And if the Spirit is God, too, then don't we have three Gods? Or is Jesus God the Father himself come to earth for the salvation of the world? If so, then when Jesus prayed to God, was he speaking to himself?

And what was it about Jesus that brought salvation? His public teachings, which if followed provide the way to eternal life? His secret teachings, meant only for the spiritually elite, whose proper understanding is the key to unity with God? His way of life, which is to be modeled by followers who like him must give up all they have for the sake of the kingdom? His death on the cross? Did he die on the cross? Why would he die on the cross?

The questions may have seemed endless, but their importance was eternal. For once it began to matter just *what* a person believed—so important that eternal life depended on it—the debates began. And different points of view emerged. All of the viewpoints claimed support, of course, in the teachings of Jesus—even the views that claimed there were 365 gods, that Jesus was not really a human being, that his death was simply a ruse meant to deceive the cosmic powers. Today we might think it nonsense to say that Jesus and his earthly followers taught such things, since, after all, we can see in the New Testament Gospels that it simply is not true. But we should always ask the historical questions: Where did we get our New Testament Gospels in the first place, and how do we know that *they*, rather than the dozens of Gospels that did *not* become part of the New Testament, reveal the truth about what Jesus taught? What if the canon had ended up containing the Gospels of Peter, Thomas, and Mary rather than Matthew, Mark, and Luke?

From the historians' perspective it is striking that all forms of early Christianity claimed authorization of their views by tracing their lineage back through the apostles to Jesus. The writings of Jesus himself, of course, were never an issue, because so far as we know, he never wrote anything. For this reason, apostolic authorship assumed a paramount importance to the earliest Christians. No wonder so much forgery was occurring among all groups, the proto-orthodox included.

But what of these other groups? We have looked at some important writings from the early Christian centuries, Gospels of Peter and Thomas, and, if it be authentic, (Secret) Mark, the Acts of Paul and Thecla, the Acts of Thomas, the Acts of John, an Apocalypse of Peter, and several other important books, lost and now found. There will be many more for us to consider as we proceed with our study. Not only are these documents important in themselves, however; so too are the social groups that produced, read, and revered them. For there were many early Christian groups, most of them recognizing the eternal significance of the theological truths that they claimed, and yet most of them also at odds—not just with the Roman religions surrounding them and the Jewish religion from which they emerged but also with one another. These internal disputes over which form of the religion was "right" were long, hard, and sometimes ugly.

Among the fascinating "discoveries" by scholars in modern times has been the realization of just how diverse these Christian groups were from one another, just how "right" each one felt it was, just how avidly it promoted its own views over against those of the others. Yet only one group won these early battles. Even this one group, however, was no monolith, for there were enormous untracked territories and gigantic swaths of doctrinal penumbrae within the broad contours of theological consensus it managed to create, shady areas where issues remained unresolved until later rounds of trial and error, dogmatism and heresy hunting, led to yet further debate and partial resolution. We will not be plumbing the depths of those later debates from the fourth century and later. Their nuances are difficult for many modern readers to appreciate or even fathom. Instead, we will focus our attention on the earlier centuries, when some of the most fundamental issues of early Christian doctrine were debated: How many gods are there? Was the material world created by the true God? Was Jesus human, divine, or both? These issues, at least, were resolved, leading to the creeds still recited today and the standardized New Testaments now read by millions of people throughout the world.

In this second part of our study, we will consider various groups that held wide-ranging opinions on such matters, groups attested in numerous ancient sources, including the writings of their Christian opponents who found their views offensive at best and damnable at worst. Four groups will occupy our attention in the chapters that follow: the Jewish Christian Ebionites, the anti-Jewish Marcionites, some early Christian Gnostics, and the group we have already labeled the proto-orthodox. Once we have described the various beliefs and, to a lesser extent, the known practices of these groups, we will be able to proceed in part 3 to consider how they engaged in their battles for dominance, leading to the virtual elimination of all groups from the Christian world through the victory of the one group that then successfully declared itself orthodox.

Chapter Five

At Polar Ends of the Spectrum: Early Christian Ebionites and Marcionites

To say that one of the ensured results of historical scholarship is that Jesus was a Jew may sound a bit trite, like saying that one of the assured results of modern science is that paper is combustible. Still, not even a century ago, the Jewishness of Jesus was a matter of real dispute among serious scholars of ancient Christianity. Moreover, throughout the history of the Christian church, even when Jesus' Jewish identity has not been denied it has been compromised, overlooked, or ignored. No one who working in the field of New Testament scholarship today, however, sees Jesus' Jewishness as contentious on the one hand or insignificant on the other. Jesus was Jewish, and any evaluation of his words, deeds, and fate needs to keep that constantly in mind.

Of course, determining what *kind* of Jew he was is another matter, and here the scholarly debates can be prolonged and harsh for insiders and a bit perplexing for outsiders. Is the historical Jesus best understood as a Jewish rabbi, who, like other rabbis, taught his followers the true meaning of the Law of Moses? Or as a Jewish holy man, who, like other holy men, could claim a special relationship with God that gave him extraordinary powers? Or as a Jewish revolutionary, who, like other revolutionaries, urged an armed rebellion against the Roman imperialists? Or as a Jewish social radical, who, like other social radicals, promoted a countercultural lifestyle in opposition to the norms and values of the society of his day? Or as a Jewish magician, who, like other magicians, could manipulate the forces of nature in awe-inspiring ways? Or as a Jewish feminist, who, like other feminists, undertook the cause of women and urged egalitarian structures in his world? Or as a Jewish prophet, who, like other prophets, warned of God's imminent interaction in the world to overthrow the forces of evil and bring in a new Kingdom in which there would be no more suffering, sin, and death?[1]

All of these options have their proponents among competent scholars who have devoted years of their lives to the matter yet cannot agree about some of the most basic facts about Jesus, except that he was Jewish. That at least is a start, however, and for our purposes here it is probably enough. Moreover, most scholars today acknowledge not only that Jesus was a Jew but that he was raised in a Jewish household in the Jewish hamlet of Nazareth in Jewish Palestine. He was brought up in a Jewish culture, accepted Jewish ways, learned the Jewish tradition, and kept the Jewish Law. He was circumcised, he kept Sabbath and the periodic feasts, and he probably ate kosher. As an adult he began an itinerant preaching ministry in rural Galilee, gathering around himself a number of disciples, all of whom were Jewish. He taught them his understanding of the Jewish Law and of the God who called the Jews to be his people. Most scholars would agree that some of these disciples, probably while Jesus was still living, considered him to be the Jewish Messiah, come to deliver God's people from the oppressive power of Rome to which they were subject. For one reason or another, the leaders of his people, the power players in Jerusalem, considered him a troublemaker, and when he appeared in the capital city for a Passover feast around 30 CE, they arranged to have him arrested and handed over to the Roman governor, who put him on trial for sedition against the state and executed him on charges of claiming to be king of the Jews.

And so Jesus was Jewish from start to last. His disciples were as well: born and bred Jews. Not long after his death, some or all of them came to understand Jesus as something more than a Jewish teacher (or holy man or revolutionary or social reformer or feminist or magician or prophet or whatever else he may have been). For them, Jesus was the one who had brought about a right standing before God for others. Some of his followers thought this salvation came through Jesus' death and resurrection; others said it came through his divine teachings. In any event, his followers soon came to proclaim that the salvation brought by Jesus was not for Jews alone, but was for all people, both Jew and Gentile.

Paul and His Judaizing Opponents

No one was more central to this proclamation to the non-Jew, the Gentile, than the apostle Paul. Paul was originally a Jewish Pharisee from outside Palestine, who had heard the Christian proclamation of Jesus, found it blasphemous, and worked to oppose it with all his heart and strength, one of the first and most forceful persecutors of the new faith (Gal. 1:13; cf. Acts 8:3). But Paul himself then had some kind of visionary experience of Jesus (Gal. 1:15–16; 1 Cor. 15:8–11) and changed from being the Christian movement's chief adversary to being its chief advocate, transformed from persecutor to proclaimer. Specifically, Paul saw himself as the apostle of Christ to the Gentiles.

Early on in Paul's efforts to take the gospel to the Gentile mission field, a major problem emerged. Gentiles, of course, were "pagans," that is, polytheists who worshiped numerous gods. To accept the salvation of Jesus, they had to renounce their former gods and accept only the God of Israel and Jesus his son, whose death and resurrection, Paul proclaimed, put them in a right standing with God. But in order to worship the God of the Jews, did they not have to become Jewish? The Jewish God, after all, had given the Jewish Law to the Jewish people. And the way his people *knew* they were his people was by keeping his Law, a Law that gave specific guidelines, say, about how they were to worship and live together in community. This Law stipulated that God's people should avoid worshiping pagan idols and should obey certain broadly acceptable ethical regulations, such as not murdering or committing adultery. But it also indicated that his people should be set apart from all other peoples in distinctive ways, for example, by keeping the seventh day holy, free from work, so as to worship him; by following certain dietary laws and avoiding such foods as pork and shellfish; and, if they were male, by receiving the sign of the covenant God had made with his people, the sign of circumcision.

And so the problem Paul faced in converting Gentiles to faith in Jesus, the son of the Jewish God. Did Gentiles who came to believe in Jesus need to become Jewish in order to be Christian? Did they need to adopt the Jewish Law for themselves? One can imagine that it was a rather pressing issue, especially for Gentile men, the vast majority of whom were uncircumcised.

Some of Jesus' Jewish followers insisted that converts were to adopt the ways of Judaism. Paul, however, appears to have been the leading advocate of a moderating line on the issue. Paul did insist that Gentiles who became followers of Jesus had to accept the God of the Jews and worship him only. But he was equally emphatic that they did not need to adopt "Jewish ways" or, as we might call them, "Jewish boundary markers" as spelled out in the Jewish Law. They did not need to observe the Sabbath or Jewish festivals, keep kosher, or be circumcised. In fact, in Paul's view, for Gentiles to adopt the ways of Judaism meant to call into question the salvation God had provided by the death of Jesus; it was Jesus alone, not the Jewish Law, that brought a person into a right standing before God (Rom. 3:10, 8:3; Gal. 2:15–16).

Looking back on these debates, as recorded even in the pages of the New Testament, we tend to think that the matter was easily, quickly, and effectively resolved. In point of fact, even the New Testament texts that discuss the issue show that it was not such a simple affair and that Paul's view was not universally accepted or, one might argue, even widely accepted. The account of the conference that met to decide this issue in Jerusalem, part way through Paul's missionary activities among the Gentiles (Acts 15), indicates that unnamed groups of Christians argued the alternative line, that Gentile converts wanting to become Christians first had to become Jews. Even more striking, Paul's own letters indicate that there were outspoken, sincere, and active Christian leaders who vehemently disagreed with him on this score and considered Paul's views to be a corruption of the true message of Christ. Some such leaders appeared among Paul's churches in Galatia and convinced the Christian men there that they had to be circumcised if they wanted to be full members of God's people. And they could quote Scripture to support their views, since God had given the sign of circumcision to the father of the Jews, Abraham, and told him both that it was an *eternal* covenant (not just a part-time agreement, to be annulled later) and that it applied not just to those born Jewish but also to anyone from outside the ranks of Israel who wanted to belong to the people of God (cf. Gen. 17:9–14).

Paul fired off a white-hot anger letter in response to his "Judaizing" opponents in Galatia, in which he went on the attack against these "false teachers" who, in his judgment, had corrupted the true gospel of Christ and stood accursed before God. This letter, of course, made it into the New Testament, and so most people simply take it at face value: Paul's opponents were corrupters of the Gospel and accursed by God. But surely they themselves did not see it this way. They were, after all, Christian missionaries, intent on spreading the gospel of Jesus throughout the world. One of our greatest losses is a written response from one of them. But if any such reply was made, it has disappeared forever. That does not necessarily mean, however, that, at the time, they took the minority position. One should always bear in mind that in this very letter of Galatians Paul indicates that he confronted Peter over just such issues (Gal. 2:11–14). He disagreed, that is, even with Jesus' closest disciple on the matter. What would Peter have said in response? Regrettably, once again, we can never know, since all we have is Paul's version.[2]

According to Paul, a person is made right with God *only* by faith in Jesus' death and resurrection, not by following any of the deeds prescribed by the Jewish Law. And this applies to both Jews and Gentiles. Since Jesus alone is the way of salvation, then anyone who tries to follow the Law in order to be right with God has misunderstood the gospel and probably lost his or her salvation (Gal. 1:6–9, 5:4). Here is a stark alternative: No one in early Christianity could surpass Paul in making an issue both clear and compelling.

At the same time, whereas only Paul's account of his confrontation with Peter and the Judaizing missionaries of Galatia survives, at one time numerous positions were represented. Even though most of the others have been lost, it is possible that not all of them have been. A close reading of our surviving sources shows that one of our Gospels, at least, appears to represent an alternative point of view.

With good reason, Matthew's Gospel is frequently thought of as the most "Jewish" of the Gospels of the New Testament. This account of Jesus' life and death goes to extraordinary lengths to highlight the Jewishness of Jesus. It begins by giving a genealogy of Jesus that extends through David, the greatest king of the Jews, to Abraham, the father of the Jews. Time and again it quotes the Jewish Scriptures to show that Jesus was the Jewish Messiah sent from the Jewish God in fulfillment of the Jewish Scriptures (cf. Matt. 1:23; 2:6, 18). Not only does Jesus fulfill the Scriptures here (a point Paul himself would have conceded); Matthew also insists, contrary to Paul, that Jesus' followers must do so as well. In one of the most trenchant statements of the Gospel, found only in this Gospel in the New Testament, Jesus is recorded as saying:

> Do not think that I have come to destroy the Law and the prophets; I did not come to destroy but to fulfill. For truly I say to you, until heaven and earth pass away, not the smallest letter or the smallest stroke of a letter will pass away from the Law until all has taken place. Whoever lets loose one of the least of these commandments and teaches others to do likewise will be called least in the kingdom of heaven; but whoever does them and teaches them will be called great in the kingdom of heaven. For I say to you that if your righteousness does not exceed that of the scribes and Pharisees, you will not enter the Kingdom of Heaven (Matt. 5:17–20).

For Matthew, the entire Jewish Law needs to be kept, down to the smallest letter. The Pharisees, in fact, are blamed not for keeping the law but for not keeping it well enough. It is worth noting that in this Gospel, when a rich man comes up to Jesus and asks him how to have eternal life, Jesus tells him that if he wants to live eternally he must keep the commandments of the Law (19:17). One might wonder: If the same person approached Paul with the same question twenty years later, what would he have said? Would he have told him to keep the Law? His own writings give a clear answer: decidedly *not* (cf. Rom 3:10; Gal. 2:15–16).

It is hard to imagine Paul and Matthew ever seeing eye to eye on this issue. In any event, from a historian's perspective it is interesting to note that after they both died, advocates of their respective positions on the Law developed these views at some considerable length. By the mid-second century, we know of Christian groups taking stands on Judaism that were at polar ends of the spectrum, some groups insisting that the Jewish Law was to be followed for salvation and others insisting that the Jewish Law could not be followed if one wanted salvation. All of these groups claimed to be representing the views of Jesus himself.

Christians Who Would Be Jews: The Early Christian Ebionites

Through sources dating from the second to the fourth centuries, we know of Christians called the Ebionites.[3] We do not know for certain where the name came from. The proto-orthodox heresiologist (opponent of heresy) Tertullian claimed that the group was named after its founder, Ebion. That seems like a poor guess, however, probably based on Tertullian's assumption that every heresy begins with a heretic who can be named. Other heresiologists, such as Origen of Alexandria, were probably closer to the mark when they derived the name from the Hebrew term *ebyon,* which means "poor." Origen and other proto-orthodox writers had a field day with the name, indicating that the

Ebionites were "poor in understanding."[4] That is almost certainly not what they thought about themselves. Possibly the name goes back to the earliest days of the community. It may be that members of this group gave away their possessions and committed themselves to lives of voluntary poverty for the sake of others, like the earliest communities mentioned in Acts 2:44–45, 4:32–37. Jesus himself, of course, was poor. Maybe these were people who took him seriously when he said they were to love their neighbors as themselves, realizing they could scarcely do so while living in relative luxury while people around them were starving.

In any event, they were called the Ebionites, and by the second century none of their opponents appears to have understood why. And since we do not seem to have any writings from anyone who belonged to the group, we cannot be certain either. This lack of primary source material is much to be regretted. Surely some of these people wrote treatises that advanced their views and defended them as necessary. But as no such writing survives, we must base our understanding on the words of their opponents, sometimes taking their claims with a pound of salt. Since some of these reports are inconsistent with others, it may be that there were a variety of Ebionite groups, each with its own distinctive understanding of some aspects of their faith.

Proto-orthodox authors clearly agree that the Ebionites were and understood themselves to be Jewish followers of Jesus. They were not the only group of Jewish-Christians known to have existed at the time, but they were the group that generated some of the greatest opposition. The Ebionite Christians that we are best informed about believed that Jesus was the Jewish Messiah sent from the Jewish God to the Jewish people in fulfillment of the Jewish Scriptures. They also believed that to belong to the people of God, one needed to be Jewish. As a result, they insisted on observing the Sabbath, keeping kosher, and circumcising all males. That sounds very much like the position taken by the opponents of Paul in Galatia. It may be that the Ebionite Christians were their descendants, physical or spiritual. An early source, Irenaeus, also reports that the Ebionites continued to reverence Jerusalem, evidently by praying in its direction during their daily acts of worship.[5]

Their insistence on staying (or becoming) Jewish should not seem especially peculiar from a historical perspective, since Jesus and his disciples were Jewish. But the Ebionites' Jewishness did not endear them to most other Christians, who believed that Jesus allowed them to bypass the requirements of the Law for salvation. The Ebionites, however, maintained that their views were authorized by the original disciples, especially by Peter and Jesus' own brother, James, head of the Jerusalem church after the resurrection.

One other aspect of the Ebionites' Christianity that set it apart from that of most other Christian groups was their understanding of who Jesus was. The Ebionites did not subscribe to the notion of Jesus' preexistence or his virgin birth. These ideas were originally distinct from each other. The two New Testament Gospels that speak of Jesus being conceived of a virgin (Matthew and

Luke) do not indicate that he existed *prior* to his birth, just as the New Testament books that appear to presuppose his preexistence (cf. John 1:1–3, 18; Phil. 2:5–11) never mention his virgin birth. But when all these books came to be included in the New Testament, both notions came to be affirmed simultaneously, so that Jesus was widely thought of as having been with God in eternity past (John, Paul) who became flesh (John) by being born of the Virgin Mary (Matthew and Luke).

Ebionite Christians, however, did not have our New Testament and understood Jesus differently. For them, Jesus was the Son of God not because of his divine nature or virgin birth but because of his "adoption" by God to be his son. This kind of Christology is, accordingly, sometimes called "adoptionist." To express the matter more fully, the Ebionites believed that Jesus was a real flesh-and-blood human like the rest of us, born as the eldest son of the sexual union of his parents, Joseph and Mary. What set Jesus apart from all other people was that he kept God's law perfectly and so was the most righteous man on earth. As such, God chose him to be his son and assigned to him a special mission, to sacrifice himself for the sake of others. Jesus then went to the cross, not as a punishment for his own sins but for the sins of the world, a perfect sacrifice in fulfillment of all God's promises to his people, the Jews, in the holy Scriptures. As a sign of his acceptance of Jesus' sacrifice, God then raised Jesus from the dead and exalted him to heaven.

It appears that Ebionite Christians also believed that since Jesus was the perfect, ultimate, final sacrifice for sins, there was no longer any need for the ritual sacrifice of animals. Jewish sacrifices, therefore, were understood to be a temporary and imperfect measure provided by God to atone for sins until the perfect atoning sacrifice should be made. As a result, if these (Christian) Jews were in existence before the destruction of the Jewish Temple in 70 CE, they would not have participated in its cultic practices; later they, or at least some of them, evidently remained vegetarian, since in the ancient world the slaughter of animals for meat was almost always done in the context of a cultic act of worship.

To what Scriptures did these Ebionites appeal in support of their views? What books did they revere and study and read as part of their services of worship? Obviously they retained the Hebrew Bible (the Old Testament) as the Scripture par excellence. These people were Jews, or converts to Judaism, who understood that the ancient Jewish traditions revealed God's ongoing interactions with his people and his Law for their lives. Almost as obviously, they did *not* accept any of the writings of Paul. Indeed, for them, Paul was not just wrong about a few minor points. He was the archenemy, the heretic who had led so many astray by insisting that a person is made right with God apart from keeping the Law and who forbade circumcision, the "sign of the covenant," for his followers.

The Ebionites did have other "Christian" texts as part of their canon, however. Not surprisingly, they appear to have accepted the Gospel of Matthew as their principal scriptural authority.[6] Their own version of Matthew, however, may have been a translation of the text into Aramaic. Jesus himself spoke Aramaic in Palestine, as did his earliest followers. It would make sense that a group of Jewish followers of Jesus that originated in Palestine would continue to cite his words, and stories about him, in his native tongue. It appears likely that this Aramaic Matthew was somewhat different from the Matthew now in the canon. In particular, the Matthew used by Ebionite Christians would have lacked the first two chapters, which narrate Jesus' birth to a virgin—a notion that the Ebionite Christians rejected. There were doubtless other differences from our own version of Matthew's Gospel as well.

We do not know what the Ebionites called their version of Matthew's Gospel. It may have been identical with a book known to some early church writers as the Gospel of the Nazareans. Nazarean was a name sometimes used for groups of Jewish Christians, of which there were others besides the Ebionites.[7]

We have evidence of yet another Gospel authority used by some or all groups of Ebionite Christians. The evidence comes to us from the fourth-century writings of a vitriolic opponent of all things heretical, Epiphanius, orthodox bishop on the island of Cyprus. In a lengthy book that details and then fervently attacks eighty different heretical groups, Epiphanius devotes a chapter to the Ebionites and quotes a Gospel that they are said to have used.[8] He gives seven brief quotations—not nearly as many as we would like, but enough to get a general sense of this now lost Gospel.[9] For one thing, this particular Gospel of the Ebionites appears to have been a "harmonization" of the New Testament Gospels of Matthew, Mark, and Luke. Evidence that it harmonized the earlier sources comes in the account that it gave of Jesus' baptism. As careful readers have long noticed, the three Synoptic Gospels all record the words spoken by a voice from heaven as Jesus emerges from the water; but the voice says something different in all three accounts: "This is my Son in whom I am well pleased" (Matt. 3:17); "You are my Son, in whom I am well pleased" (Mark 1:11); and, in the oldest witnesses to Luke's Gospel, "You are my Son, today I have begotten you" (Luke 3:23). What did the voice actually say? In the Gospel of the Ebionites, the matter is resolved easily enough. For here the voice speaks three times, saying something different on each occasion.

The antisacrificial views of the Ebionites also come through in some of the fragments that Epiphanius quotes. In one of them, the disciples ask Jesus where he wants to eat the Passover lamb with them (cf. Mark 14:12), and he replies, "I have no desire to eat the flesh of this Passover Lamb with you." In another place, he says somewhat more forthrightly, "I have come to abolish the sacrifices; if you do not cease from sacrificing, the wrath of God will not cease from weighing upon you."

Where there is no sacrifice, there is also no meat. Probably the most interesting of the changes from the familiar New Testament accounts of Jesus comes in the Gospel of the Ebionites description of John the Baptist, who, evidently, like his successor Jesus, maintained a strictly vegetarian cuisine. In this Gospel, with the change of just one letter of the relevant Greek word, the diet of John the Baptist was said to have consisted not of locusts [meat!] and wild honey (cf. Mark 1:6) but of pancakes and wild honey. It was a switch that may have been preferable on other grounds as well.

This Gospel of the Ebionites was evidently written in Greek (hence the ability to change the locusts into pancakes), based to some extent on Matthew, Mark, and Luke (hence the harmonizing tendency). It would have been used by Ebionite Christians who no longer knew Aramaic, who were, therefore, living outside of Palestine. And it would have included the Ebionites' own perspectives on the nature of true religion (hence the condemnation of animal sacrifice)—all the more reason to regret that we have such scant access to it, one more Gospel lost to posterity, destroyed or forgotten by the proto-orthodox victors in the struggle to decide what Christians would believe and read.

Christians Who Spurn All Things Jewish: The Marcionites

Living at the same time and also enjoying the unwanted attention of proto-orthodox opponents, though standing at just the opposite end of the theological spectrum, were a group of Christians known as the Marcionites.[10] In this instance, there is no question concerning the origin of the name. These were followers of the second-century evangelist/theologian Marcion, known to later Christianity as one of the arch heretics of his day, but by all counts one of the most significant Christian thinkers and writers of the early centuries. We are better informed about the Marcionites than about the Ebionites, because their opponents took them more seriously as a threat to the well-being of the church at large. As I have intimated, potential converts from among the pagans were not flocking to the Ebionite form of religion, which involved restricting activities on Saturday, giving up pork and other popular foods, and, for the men, undergoing surgery to remove the foreskin of their penises.

The Marcionites, on the other hand, had a highly attractive religion to many pagan converts, as it was avowedly Christian with nothing Jewish about it. In fact, everything Jewish was taken out of it. Jews, recognized around the world for customs that struck many pagans as bizarre at best, would have difficulty recognizing in the Marcionite religion an offshoot of their own. Not only were Jewish customs rejected, so, too, were the Jewish Scriptures and the Jewish God. From a historical perspective, it is intriguing that any such religion could claim direct historical continuity with Jesus.

Since Marcionite Christianity was seen as a significant threat to the burgeoning proto-orthodox movement, the heresiologists wrote a good deal about it. Tertullian, for example, devoted five volumes to attacking Marcion and his views. These volumes are primary sources for the conflict, to be supplemented by attacks mounted by Tertullian's successors, including Epiphanius of Salamis.

One still needs to sift through what is said; you can never rely on an enemy's reports for a fair and disinterested presentation. And once again, Marcion's own writings and those of his survivors were long ago relegated to the trash heap or bonfire. Still, we appear to get a fairly good sense of Marcion's life and teachings from the polemical sources that survive.[11]

The Life and Teachings of Marcion

Marcion was born around 100 CE, in the city of Sinope, on the southern shore of the Black Sea, in the region of Pontus. His father was said to have been the bishop of the church there—an altogether plausible claim, as it can make sense of Marcion's intimate familiarity with the Jewish Bible, which he later came to reject, and his full understanding of certain aspects of the Christian faith from an early period in his life. As an adult, he evidently was wealthy, having made his money as a shipping merchant or possibly a shipbuilder.

Later reports indicate that he had a falling out with his father, who proceeded to remove him from the church. The rumor mill indicated that it was because he had "seduced a virgin." Most scholars take that as a metaphorical seduction—that Marcion had corrupted members of the congregation (the church as the virgin of Christ) by his false teachings.

In any event, in 139 CE Marcion appears to have traveled from his native Asia Minor to the city of Rome, which, as the capital and largest city of the empire, appears to have attracted all sorts, including all sorts of Christians, in this period. He made a good impression on the church there—already one of the largest churches in the world (if not *the* largest)—by donating 200,000 sesterces for the church's mission.[12] Although recognized for his munificence, Marcion appears to have had bigger designs. But he lay low and worked out his plan over the course of five years, bringing it forth in two literary productions.

Before discussing these books, I should say a word about the theology Marcion developed, which was seen as distinctive, revolutionary, compelling, and therefore dangerous. Among all the Christian texts and authors at his disposal, Marcion was especially struck by the writings of the apostle Paul, and in particular the distinction that Paul drew in Galatians and elsewhere between the Law of the Jews and the gospel of Christ. As we have seen, Paul claimed that a person is made right with God by faith in Christ, not by doing the works of the Law. This distinction became fundamental to Marcion, and he made it absolute. The gospel is the good news of deliverance; it involves love, mercy, grace, forgiveness, reconciliation, redemption, and life. The Law, however, is the bad news that makes the gospel necessary in the first place; it involves harsh commandments, guilt, judgment, enmity, punishment, and death. The Law is given to the Jews. The gospel is given by Christ.

How could the same God be responsible for both? Or put in other terms: How could the wrathful, vengeful God of the Jews be the loving, merciful God of Jesus? Marcion maintained that these attributes could not belong to one

God, as they stand at odds with one another: hatred and love, vengeance and mercy, judgment and grace. He concluded that there must in fact be two Gods: the God of the Jews, as found in the Old Testament, and the God of Jesus, as found in the writings of Paul.

Once Marcion arrived at this understanding, everything else naturally fell into place. The God of the Old Testament was the God who created this world and everything in it, as described in Genesis. The God of Jesus, therefore, had never been involved with this world but came into it only when Jesus himself appeared from heaven. The God of the Old Testament was the God who called the Jews to be his people and gave them his Law. The God of Jesus did not consider the Jews to be his people (for him; they were the chosen of the other God), and he was not a God who gave laws.

The God of the Old Testament insisted that people keep his Law and penalized them when they failed. He was not evil, but he was rigorously just. He had laws and inflicted penalties on those who did not keep them. But this necessarily made him a wrathful God, since no one kept all of his laws perfectly. Everyone had to pay the price for their transgressions, and the penalty for transgression was death. The God of the Old Testament was therefore completely justified in exacting his punishments and sentencing all people to death.

The God of Jesus came into this world in order to save people from the vengeful God of the Jews. He was previously unknown to this world and had never had any previous dealings with it. Hence Marcion sometimes referred to him as God the Stranger. Not even the prophecies of the future Messiah come from this God, for these refer not to Jesus but to a coming Messiah of Israel, to be sent by the God of the Jews, the creator of this world and the God of the Old Testament. Jesus came completely unexpectedly and did what no one could possibly have hoped for: He paid the penalty for other people's sins, to save them from the just wrath of the Old Testament God.

But how could Jesus himself, who represented the nonmaterial God, come into this material world—created by the other God—without becoming part of it? How could the nonmaterial become material, even for such a good and noble cause as salvation? Marcion taught that Jesus was not truly a part of this material world. He did not have a flesh-and-blood body. He was not actually born. He was not really human. He only *appeared* to be a human with a material existence like everyone else. In other words, Marcion, like some Gnostic Christians, was a docetist who taught that Jesus only "seemed" to have a fleshly body.

Coming "in the *likeness* of sinful flesh," as Marcion's favorite author Paul put it (Rom. 8:3), Jesus paid the penalty for other people's sins by dying on the cross. By having faith in his death, one could escape the throes of the wrathful God of the Jews and have eternal life with the God of love and mercy, the God of Jesus. But how could Jesus die for the sins of the world if he did not have a real body? How could his shed blood bring atonement if he did not have real blood?

Unfortunately, we do not know exactly how Marcion developed the details of his theory of atonement. Possibly he, like some Christians after him, thought that Jesus' death was a kind of trap that fooled the divine being who had control of human souls lost to sin, that the God of the Jews was forced to relinquish the souls of those who believed in Jesus' death, not realizing that in fact the death was only an appearance. But we do not actually know how Marcion worked out the theological niceties.

What we do know is that he based this entire system on sacred texts that he had in his church. These included, but were not limited to, the writings of Paul. Tertullian indicates, for example, that Marcion was particularly attracted to the saying of Jesus that a tree is known by its fruit (see Luke 6:43–44): Good trees do not produce rotten fruit, and rotten trees do not produce good fruit. What happens when the principle is applied to the divine realm? What kind of God creates a world wracked with pain, misery, disaster, disease, sin, and death? What kind of God says that he is the one who "creates evil" (Amos 3.6)? Surely a God who is himself evil. But what kind of God brings love, mercy, grace, salvation, and life? A God who does what is kind and generous and good? A God who is good.

There are two Gods, then, and according to Marcion, Jesus himself says so. Moreover, Jesus explains that no one puts new wine into old wineskins; otherwise, the old wineskins burst and both they and the wine are destroyed (Mark 2:22). The gospel is a new thing that has come into the world. It cannot be put into the old wineskins of the Jewish religion.

Marcion's Literary Productions

Once Marcion had worked out his theological system, he incorporated it into his two literary works. The first was his own composition, a book that no longer survives, except in the quotations of his opponents. Marcion called the book the *Antitheses* (Contrary statements). It was evidently a kind of commentary on the Bible, in which Marcion demonstrated his doctrinal views that the God of the Old Testament could not be the God of Jesus. Some of the book may well have consisted of direct and pointed antithetical statements contrasting the two Gods. For example, the God of the Old Testament tells the people of Israel to enter into the city of Jericho and murder every man, woman, child, and animal in the city (Joshua 6); but the God of Jesus tells his followers to love their enemies, to pray for those who persecute them, to turn the other cheek (Luke 6:27–29). Is this the same God? When Elisha, the prophet of the Old Testament God, was being mocked by a group of young boys, God allowed him to call out two she-bears to attack and maul them (2 Kings 2:23–24). The God of Jesus says, "Let the little children come to me" (Luke 18:15–17). Is this the same God? The God of the Old Testament said, "Cursed is anyone who hangs on a tree" (Deut. 27:26; 28:58). But the God of Jesus ordered him, the one who was blessed, to be hanged on a tree. Is this the same God?

Many Christians today might be sympathetic with Marcion's view, as one often hears even still about the wrathful God of the Old Testament and the loving God of the New. Marcion, however, drove the idea to its limit, in a way many moderns could not accept. For him, there really were two Gods, and he set out to demonstrate it by appealing to the Old Testament. In this book of *Antitheses*, Marcion showed that he was not willing to explain away these passages by providing them with a figurative or symbolic interpretation; for him, they were to be taken literally. And when so read, they stood in stark contrast with the clear teachings of Jesus and his gospel of love and mercy.

Marcion's second literary creation was not an original composition but a new edition of other texts. Marcion put together a canon of Scripture, that is, a collection of books that he considered to be sacred authorities. Marcion, in fact, is widely thought to have been the first Christian to have done so, to construct a closed, that is, a finalized, canon of Scripture, long before the New Testament that we know was established. Some scholars think that Marcion's decision to create a canon may have spurred on efforts of proto-orthodox Christians to follow suit.

Of what did Marcion's canon consist? First and most obviously, it did not include any of the Jewish Scriptures (the "Old" Testament). These were books written by and about the Old Testament God, the creator of the world and the God of the Jews. They are not sacred texts for those who have been saved from his vengeful grasp by the death of Jesus. The New Testament is *completely* new and unanticipated.

Marcion's New Testament consisted of eleven books. Most of these were the letters of his beloved Paul, the one predecessor whom Marcion could trust to understand the radical claims of the gospel. Why, Marcion asked, did Jesus return to earth to convert Paul by means of a vision? Why did he not simply allow his own disciples to proclaim his message faithfully throughout the world? According to Marcion, it was because Jesus' disciples—themselves Jews, followers of the Jewish God, readers of the Jewish Scriptures—never did correctly understand their master. Confused by what Jesus taught them, wrongly thinking that he was the Jewish Messiah, even after his death and resurrection they *continued* not to understand, interpreting Jesus' words, deeds, and death in light of their understanding of Judaism. Jesus then had to start afresh, and he called Paul to reveal to him "the truth of the gospel." That is why Paul had to confront Jesus' disciple Peter and his earthly brother James, as seen in the letter to the Galatians. Jesus had revealed the truth to Paul, and these others simply never understood.

Paul understood, however, and he alone. Marcion therefore included ten of his letters in his canon of Scripture, all, in fact, of those that eventually came to be found in the New Testament with the exception of the Pastoral epistles: 1 and 2 Timothy and Titus. We may never know why these three were not included as well. It may be that they were not as widely circulated by Marcion's time and that he himself did not know of them.[13]

Paul, of course, speaks of his "gospel," by which he means his gospel message. Marcion, however, believed that Paul actually had a Gospel book available to him. As a consequence, Marcion included a Gospel in his canon, a form of the Gospel of Luke. It is not clear why Marcion chose Luke as his Gospel, whether it was because its author was allegedly a companion of the apostle Paul,[14] or because it showed the greatest concern for Gentiles in the ministry of Jesus, or, perhaps more plausibly, because it was the Gospel he was raised on in his home church of Sinope.

In any event, this Gospel along with the ten Pauline letters formed Marcion's sacred canon of Scripture. Even such a short canon—no Old Testament and only eleven other books—created a problem for Marcion, for these eleven books do appear to affirm the material world as the creation of the true God, they quote passages from the Old Testament, and they show ties with historical Judaism. Marcion was fully aware of this problem and worked hard to resolve it. In his view, the reason these books had such passages is not because their authors were deceived into thinking that Judaism was important to the message of Jesus. No, it was only after the authors had produced these works that the offensive passages had been inserted into copies of their books, inserted by scribes who still did not understand Jesus' true message.

In order to present the Scriptures in their original pristine form, then, Marcion was driven by the logic of his system to edit the passages that affirmed the material world as the creation of the true God, that quoted the Old Testament, that smacked of Judaism. In a manner reminiscent of the later Jefferson Bible, Marcion removed all the passages offensive to his views. In the words of his proto-orthodox opponent, Tertullian, Marcion interpreted his scripture "with a pen knife" (*Prescription*, 38).

Marcion's Fate

Once Marcion had completed his literary creations, he strove to have his views accepted by the Christian world at large. Possibly that was part of the motivation for his relocation to Rome, the capital city, in the first place. It appears that Marcion called a council of church leaders together in Rome to present his views—the first such Roman church council of record. But after hearing what he had to say, the Roman elders, rather than welcoming his views with open arms, chose to excommunicate him from their community, refunding his large donation and sending him on his way. Marcion left the church of Rome, momentarily defeated but none the worse for wear and none the less convinced of the truth of his gospel.

Marcion returned to Asia Minor to propagate his version of the faith, and he was fantastically successful in doing so. We cannot be sure exactly why, but Marcion experienced an almost unparalleled success on the mission field, establishing churches wherever he went, so that within a few years, one of his proto-orthodox opponents, the apologist and theologian in Rome, Justin, could say that he was teaching his heretical views to "many people of every nation" (*Apology* 1.26). For centuries Marcionite churches would thrive; in some parts of Asia Minor they were the original form of Christianity and continued for many years to comprise the greatest number of persons claiming to be Christian. As late as the fifth century we read of orthodox bishops warning members of their congregations to be wary when traveling, lest they enter a strange town, attend the local church on Sunday morning, and find to their dismay that they are worshiping in the midst of Marcionite heretics.[15]

Christianities in Contrast and Competition

We might do well in this, our opening move into some of the diverse forms of Christianity of the second and third centuries, to consider a set of contrasts between the two groups of Christians we have considered here. Both the Ebionites and the Marcionites claimed to be followers of Jesus and through him of the true God; both of them thought that Jesus' death was the way of salvation (on this they would disagree with other groups—cf. the Gospel of Thomas); both of them claimed to trace their views back to Jesus through his apostles. But in most other respects, they stood at opposite ends of the theological spectrum.

- The Ebionites were Jews who insisted that being Jewish was fundamental to a right standing before God. The Marcionites were Gentiles who insisted that Jewish practice was fundamentally detrimental for a right standing before God.
- The Ebionites insisted there was only one God. The Marcionites maintained that there were two.
- The Ebionites held to the laws of the Old Testament and saw the Old Testament as the revelation of the one true God. The Marcionites rejected the laws of the Old Testament and saw it as a book inspired by the inferior God of the Jews.
- The Ebionites saw Jesus as completely human and not divine. The Marcionites saw Jesus as completely divine and not human.
- The Ebionites saw Paul, with his teaching of justification by faith in Christ apart from the works of the law, as the arch heretic of the church. Marcion saw Paul as the one and only true apostle of Christ.
- The Ebionites accepted a version of Matthew as their Scripture (without its first two chapters, which show that Jesus was born *of a virgin*), possibly along with other books, such as their own Gospel of the Ebionites. Marcion accepted a version of Luke as his Scripture (again, possibly without its first two chapters, which show that Jesus was *born*), along with ten letters of Paul.

Here we have two groups with diametrically opposed views, both claiming not just to be Christian but to be *true* Christians. Both ultimately came to be condemned as heretical, not just by each other but also by the group that defeated them both, the proto-orthodox Christians who established themselves as dominant and determined what future Christians would think about God, Christ, salvation, and the Bible.

What if it had turned out differently? What if the Ebionites had won these battles, or the Marcionites?

From a historian's perspective, with all the advantages and disadvantages of hindsight, it has to be admitted that it is difficult to imagine either of these groups establishing itself as one of the dominant religions, let alone the "official" religion, of the Roman Empire in the way proto-orthodox Christianity eventually did.

If the Ebionites *had* established themselves as dominant, then things would be radically different for Christians today. Christianity would be not a religion that was separate from Judaism but a sect of Judaism, a sect that accepted Jewish laws, customs, and ways, a sect that practiced circumcision, observed Jewish holy days such as Yom Kippur and Rosh Hashana and other festivals, a sect that kept kosher food laws and probably maintained a vegetarian diet.

As a sect within Judaism, Christianity would have had its principal battles internally with other Jews who did not accept Jesus as Messiah; anti-Semitism as it developed, with Christians opposing Jews, members of a different religion, might well have never occurred. What we think of as historical developments from the fall of ("Christian") Rome to the early and later Christian Middle Ages would never have transpired as they did, nor would the Renaissance and the Protestant Reformation, historical developments that arose out of a specific set of circumstances of medieval Christianity. One could argue that the modern world would have been totally unrecognizable.

All of this, of course, is rank speculation. We have no idea what exactly might have happened, whether life in our world would have been better, worse, or about the same. But it would have been wildly different. At the same time, as I have pointed out, it is hard to imagine it happening at all. Ebionite Christianity was at a serious disadvantage when it came to appealing to the masses. It attracted some Jews and some non-Jews who found Judaism appealing. But such people were never in the majority in the ancient world. The idea of large-scale conversions to a religion that required kosher food laws and circumcision seems a bit far-fetched. Had Ebionite Christianity "won" the internal battles for dominance, Christianity itself would probably have ended up as a footnote in the history of religion books used in university courses in the West.

In any event, Ebionite Christianity was "left behind" at a fairly early moment in the history of the church. Proto-orthodox fathers like Irenaeus and Tertullian mention it and say a few things about it, but they do not see it as a serious threat, already by the end of the second century.

What about Marcionite Christianity? Here one can both imagine and argue for real success within Christianity itself. Marcionite Christianity was a forceful movement in the early church, and one can readily see why. It took what most people in the empire found most attractive about Christianity—love, mercy, grace, wonder, opposition to this harsh, material world and salvation from it—and pushed it to an extreme, while taking Christianity's less attractive sides—law, guilt, judgment, eternal punishment, and, above all, association and close ties with Jews and Judaism—and getting rid of them. Had Marcionite Christianity succeeded, the Old Testament would be seen by Christians today not as the Old Testament but as the Jewish Scriptures, a set of writings for the Jews and of no real relevance to Christianity. So, too, Christians would not see themselves as having Jewish roots. This may well have opened the doors to heightened hostilities, since Marcion seems to have hated Jews and everything Jewish; or possibly even more likely, it may have led simply to benign neglect as Jews and their religion would have been considered to be of no relevance and certainly no competition for Christians. The entire history of anti-Semitism might have been avoided, ironically, by an anti-Jewish religion.

Once again, other aspects of the history of the West would have been quite different, but it is not easy to see how. Certainly, the intellectual tradition of Christianity would have been distinctly different, as the Old Testament would not have been an issue of ongoing concern, and figurative, spiritual, allegorical modes of interpretation might not have developed within Christian circles (as Marcion was a literalist), leading to a history of literary analysis and a set of reading practices entirely different from what we have inherited. Economic and political history might have turned out to be quite different, since there would have been nothing in the sacred Scriptures, for example, to oppose lending money at interest or to promote the system of an eye for an eye and a tooth for a tooth. Who knows what would have happened to the environment, given the circumstance that so much of modern environmental concerns stem ultimately from a conviction, filtered through many layers, but with Judeo-Christian roots, that God is the creator of this world and that we are its caretakers. Different, too, would have been so much of modern socialism, even (odd as it may seem) so much of Marxist theory, as it is ultimately rooted in notions of economic justice, fairness, and opposition to oppression that trace their lineage back to the Hebrew prophets.

But once again, it is impossible to know where we would be if Marcionite Christianity had won the internal debates among Christian groups. At the same time, even if the Marcionites had established their supremacy within Christianity, it is extremely difficult to imagine them succeeding in becoming the dominant religion of the Roman Empire, the way proto-orthodox Christianity did. This is because of a unique feature that made Christianity initially palatable to Roman religious tastes (and to become ultimately successful, of course, something first has to be palatable). Unlike today, in the ancient Roman world there was wide-ranging suspicion of *any* philosophy or religion that smacked of novelty. In the fields of philosophy and religion, as opposed to the field of military technology, it was the *old* that was appreciated and respected, not the new. One of the most serious obstacles for Christians in the Roman mission field was the widespread perception—and it was entirely valid—that the religion was "recent." Nothing new could be true. If it were true, why was it not known long ago? How could it be that no one until now has understood the truth? Not even Homer, Plato, or Aristotle?

The strategy that Christians devised to avoid this obstacle to conversion was to say that even though Jesus did live just decades or a century or so ago, the religion based on him is much, much older, for this religion is the fulfillment of all that God had been predicting in the oldest surviving books of civilization. Starting with Moses and the prophets, God had predicted the coming of Jesus and the religion founded in his name. Moses lived four centuries before Homer, eight centuries before Plato. And Moses looked forward to Jesus and the salvation to be brought in his name. Christianity is not a new thing, of recent vintage, argued the (proto-orthodox) Christian thinkers. It is older than anything that Greek myth and philosophy can offer; it is older than Rome itself. As an ancient religion, it demands attention.[16]

By embracing "true" Judaism, that is, by taking over the Jewish Scriptures and claiming them as their own, Christians overcame the single biggest objection that pagans had with regard to the appearance of this "new" religion. Had Christians not been able to make a plausible case for the antiquity of their religion, it never would have succeeded in the empire.

But what about Marcion and his followers? They claimed that Jesus and the salvation that he brought were brand-new. God had never been in the world before. He was a Stranger to this place. There were no ancient roots to this religion, no forerunners, no antecedents. The salvation of Christ came unlooked for and unexpected, unknown to all ancient philosophy and unlike anything found in ancient religion. Given the reverence for antiquity in antiquity, in its quest for ultimate dominance, Marcionite Christianity probably never had a chance.

Chapter Six

Christians "In the Know": The Worlds of Early Christian Gnosticism

No form of lost Christianity has so intrigued modern readers and befuddled modern scholars as early Christian Gnosticism. The intrigue is easy to understand, especially in view of the discovery of the Nag Hammadi library (see pp. 51–55). When that group of fieldhands headed by Mohammed Ali uncovered this cache of books in Upper Egypt, the world was suddenly presented with hard evidence of other Christian groups in the ancient world that stood in sharp contrast with any kind of Christianity familiar to us today. There was no Jesus of the stained glass window here, nor a Jesus of the creeds—not even a Jesus of the New Testament. These books were fundamentally different from anything in our experience, and almost nothing could have prepared us for them.

The Nag Hammadi Library

The library contained a wide array of books, many of them with understandings of God, the world, Christ, and religion that differed not only from the views of proto-orthodoxy but also from one another.[1] There were new Gospels recording Jesus' words, some of them containing his secret and "truer" teachings, delivered after his resurrection from the dead, Gospels allegedly written by his disciples Philip and John the son of Zebedee, by his brother James, by his twin brother Thomas. Even though forged, these books were obviously written seriously and meant to be taken seriously, as providing a guide to the truth. So, too, the other books in the collection, including several different and internally diverse mystical reflections on how the divine realm came into being. Most of these documents assumed that there was not simply one God over all who had created the world and made it good. Some of them were quite explicit: This creation was not good, not in the least. It was the result of a cosmic catastrophe, brought into being by an inferior and ignorant deity who erroneously imagined he was God Almighty.

Such documents thus gave expression to what so many people over the course of history have known so well firsthand—the starving, the diseased, the crippled, the oppressed, the deserted, the heartbroken. This world is miserable. And if there is any hope for deliverance, it will not come from within this world through worldly means, for example, by improving the welfare state, putting more teachers in the classroom, or devoting more national resources to the fight against terrorism. This world is a cesspool of ignorance and suffering, and salvation will come not by trying to make it better but by escaping it altogether.

Some of the documents of the Nag Hammadi library not only express this view of the world; they also describe how such a world came into being in the first place, how we humans came to inhabit it (another cosmic catastrophe), and how we can escape. For many of these texts, this deliverance from the material world can happen only when we learn the secret knowledge that can bring salvation. (Recall: *gnosis* is the Greek word for knowledge; Gnostics are the ones who "know.") Some of these texts—ones that are most clearly Christian in their orientation[2]—indicate that Jesus is the one who brings this knowledge. But knowledge of what? It is not the kind of knowledge that one can attain by empirical observation and experimentation, not the knowledge of external phenomena and how to manipulate them. It is knowledge of ourselves. Many of these texts preserve and present the view known to be held by groups of early Gnostics, that saving knowledge is "knowledge of who we were and what we have become, of where we were and where we have been made to fall, of where we are hastening and from where we are being redeemed, of what birth is and what rebirth."[3]

According to this view of things, we do not belong here in this awful world. We have come from another place, the realm of God. We are trapped here, imprisoned. And when we learn who we are and how we can escape, we can then return to our heavenly home.

No wonder these expressions of Gnostic religiosity have struck a resonant note among modern readers, many of whom also feel alienated from this world, for whom this world does not make sense, readers who realize, in some very deep and significant way, that they really don't belong here. For some groups of early Christian Gnostics, we in fact do not belong here. Our alienation is real; this is not our home. We have come from above, and above we must return.

Despite their inherent interest, many of these Gnostic texts are not simple to understand. And that, of course, is as it should be: If the knowledge necessary for salvation were simple and straightforward, we all would have figured it out long ago. But this is secret knowledge reserved for the elite, for the few, for those who really do have a spark of the divine within them, a spark that needs to be rekindled and brought to life through the gnosis (knowledge) from on high, brought from one who has come down from the divine realm to remind us of our true identity, our true origin, and our true destiny. This divine emissary is no mere mortal. He is a being from the realm above, a divine emissary sent from the true God (not the ignorant creator who made this hateful material world in the first place) to reveal to us the true state of things and the means of escape. Those who receive, and understand, and accept these teachings will then be "Gnostics," those "in the know."

The intrigue of these Gnostic systems for general readers is thus obvious. But why, as I indicated at the outset, have they created such scholarly befuddlement? Maybe the easiest explanation is that while it is one thing to summarize the gist of the teachings of one Gnostic group or another, it is another thing to plumb the depths of the texts themselves. And there is scarcely any religious literature written in any language at any time that can be more perplexing and deliberately obscure than some of the Gnostic writings of Christian antiquity. To be sure, these are all available in good English translation. But even as translators try to present these texts in terms comprehensible to modern readers, they remain obtuse in places, as, for example, they detail the complex relations of incalculable divine beings described in the subtle nuances of highly symbolic language. Sometimes you may suspect the translation is bad, but in fact, most of the time the English translation is clearer than the Coptic of the texts themselves.

Not only are some of these original materials difficult to understand individually: they are also difficult to place in relationship with one another. Scholars have concluded that there are *numerous* religious perspectives represented in the various Gnostic documents surviving from antiquity and that these perspectives are not always consistent with one another. Probably different documents come from different communities with different worldviews, mythological systems, beliefs, and practices. Some of the texts found at Nag Hammadi present or presuppose religious systems unrelated to anything else known from the ancient world; some of them are evidently not even Gnostic; some are almost certainly not Christian. Rather than one thing, then, the Nag Hammadi library contains numerous things, various perspectives presented in an array of texts including a whole host of lost Christianities. It is impossible to synthesize the views, presuppositions, religious perspectives of these into one monolithic system.[4]

As a result, scholars have enormous and ongoing disputes over them, in terms of the individual documents and the overall phenomenon traditionally called Gnosticism. Some of the major questions are: Is *Gnosticism* an appropriate term for all the religions that we normally subsume under this name? Or are these religions so different from one another that we level out their differences by calling them all Gnostic? When did these various religions come into being? Were some of them in existence before Christianity? Do they spring from some kind of Judaism? Or are they offshoots of Christianity? Or are they religions that sprang up at the same time as Christianity and were mutually influential with it (i.e., with non-Gnostic Christians picking up ideas from

Gnostics and Gnostics picking up ideas from non-Gnostic Christians)? Can we assign certain Christian Gnostic texts to known Christian Gnostic sects? Were there scores of Gnostic myths or just one overarching myth that was told in a variety of ways? And so on.[5]

Fortunately, I do not need to delve into these questions of scholarship here, many of which revolve around highly technical issues. My interests are much broader. I will be assuming that Gnosticism is a complex phenomenon with numerous manifestations (like Christianity, past and present), but that a number of the texts of the Nag Hammadi library cohere together because they were rooted in the same basic Gnostic view of the world—even when that view comes to be manifested in a variety of ways. Moreover, I will assume that, based on these texts which do cohere (as opposed to others which assume different perspectives), we can describe general characteristics of some Gnostic religions (while acknowledging that other characteristics might apply to other kinds of Gnostic religion), that these characteristics can in turn help explain the texts, and that we can get a general idea of how some forms of Gnostic Christianity relate to non-Gnostic Christianities, whether or not there were Gnostic groups before or independent of early Christianity. When I speak of the "Gnostic texts" in the discussion that follows, then, I will be referring only to those documents (mainly from Nag Hammadi) that cohere together and appear therefore to represent a particular religious perspective. It must always be borne in mind that even as I speak of one form of the Gnostic religion, I do not thereby mean to say that Gnosticism was only one thing any more than Christianity was.

The Origins of Gnosticism

Before discussing further the major tenets of the one kind of Gnosticism we will be focusing on, I should say a few words about where it appears to have come from and give a more extensive account of how we now can know about it.

The "where it came from" question has intrigued scholars for a very long time.[6] Two features of Gnostic texts in particular have caused a good deal of puzzlement. On the one hand, these texts clearly suppose that the material world is not a good place, that it is not the creation of the good God who made all things and then declared them "good," as in Genesis. To be sure, Jews and Christians have never thought the world was perfect, not even the Jews and Christians responsible for writing the Bible. Evil and suffering are constantly on their minds and usually at the forefront of their writings. But for the most part, the biblical writers maintain that the evil in this world results from human sin, which brought about a corruption of the good creation of God. Most Gnostic authors assume, however, that evil is written into the fabric of the material world itself. This may sound like an *anti*-Judeo-Christian view. On the other hand, these Christian Gnostic texts are filled with Jewish and Christian materials; Christ is the ultimate redeemer, the creator God is assumed to be the God of the Old Testament, and a number of the texts are actually expositions of the early chapters of Genesis (creation, Adam and Eve, the flood, etc.).[7] If the writers were anti-Jewish, why did they presuppose the teachings of Judaism? If they came from an anti-Jewish milieu, why did they write commentaries on Genesis?

One way to solve this problem is to situate the origins of Gnostic Christianity not outside of Judaism but *inside* it, as a kind of reaction movement to forms of Judaism that had developed by the time Christianity emerged, forms of Judaism that influenced Jesus and his followers. To give even a simplified picture of how it works, we need to start way back, as far back as we have records among Jewish theologians who were trying to understand why there was suffering in the world. This is as far back as we have records of Jewish theologians—hundreds of years before Jesus.

In one way or another, a significant amount of Jewish theology goes back to the traditions about the Exodus from Egypt under Moses, as recounted in the early books of the Hebrew Bible. According to the accounts, after the children of Israel had been enslaved for centuries, God heard their cry and raised up for them a prophet, Moses, whom he used to oppose the Egyptian Pharaoh, working ten plagues against the Egyptians to force his hand and set the people free. After the Israelites escaped, Pharaoh pursued his former slaves, only to be soundly defeated at the Red Sea, when the waters miraculously parted, the children of Israel crossed on dry land, and the Egyptian armies were destroyed by the floods when the waters returned. For ancient Jews, this Exodus tradition was theologically significant. It showed, in broad terms, that God had chosen Israel to be his people and that he would intervene on their behalf when they were in dire straits.

What were theologians, and others, to think, then, when in later times the people of Israel suffered but God did not intervene? Much of the Hebrew Bible is taken up with this question. The standard answer comes in the writings of the Hebrew prophets, such as Isaiah, Jeremiah, Ezekiel, Hosea, and Amos. For these writers, Israel suffers military, political, economic, and social setbacks because the people have sinned against God and he is punishing them for it. But when they return to his ways, following the directions for communal life and worship that he had given to Moses in the Law, he would relent and return them to their happy and prosperous lives.

This "classical" view of suffering continued to affirm the Exodus theology, that God is the God of Israel who will intervene on their behalf, and yet it explains the ongoing problem of suffering. But what happens when the people do return to God, do try to keep his ways, and still suffer? The difficulty with the classical, prophetic view is that it does not explain why the wicked prosper and the righteous suffer. This shortcoming led to a number of variant theologies in ancient Israel, including those of the books of Job and Ecclesiastes (both directed against this prophetic view) and to that of a group of Jewish thinkers that modern scholars have called "apocalypticists." The term comes from the Greek word *apocalypsis,* which means an "unveiling" or a "revealing," used of these people because they believed God had "revealed" to them the ultimate secrets of the world that explain why it contains such evil and suffering.[8]

Jewish apocalypticism arose in a context of intense suffering, some two hundred years before Jesus, when the Syrian ruler who had control of Palestine, the Jewish homeland, persecuted Jews precisely for being Jewish.[9] For example, circumcision—the central sign of covenant union with God—was forbidden on pain of death. Clearly, for many Jewish thinkers, this kind of suffering, contrary to the classical view of the prophets, could not come from God, since it was the direct result of trying to follow God. There must be some other reason for the suffering, then, and some other agent responsible for it. Jewish apocalypticists developed the idea that God had a personal adversary, the Devil, who was responsible for suffering, that there were cosmic forces in the world, evil powers with the Devil at their head, who were afflicting God's people. According to this perspective, God was still the creator of this world and would be its ultimate redeemer. But for the time being, the forces of evil had been unleashed and were wreaking havoc among God's people.

Jewish apocalypticists maintained, however, that God would soon intervene and overthrow these forces of evil in a cataclysmic show of force, that he would destroy all that opposed him, including all the kingdoms that were causing his people to suffer, and that he would then bring in a new kingdom, in which there would be no more sin, suffering, evil, or death. These apocalypticists maintained that those who were suffering needed to hold on just a little while longer, for God would soon vindicate them and give them an eternal reward in his Kingdom. How soon would this be? "Truly I tell you, some of you standing here will not taste death until you see the Kingdom of God having come in power." These are the words of Jesus (Mark 9:1), probably the best-known Jewish apocalypticist of antiquity. Or as he says later, "Truly I tell you, *this generation* will not pass away until all these things take place" (Mark 13:30).

Jesus and his earliest followers were Jewish apocalypticists, expecting the imminent intervention of God to overthrow the forces of evil. To this extent they were like many other Jews of the first century, including those who produced the Dead Sea Scrolls. Jesus appears to have thought that God was soon to send the Son of man from heaven as a judge against all those who align themselves against God (cf. Mark 8:38–9:1, 13:24–30); in this, too, he agreed with other apocalyptic prophets of his own day. But after Jesus died, his followers came to think that it was Jesus himself who would soon return from heaven on the clouds as a cosmic judge of the earth. The apostle Paul, our earliest Christian author, believed that Jesus would return in judgment in his own lifetime (see 1 Thess. 4:14–18; 1 Cor. 15:51–52).

What would happen to an apocalyptic worldview if, contrary to expectation, the end did not come "soon"? Or, worse, if it never came at all? What would people firmly committed to an apocalyptic view of the world do then? How would their thinking change?

Some such people might well experience another radical modification in their thinking, at least as radical as that from the prophetic view (God is causing suffering) to the apocalyptic (God's enemy, the Devil, is causing suffering). Both of these earlier views presuppose that the world was created by God, who is the good and all-powerful divine force behind it. But if these views are called into question by the ongoing realities of suffering in the world, what then? Maybe in fact the entire assumption is wrong. Maybe this world is not the creation of the one true God. Maybe the suffering in this world is not happening as a punishment *from* this good God or *despite* his goodness. Maybe the God of this world is not good. Maybe he is causing suffering not because he is good and wants people to share in his goodness but because he is evil, or ignorant, or inferior, and he *wants* people to suffer or doesn't *care* if they do, or maybe he can't do anything about it. But if that's true, then the God of this world is not the one true God. There must be a greater God above this world, one who did not create this world. In this understanding, the material world itself—material existence in all its forms—is inferior at best or evil at worst, and so is the God, then, who created it. There must be a nonmaterial God unconnected with this world, above the creator God of the Old Testament, a God who neither created this world nor brought suffering to it, who wants to relieve his people from their suffering—not by redeeming this world but by delivering them from it, liberating them from their entrapment in this material existence.

That is a Gnostic view. It may well have derived, ultimately, from a kind of failed apocalypticism. No wonder, then, that it is so taken up with Jewish texts. It derives from a Jewish worldview. And no wonder that in its Christian forms it gives such a central role to Christ, reinterpreting him away from his own apocalyptic roots.

It would be a mistake, however, to see Gnosticism as failed apocalypticism, pure and simple, for there are other factors that appear to have affected the complicated "mix" that we find in the Gnostic religions. Here I will mention just one other. One of the most striking features of Gnosticism is its radical dualism, in which the material world is evil and the world of the spirit is good. Where did this idea come from? Some readers are immediately struck by the parallels to certain kinds of eastern religion, and there may be something to that connection. But scholars of antiquity are usually struck even more by the similarities to other philosophical notions known from the period, especially among thinkers who stood within the Platonic tradition. Plato, too, had emphasized a kind of dualism of shadow and reality, matter and spirit. And there were a number of philosophers from the first and second centuries of the common era who expanded Plato's views and developed entire cosmologies—explanations for our world—that were dependent on him. These thinkers are usually called "Middle Platonists," to differentiate them from the older Platonists immediately following Plato (who died in the fourth century BCE) and the even better known Neoplatonists of the third and following centuries CE.[10]

Like the Gnostics, Middle Platonists thought that there was an ultimate deity far removed from anything we could think or imagine, completely ineffable (i.e., words cannot describe this God—even the loftiest words we can muster), absolutely perfect, totally removed from this world and its categories. He is complete and eternal within himself, not in relation to something else, not limited by space or time, and not intrinsically connected with anything in space and time. You cannot say that he is "great," because that would mean that he participates in something other than himself, called "greatness." You can't really say that he is "good," for the same reason. He is not big, because that would imply he has size.

Like Gnostics, the Middle Platonists were obsessed with understanding how this material world could come into being, if in the beginning the only thing that existed was this self-existent, perfect One. They developed mythological systems to explain how it happened. These myths did not suggest that the one God decided to create the world. Instead, they maintained that from this One there emanated a bewildering series of other divine beings, spilling outwards like water from a fountain, so that between the One True Spirit and this material world there were large numbers and various kinds of divine intermediaries, separating us from that One by an unbridgeable chasm.

These Middle Platonists were especially enthralled with Plato's dialogue, the *Timaeus*, in which Plato himself describes the creation of the material world from the world of nonmatter. It is interesting that one of the most philosophically astute Jews of the first century, Philo of Alexandria, wrote a commentary on the book of Genesis in which he tried to show that, when properly understood, Moses stood in direct continuity with Plato. Philo himself can be understood as a Middle Platonist, taking the Middle Platonic notions of the One supreme spiritual God and the realm of divine intermediaries between that God and this world, and applying them to his interpretation of Scripture.

Maybe Gnostics stood in that intellectual line, deriving their understanding of the world from Middle Platonism, in light of a transformation of a traditional view of Judaism, driven by the failure of apocalyptic hopes to materialize. The Christian form of Gnosticism, then, would have been influenced by the Christian claims about Christ, as the one through whom salvation comes, the one who reveals the truth, the one who comes from God above to us below (see, e.g., John 3:12–13, 6:41–42, 8:32).

This, then, is at least one way of understanding where this puzzling worldview of early Christian Gnosticism came from.

The Sources of Our
"Knowledge" of Gnosticism

What, more precisely, was this Gnostic view? One of the difficulties in summarizing it has to do with the ancient sources that are available. For centuries—in fact, all the time prior to the discovery of original Gnostic documents—our only sources of information about Gnosticism were the writings of the orthodox and proto-orthodox church fathers who opposed it, writers like Irenaeus, bishop of Lyons, who around 180 CE composed a five-volume work, *Refutation and Overthrow of Gnosis, Falsely So-Called* (usually simply called *Against Heresies*); Tertullian of Carthage, who about twenty years later wrote a number of treatises against various heretics; and his contemporary, Hippolytus of Rome, whose own work, *Refutation of All Heresies,* was itself discovered only in the nineteenth century. These writers give full, sometimes interminable, descriptions of Gnosticism. But they have nothing good to say about it. Gnostics are consistently ridiculed for espousing absurd and absurdly complex myths, for corrupting the clear teachings of Scripture (clear, that is, to the proto-orthodox), for espousing self-contradictory views, for encouraging wild and licentious activities that reveal their true colors as reprobates and deviants from the truth.

We will look at some of these lively polemics in a later chapter. For now it is enough to note that if we want to know what Gnostics really believed, it is difficult to trust the claims of their sworn enemies. It is true that these proto-orthodox authors sometimes used actual Gnostic documents and appear, on occasion, to have summarized them more or less accurately. When they do so, all to the good. But it is not always easy to know when we have reliable reportage and when we have scurrilous slander, or a clever mixture of the two.

Fortunately, we do have other sources available for our study of Gnostic Christianity. Several original Gnostic documents were available even before the discovery of the Nag Hammadi library, documents discovered in the eighteenth and nineteenth centuries. At the time of their discovery, however, these documents made little impact on the world of scholarship (let alone the rest of the world), partly because the accounts found in them did not readily square with those provided by the proto-orthodox heresiologists, Irenaeus and his successors. In a remarkable move that I suppose we should be accustomed to by now, scholars studying the phenomenon decided that these original Gnostic texts were less to be trusted than the reports of the proto-orthodox enemies of Gnosticism, that the Gnostic texts must in some way be aberrations from the Gnostic "norm." And so they shunted them to one side.

That is no longer possible, since the discovery of the texts near Nag Hammadi, many of them written by Gnostics, for Gnostics, presupposing Gnostic perspectives.

Not even these documents, however, are problem-free for trying to make sense of the phenomenon. For one thing, the very fact that some of these texts *presuppose* Gnostic views make them difficult to understand. It is somewhat like reading the sports page. An article about the first game of the World Series will not give a detailed account of the history and rules of baseball. It is written for insiders who already have all the background information they need to make sense of the report. So it is with many of the Gnostic texts from Nag Hammadi. They are books for insiders who—unlike us—already have all the background information they need.

And there are other problems. Some of these texts are incomplete, in that over the centuries since their production they have been worn out in places. Many of the manuscripts are riddled with holes, their missing words needing to be filled in. Sometimes restoring these texts is not overly difficult, but on other occasions we cannot be sure what was in the gaps. In the Gospel of Philip, for example—which is a seemingly random series of reflections and dialogues of Jesus and his disciples about the secrets of the universe, the meaning of the world, and our place in it—the disciples are upset about Jesus' relationship with Mary Magdalene and ask, "Why do you love her more than all of us?" They are responding to something Jesus has done, but what is it? The preceding text is full of holes, as follows: "And the companion of the [small gap in the manuscript] Mary Magdalene [small gap] her more than [small gap] the disciples [small gap] kiss her [small gap] on the [gap]" (*Gospel of Philip* 55). Our curiosity notwithstanding, we simply cannot know what was in the gaps.

Probably the biggest problem with the Nag Hammadi texts, however, is the one I have already alluded to, that they do not contain one coherent picture of Gnostic myth, belief, and practice, but represent widely divergent and disparate understandings of the world, the divine realm, humans, Christ, and so on. We should probably speak of Gnosticisms rather than Gnosticism.[11]

Still, there do seem to be some wide-ranging agreements in basic worldview among many of these texts and the systems that appear to presuppose, as we can patch them together both from the texts themselves and the descriptions of their enemies. Here I will lay out some of the overarching tenets that appear to apply to these particular Gnostic systems, discuss some of the mythologies used to present these perspectives, and provide an overview of several of the more interesting texts that have been discovered.

The Tenets of Gnosticism

As we have seen, Gnostic Christians maintained that in the beginning there was only One. This One God was totally spirit, totally perfect, incapable of description, beyond attributes and qualities. This God is not only unknown to humans; he is unknowable. The Gnostic texts do not explain why he is unknowable, except to suggest that he is so "other" that explanations—which require making something unknown known by comparing it to something else—simply cannot work.

According to sundry Gnostic myths, this one unknowable God, for some unknowable reason, generated a divine realm from himself. In some of these myths, the perfect essences of this One become themselves, somehow, self-existent. So, for example, this One spends eternity thinking. He thinks, of course, only of himself, since he is all there is. But his thought itself must exist, since he thinks. And so his thought becomes its own entity. Moreover, this One always exists. And so his eternal existence, his eternality, exists. And so it becomes its own entity. This One is living; in fact, he is Life. And so his life itself exists. Life then becomes its own entity. And so on.

Thus there emerge from this One other divine entities, emanations from the one, called aeons (Thought, Eternality, Life, etc.); moreover, some of these aeons produce their own entities, until there is an entire realm of the divine aeons, sometimes called the Fullness or, using the Greek term, the Pleroma.

The Gnostic myths are designed to show not only how this Pleroma came into existence in eternity past but how the world we live in came into being and how we ourselves came to be here. What these myths appear to have in common is the idea that there is a kind of downward movement from spirit to matter, that matter is a denigration of existence, the result of a disruption in the Pleroma, a catastrophe in the cosmos. In some of these systems, it is the final aeon who is the problem, an aeon called Wisdom or, using the Greek term, Sophia. The myths have different ways of explaining how Sophia's "fall" from the Pleroma led to the awful consequences of the material world. One of the more familiar myths is found in the *Secret Book of John*, an account of a revelation given to John the son of Zebedee by Jesus after his resurrection. This book was one of those discovered (in several versions) near Nag Hammadi in 1945; a version of its myth can also be found in the summaries of Irenaeus. In this Gnostic myth, Sophia decides to generate a divine being apart from the assistance of her male consort, leading to a malformed and imperfect offspring. Fearful that her misdeed will be uncovered, she removes her offspring from the divine realm into a lower sphere where no one can see him, and she leaves him then to his own devices. She has named him Yaldabaoth, a name reminiscent of "Yahweh, Lord of Sabbaths," from the Old Testament, for this malformed and imperfect divine being is the Jewish God.

According to this form of the myth, Yaldabaoth somehow manages to steal divine power from his mother. He then moves far off from her and uses his power to create other lesser divine beings—the evil cosmic forces of the world—and the material world itself. Since he is the creator, he is often called the Demiurge (Greek for "maker"). Yaldabaoth is ignorant of the realm above him, and so he foolishly declares, "I am God and there is no other God beside me" (Isa. 45:5–6). But he, along with his divine henchmen who have helped him create the world, are shown a vision of the one true God; they then declare among themselves, "Let us create a man according to the image of God" (i.e., the *true* God they have just seen—cf. Gen. 2:7). And so they make Adam. But Adam, not having a spirit within him, is completely immobile. The one true

God then tricks Yaldabaoth into conveying the power of his mother into this inanimate being, by breathing the breath of life into it, thereby imparting the power of Sophia into humans, making them animate and giving them a power greater even than the lesser cosmic forces that Yaldabaoth had created. When the cosmic forces realize that the man who was created is greater than they, they cast him into the realm of matter. But the one true God sends his own Thought into man, to instruct him concerning his true divine nature, the manner of his descent into the realm of matter, and the way in which he can reascend.

Other myths have other ways of describing the creation of the material world and the creation of humans. What they share is the notion that the world we live in was not the idea or creation of the One true God, but the result of a cosmic disaster, and that within some humans there resides a spark of the divine that needs to be liberated in order to return to its real home.

The only way this salvation can occur is for the divine spark to learn the secret knowledge that can bring liberation from its entrapment in the world of matter. Knowledge is thus central to these systems, knowledge of who one really is. As Jesus indicates to his brother, Judas Thomas, in one of the Nag Hammadi tractates, "While you accompany me, although you are uncomprehending, you have in fact already come to know, and you will be called the 'one who knows himself.' For he who has not known himself has known nothing, but he who has known himself has at the same time already achieved knowledge about the depth of the all" (*Book of Thomas the Contender* 2.138.14–18).[12]

This knowledge can come only from revelation. One cannot simply look at the world and figure out how to be saved. This world is evil, and any knowledge acquired within it is simply material knowledge. True knowledge comes from above, by means of a revelation. In Christian Gnostic circles, it is Christ who provides this knowledge. In the words of a Gnostic hymn by a group known as the Naassenes, quoted by the heresiologist Hippolytus,

> But Jesus said: "Look, Father, upon this being [i.e., the human] pursued by evils, which on the earth wanders about, far from your breath. It seeks to escape from the bitter chaos and knows not how it shall win through. For its sake send me, Father! Possessing the seals I will descend, all the aeons will I pass through, all secrets will I reveal, the forms of the gods will I disclose, and the hidden things of the holy way, which I have called 'knowledge,' will I impart" (*Refutation* 5.10.2).[13]

But how can Christ enter into this world of matter and not be tainted by it? That is one of the puzzles the Gnostics had to solve, and different Gnostic thinkers did so in different ways. Some took the line we have already seen in Marcion and others, maintaining that Jesus was not a flesh-and-blood human being, but only appeared to be so. These Gnostics took the words of the apostle Paul quite seriously: Christ came "in the *likeness* of sinful flesh" (Rom. 8:3). As a phantom sent from the divine realm, he came to convey the gnosis neces-

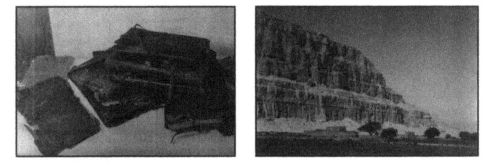

The Gnostic books discovered in 1945, and Nag Hammadi, Egypt, the place where they were found.

sary for salvation, and when he was finished doing so, he returned to the Pleroma whence he came.

Most Gnostics, however, took another line, claiming that Christ was a divine emissary from above, totally spirit, and that he entered the man Jesus temporarily in order to convey the knowledge that can liberate sparks from their material imprisonment. For these Gnostics, Jesus himself was in fact a human, even though some thought that he was *not* made like the rest of us, so that he could receive the divine emissary; some, for example, thought that he had a "soul-body" rather than a "flesh-body." In any event, at the baptism, Christ entered into Jesus (in the form of a dove, as in the New Testament Gospels); and at the end he left him to suffer his death alone. That is why Jesus cried out, "My God, my God, why have you forsaken me?" (literally, "Why have you left me behind?") Or, as stated in the Gospel of Philip, "'My God, my god, why O lord have you forsaken me?' He spoke these words on the cross; for he had withdrawn from that place" (G. Phil. 64).[14] According to one of the myths reported by Irenaeus, once Jesus had died, the Christ then came back and raised him from the dead (*Against Heresies* 1.30.13).

In either system, Christ provides the knowledge necessary for salvation. As the Gospel of Philip says, "The one who possesses the knowledge (gnosis) of the truth is free" (G. Phil. 93). Not everyone, however, can expect this liberating knowledge. In fact, most people have obviously never received it and never will. Some Christian Gnostics maintained that there were three kinds of humans. Some are the creations of the Demiurge, pure and simple. Like other animals, they have no spirit within; like them, when they die, their entire existence is annihilated. Other people have a soul within, but not a spark of the divine spirit. Such people have an opportunity for an afterlife, if they have faith and do good deeds. These in fact are regular Christians, those who believe in Christ but do not have the full understanding of the secret knowledge that leads to ultimate salvation. The third group of people have this knowledge. They are the Gnostics, those "in the know," who have within them a spark of the divine, who have learned who they really are, how they got here, and how they can return. These people will have a *fantastic* afterlife, in that they will return to the Divine realm from which they came and live eternally in the presence of God as part of the Pleroma.

One might think that Christians who held some such view, in which the point of salvation was to escape the body, might urge, or at least allow, a rather cavalier approach to bodily existence. If the body does not matter, then surely it does not matter what you do with your body! And, in fact, that is precisely the charge leveled against Gnostics by their proto-orthodox opponents, as we will later see (chap. 9). But as it turns out, Gnostic Christians themselves appear to have taken just the opposite perspective. This is one aspect of the Gnostic religions that their enemies appear to have misunderstood (or, possibly, misrepresented). As far as we can tell from the Nag Hammadi writings, instead of taking a libertine view of ethics (anything goes, since nothing matters), Gnostics were ascetic, advocating the strict regulation and harsh treatment of the body. Their logic was that since the body is evil, it should be punished; since attachment to the body is the *problem* of human existence, and since it is so easy to become attached to the body through pleasure, the body should be denied all pleasure. Thus it appears that the typical Gnostic stand on how to treat the body was rather strict.

Before turning to several of the interesting Gnostic texts, what can we say about the various Gnostics Christians as social groups? The Marcionites and the Ebionites appear to have had their own churches, separate from those of the other, obviously, and from those of the proto-orthodox. What about the Gnostics?

One of the striking features of Christian Gnosticism is that it appears to have operated principally from *within* existing Christian churches, that Gnostics considered themselves to be the spiritually elite of these churches, who could confess the creeds of other Christians, read the Scriptures of other Christians, partake of baptism and Eucharist with other Christians, but who believed that they had a deeper, more spiritual, secret understanding of these creeds, Scriptures, and sacraments. This may well be why proto-orthodox church fathers found them so insidious and difficult to deal with, as we will see later in chapter 10. Gnostics were not "out there" forming their own communities. The Gnostics were "in here," with us, in our midst. And you couldn't tell one simply by looking. It seems likely that these Gnostic "inner circles" were prevalent in some parts of Christianity. In addition to the Scriptures used by the church at large, interpreted in Gnostic ways (for example, in the reinterpretations of Genesis I've mentioned above), they used their own writings, including some of the mythological treatises and mystical reflections now discovered in Nag Hammadi. They may have had additional sacraments: The Gospel of Philip, for example, alludes to five of them, without explaining what they were or how they worked: baptism, anointing (with oil), Eucharist, ransom, and bridal chamber (G. Phil. 60). It is difficult to know what all these involved—especially the sacrament of the "bridal chamber." Unfortunately, the Gospel of Philip simply mentions it, presumably because its readers knew full well what it was.

Some of the Gnostic Texts

I have already discussed several Gnostic texts and mentioned others in passing, for example, the Gospel of Thomas (which, as I've indicated, I take as Gnostic), the Gospel of Mary, the Secret Book of John, the Gospel of Philip. One way to gain a fuller appreciation of this form of lost Christianity—or rather of the various forms that it takes—is to consider several other interesting texts. Here I will discuss three that illuminate key aspects of the Gnostic religions, and consider several others, such as the Coptic Apocalypse of Peter and the Second Treatise of the Great Seth, in later chapters.

The Gospel of Truth

One of the most intriguing documents found in Nag Hammadi comes without a title. Based on its opening lines, it is usually called the Gospel of Truth. These opening lines put the lie to those who may think of Gnosticism as some kind of dour, intellectualizing, morally dubious kind of religion, for here the joy of salvation is celebrated with abandon:

> The gospel of truth is joy for those who have received from the Father of truth the grace of knowing him, through the power of the Word that came forth from the Pleroma, the one who is in the thought and the mind of the Father, that is, the one who is addressed as the Savior. (G. Truth 16)[15]

We don't know for certain who wrote this terrific little treatise, which lays out a Gnostic understanding of salvation in unusually clear terms. But its point of view coincides in many ways with the teachings of a famous Gnostic teacher from the second century, who taught in Rome and, because of his charismatic presence and rhetorical power, acquired a large following among Christians there, a man named Valentinus. Valentinian Christianity was seen as one of the main enemies by proto-orthodox authors like Irenaeus and Tertullian, but whether it was, as they claimed, an insidious attempt to pervert the truth is another matter. The few fragments that we have from the hand of Valentinus himself are both thoughtful and thought provoking. Many scholars think that this Gospel of Truth also came from his pen.[16]

Although called a Gospel, this is not an account of Jesus' words and deeds. It is instead a celebration of the salvation that Jesus has brought into the world by delivering the truth that can free the soul from its bondage to material things. A number of central issues are discussed in the writing: the nature of God, the character of the world, the person of Christ, the work of salvation he brought, and how to respond to it. Notably, its views stand diametrically opposed to those that eventually became dominant in Christianity and that have been handed down to Christians today.

"Orthodox" Christianity maintained that this world was the intentional creation of the one true God, and as such was made good—even if sin later came into the world and corrupted it. This Gnostic Gospel claims that the material world came about, instead, by a conflict in the divine realm, resulting in ignorance, terror, anguish, and error:

> Ignorance of the Father [i.e., the opposite of "gnosis"] brought about anguish and terror; and the anguish grew solid like a fog so that no one was able to see. For this reason error became powerful; it worked on its own matter foolishly, not having known the truth. It set about with a creation, preparing with power and beauty the substitute for the truth. (G. Truth 17)

"Orthodox" Christianity claimed that Christ died for the sins of the world and that his death and resurrection are what brings salvation. This Gospel, however, maintains that Jesus brought salvation by delivering the truth that could set the soul free. Moreover, it was out of anger for his deliverance of this knowledge that the ignorant rulers of this world erroneously put him to death:

> Jesus, the Christ, enlightened those who were in darkness through oblivion. He enlightened them; he showed them a way; and the way is the truth which he taught them. For this reason error grew angry at him and persecuted him. . . . He was nailed to a tree and he became a fruit of the knowledge of the Father. (G. Truth 18)

"Orthodox" Christianity insisted that people are made right with God by faith in Jesus' death and resurrection. This Gospel maintains that people are saved by receiving the correct knowledge of who they really are.

> There came the men wise in their own estimation, putting him to the test. But he confounded them because they were foolish. They hated him because they were not really wise. After these, there came the little children also, those to whom the knowledge of the Father belongs. Having been strengthened, they learned about the impressions of the Father. They knew, they were known; they were glorified, they glorified. . . . But those who are to receive teaching are the living who are inscribed in the book of the living. It is about themselves that they receive instruction. (G. Truth 19–21)

"Orthodox" Christianity understood that God would redeem this sinful world, create it anew as a utopian place of eternal life. This Gospel states that once saving knowledge comes to souls entrapped in this world, the world of ignorance will pass away.

> Since the deficiency came into being because the Father was not known, therefore, when the Father is known, from that moment on, the deficiency will no longer exist. As in the case of the ignorance of a person, when he comes to have knowledge, his ignorance vanishes of itself, as the darkness vanishes when light appears, so also the deficiency vanishes in the perfection. (G. Truth 24–25)

The book concludes with an exhortation for its hearers to share the true knowledge of salvation with those who seek the truth, and not to return to their former (proto-orthodox?) beliefs, which they have already transcended.

> Say, then, from the heart that you are the perfect day and in you dwells the light that does not fail. Speak of the truth with those who search for it and of knowledge to those who have committed sin in their error. . . . Do not return to what you have vomited to eat it. Do not be moths. Do not be worms, for you have already cast it off. . . . Do the will of the Father, for you are from him. For the Father is sweet and in his will is what is good. (G. Truth 32)

Whatever one might say about this form of Christianity, I don't think we can call it insincere or wanting of feeling. It is warm and intense, full of joy and passion. Its enemies found it heinous, though, and did their utmost both to destroy it and to sully the reputation of its author.

Ptolemy's Letter to Flora

We have seen that Gnostic Christians, in addition to utilizing their own writings, had no difficulty accepting on some level the Scriptures used by other Christians as well. But how did they understand these other texts? One of the most interesting Gnostic documents that we have is a letter written by one of Valentinus's main followers, a teacher named Ptolemy, who bore the brunt of much of the attack of Irenaeus's lengthy five-volume work against the Gnostics. The letter is addressed to an otherwise unknown woman named Flora, who was evidently a proto-orthodox Christian who had inquired into the Gnostic understanding of Scripture. The letter is not cited by Irenaeus, however, nor was it discovered among the writings at Nag Hammadi. It is instead known from the work of that doughty defender of orthodoxy, the fourth-century Epiphanius of Salamis, who quotes the letter in toto.

The letter provides a clear and coherent exposition of this particular Gnostic's understanding of the Old Testament. It is striking that Ptolemy does not simply state his views as the "gospel truth." Instead, he reasons with his reader, urging her to see that his views are completely sensible and even persuasive. We should recall that there were a range of understandings of the Old Testament among early Christian groups: For Ebionite Christians, they were the sacred Scriptures par excellence, the heart and soul of the Christian canon; for Marcion, they were the Scriptures of the Jewish God, not of the God of Jesus, and they were not to be accepted as in any way canonical. Ptolemy's understanding of the Old Testament is based on both his Gnostic assumptions and the words of Jesus. His focus is on the Law of Moses, the first five books of the Old Testament (the Torah, also known as the "Pentateuch").

Ptolemy begins by indicating views of Scripture that he considers to be absolutely wrong. Some people, he points out, claim that the "law was ordained by God the Father," whereas others insist that "it has been established by the adversary, the pernicious devil."[17] The first view, we might suppose, is that of most Jews and proto-orthodox Christians (and Ebionites, etc.). The second view is not exactly that of Marcion; possibly it was held by other Gnostics. In any event, Ptolemy insists that both views "are utterly in error . . . and miss the truth of the matter."

On the one hand, the Old Testament could not have been inspired by the one true God, since it is not perfect. The Old Testament, for example, contains commandments that are not appropriate to God, such as when God gives his people, the Israelites, the promised land and orders them to murder in cold blood the Canaanites already living there. Moreover, since some of the Old Testament had to be "fulfilled" by Jesus (e.g., the prophecies that the Messiah was to be born in Bethlehem to a virgin), this shows that parts of the Old Testament were incomplete and therefore imperfect. But neither could the Old Testament have been inspired by the Devil, since it contains laws that are just and good. An evil being cannot produce something that is contrary to its nature.

The payoff is that the Old Testament must have been inspired by some other divine being, neither the one true perfect God nor his nemesis, the Devil, but a deity between the two. One can see, here, the "logic" of the need for intermediaries between God and the cosmic forces of this world.

Ptolemy goes on to insist, on the basis of Jesus' own words, that there are in fact three kinds of laws found in the Old Testament:

> Indeed, our savior's words teach us that the Law of the Old Testament divides into three parts. For one division belongs to god himself and his legislations [Ptolemy means here the intermediary god, not the one true God], while another division belongs to Moses . . . not as god himself ordained through him, rather based upon his own thoughts . . . and yet a third division belongs to the elders of the people. (4:1–2)

As he explains, the Ten Commandments must have been given by (the intermediary) God. But there are other laws that Jesus clearly indicates did not come from God, for example, the law of divorce, which Jesus disallowed by saying, "For your hardness of heart Moses allowed divorce. . . . But from the beginning it was not so" (4:4; quoting Matt 19:8). This kind of law comes, then, not from God but from Moses. And other laws come not from Moses but from "the elders of the people," for example, the law which indicates that a gift that might benefit one's parents could be donated instead to the Temple; Jesus claims that this law "from the elders" violates God's commandment to "honor your father and mother" (4:11–12, quoting Matt 15:4–5).

And so only some laws of Scripture actually come from (the intermediary) God. But even these divine laws are of three kinds. Some of them are perfect, for example, the Ten Commandments. Others are tainted by human passion. For example, the law of retaliation, "an eye for an eye and a tooth for a tooth," is "interwoven with injustice," since, as Ptolemy points out, "the one who is second to act unjustly still acts unjustly, differing only in the relative order in which he acts, and committing the very same act" (5:4). Third, there are some laws of Scripture that are clearly meant to be taken symbolically, not literally. The law of circumcision is not about cutting the foreskin off baby boys but about setting aside one's heart for God; the law of Sabbath is not about refraining from work on the seventh day but about refraining from doing what is evil; the law of fasting is not about going hungry but about abstaining from bad deeds (5:11–13).

Ptolemy concludes that Jesus' teaching of the Law therefore presupposes a just divine being who is not the one true perfect God. This one is the Demiurge, the maker of the world, in an intermediate state between God and the Devil, "inferior to the perfect God" but "better and more authoritative than the Devil" (7:6; note: Ptolemy here differs from other Gnostics in giving a rather positive evaluation of the Demiurge). He ends his letter by indicating that in a future treatise he will explain this divine world inhabited by more than one God, urging that his views come from the "apostolic tradition" and are founded on "our savior's teaching" (7:9).

Clearly, here is a sincere believer who understood his views to be those of the apostles and, through them, of Jesus. This applies not just to his views of Scripture but to those of the divine world and of the human's place in it. Here we have additional evidence, as if more were needed, that the losers in the battle to establish the "true" form of Christianity were intent on discovering the truth and were certain that their understanding of the faith resided in the teachings of Jesus' own apostles. Had his views not been quoted in the writings of Epiphanius, who set them forth simply in order to attack them, we might never have realized just how clear, passionate, and earnest they really were.

The Treatise on the Resurrection

One of the issues naturally raised by a Gnostic understanding of the world involves the character of the afterlife. If salvation comes by *escaping* the body rather than while *in* the body, what kind of existence awaits us after death? How can a bodiless existence be imagined? Moreover, if Christianity in any sense is based on the notion that Christ was "raised from the dead," what exactly could that mean for someone who did not think that Christ had a fleshly body to begin with, or for someone who maintained that Jesus and Christ were two separate beings?

These are the sorts of questions dealt with by another surviving Gnostic letter, again addressed to a non-Gnostic Christian. This letter, however, appeared for the first time among the writings of Nag Hammadi. It is sometimes called by the name of its recipient, Letter to Rheginus, but is more commonly entitled Treatise on the Resurrection. It is a short work, meant to argue that the resurrection is not at all an illusion, but that neither does it involve some kind of crass revivification of the material body, which itself is illusory. No, the resurrection involves the salvation of the spirit as it rises up to its heavenly home.

The letter addresses itself to questions raised by Rheginus, concerning "what is proper concerning the resurrection."[18] The author indicates that Christ was both Son of God and Son of man, "possessing the humanity and the divinity . . . originally from above, a seed of the truth, before this structure of the cosmos had come into being" (Treat. Res. 44). He claims that at Jesus' resurrection, "the Savior swallowed up death . . . for he put aside the world which is perishing. He transformed himself into an imperishable aeon and raised himself up, having swallowed the visible by the invisible, and he gave us the way of our immortality" (Treat. Res. 45). In other words, what is eternal is the invisible; that which is perishable is done away with, for the life of immortality. And Jesus' resurrection then paves the way for that of the Christians: "We are drawn to heaven by him, like beams by the sun, not being restrained by anything. This is the spiritual resurrection. . . . The thought of those who are saved shall not perish. The mind of those who have known him shall not perish" (Treat. Res. 45–46).

The author continues by pointing out that before they appeared in this world, people were not in the flesh, and once they leave this world, they will leave the flesh behind (v. 47). Not that which is dead (the flesh) will be saved, but only that which is alive (the spirit) (v. 48). Yet the author insists that even though it is the invisible which is raised, the resurrection is no illusion. On the contrary, it is this world which is the illusion, falsely lulling people into thinking that it is the ultimate reality. But this material world will pass away; it is the spirit that will live on (v. 48).

This doctrine that the flesh will pass away but the spirit will live has clear ethical implications for the author: "Therefore do not, O Rheginus, live in conformity with this flesh . . . but flee the divisions and the fetters and already you have the resurrection. . . . It is fitting for each one to practice in a number of ways, and he shall be released from this Element that he may not fall into error, but shall himself receive again what at first was" (Treat. Res. 49).

And so, to achieve this return to the realm whence we came, we must refuse to satisfy the longings of our flesh. This is scarcely the ticket to flagrant immorality that the proto-orthodox thought; instead, it is a life of freedom of the spirit, no longer yielding to the demands of the body.

Gnostic Religions and the Question of Dominance

So much more could be said about Gnostic forms of Christianity. But perhaps enough has been said to give a taste of this strange, even inviting set of religious practices and beliefs.

Christianity in nearly all its forms has always had its spiritual elite, the insiders who have a special insight into the true meaning of the faith, a cut above the rest of us in their nuanced understanding of God, the world, and our place in it. The Gnostics virtually fetishized this notion of an elite, a group of people in the know, who recognized the true nature of the church's profession of faith, of its Scriptures, of its sacraments. Those outside the inner circle often felt threatened by it, so much so that the ones claiming to be in the know became the object of scorn and derision. We will observe some of these reactions in a later chapter, and we will see how some of the Gnostics answered in turn. For it was not only the proto-orthodox who felt that they themselves were right and all others were wrong. Every group felt the same, whether relatively small, established, and marginalized groups like the Ebionites, or fast-growing and progressive groups like the Marcionites, or insider, elitist groups like the Gnostics.

Is it conceivable that Gnostic Christianity could have eventually won out in this struggle for dominance? Certainly the proto-orthodox leaders felt the pressure of these groups; otherwise, we would be hard-pressed to explain the massive expenditure of time and energy devoted to rooting out the Gnostic "heretics," spurning their views, maligning their persons, destroying their writings, eliminating their influence. And one can certainly see why the Gnostic views won a following. Here were Christian groups that were fearless in their denunciation of our material existence: This world is not just fallen; it is inherently evil, a cosmic catastrophe; it is a place to be escaped, not enjoyed. It may seem acceptable on one level simply to say that humans have corrupted it. You can account for war and oppression and injustice simply by pointing the finger at someone else. But the suffering of this world is far deeper than that: droughts that bring massive starvation, unstoppable floods, volcanoes that devastate entire populations, rampant disease, pain that wracks the body, infirmity, death. The Gnostics took the suffering of this world seriously, and they turned their backs on it. This, they argued, cannot be laid at the feet of God.

God is good, true, and perfect. And some of us belong to him. We may feel alienated here. If so, it is for good reason. We *are* alienated here. We are not of this world; we belong to another world. The story of how we got here is filled with mystery; it can be told only as a myth, not as a propositional statement of historical fact. We came to be here by a cataclysmic rip in the fabric of reality, a cosmic disaster, a tragic mistake. But we can escape this world and all that it holds; we can return to our heavenly home; we can become united with God, once again, as we originally were.

It is a powerful message. It was obviously attractive. But I don't know if it could ever have won out. One of the problems with religions that stress the importance of the spiritually elite is that they have trouble winning over the (nonelite) masses.

Had Gnostic Christianity done so, it would have made for quite a few changes in our world. Who knows what kind of social agenda could have been formed in the long run by a group that rejected the importance of the ongoing life of society? Would they have been able to address problems of poverty and disease, injustice and oppression, when they thought the flesh was to be escaped rather than endured? It is a genuine question, since other "other-worldly" groups have strived to improve life on earth. On a less pressing but more fundamental level: Who knows how common modes of discourse would have developed had secret revelatory knowledge, accessible to only a few and confusing, no doubt, even to them, proved to be the ultimate arbiter of truth? Would a western form of philosophy rooted in the likes of Aristotle, which provide us today with what we think of as "common sense" (for example, in the Aristotelian "law of noncontradiction"), have seemed bizarre or even quaint? Who knows how the ways of reading texts that strike us as obvious and straightforward, literal readings in which we follow the words in sequence and accept their commonly accepted meanings within their own contexts—who knows how our ways of reading texts would have altered if a group that insisted on figurative understandings as the primary modes of interpretation had won out and established sway in our forms of civilization?

On the other hand, maybe hatred of the world would have led people to work to change the world instead of abandon it. Maybe devaluation of the body would have ultimately led people to work to control the body. We don't know. What we do know is that these precious systems of belief and practice, these alternative forms of Christianity, had a lot to say to the world of antiquity, and evidently they have a lot to say to people even today, given the fascination about Gnosticism among those interested in early Christianity. They nonetheless came to be roundly defeated in the battles for dominance among early Christian groups. As a result, they were virtually lost to the world except in their polemical refutations by proto-orthodox adversaries, until some of their texts reappeared by sheer serendipity in modern times.

Chapter Seven

On the Road to Nicaea: The Broad Swath of Proto-orthodox Christianity*

In America today, Christians new in town sometimes find it difficult to choose the right church. If they are Episcopalian, do they prefer high church or low church? If Methodist, socially liberal or ethically conservative? If evangelical, large and technologically sophisticated or small and intimate? Should it be a Bible-preaching church or a liturgically oriented church? Politically active or spiritually focused? Strong music program or thoughtful sermons? Should it have a solid social ministry? Active youth group? Vibrant outreach program? The questions go on and on for those concerned about such things.

Imagine the choices facing Christians in the second century. Which is better: the Ebionite church or the Marcionite? Gnostic or proto-orthodox? A church that believes in one god or twelve or thirty? A church that accepts the Gospels of Matthew, Mark, and Luke or the Gospels of Thomas, Philip, and Mary? A church that believes God created the world or that the world is a cosmic mistake? A church that adheres to the Jewish laws of kashrut, Sabbath observance, and circumcision or a church that condemns these laws as inspired by an inferior deity?

It makes the choice of a good music program pale a bit by comparison.

We have talked about several of the early Christian groups, but as we have seen, there were in fact many more. Gnostic groups alone had so many perspectives, theologies, and mythological systems that not even the heresy hunters could

---

*By "Nicaea" I refer to the council called in the city of Nicaea by the emperor Constantine in 325 CE, a council that established a creed that became the basis of Christian orthodoxy for centuries to follow. Eventually this creed developed into the Nicene Creed; see chap. 9.

track them all down. And there were interminglings: Jewish Christians influenced by Gnostics, Gnostics influenced by Marcionites, proto-orthodox influenced in one way or another by everyone.

But only one form of Christianity, this group we have been calling proto-orthodox, emerged as victorious, and it is to this victory that we owe the most familiar features of what we think of today as Christianity. This victory bequeathed to us four Gospels to tell us virtually everything we know about the life, death, and resurrection of Jesus. In fact, it handed down to us the entire New Testament, twenty-seven books, the only books produced by Christians accepted as Scripture. Along with these "new" Scriptures was the "Old" Testament, still accepted as canon, even though sometimes considered to have been superseded by the New. The proto-orthodox victory also passed along a church hierarchy—different kinds of hierarchy in different denominations now. But for centuries (in parts of the church) it was as widely accepted and unproblematic as the branches of the federal government in the United States today, a hierarchy of bishops, elders, and deacons and eventually offices still higher up, to the rank of pope, and lower down.

In addition, the proto-orthodox victory conferred to Christian history a set of practices and beliefs. These include "sacraments" practiced by Christians almost everywhere: baptism and eucharist. And they include doctrines familiar to anyone conversant with Christianity: Christ as both divine and human, fully God and fully man. And the sacred Trinity, the three-in-one: Father, Son, and Holy Spirit, three persons, but only one God, the mystery at the heart of traditional Christian faith.

All this, and much more, was bequeathed to the world by the victory of proto-orthodoxy. We are now in a position in our study to take a closer look at what the proto-orthodox stood for and, to some extent, see what they stood against. In many respects, it was their opposition to alternative perspectives that drove proto-orthodox Christians to adopt the views they did. But rather than focusing on the conflicts with other groups, for the moment we will consider some of their major perspectives on their own terms, as reflected in the proto-orthodox writings. As was true of the other forms of Christianity we have examined, this group was no monolith. Here also we find a wide range of perspectives, even though they all fall within certain parameters, boundary markers that separated the proto-orthodox from other groups and that determined their acceptability to later Christians who established the creeds and scriptural canon of Christianity. But within these broader parameters there were multiple views represented—not a solitary perspective that could be traced all the way back to Jesus and his apostles, despite the claims of the proto-orthodox themselves, claims they sometimes made, ironically enough, even when expressing views that their fellow proto-orthodox found dubious or problematic.

Moreover, not even the parameters of proto-orthodoxy were hard and fast, static boundary markers that were never moved. They evolved over time, with new boundaries occasionally being set up and old ones shifted accordingly.

Still, we can acquire a good sense of the broad contours of proto-orthodox Christianity by examining the writings of some of its earliest champions, authors who were later embraced as the forebears of orthodoxy. Of these, no one can serve our purposes better than Ignatius of Antioch, whose letters adumbrate many of the issues to be taken up by his successors among the proto-orthodox.

Proto-orthodox Martyrs as
Witnesses to the Truth

Ignatius has long been a source of fascination for students of early Christianity, both for what he says in his letters and for the context in which he said them.[1] Bishop of Antioch at the beginning of the second century, Ignatius had been arrested, evidently for Christian activities, and sent to Rome for execution in the arena, where he was to be thrown to the wild beasts. We are not sure why he was sent to Rome for the occasion, rather than executed on the spot, as more typically happened with convicted criminals in the Roman provinces. It may be that the governor of Syria chose to send him, possibly along with some others, as a gift for the Roman hunting games, in which convicted criminals were made to "fight" fierce and exotic animals as part of a public spectacle before a crowd of delighted onlookers. American football is a mere shadow of that particular reality.

In any event, it seems reasonably clear that Ignatius was *not* going to Rome under conditions similar to those of his own hero, the apostle Paul, who, according to Acts, appealed to the emperor for a fair trial as a Roman citizen, and so was sent to the capital to receive due process (see Acts 25:10–12). Ignatius is not concerned about due process or a fair trial. He speaks of himself as already condemned, not under judicial review, and is clearly not interested in an appeal for clemency. One of his letters is addressed to the Christians of Rome, in which he urges them not to intervene in the proceedings, because he is eager to be devoured by the wild beasts: By suffering that kind of death he will "attain to God." To most modern ears, his passion for a violent death borders on the pathological:

> Allow me to be bread for the wild beasts; through them I am able to attain to God. I am the wheat of God and am ground by the teeth of the wild beasts, that I may be found to be the pure bread of Christ. Rather, coax the wild beasts, that they may become a tomb for me and leave no part of my body behind, that I may burden no one once I have died. (Ign. Rom. 4)
>
> May I have the full pleasure of the wild beasts prepared for me; I pray they will be found ready for me. Indeed, I will coax them to devour me quickly. . . . And even if they do not wish to do so willingly, I will force them to it. . . . May nothing visible or invisible show any envy toward me, that I may attain to Jesus Christ. Fire and cross and packs of wild beasts, cuttings and being torn apart,

the scattering of bones, the mangling of limbs, the grinding of the whole body,
the evil torments of the devil—let them come upon me, only that I may attain to
Jesus Christ. (Ign. Rom. 5)

One person's pathology, however, is another person's common sense. For
Ignatius, and other martyrs following in his steps, wanting to die a violent
death for the faith was not at all unreasonable. It was a way to imitate the Son
of God and to show the world that neither the pains nor the pleasures of this life
were anything compared with the glories of salvation awaiting those who gave
themselves over not to this world but to the world above, the world of God.[2]

Proto-orthodox authors considered this willingness to die for the faith one
of the hallmarks of their religion, and in fact used it as a boundary marker,
separating true believers (i.e., those who agreed with their theological perspectives) from the false "heretics" they were so concerned about. Some of their
opponents agreed that this was a distinctive boundary marker: One of the Gnostic
tractates from Nag Hammadi, for example, *The Testimony of Truth,* takes just
the opposite position, maintaining that martyrdom for the faith was ignorant
and foolish. From this Gnostic perspective, a God who required a human sacrifice for himself would be completely vain (*Test. Truth* 31–37).

We do not have a historical account of Ignatius's own martyrdom, although
we do have a later, legendary account forged by some of his proto-orthodox
successors. In this account Ignatius is shown standing trial before the emperor
Trajan himself (who just happens to be in Antioch at the time) and making a
profession of his faith, filled with proto-orthodox notions. Condemned then to
the amphitheater in Rome, he undertakes his travels and is thrown to the wild
beasts, fulfilling his every desire. Or almost every desire. For according to this
later account, the beasts did *not* completely consume his body (recall what he
wrote to the Romans: "I wish that they leave no part of my body behind"): Some
of the "harder portions of his holy remains were left." And, as appropriate in a
period that saw a rising passion for relics of the saints, these were wrapped in
linen and taken back to Antioch as an object of veneration (Mart. Ign. 6).

Martyrologies—that is, written accounts of martyrdom—became common in
proto-orthodox circles after Ignatius. The first full account of a Christian being
condemned to execution for his faith is based on an eyewitness report of the
death of Polycarp, bishop of Smyrna in Asia Minor, the one individual, as it
turns out, to receive a letter of Ignatius (the others were all written to churches).
Ignatius's letter to Polycarp was written, as were the others, while Ignatius was
on his journey to his martyrdom. This was probably around 110 CE, just after
most of the books of the New Testament had been written. Polycarp was a
middle-aged bishop at the time, and he lived for another forty-five years before
becoming the victim of a local persecution that culminated in his death.

The account of the Martyrdom of Polycarp is intriguing for both its historical character and its legendary accretions.[3] On the historical side, it shows that

Polycarp was not *eager* to be martyred for his faith. When the authorities decide to arrest him, he goes into hiding, at the encouragement of his parishioners. On the other hand, he refuses to be intimidated and makes no serious attempt to resist the forces that want him dead, principally the mobs in town who evidently see Christians as a nuisance and social disease, and who want to be rid of them and, particularly, their cherished leader. Rather than stay on the run, Polycarp allows himself to be captured in a farmhouse in the countryside. And when taken into the arena and threatened with death, rather than defend himself, he stoutly refuses to do what is required: deny Christ and make an offering for the emperor. He is threatened with torture and wild beasts, but nothing fazes him. The governor orders his death by burning at the stake, and the sentence is immediately carried out.

As I have indicated, the account appears to be written by an eyewitness, and there is no reason to doubt that in its essentials it is accurate. At the same time, the author expressly states that he intends to show how Polycarp's death was "in conformity with the Gospel" (Mart. Pol. 1.1) and, indeed, there are important similarities here with the death of Jesus: Like Jesus, Polycarp did not turn himself in, but waited to be betrayed; he knew about his coming execution in advance and predicted it to his followers; he prayed intensely before his arrest; he asked that "God's will be done"; the official in charge of his arrest, remarkably enough, was named Herod; he rode into town on a donkey, and so on. Moreover, God works a miracle for this proto-orthodox champion of the faith: Polycarp receives such divine succor that he appears to feel no terror and experiences no anguish. When burned at the stake, he does not need to be secured to the upright with nails but is only tied, standing of his own volition. When the conflagration begins, a miracle occurs: The flames do not touch his body but envelop him like a sheet. And rather than emitting a stench of burning flesh, his body seems to exude a sweet odor like perfume. When the flames fail to consume his body, an executioner administers the coup de grâce by stabbing him with a dagger, which has the effect of releasing a dove from his side (his "holy" spirit, returning to heaven?), along with such a quantity of blood that it douses the flames.

The legendary details of the account, in other words, are designed to show God's stamp of approval on a martyrdom of this kind. This was the sort of death for the faith celebrated by the proto-orthodox authors whose writings have survived, including other martyrologies of the period and essays written about martyrdom by those who were spared. No one is more forthright in his insistence that martyrdom is a sign of the truth than Tertullian, who wrote several treatises touching on the matter, including one that urges the martyrs on to their deaths. In language reminiscent of his archenemies, the Gnostics, Tertullian speaks of the world, not the dungeon, as the real prison to be escaped: "Nor let this separation from the world alarm you; for if we reflect that the world is more really the prison, we shall see that you have gone out of a prison rather than into one" (*To the Martyrs* 2). Christians should reflect on their heavenly home, even when in chains here, for "the leg does not feel the chain when the mind is in the heavens." This may sound a bit like armchair theology: It is well enough to claim that being tortured to death is not a matter of ultimate concern, when you yourself are destined to live long and reasonably well. But there is more to it than that. For Tertullian, like other proto-orthodox writers before and after him, the divine succor afforded true martyrs in the time of torment was proof positive of the validity of their faith.

And so it is no accident that Tertullian uses proto-orthodox martyrdoms as a point of differentiation between true and false believers. As he indicates, "heretics" refuse to pay the ultimate price for their faith. In his essay "The Remedy for the Scorpion's Sting" (the scorpion being "heresy"), Tertullian indicates that Gnostics—not true believers in any sense for Tertullian—avoid martyrdom, reasoning that Christ died precisely so that they would not have to and that it is better to deny Christ and repent of it later than to confess Christ and pay the ultimate price.

We have no way of knowing how many proto-orthodox Christians were actually martyred or, conversely, how many chose to deny Christ under oath rather than face executioners renowned for their creativity in the technology of torture. Nor, for that matter, do we know how many Gnostics, Marcionites, Ebionites, or others were willing to brave death for the sake of what they held to be true. But it is clear that one of the distinguishing marks of the proto-orthodox, at least in their own minds, was their claim not only to represent the truth but also to be willing to die for it. In this, as in so many other ways, Ignatius shows us a clear boundary marker for proto-orthodox Christianity in the early centuries.

Apostolic Successors in the Proto-orthodox Tradition

We have already seen that at a much later time, in the early seventeenth century, the letters of Ignatius became a hotbed of contention, not for their stance on martyrdom but for their view of church organization. This was especially true in England, where, in the wake of the Reformation, traditionalists and nonconformists were at loggerheads concerning the validity of the "church offices." Anglicans like James Ussher, one of the most erudite scholars of his age, argued that the earliest Christian writings, such as those of Ignatius, demonstrate that the office of the bishop had been in place virtually from the beginning.[4] His opponents, including the young and already feisty John Milton, argued that the letters of Ignatius were forgeries of later times, fabricated, in part, precisely in order to justify the later creation of the office. Among all the participants in this debate, it was Ussher himself who cut through the Gordion knot by showing that of the thirteen widely circulated letters of Ignatius, six were forgeries and the rest had undergone illicit expansion by the author of the forgeries. But there were authentic Ignatian letters as well, and we still have them, preserved in their shorter, more original form in several surviving manuscripts.

This judgment, with some slight modification, is still the consensus among scholars who work in the field today.[5] We have seven of Ignatius's letters. And even stripping away the fabricated expansions, these give a clear picture of one proto-orthodox author's view of church structure. Ignatius was an avid and outspoken advocate of the monepiscopacy (single bishop). Each Christian community had a bishop, and this bishop's word was law. The bishop was to be followed as if he were God himself. As Ignatius urges his readers in various churches: "Be subject to the bishop as to the commandment" (Ign. Trall. 13.2); "We are clearly obliged to look upon the bishop as the Lord himself" (Ign. Eph. 6.1); "You should do nothing apart from the bishop" (Ign. Magn. 7.1).

This then was a mark of the proto-orthodox tradition, an emphasis on church order guaranteed by a rigid church structure, with one person at the top making the key decisions. Things had not always been that way. Sixty years or so before Ignatius, when the apostle Paul had written to the church of Corinth, a church wracked with problems of division, infighting, flagrant immorality, chaotic gatherings, and doctrinal error, he did not address the "pastor" of the church or the "bishop," telling him to resolve the church's problems. He wrote the entire church with instructions concerning how to handle the situation. But why did he not write the person in charge? It was because there *was* no person in charge. Paul's churches, as evident from 1 Corinthians itself, were organized as charismatic communities, directed by the Spirit of God, who gave each member a special gift (Greek: *charisma*) to assist them to live and function together as a communal body, gifts of teaching, prophesying, giving, leading, and so on (1 Cor. 12).

An organization like that may work for the short term, for example, in what Paul imagined to be the brief interim between Jesus' resurrection and his imminent return in glory. But if Jesus were not to return immediately, and as a result, the church has time to develop and grow, having no one in charge can lead to serious chaos. And it did lead to serious chaos, especially in Corinth.

After Paul's death, an aspiring author in one of his churches wrote the Pastoral epistles (1 and 2 Timothy and Titus) in Paul's name.[6] These books are addressed not to troubled churches but to the *pastors* of troubled churches, who are told to deal with the problems and to bring their people into proper order. These books also give instructions for church leaders, indicating qualifications for the offices of bishop and deacon, for example, and directives for church life together. Here we are on the road to a proto-orthodox church hierarchy.

It is interesting to note that the road ran through Corinth. One of the most intriguing proto-orthodox documents from early times is an anonymous letter written by the church of Rome to the church of Corinth, traditionally called 1 Clement.[7] This was a very important book to many of the proto-orthodox of the second and third centuries. It was evidently read as Scripture during worship services in Corinth in the 170s; so reports Dionysius, the bishop of Corinth at the time (Eusebius *Church History* 4, 23). And later still, some orthodox Christians continued to regard 1 Clement as one of the books of the New Testament. It is included, for example, as part of the canon in one of our oldest surviving manuscripts of the New Testament, the fifth-century Codex Alexandrinus.

Although the book is anonymous, it was later attributed to a man named Clement, who was thought to be the bishop of Rome. Tertullian indicated that Clement was the second bishop there, ordained by the apostle Peter himself (*Prescription* 32); more commonly it was thought, as early as Irenaeus, that he was the third bishop, following Linus and Anacletus (thus Irenaeus in *Against Heresies* 3.3.1). The book itself, however, does not claim Clement as its author or, in fact, even mention his name. It was probably written near the end of the first century. Its significance lies not only in being a proto-orthodox writing at least as old as some of the books that became part of the canon, but also in being one of the earliest instances of one church helping with (or interfering with, depending on one's perspective) the internal problems of another. Scholars have not been slow to notice that it was precisely the *Roman* church doing this, the church that later was to become the center of Christendom, the church whose bishop was in fact to become the pope. Possibly this letter marks the beginning of bigger things.

In any event, there was a situation in Corinth that called for intervention. The church leaders (presbyters, or elders) had been removed from office, and others had taken their place (1 Clement 3, 4, and 47). We don't know whether it was a violent coup (which seems a bit unlikely), a failed election (which seems a bit anachronistic), or some other kind of power play. But the Roman Christians who wrote the letter did not approve of the situation, and they wanted it reversed. The letter upbraids the Corinthian church for its disunity, convicts members of the guilty party of the error of their ways, and urges them to return the deposed presbyters to their positions of authority.

In addition to providing extensive citations of Scripture, principally the Old Testament, in order show the atrocity of the jealousy and strife at the center of the dispute, the letter mounts a particular argument for reinstating the church leaders. This is an argument that, in suitably modified form, was destined to become part and parcel of the proto-orthodox understanding of church structure. Within a century or so after the writing of 1 Clement, proto-orthodox Christians had become accustomed to opposing "aberrant" forms of Christianity by arguing that the bishops of the leading churches in the world could trace their lineage back through their personal predecessors to the apostles themselves, who had appointed them. This argument from "apostolic succession" is not found yet in full form in 1 Clement, as there is no evidence in the letter of a solitary bishop over the churches in either Rome or Corinth. But the argument is already here *in nuce:* According to the author, Christ chose the apostles, who appointed the leaders of the churches, who then handpicked their successors (chaps. 42, 44). Since the (deposed) presbyters of Corinth stood in the lineage of leaders chosen by the apostles, to oppose them meant to set oneself against the handpicked successors of the apostles, who had been chosen by Christ, who had been sent from God.

A powerful argument, this, especially when the leaders of the churches you have in mind happen to agree with your own understanding of the faith.[8] Within proto-orthodox circles there came to be a heightened emphasis both on having a strict hierarchy of authority, in which the bishop oversaw the work of the presbyters and the deacons (who may have dealt, respectively, with the more spiritual matters of the church and the more material side of things), and on making certain that only those with the proper understanding of the faith be allowed to serve in that capacity. Administrative skill was important, but a correct understanding of the Truth was a sine qua non. In the course of these developments, Irenaeus, Tertullian, and their successors were to use the argument of "apostolic succession" to counter any claims of the Gnostics, or others, to the truth: No one except the bishops appointed by the heirs of Christ could possibly be right about the precious truths of the faith.

The argument overlooked the uncomfortable circumstance that already in the second and third centuries there were bishops—including bishops of Rome—who were themselves declared heretical by well-intentioned (and often ambitious) proto-orthodox theologians. But an argument's rhetorical force should never be confused with the practical realities compromising its logic, as anyone conversant with modern political debates knows full well.

Proto-orthodoxy and the Jewish Traditions

Some proto-orthodox writings try to resolve church conflict by pressing for the authority of church officials ("Obey the bishop!") without going into the content of the disputes, on the assumption that if the right people are in charge, they will know what to do. That is the tack taken, for example, by the Pastoral epistles, 1 and 2 Timothy and Titus, far more concerned with getting the right kind of leaders in office than in explaining why the erroneous views that need to be overthrown are a problem. Ignatius is different, though. Ignatius deals with problems head on and argues a case.

Apart from his letter to the Christians in Rome, in which he urges them not to intervene with his bloody ordeal soon to come, Ignatius's letters are all addressed to churches (and one individual, Polycarp) that he has encountered on his way to martyrdom either personally, by passing through town, or indirectly, by meeting representatives sent to greet him and provide moral support. In these encounters he has learned of various problems in the churches. Some of these could be resolved simply by unleashing the authority of the bishop and insisting that everyone follow his lead. But others needed to be addressed. One of the most interesting involved the relationship of true Christianity to Judaism. This was a problem the proto-orthodox dealt with in a way quite different from the Ebionite Christians (who continued to embrace Judaism more or less wholesale), the Marcionites (who rejected all things Jewish), and various groups of Gnostics (who rejected historical Judaism but read the sacred Jewish texts through the lenses of their own complicated mythologies). Even among the proto-orthodox there were various attitudes and approaches to Jews and their Scripture, within broad parameters. Ignatius clearly understands those parameters, here already at the outset of the proto-orthodox movement.

One of the final letters Ignatius wrote was addressed to the Christians in the Asia Minor city of Philadelphia, which he had passed through on his journey to Rome. As is typical, he speaks highly of the bishop of Philadelphia and is eager that the church be united behind him. It appears that when he was there, Ignatius had seen divisions in the church and recognized a simple solution for them: "I cried out while among you, speaking in a great voice, the voice of God, 'Pay attention to the bishop and the presbytery and the deacons!'" (7:1). He urged the community to "do nothing apart from the bishop; keep your flesh as the temple of God; love unity; flee divisions" (7:2).

The divisions were evidently rooted in different theological and practical perspectives advanced by some members of the congregation. Among the Philadelphians were Gentile believers who had come to think that Christians needed to follow the practices of Judaism. It is difficult to know whether these people were spiritual descendants of Paul's opponents in nearby Galatia,[9] converts to Ebionite Christianity, or just Jewish sympathizers with an agenda of their own. In any event, their position could elicit small sympathy from Ignatius, who argued: "If anyone should interpret Judaism to you, do not hear him. For it is better to hear Christianity from a man who is circumcised than Judaism from one who is uncircumcised" (6:1).

And when his opponents claimed not to accept anything as true that was not supported in their "ancient records" (i.e., the Hebrew Bible), Ignatius insisted that "Jesus Christ is the ancient records" (8:2). Although he obviously doesn't say so, their reply (which he does record) may have cut him to the quick: "That is just the question!" But for Ignatius, the Old Testament patriarchs and prophets were looking forward to Christ and had salvation only through him (9:1–2).

Proto-orthodox Christians found themselves in a difficult situation when it came to the Jewish Scriptures. On the one hand, they were not at all inclined to adopt the ways of Judaism. Even by the time of Ignatius, the vast majority of Christians had converted from paganism and saw Jews and their religion as something distinct from the salvation wrought by Christ. At the same time, as they themselves knew, Jesus had been Jewish, as had his followers, and from the beginning, the Jewish Bible had been the Christian Scriptures, the revelation of the one true God, the God of the Jews. Moreover, as we have seen, without the Jewish Scriptures, Christians lacked the one thing they needed for religious legitimacy in the ancient world: a claim to antiquity. It was only by claiming to be rooted in the ancient traditions that they had inherited—found in the Jewish Scriptures, whose oldest parts were produced long before Homer, let alone Plato—that Christians could be seen as respectably ancient, in an ancient world that set a high premium on antiquity. But actually to follow the laws of Judaism and become Jews—that was out of the question.

How were proto-orthodox Christians to solve the problem? The most common road taken is that presumed by Ignatius, who wrote that Christ is himself the point of the Jewish Bible. This may not have sounded plausible, let alone convincing, for non-Christian Jews, but it became a trademark for non-Jewish Christians among the proto-orthodox. And as one might imagine, this perspective led to enormous tensions with Jewish neighbors, who thought Christians were trying to usurp their traditions: How can *you Christians* claim to be heirs of the Jewish Scriptures, when you don't even keep its laws?

That's exactly what Christians claimed, however, sometimes in ways that in hindsight may appear insidious and inflammatory. We are still living with the repercussions of this incipient anti-Judaism today.

One of the most famous proto-orthodox writings to deal with the issue is another book that nearly made it into the New Testament. The Epistle of Barnabas was sometimes quoted as Scripture in the early centuries of the church, and it was included among the books of the New Testament in one of our most ancient manuscripts, this time the famous Codex Sinaiticus.[10] The epistle came to be attributed to Barnabas, the traveling companion of the apostle Paul, even though it is written anonymously. Had it been finally admitted into the canon, the history of Jewish-Christian relations might have been even more horrendous than it was. Among all the early Christian writings vying for a spot in the sacred canon, this is the most virulently anti-Jewish in its message, arguing that it is Christians, not Jews, who are heirs of the covenantal promises made to the patriarchs of Israel, that the "Old Testament" is a Christian, not a Jewish book, and that, as a result, the Jews have always adhered to a false religion.[11]

As became typical among his proto-orthodox successors, the author of the letter does not spurn the Jewish Scriptures per se. He instead embraces them, insisting that when the prophets of Scripture attack the people of Israel for their opposition to God, their words are to be taken as literal truth. Because Jews rebelled against God from the very beginning, this author claims, they were misled into thinking that scriptural laws concerning how to live and worship were to be taken literally (4:6–8). But these biblical laws concerning sacrificial rites, ritual practices, and sacred institutions, he avers, were meant to be taken figuratively, pointing forward to the salvation to be brought to the world by Christ.

And so the author provides a "true" interpretation of key passages, informed by the special knowledge (interestingly enough, he uses the word *gnosis*) that he claims to have received from God, in order to discount the Jews' understanding of significant aspects of their own religion: the covenant, fasting, sacrifices, circumcision, kosher food laws, Sabbath, the Temple, and so on. The

Jews' misunderstanding, the author maintains, can be traced to the very beginning, when Moses received the Law of God on Mount Sinai. Learning that the people, who had just been delivered from their slavery in Egypt, had already turned to worship foreign gods, Moses angrily smashed the two tablets containing the covenant given him by God. For this author, once the covenant was broken, it was never restored—until the coming of Christ and the formation of the true people of God, his followers (4:6–8, 14:1–5). The Jews, on the other hand, were excluded from their covenant and misled by an evil angel into thinking that they were members of God's covenantal community and that the laws they inherited were to be interpreted literally (9:4).

Barnabas devotes most of his energies to driving home this basic point, time and again giving the "true" interpretation of the Jewish Law in opposition to their own literal understandings of it. For example, when God spoke of honoring the Sabbath day and keeping it holy, he did not mean that Jews should refrain from work on the seventh day. As unholy people, Barnabas claims, Jews could not possibly keep the day itself holy. God was instead referring to his own act of creation in which he spent six days making the world before resting on the seventh. Moreover, as the Scriptures themselves testify, "With the Lord a day is as a thousand years and a thousand years as one day" (2 Pet. 3:8; cf. Ps. 90:4). The "six days" of creation, then, refer to a period of six thousand years in which God is actively involved with the world, to be followed by a "seventh day" of rest, in which he will finally put an end to sin and bring peace on earth once and for all. The injunction to keep the Sabbath day holy is therefore not to be interpreted as a commandment to refrain from work; it is an instruction concerning the future apocalypse in which God's millennial kingdom will come to earth. Only then will there be a completely holy people who can keep "the day" holy (15:1–8). This is the first instance in which a Christian writer indicates that the world would last six thousand years.[12]

Barnabas is especially intent on showing that Jews are wrong to take the dietary laws of the Old Testament literally. God did not mean that his people were not to eat pork or rabbit or hyena, all of which are proscribed in the Torah. The injunction not to eat pork means not to live like swine, who grunt loudly when hungry but keep silent when full. People are not to treat God in this way, coming to him with loud petitions when they are in need but ignoring him when they are not (10:3). Not to eat rabbit means not to live like those wild creatures, who with every passing year increase their sexual appetites and— Barnabas tells us, in a very strange passage—every year grow another orifice, allowing them to propagate at random and even commit incest (10:6). So too, not to eat hyena means not to live licentious lives, like those promiscuous animals who were "known" to change their gender every year, alternately becoming male and female (10:7). Yet more peculiar is the command not to eat weasel.[13] Barnabas points out (based, probably, as in the other instances, on evidence provided by an ancient bestiary) that the weasel conceives through the mouth; he takes this command, then, to forbid oral sex. Do not, he says, "be like those who are reputed to perform a lawless deed in their mouth because of their uncleanness, nor cling to unclean women who perform the lawless deed in their mouth" (10:9).

For Barnabas, the laws of God are meant to induce ethical behavior and are totally misread if taken literally. This also applies to the most distinctive Jewish law of all, the law of circumcision, for God did not literally want his people to cut the foreskins off the penises of their baby boys. The sign of circumcision given to Abraham was in fact something quite different: It was the sign that salvation would be given to the world through the cross of Jesus. To derive this rather unusual interpretation, Barnabas points to the first account of circumcision in the Bible, where the father of the Jews, Abraham, took his 318 servants into the wilderness to rescue his nephew Lot, who had been captured by an army of invading kings (Genesis 14). Prior to going into battle, Abraham had these 318 members of his household circumcised (a conflation of Gen. 14:14 and 17:23). What is significant for Barnabas is the number 318 itself, a mysterious and significant number that he explains by the method of interpretation known in ancient Jewish sources as "gematria."

Gematria was a way of interpreting words in light of their numerical value. In ancient languages, the letters of the alphabet performed double duty as numerals—unlike English, where we use Roman letters but Arabic numerals (except when we use Roman numerals). In the case of both ancient Greek and ancient Hebrew, every letter had a numerical value, so that in Greek, for example, Alpha was one, Beta two, Gamma three, etc. For this reason, every word written in these languages had a numerical equivalent—the sum of the numbers represented by its letters. Conversely, every number was represented by a sequence of letters.

What, then, is the point of Abraham's circumcision of his 318 servants? In Greek, 318 is represented by the letters Tau, Iota, and Eta (T I H). For Barnabas, this number is quite significant because it clearly shows that circumcision prefigures the Christian religion. The Tau (T), he points out, is made in the shape of the cross, and Iota Eta (I H) are the first two letters of the name "Jesus" (IHSOUS in Greek). The true circumcision is thus not the literal cutting of the flesh of the foreskin. It is the cross of Jesus. Adherence to the cross is what makes a person a member of the people of God. And according to Barnabas, this is found in the Jewish Scriptures in the story of Abraham, the father of circumcision (9:1–8). Barnabas assures his readers that no one had ever heard a more excellent lesson from him (9:8).

The letter of Barnabas was probably written around 130 CE. Somewhat later proto-orthodox writers followed its basic strategy of rejecting Judaism but accepting the Jewish Scriptures not only for their witness to Christianity but, notably enough, also for their rejection of Jews. Both Justin Martyr and Tertullian, for example, admitted that circumcision was given as a sign to set Jews apart from all other peoples. But for Justin it was to set them apart for persecution, and for Tertullian it was to show who would not be allowed into the holy city. (Tertullian was writing after the Romans had made it illegal for Jews to live in Jerusalem after the violence of the second Jewish uprising in 132–35 CE.)

Other authors raised the ante even higher. One of the most eloquent homilies of the second century derives from a proto-orthodox orator named Melito, who lived in the city of Sardis in Asia Minor. His sermon text is the story of the Passover in the book of Exodus, and his mode of interpretation is figurative. He sees Jesus as the real Passover lamb, rejected and killed by his own people. But for Melito, Jesus was more than this; he was also God himself. The implications, for Melito, are severe: Israel is guilty of murdering its own God. Indeed, Jews who continue to reject Christ are themselves culpable of this hateful deed.[14]

With Melito we are at the beginning of a form of anti-Jewish hatred that had not appeared on the stage of human history prior to the advent of Christianity, built on a proto-orthodox view that the Jewish Scriptures witness to Christ, who was rejected by his own people and whose death, in turn, leads to their condemnation.

Proto-orthodoxy and the Prophetic Tradition

Clearly the Scriptures—originally the Old Testament, and eventually the books that came to form the "New" Testament—were ultimate authorities for the proto-orthodox Christians. But doesn't God speak in other ways as well, apart from these written texts?

Ignatius appears to have thought so. Again, in his letter to the Philadelphians, he indicates that he himself was a direct recipient of a revelation from the Spirit of God, a revelation that confirmed his own convictions about the importance of the bishop:

> For even if some people have wanted to deceive me according to the flesh, the Spirit is not deceived, since it comes from God. For it knows whence it comes and where it is going, and it exposes the things that are hidden. I cried out while among you, speaking in a great voice, the voice of God, "Pay attention to the bishop and the presbytery and the deacons!" But some suspected that I said these things because I knew in advance that there was a division among you. But the one in whom I am bound is my witness that I knew it from no human source; but the Spirit was preaching, saying: "Do nothing apart from the bishop; keep your flesh as the Temple of God; love unity; flee divisions; be imitators of Jesus Christ as he is of his Father." (Ign. Phil., 7)

Ignatius was standing in a solid tradition here, once again, as Christians connected with the Pauline churches—the earliest Christian churches of which we have any written record—understood themselves to be under the direction of the Spirit. Some in those churches had the gift of "prophecy," that is, the ability to speak direct revelation from God under the spontaneous influence of the Spirit (see 1 Cor. 14).

For a time, this emphasis on direct revelation enjoyed success among proto-orthodox Christians. Some of their revelations came to be written down. Most famous, of course, is the revelation given to a prophet named John which, after some considerable controversy between those who valued the book and those who suspected it, came to be included in the canon of Scripture as the final book of the New Testament. But there were other revelations as well, including the one allegedly given to Peter in the Apocalypse of Peter, the guided tour of heaven and hell discussed earlier which also nearly made it into Scripture.

And there was a series of visions given to a proto-orthodox prophet, Hermas, whose written account, the *Shepherd*, was accepted as an authoritative book by many Christians of the early centuries.[15] Quoted by several church fathers as Scripture, the book, like the Epistle of Barnabas, was included as one of the books of the New Testament in the fourth-century Codex Sinaiticus. It was eventually excluded, however, in part because it was known to have been written not by an apostle but by the brother of Pius, bishop of Rome in the mid-second century.

The book takes its name from an angelic mediator who appears to Hermas in the form of a shepherd. Other angelic beings appear here as well, in particular an old woman who identifies herself as the personification of the Christian Church. These various figures communicate divine revelations to Hermas and, upon request, interpret their meaning to him.

It is a long book—the longest Christian text to survive from the first two centuries—divided into a series of five visions, twelve sets of commandments, and ten extended parables. The visions and parables are enigmatic and symbolic; they are usually explained to Hermas as having a spiritual significance for Christians here on earth. The sets of commandments are somewhat easier to interpret, consisting mainly of direct exhortations to speak the truth, give alms, do good, and avoid sexual immorality, drunkenness, gluttony, and other vices.

Indeed, the entire book is driven by an ethical concern: What can Christians do if they have fallen into sin after being baptized? A number of proto-orthodox Christians insisted that those who returned to lives of sin after joining the church had lost any hope of salvation (cf. Heb. 6:4–6). An alternative view is advanced by the *Shepherd*. This book maintains, on the basis of its divine revelations, that Christians who had fallen again into sin after their baptism had a second chance (but only one second chance) to repent and return to God's good graces. Those who refused to avail themselves of this opportunity, however, or who reverted to sin, would be forced to face the judgment of God on the day of reckoning that was soon to come.

This was not the only "prophetic movement" in proto-orthodox Christianity driven by strict ethical concerns. The most famous one is of particular interest, because even though completely orthodox in its theological views, it came to be viewed as sectarian by its fellow proto-orthodox, in part because of its reliance on direct revelation from God rather than on written Scripture. The movement was called Montanism by its opponents, and its orthodoxy is made obvious by its constituency.[16] Its most famous convert was none other than Tertullian, a strict moralist whose theological credentials no proto-orthodox Christian could deny.

The Montanists received their name from a proto-orthodox Christian named Montanus, a figure about whom we do not know a good deal. Later reports indicate that Montanus came from the town of Pepuza, a small and rather insignificant place in the province of Phrygia, in what is now west-central Turkey. He understood himself to be a prophet who received revelations directly from God. Old traditions indicate that early on Montanus acquired two female prophetesses as followers, Maximilla and Prisca. We know of their prophetic utterances almost entirely as these came to be quoted in the writings of later authors. None of their own books survive—yet more early Christian texts lost to posterity.

As might be expected of a group to which Tertullian was attracted, the Montanists were ethically quite strict, insisting, for example, that a Christian should not remarry after the death of a spouse but should be completely devoted to the church instead. Tertullian himself embraced this idea, and in fact wrote a letter to his own wife forbidding her to remarry should he precede her in leaving this mortal coil.[17] These strict ethics may have derived from the Montanists' view—evidently the burden of their revelatory utterances—that the end of all things was near and that people needed to prepare for it. To be sure, one could imagine that the expectation of the imminent end of all things might lead some people to enjoy themselves while they can ("eat, drink, and be merry, for tomorrow we die"); but this does not apply to those who expect the end to be a time of judgment rather than the point of annihilation. The Montanists urged people to prepare to meet their maker, with the full recognition that this might not be a happy prospect. In particular, Montanus believed that the new Jerusalem, to replace the old one characterized by the unbelief of the Jews, was to descend from heaven to Pepuza. That is where the Kingdom of God would arrive and Christ would then reign. Christians should devote themselves to its coming, standing up for their faith, even to the point of being martyred if necessary. Moreover, this end of the age was to arrive very soon. In the words of the prophetess Maximilla, "After me there will be no more prophecy, but the End."

The end did not come, however, and that created problems. In a quite specific way, it created problems for prophets who had claimed a divine insight into the future course of events. There is nothing like a radical disconfirmation to make your group a laughing stock. But in more general terms, the failure of prophecy to materialize raised the awareness of a bigger problem of direct revelation for proto-orthodox Christians. How can we imagine that God has spoken to his prophets, even his theologically correct prophets, if their predictions do not come true? Moreover, how can divine teaching be controlled if it is a matter of personal inspiration? What prevents one person, even if well-intentioned and completely orthodox, from claiming a divine revelation that stands completely at odds with someone else's divine revelation? Or worse yet, what should be done with a direct personal revelation that contradicts the written revelation of Scripture? And what kind of tactical handles can be applied to heretics who claim revelation, direct from God? The Gnostics, of course, claimed secret knowledge. Why were their claims any less plausible than those of the proto-orthodox? In short, how can one determine whether a "prophecy" is from God or not? If it agrees with Scripture? But if Scripture is the key to everything, why does one need prophecy at all?

It was not long before the proto-orthodox began asking these questions and started to recognize the problem with Montanism and other movements that stressed the direct inspiration of divine prophets. As a result, the movement was soon marginalized within proto-orthodoxy, despite its advocacy by so great a spokesperson as Tertullian. Inspired utterances were demoted from an authoritative position to a completely secondary, and highly dubious, status. In proto-orthodox circles, it was the written word, the texts of Scripture, that became the ultimate arbiter of theological and practical Truth.[18]

The Development of
Proto-orthodox Theology

In this brief survey of the major defining marks of proto-orthodoxy, I have saved for last the matter that many people consider the most important of all. "Orthodoxy" and "proto-orthodoxy," of course, are theological categories, as are their negative counterparts, "heterodoxy" (other opinion) and "heresy." Orthodoxy and heresy refer to views that are theologically correct and theologically incorrect. Theological categories are not necessarily the best way to describe social groups—Presbyterians and Episcopalians, for example, are classified not according to who is theologically right and wrong but according to their ecclesiological structures, as having churches governed, ultimately, by elders (presbyters) or bishops (episcopoi). And debates in Christian antiquity among various Christian groups also involved ecclesiological structures, just as they involved ethics, liturgical practices, patterns of authority, and numerous other matters. But a major component of these debates was theology in the purer sense—doctrines to be ascribed to, beliefs to be affirmed. In fact, probably nothing was more important in the early centuries of proto-orthodox Christianity than affirming the proper belief about God and Christ.

It was the development and refinement of these proper beliefs that ultimately led to the orthodox doctrine of Christ as fully God and fully man and to the hallmark of orthodox belief, the doctrine of the Trinity, one God in three persons, distinct in number but equal in substance.

We can trace the debates over doctrine to the earliest stages of proto-orthodoxy, again starting with Ignatius. Ignatius spoke of Christ as divine, for example,

referring to "our God Jesus Christ, [who] is in the Father" (Ign. Rom. 8:3), or
as "God come in the flesh" (Ign. Eph. 7:2), or of "the blood of God," by which
he means the blood of Christ (Ign. Eph. 1:1). But he was equally and passion-
ately committed to Christ being human, as is evident in two of his letters, one
sent to the Christians of Tralles and the other to those of Smyrna. He knew that
in both cities there was opposition to the proto-orthodox view that Jesus was
somehow both divine and human; the opponents were docetists, who maintained that Jesus was divine and not at all human.

And so in his letter to the Trallians, Ignatius warns against those who claim
that Jesus "only appeared to suffer" (10:1) and insists, in response, that Jesus
"was truly born, both ate and drank; was truly persecuted at the time of Pontius
Pilate, was truly crucified and died . . . and was also truly raised from the dead"
(9:1–2). So, too, in the letter to the Smyrneans, Ignatius attacks those who
claimed that Jesus' passion was a sham, that he was not an actual flesh-and-blood
human being who really suffered (2:1). Ignatius again denies that such persons
are "believers" (2:1) and warns his readers not even to meet and talk with them
(4:1). In opposition to their views, he insists that Jesus was "actually born"
(1:1) and was "actually crucified . . . in the flesh" (1:2), and he "genuinely
suffered" and "genuinely raised himself" (2:1). Even after his resurrection he
was "in the flesh" (3:1), as evidenced by the fact that his disciples touched him
and observed him eating and drinking (3:2–3).

Some people have suggested that Ignatius may have been personally troubled
by this christological issue because of how it related to his own situation.[19] He
himself was on the road to martyrdom. If Christ did not actually suffer in the
flesh, there would be little reason for Ignatius himself to do so: "If what our
Lord did is a sham, so is my being in chains. Why then have I given myself
completely to death, fire, sword, and wild beasts?" (4:2). This appears to be
part and parcel of the broader proto-orthodox agenda: The emphasis on Jesus'
real flesh-and-blood existence and, as a consequence, his real suffering is tied
to the claim that willingness to suffer physical martyrdom is somehow a proof
of one's theological views.

Some of the proto-orthodox, though, pushed the humanity of Jesus to an
extreme and as a result came to be expelled from the church. We have already
seen outsiders who did so, for example, Ebionites, who understood Jesus to
have been fully human and not divine. We can never know for certain what
drove them to insist on the point, although one might suspect that their resilient
Jewishness forced them to affirm monotheism to such an extent that they could
not conceive of Jesus also as God. But they were not the only ones in this
particular camp. Sometime near the end of the second century, there appeared
in Rome, from among the proto-orthodox ranks, a man named Theodotus, a
cobbler by trade, but evidently an inordinately thoughtful and learned one.
Claiming that his views represented those passed down by the disciples of
Jesus to true believers ever since, Theodotus maintained that Jesus was "a mere
man," born of the sexual union of Joseph and Mary, but chosen by God at his

baptism to be the savior of the world. Theodotus acquired quite a following in Rome, especially, as it turns out, among intellectuals who knew their secular logic, mathematics, and philosophy, and applied them to their theological perspectives. And the Theodotians' claim to represent the opinion of Christians high in the Roman hierarchy down to the time of Bishop Victor (189–98 CE) was taken seriously enough to be attacked by one of the leading Roman heresiologists of the day.[20]

These Roman "adoptionists" were eventually weeded out and their views castigated by those who insisted that, even though Jesus Christ was a man, he was not a "mere man"; he was also God. With that Ignatius, too, would have agreed.

But if Christ is God, and God is God—how can there be only one God? This also caused huge problems for the proto-orthodox in Rome and elsewhere, bringing considerable dissension in their ranks. No one was more central to the dispute than Hippolytus of Rome, who maintained in *Against Noetus* that, after the Theodotians, the Roman church leadership had gone too far in the other direction in affirming Jesus' divinity and close connection with God; even the bishop of Rome (the "pope") was included in his castigation. The result of the outcome was remarkable. This was the first known split in the upper echelons of the Roman church leadership. Hippolytus, supported by his own followers, set himself up as the first antipope—the first, that is, to claim that the real pope's theological views had disqualified him from office and to step in, then, to assume the papal duties.

The Roman bishops in question were Victor's successor, Zephyrinus (bishop 198–217 CE) and Zephyrinus's successor Callistus (217–22 CE). Hippolytus himself is one of our main sources of information for the conflict, and he has the honesty to admit that the majority of Christians in Rome supported the christological view he opposed. Both sides in the dispute, I should stress, agreed with the essential proto-orthodox notion that Christ was both God and man. And both were firmly committed to monotheism: There is only one God. But how can Christ be God and God the Father be God if there is only one God? Hippolytus's opponents solved the problem rather neatly. Christ was God the Father himself, come in the flesh to save the world that he created.

Hippolytus was not the only proto-orthodox Christian to find this view untenable. Equally vocal in opposition was Tertullian. Together they raised a number of biblical and logical objections: Why does Scripture say that God sent his son, rather than that he sent himself? How can anyone be his own father? To whom is Jesus speaking when he prays? How can Jesus talk about going to his Father (John 20:17) if he *is* the Father? And is it really conceivable that God the Father was killed? This last issue became a rallying point for those who opposed the view. They mocked to those who thought the "Father suffered," and coined the term "patripassianist" (father-sufferers) to refer to anyone who subscribed to such a notion.[21]

The other side, of course, refused to be mocked and pointed out that the alternative was not at all acceptable. Scripture repeatedly affirms there is only one God (e.g., Isa. 44:6, 45:18). If Christ is God, he must be that one. If he is a different one, then in fact there are two gods. Whoever thinks so is no longer a monotheist but a dytheist.

As it turns out, Zephyrinus and Callistus were to lose that debate, as proto-orthodox thinkers came to consider the relationship of God the Father and God the Son to be more complicated than an exact identification. Christ may be equal with Father, but he is not identical with the Father. And that is a big difference. But how could he have equal standing with God, so that he too is God, if there is only one God?

The theologians who began working on this problem are the ones who developed the traditional doctrines of the Trinity. Not only were Christ and the Father separate persons, both equally divine; there was also the matter of the Spirit, whom Jesus spoke of as "another Comforter" who was to come in his stead (John 14:16–17, 16:7–14) and who was seen as the Spirit of God already at the beginning of Genesis, where "the Spirit of God was brooding over the waters" (Gen. 1:2). Scripture passages dealing with Christ, his Father, and the Spirit were carefully examined, combined, amalgamated—all in order to make sense of the trinitarian mystery. And so, as the Scripture affirmed, Christ and the Father were "one" (John 10:30), so that "whoever has seen me has seen the Father" (John 14:9). And yet the Father was "in" Christ just as Christ was "in" the Father (John 14:11), and the Father "sent" Christ just as later he was to "send" the Spirit (John 14:26). Somehow or other there are three beings—not just one and not just two—all of whom are closely related and yet distinct. Equal but not identical.

How can that work? Earlier proto-orthodox Christians developed models for understanding the Godhead that struck their intellectual descendants as moving in the right direction but completely unnuanced. Ignatius, for example, appears never to have worked out a precise understanding of how Christ could be both divine and human. Possibly he did not have the requisite intellectual gifts, as it is a rather difficult philosophical conundrum. In any event, his own paradoxical formulation would have seemed hopelessly unrefined to later generations of the proto-orthodox:

> For there is one physician, both fleshly and spiritual, born and unborn, God come in the flesh, true life in death, from both Mary and God, first subject to suffering and then beyond suffering, Jesus Christ our Lord. (Ign. Eph. 7:2)

Somewhat later times saw various attempts to solve the problem, some of them completely acceptable among the proto-orthodox of the moment, only to be condemned as heretical by orthodox theologians in later centuries. The best example comes from the most learned, prolific, and famous theologian of the first three Christian centuries, Origen of Alexandria (185–254 CE).[22] Origen was a true genius, whose capacious learning and inordinate abilities were recognized by a wealthy Christian in Alexandria, Ambrose, who became his patron, providing him with extensive resources to allow him to pursue his theological endeavors. Origen wrote massive commentaries on Scripture, both Old and New Testaments, copious homilies on specific texts, an extensive "apology" defending the faith against its intellectual despisers, antiheretical works against those who espoused false doctrines, and erudite theological treatises dealing with the leading issues of his day. He appears to have written as many as a thousand books—assisted by Ambrose, who supplied him with a small army of stenographers to record his dictated reflections and calligraphers to set them up for publication. Most of these books, regrettably, have been lost or destroyed. Although Origen was the champion of orthodoxy in his own day, he came to be condemned as heretical in later times, and his works were banned. Not surprising for someone trying, for the first time, to work out the mysteries of the universe on a new theological basis.

Origen's theology was biblically rooted from start to finish. He subscribed to the notion that God was the creator of all things. And he believed that to mean *all* things, including Christ. The essence of Christ came into being at some point in eternity past. In fact, it came into being when all the intelligent beings of the divine realm came into being—angels, archangels, demons, the devil, human souls. All these creatures of God were originally disembodied minds, created to adore God forever, and yet they were given the free will to choose to do otherwise. Some minds chose to depart from God—for example, the devil and his demons, whose lust for power led to their "fall." Others simply could not sustain the worship of God for eternity; these, too, fell from their divine place and became souls that were placed in human bodies as a discipline and punishment, prior to their redemption. One mind, however, stayed in direct and intensely focused contact with God, from eternity past. So connected with God was this mind that it became one with God. Just as the iron placed in a hot fire eventually takes on all the characteristics of the fire, this one took on all the characteristics of God, became so infused with God's wisdom that it became God's wisdom, so infused with God's word that it became God's word. In a very real sense, then, to all outward appearances and to the depth of its being, this mind was God. This mind then became a soul that took on human flesh and dwelt among us in the form of a human. Christ is the incarnation of this divine being that came into existence in eternity past; Christ is God's Word made flesh; Christ is God, one with the Father, distinct in person but equal in substance, the one through whom God made the world (Origen *On First Principles* 2:6). But—this is a key point—he is equal with God by the *transference* of God's being; ultimately, he is subordinate to God and is "less than the Father" (*On First Principles* 1:3)

Origen eventually was condemned for this innovative resolution of the relationship of God and Christ when orthodox thinkers in later centuries refined their categories and came to reject *any* notion of Christ's subordination to God, which necessarily, for them, meant that in his essence he was *not* equal with God. Origen came to be condemned for other ideas as well, especially his views that souls preexisted and that all creation, including the devil, will ultimately yield to the sovereignty of God and thus be saved.[23]

If nothing else, Origen shows that in the second and third centuries, not only are there clearly defined boundaries between the proto-orthodox and the "heretics"; there are also some vague boundaries between what counts as orthodox and what does not. The orthodoxy of one age can become the heresy of the next. The Ebionites were arguably the first to learn this theological maxim, as those who represented a very ancient form of Christianity, possibly rooted in the beliefs of Jesus' own Jewish apostles. They had numerous unlucky successors in later ages, advocates of once acceptable views later to be condemned as heretical.

The Beginnings of the Trinity

Neither Tertullian nor Hippolytus approached the questions of the nature of Christ as God and man and of the relationship of the divine members of the Godhead with the erudition, nuance, and acumen of Origen. But in some ways, their less daring approaches became more useful to orthodox thinkers of later times. Their opposition to patripassianist understandings (the belief that "the Father suffered") forced them to think in trinitarian terms, of God being distinctively three in expression though one in essence. As Hippolytus puts it, "With respect to the power, God is one; but with respect to the economy [i.e., to how this power expresses itself], the manifestation is triple" (*Refutation* 8:2). In Tertullian's formulation, God is three in degree, not condition; in form, not substance; in aspect, not power (*Against Praxeas*, 2). Tertullian was the first Latin theologian to use the term *Trinity*.

Within the broad contours of proto-orthodoxy, then, one can see development and variety. As time progressed, theologians became more entranced with the mystery of the Trinity and developed a more highly refined vocabulary for dealing with it. But that was long after the major issues had been resolved, of whether Christ was man but not God (Ebionites; Theodotians), God but not man (Marcionites, some Gnostics), or two beings, one man and one God (most Gnostics). The proto-orthodox opted for none of the above. Christ was God and man, yet he was one being, not two.[24]

Once that was acknowledged, the details still had to be worked out. And they were worked out for centuries. If it were easy, it would not be a mystery. Theologians began to be obsessed with the question of how and in what way Christ could be both human and divine, completely both. Did he have a human soul but a divine spirit? Did he have a divine soul instead of a human soul? Was his body really like everyone else's body? How could God have a body? Was he subordinate to the Father, as in Origen?[25] If he was not subordinate to the

Father, why was *he* the one sent, rather than the other way around? And so on, almost ad infinitum.

In this earlier period, however, the debates were both more basic and more fundamental. As a result, the alternatives *within* the proto-orthodox tradition—as opposed to the alternatives that separated the proto-orthodox from everyone else—were less clear and less obvious. All that was to change when the proto-orthodox found themselves to be the last ones standing and were forced then to move forward into the orthodox forms of Christianity of the fourth and fifth centuries.

Part Three

WINNERS AND LOSERS

Now that we have examined some of the forged texts of early Christianity (part 1) and observed several groups of early Christians who produced these and other texts (part 2), we are able to consider in greater detail the conflicts that arose among these groups and to reflect on the strategies that proved effective in their struggles for dominance. The outcome of these internecine Christian battles was significant. The group that emerged as victorious and declared itself orthodox determined the shape of Christianity for posterity—determining its internal structure, writing its creeds, and compiling its revered texts into a sacred canon of Scripture. Had things turned out otherwise, not just the Christian Church but all of history would have been quite different. Before addressing the specifics of these internal disputes, I should say a word about such conflicts more generally.

By the second century, of course, there was already a long history of quarrels in the Christian tradition. Jesus himself had enemies, and they tended to be those with whom he had a good deal in common. Chief among his opponents during his public ministry were Pharisees, a group of Jews who insisted on keeping God's Law fully and completely. Pharisees were not professional hypocrites, as is sometimes made out in later Christian tradition. They were experts in the laws God had given to Moses—laws that God gave precisely in order to be followed—who believed these laws should be observed.[1] Pharisees developed a set of traditions that assisted them in keeping the laws. If Sabbath is to be kept holy, and work is therefore not to be done on Sabbath, then one needs to determine what it is that constitutes work so as to avoid doing it. If tithes are to be given to the priests in the Temple, one needs to determine what is to be tithed and how a person can be certain that it has been tithed. And so on.

Pharisees had serious disputes among themselves concerning how to interpret and implement these laws. Jesus had disputes with them as well. Some of the things said in the heat of the battle were not kind. Within the Christian tradition, the Pharisees came to be known as "whitewashed sepulchres" (Matt. 23:27)—clean and attractive on the outside but filled with rotting flesh within. They were hypocrites, who strained a gnat out of their drink but then swallowed a camel (Matt. 23:24). No doubt these Christian slurs were reciprocated by the Pharisees, who were, after all, doing the best they could to understand and practice what God wanted. In religious conflict, it is always a matter of give and take. Even so, it should not be imagined that Jesus opposed the Pharisaic interpretations because they stood so far apart on most issues. In fact, they were extremely close. Hence the emotional rhetoric. We tend to argue most frequently and fervently with those closest to us.

When we move the calendar forward twenty years to Jesus' outspoken apostle, Paul, we find a comparable situation, only now the "internal" conflicts involve battles within the Christian community, founded after Jesus' death. Every church that Paul established appears to have become embroiled in turmoil. His letters were meant to solve the problems. Throughout these letters we find harsh and forthright opposition to false teachers. But it is important to note that these are *Christian* false teachers, who are in *Paul's* churches. Sometimes readers neglect to consider the implication: These "false" teachers understand themselves to be continuing on in the same Christian tradition as Paul, bringing out the implications of the gospel message, providing a fuller account of what Paul had taught while passing through town making converts. Paul, however, sees them as standing over and against his gospel message, and so he attacks them with a vehemence unparalleled in his comments about pagans or Jews.

Nowhere can this seen more clearly than in the letter to the Galatians. Paul established churches in this central region of Asia Minor, based on his gospel that the death and resurrection of Jesus are God's way of salvation to all people, Jew and Gentile. He left then to take the mission elsewhere, and other Christian missionaries arrived. They evidently attempted to "correct" some of the things Paul had taught and added some important information. In particular, they insisted that to be full members of the people of the Jewish God, converts needed to become Jewish. For many of their hearers, this view made considerable sense: They were worshiping the God of the Jews, who gave the Jewish Law, and who ordered all of his people—insiders as well as outsiders—to keep his commandments, including the commandment of circumcision for the men. Surely the sovereign Lord of all would not change his mind concerning how his people were to relate to him, especially when he called the agreement that he made with the Jewish ancestors an "eternal" covenant. To worship this God and believe in his Messiah, argued the Christian missionaries who arrived in Paul's wake, followers of Jesus need to join his people in the ways he set forth in his Scriptures.[2]

These "opponents" had a good deal in common with Paul. They worshiped the God of the Jews. They saw Jesus as the Messiah sent from God to the Jews. They believed that Jesus' death and resurrection were part of God's plan for salvation. They believed this salvation was a fulfillment of the promises found in Scripture. And they believed it applied to all people, Jew and Gentile.

So similar. But they differed on a key point: whether Gentiles were to become Jews in order to be "Christians." The difference was enough to infuriate Paul. His letter to the Galatians seethes with white-hot anger. His opponents are false teachers who stand under God's curse. They have "bewitched" their hearers. Those who follow their instruction will lose their salvation. Paul hopes that when they themselves are circumcised the knife slips and they castrate themselves (Gal. 1:6–9; 3:1–5; 5:2–4, 12). One can only wonder what they may have said in return.

The tradition of such vitriolic attacks was to continue past Paul into other writings that eventually became part of the New Testament and on into the second and third centuries, as Christians argued against those with whom they had the most in common, whom they could recognize as almost, but not quite, their fellow Christians. These arguments often focused on which beliefs to affirm and which practices to follow. Every side understood that its views were right. And they believed that being right mattered—not just for life on earth but also for rewards in heaven. The losers of these battles would pay an eternal price. And so the fights were hard and drawn out. When they ended, the winners chose which records of the affair to keep and decided how to tell the history of the conflict. Only in modern times have the voices of the losers begun to be heard with any kind of clarity.

Chapter Eight

The Quest for Orthodoxy

There was a time, not so long ago, when *orthodoxy* and *heresy* were not problematic terms and the relationship between them was uncomplicated. Orthodoxy was the right belief, taught by Jesus to his disciples and handed down by them to the leaders of the Christian churches. In its most basic form, this orthodoxy came to expression in the words of the famous creeds of the Church, for example, the Nicene Creed, as it emerged from the great church councils of the fourth century and was later refined into words familiar to many Christians today:

> We believe in one God, the Father, the Almighty, maker of heaven and earth, of all that is, seen and unseen.
> We believe in one Lord, Jesus Christ, the only Son of God, eternally begotten of the Father, God from God, Light from Light, true God from true God, begotten, not made, of one Being with the Father. Through him all things were made. For us and for our salvation he came down from heaven: By the power of the Holy Spirit he became incarnate from the Virgin Mary and was made man. For our sake he was crucified under Pontius Pilate; he suffered death and was buried. On the third day he rose again in accordance with the Scriptures; he ascended into heaven and is seated at the right hand of the Father. He will come again in glory to judge the living and the dead, and his kingdom will have no end.
> We believe in the Holy Spirit, the Lord, the giver of life, who proceeds from the Father and the Son. With the Father and the Son he is worshiped and glorified. He has spoken through the Prophets. We believe in one holy catholic and apostolic Church. We acknowledge one baptism for the forgiveness of sins. We look for the resurrection of the dead and the life of the world to come. Amen.[1]

Heresy was any deviation from this right belief, in evidence, for example, among those who would claim that instead of one God there were two, or twelve, or thirty. Or those who would deny that Christ was fully God, or that he became a real human being, or that he was born of a virgin, or that he was raised from the dead. Or those who denied the future resurrection.

According to this view, any *falsified* doctrine necessarily existed before its falsification, and any heretic who corrupted the truth must have had the truth itself available to corrupt. For this reason, orthodoxy was seen to be prior to heresy and true believers prior to false. By definition, then, orthodoxy was the original form of Christian belief, held by the majority of believers from the beginning, and heresy was a false perversion of it, created by willful individuals with small and pestiferous followings. Thus, in this view, *orthodoxy* really does mean what its etymology suggests: "right belief." Moreover, it implies both originality and majority opinion. *Heresy,* from the Greek word for "choice," refers to intentional decisions to depart from the right belief; it implies a corruption of faith, found only among a minority of people.

Orthodoxy and Heresy:
The Classical View

These views of the relationship of orthodoxy and heresy dominated Christian scholarship for many centuries. Their classical expression can be found in the earliest written account of church history—including the history of internal Christian conflicts—written by the "father of church history," Eusebius of Caesarea. In ten volumes, Eusebius's *Church History* narrates the course of Christianity from its beginning up to his own time (the final edition was produced in 324/25).[2]

The account actually begins *before* Jesus' birth, with a statement concerning the twofold nature of Christ, both God and man, and a discussion of his preexistence. That is an unusual way to begin a historical narrative, and it serves to show the account's theological underpinnings. This is not a disinterested chronicle of names and dates. It is a history driven by a theological agenda from beginning to end, an agenda involving Eusebius's own understandings of God, Christ, the Scriptures, the church, Jews, pagans, and heretics. The orientation is clearly orthodox, with Eusebius opposing anyone who advocates an alternative understanding of the faith. This opposition determined both what Eusebius had to say and how he said it.

A remarkably sanguine picture of Christianity's first three hundred years emerges in Eusebius's account, a picture all the more striking in view of the external hardships and internal tensions Christians actually had to endure in the period. But Eusebius could detect the hand of God behind the scene at every stage, directing the church's mission and destiny. Believers who were controlled and sustained by God's Spirit faced persecution fearlessly, so that the church grew despite opposition.[3] And "heresy" was quickly and effectively overcome by the original and apostolic teaching of the church's vast majority, a teaching that, for Eusebius, was by definition orthodox.

Like many of his predecessors among the heresiologists, Eusebius maintained that Christian heresy began with a shadowy figure mentioned in the New Testament book of Acts, Simon Magus. Acts, a canonical book for Eusebius, indicates that Simon was a great magician in the city of Samaria, who used his deft powers to convince the Samarians that he himself was "the Power of God that is called Great." But then, according to Acts 8, someone with real power arrived in town, the Christian evangelist Philip, who preached the gospel of God, leading many to convert and be baptized. This included Simon, who was astounded by Philip's miracles, which were truly divine, not manipulations of magic (Acts 8:9–13).

When the apostles of Jerusalem learned that Samarians had converted to follow Christ and had been baptized, they sent two of their own, Peter and John, to provide the converts with the gift of the Spirit through the laying on of hands (8:14–17).[4] We are not told how the Spirit's presence was manifest at this point, but if its first appearance on the Day of Pentecost (Acts 2) is any indication, it must have been a spectacular moment. Simon in particular was impressed, but his wicked nature again took over. He tried to bribe the apostles to bring him into the inner circle and make their power available to him: "Give me also this power, that any one on whom I lay my hands may receive the Holy Spirit" (8:19). Peter upbraided him for his insolence and sent him off with a reproach, urging him to repent of his wickedness. In humility, Simon asked that the apostles pray for him.

That is the end of the story in Acts. But it came to be expanded considerably in later Christian tradition. By the mid-second century Christians told legends about Simon that indicated he never did repent but continued in his sinful ways, focusing on supernatural power and on convincing others that he had it. According to Justin Martyr, living in mid-second-century Rome, Simon became entirely persuasive in his claims that he was a divine being. Justin notes that the Romans set up a statue to Simon on the Tiber island, with a Latin dedicatory inscription that read, "Simoni Deo Sancto," meaning "To Simon, the Holy God" (*Apology* 1.26). Unfortunately, Justin appears to have gotten things muddled. As it turns out, the inscription was discovered many centuries later, in 1574. It actually read, "Semoni Sanco Sancto Deo." What a difference a word makes. Semo Sancus was in fact a pagan deity worshiped by the Sabines in Rome, and this was a statue dedicated to him. Justin mistook the inscription as referring to the Holy Simon.[5]

The early Christian heresiologists narrated yet more extensive accounts of Simon after his brusque dismissal by the apostles. According to Irenaeus and his successors, Simon was the original Gnostic, who taught that he was personally the divine redeemer sent from the heavenly realm to reveal the truths necessary for salvation. Moreover, he had brought his "Primal Thought" with him, the first aeon that emanated from the one true God. This Primal Thought came embodied as a woman named Helen, whom, the heresiologists tell us, Simon had acquired at a local brothel. For these heresiologists, who delight in stressing the point, Gnostics have prostituted themselves in more ways than one.[6]

A Roman inscription to Semo Sancis, a Sabine diety worshiped in Rome. This inscription was mistakenly taken to refer to "the holy Simon (Magus)" by Justin Martyr. (Vatican)

Eusebius takes these stories found in Acts, Justin, and Irenaeus and develops them even further, establishing a precedent for the portrayal of heretical teachers throughout his ten-volume account. According to Eusebius, Simon was a demonically inspired opponent of the apostles who appeared in the course of the early Christian mission, performing black magic and misleading others to believe that he was divine. Not only did Simon advocate blasphemous and false doctrines; he also led a profligate life, openly consorting with the prostitute Helen and engaging in secret and vile rituals. Those he misled accepted his heretical teachings and, like him, indulged in scandalous practices: "For whatever could be imagined more disgusting than the foulest crime known has been outstripped by the utterly revolting heresy of these men, who make sport of wretched women, burdened indeed with vices of every kind" (*Church History* 2.13.8).[7]

Eusebius indicates, however, that God had an answer for this scurrilous heretic and raised up the apostle Peter to encounter him in Judea,

> extinguishing the flames of the Evil One before they could spread. . . . Consequently neither Simon nor any of his contemporaries managed to form an organized body in those apostolic days, for every attempt was defeated and overpowered by the light of the truth and by the divine Word Himself who had so recently shone from God on humans, active in the world and immanent in His own apostles. (*Church History* 2.14.2–3)

Defeated in Judea, Simon then fled to Rome, where he achieved no little success, until Peter again appeared on the scene and once and for all dispensed with this henchman of Satan through a radiant and powerful proclamation of the truth.

There is more vitriol than substance in Eusebius's account of Simon. The account nonetheless presents a schematic framing of the nature of Christian heresy, a framework that would prevail among church historians from late antiquity, down into the Middle Ages, and on up to the modern period. This is the "classical" view of internal doctrinal conflicts discussed above, in which orthodoxy is the "right opinion" taught by Jesus and his apostles and held by the majority of believers ever since, and heresy is "false belief" created by willful persons who have perverted the truth and convinced a minority of equally willful persons of their lies. In many of these accounts the corruptions of truth occur under the pressure of other, non-Christian influences, either Jewish traditions or, more commonly, pagan philosophy.

Although Eusebius was chiefly responsible for popularizing this view, by no stretch of the imagination was he the first to express it. In fact, as I have intimated, a similar perspective may be found already in the New Testament book of Acts, which portrays the true faith as based on the eyewitness testimony of the apostles, who spread this faith throughout the world by the power of the Holy Spirit. The churches they establish—all of them, necessarily, apostolic churches—stand in complete harmony with one another in every important point of doctrine and practice; even relative latecomers such as Paul agree with Jesus' original followers in all the essentials of the faith. To be sure, internal problems arise on occasion. But for Acts, in almost every instance these problems derive from the greed and avarice of individual Christians (such as the infamous Ananias and Sapphira; 5:1–11) or from the thirst for power of outsiders who have come to infiltrate the church (such as Simon Magus; 8:4–25). Most converts are said to remain true to the apostolic message. And theological issues are readily resolved by an appeal to apostolic authority, which, even after serious debate and reflection, reveals the most remarkable of all unities.[8] According to Acts, disunities in the church can be attributed to the false teachings of degenerate individuals, portrayed as ravenous wolves who infiltrate the flock of Christ's sheep to do great damage but who cannot, ultimately, overcome a church unified behind the original apostolic teaching (10:28–31).

This view, afforded canonical status by Acts, became standard among proto-orthodox Christians of the second and third centuries, who, as we have seen, developed the notion of apostolic succession into a powerful weapon with which to fight their battles for truth.

Assaults on the Classical View

The "classical" understanding of the relationship of orthodoxy and heresy remained unchallenged, for the most part, until the modern period. Rather than present an exhaustive history of scholarship, I have decided to focus on three key moments in the history of its demise, each involving a fundamental question: Did Jesus and his disciples teach an orthodoxy that was transmitted to the churches of the second and third centuries? Does Acts provide a reliable account of the internal conflicts of the earliest Christian church? And does Eusebius give a trustworthy sketch of the disputes raging in the post-apostolic Christian communities? The answer to all three questions, as now known, is probably No. Scholars who first propounded these answers engaged in daring, even risky, historical work. But their conclusions are now so widely held as to be virtually commonplace.

H. Reimarus, the Historical Jesus, and the Gospels

The first question involves the teachings of Jesus and his apostles and the reliability of the New Testament documents that convey them. Serious concerns about the historical accuracy of the Bible began to appear during the Enlightenment, when supernatural doctrines of divine revelation that guaranteed the truth of Scripture became matters of scholarly debate. Doubts that surfaced affected not only the increasingly secular discourses of science but also internal Christian reflections on the nature of Truth, the value of history, and the importance of human reason. The skepticism about church doctrine that came to a fevered pitch among western intellectuals in the eighteenth century found its way into the ranks of biblical and ecclesiastical scholarship, not just among those who saw themselves as standing outside the Christian tradition but especially among those within.

In some ways the beginning can be traced to a remarkable book published in German in a series of seven installments in 1774–78. These so-called Fragments totaled around four thousand pages and were only part of a larger work written by an erudite German scholar named Hermann Reimarus (1694–1768). Reimarus had the good professional sense not to publish the Fragments himself.[9] It was only after his death that the philosopher G. E. Lessing uncovered them and made them available to the public. He did so not because he agreed with their perspective but because they raised arguments that he believed needed to be addressed.

Reimarus, the son of a Lutheran pastor in Hamburg, had been trained in philosophy, theology, and philology, and had spent the last forty years of his life as a professor of Hebrew and Oriental languages at the Hamburg Gymnasium (comparable to an advanced high school). The position afforded him time to write, and he produced several important works in a range of academic fields. But nothing proved so influential as these posthumous fragments on religion, the Bible, and the history of early Christianity. And among the fragments, none proved so controversial as the last, "The Intention of Jesus and His Disciples."[10]

Early in his academic life Reimarus had traveled to England, where he became intrigued by the ideas propounded by English Deists. With them, he came to affirm the supremacy of human reason over a purported divine revelation. He rejected the existence of miracles and insisted that contradictions in historical narratives even when in the Bible compromise their reliability. These principles were rigorously applied in his discussions of the New Testament in the Fragments, leading to a complete rejection of the historical reliability of the Gospel accounts of Jesus' resurrection (which, when compared carefully with one another, appear to be filled with discrepancies) and of the apostles' claims that Jesus was a supernatural being.

According to Reimarus, Jesus did proclaim the coming Kingdom of God. But for Jesus, as for all Jews living at the time, this was to be a political entity, a real "kingdom" here on earth. Jesus maintained that there would be a victorious uprising by the Jews against the oppressive Romans leading to a new political state in Israel. Jesus himself would be at its head as the Messiah. This would happen in the near future, when the Jewish masses rallied around Jesus in support of their own liberation. Unfortunately, when the Roman authorities learned of Jesus' revolutionary preaching, they ruthlessly and effectively removed him from public view, crucifying him as a political incendiary.

The disciples, however, had grown accustomed to their itinerant lives as followers of Jesus. Intent on perpetuating the cause, they decided to found a religion in Jesus' name. And so they invented the idea that Jesus was the Messiah—not the political Messiah that everyone expected, but a spiritual Messiah who had died for sin and been raised from the dead. To prevent the refutation of their claims, they stole Jesus' body from the tomb, as hinted at still in the Gospel accounts (Matt. 28:13). Thus, for Reimarus, the disciples started the Christian religion. And this was not at all what Jesus intended. Jesus, then, was clearly not the Messiah in either the physical or spiritual sense—let alone the preexistent son of God or, as later theologians would have it, God himself, of the "same substance as the Father." Jesus was a Jew who preached a revolutionary message that placed him on the wrong side of the law and that led to his violent death. And that was the end of his story.

No scholar today agrees with this reconstruction of the historical Jesus.[11] But as Albert Schweitzer noted in his classic 1906 study, *The Quest of the Historical Jesus,* more than anyone else Reimarus began the critical quest to establish what really happened in Jesus' life, based on the premise that the Gospel narratives are not accurate reports but later accounts written by believers with a vested interest in their claims.[12]

The basic evidence for this point of view involves some of the major points that Reimarus himself made: There are differences among the Gospel accounts that cannot be reconciled. Some of these differences are minor discrepancies in details: Did Jesus die the afternoon before the Passover meal was eaten, as in John (see 19:14), or the morning afterwards, as in Mark (see 14:12, 22; 15:25)? Did Joseph and Mary flee to Egypt after Jesus' birth as in Matthew (2:13–23), or did they return to Nazareth as in Luke (2:39)? Was Jairus's daughter sick and dying when he came to ask Jesus for help as in Mark (6:23, 35), or had she already died, as in Matthew (9:18)? After Jesus' resurrection, did the disciples stay in Jerusalem until he had ascended into heaven, as in Luke (24:1–52), or did they straightaway go to Galilee, as in Matthew (28:1–20)? Discrepancies like these (many of which seem minor, but which often end up being significant when examined closely) permeate the Gospel traditions.

Some of the differences are much larger, involving the purpose of Jesus' mission and the understanding of his character. What all the differences show, great and small, is that each Gospel writer has an agenda—a point of view he wants to get across, an understanding of Jesus he wants his readers to share. And he has told his stories in such a way as to convey that agenda.

But once we begin to suspect the historical accuracy of our Gospel sources, and find evidence that corroborates our suspicions, where does that lead us? With regard to our questions about the nature of orthodoxy and heresy in early Christianity, it leads us *away* from the classical notion that orthodoxy is rooted in the apostles' teaching as accurately preserved in the New Testament Gospels and *to* the realization that the doctrines of orthodox Christianity must have developed at a time later than the historical Jesus and his apostles, later even than our earliest Christian writings. These views are generally held by scholars today, based on in-depth analyses of the Gospel traditions since the days of Reimarus.[13]

F. C. Baur and the Earliest History of Christianity

The scholarly interest unleashed on the New Testament during the Enlightenment focused not just on Jesus and the Gospels but also on the historical reliability of the rest of the Christian Scripture. Of particular relevance to the traditional understanding of orthodoxy and heresy, questions arose concerning the accuracy of the description of the earliest Christian community in Acts. Another key moment in the history of scholarship came some six decades after the publication of Reimarus's Fragments, in the work of another German scholar, F. C. Baur (1792–1860).[14]

Baur was a towering figure in the history of nineteenth-century biblical and theological scholarship. Professor of New Testament and historical theology at the University of Tübingen from 1826 until his death, Baur was the founder of the so-called Tübingen School, with its distinctive understanding of the history of the first three hundred years of Christianity, including most famously a complete reevaluation of the historical trustworthiness of the New Testament writings. Discussions concerning the arguments of this "school," pro and con, dominated German- and even English-speaking scholarship for an entire generation, and they still affect research today.

Baur was a remarkable scholar in every way—brilliant, wide-ranging, and hardworking. Stories of his scholarly output are the stuff of legend. At his desk every morning at 4:00, by the end of his life he had produced the equivalent of a 400-page book every year, for forty years.

One of his earliest writings set the tone for the understanding of church history that became the keynote of his career and the writings of his students. In a work called "The Christ Party in the Corinthian Community," Baur maintained that earliest Christianity, before the books of the New Testament had been completed, was characterized by a conflict between Jewish Christians, who wanted to maintain distinctive ties to Judaism and so keep Christianity as a particularist religion (it was *Jewish*), and Gentile Christians, who wanted to sever those ties in order to make it a universalistic religion (it was for *everyone*). The conflicts were spearheaded by the two key figures of the early church, Peter, head of the Jewish-Christian faction, and Paul, head of the Gentile Christians. According to Baur, there was no clear winner in the early back and forth between these two groups. Instead, a kind of historical compromise emerged, in which aspects of both the Jewish-Christian insistence on keeping the Law and the Gentile-Christian emphasis on salvation available to all came to be melded together into what eventually became the catholic church of both Jew and Gentile.

Anyone familiar with continental philosophy will recognize here the influence of Hegel, the German philosopher who understood history to proceed dialectically, with a thesis (in this case, Jewish Christianity) encountering an antithesis (Gentile Christianity), resulting then in a synthesis (catholic Christianity). This Hegelian understanding, however, was not simply taken over by Baur in generalized terms; it was worked out in great analytical detail with specific texts. Two keys to Baur's argument were his claims that the history of the early conflict was shrouded by the emergent synthesis and that the earliest Christian writings could be situated in their genuine historical contexts only by analyzing their ideological proclivities.

The book of Revelation, for example, is thoroughly Jewish-Christian in its apocalyptic and particularist orientation (the thesis position); Paul's letters to the Galatians and Romans are harshly anti-Jewish (the antithesis).[15] These books then are all early in the conflict, representing the two competing sides. But Acts—to take a prominent and, for us, key example—is a mediating force, showing Peter and Paul in essential agreement on all major points and working out a compromising solution to the problem of particularism and universalism. It is striking, as members of the Tübingen school could point out, that the speeches of Peter (e.g., Acts 2) and of Paul (e.g. Acts 13) read almost exactly alike. Peter sounds like Paul and Paul sounds like Peter. According to the version of Acts, rather than being at loggerheads over how Jews and Gentiles are to react to each other in Christ, as they were according to Paul's own account in Gal. 2:11–14, these two apostles, and all the others, are portrayed in perfect concord on the matter (Acts 10–11; 15). Acts is thus not a historical account of what actually happened but an attempt to smooth over the acrimonious debates. It is a later work, not from the lifetime of Paul at all but written by someone who chose to reformulate the history of the early tensions within the church to show that the catholic solution had been in place from the beginning.

Again, no one subscribes to the precise views of Baur and the Tübingen school today. But the basic point is widely recognized that Acts, like the Gospels, is driven by a theological agenda that sometimes affects its historical accuracy. Probably the easiest way to demonstrate the point is to compare what Acts has to say about its main protagonist, the apostle Paul, with what Paul has to say about himself in his own letters. Not only are there small differences in detail concerning where Paul was, when, and with whom, there also are major discrepancies in important issues involving Paul's activities, the nature of his proclamation, and the overall portrayal of his character.

For instance, did Paul consult with the Apostles before going on the mission field? Acts says yes (Acts 9:26ff.), but Paul emphatically says no (Gal. 1:17). And what did Paul think about pagans who worship idols? Are they guilty before God for violating what they know to be true about him (so Romans 1:18–32), or are they innocent before God because they are ignorant of the truth about him (so Acts 17:22–31). In terms of the overall understanding of Paul's message and mission: Paul portrays himself as a missionary to the Gentiles who has abandoned, for the most part, adherence to the Jewish Law for the sake of his mission; Acts portrays Paul as a good Jew who has never done anything contrary to the Law. And what about Paul's interactions with his apostolic predecessors? Paul portrays himself as being at loggerheads with the apostles in Jerusalem, especially Peter (cf. Gal. 2:11–14); Acts portrays the entire Christian in harmony from the beginning to the end of Paul's mission (cf. Acts 15:1–24).

The significance of this evidence for our survey should be obvious. Scholars widely recognize that the Acts of the Apostles may be driven as much by a theological agenda as by a concern for historical accuracy. For that reason, it cannot be used uncritically to provide a historical basis for the classical understanding of the relationship of orthodoxy and heresy.[16]

Walter Bauer on Orthodoxy and Heresy in Earliest Christianity

The third question to be addressed concerns the reports of Eusebius himself, whether he can be trusted to give an accurate account of the relationships between proto-orthodox and heretical Christians over the course of the first three centuries. In the early days of Enlightenment scholarship, Eusebius was occasionally attacked for presenting a biased and unhistorical account.[17] With new discoveries of primary sources showing the wide varieties of early Christianity, scholars of the nineteenth century sometimes went further and argued that his narrative was inaccurate and theologically driven. But it was not until the early twentieth century that Eusebius's account came under severe scrutiny, leading to a devastating attack on his portrayal of early Christian unity and diversity.

The major study was published by yet another German scholar, of similar name to the founder of the Tübingen School, but not to be confused as a relation. Walter Bauer (1877-1960) was a scholar of great range and massive erudition; his Greek lexicon remains a standard tool for all students of New Testament Greek. His most controversial and influential work was a study of theological conflicts in the early church. *Orthodoxy and Heresy in Earliest Christianity* (1934) was arguably the most important book on the history of early Christianity to appear in the twentieth century. Its precise aim is clear: to undercut the Eusebian model for the relationship of orthodoxy and heresy. The argument is incisive and authoritative, made by a master of all the surviving early Christian literature. Some scholars recoiled in horror at Bauer's views, and others embraced them fiercely, but no one in the field has been untouched by them. The repercussions are still felt today, as Bauer's analysis has changed forever how we look at the theological controversies prior to the fourth century.[18]

Bauer argued that the early Christian church did not consist of a single orthodoxy from which emerged a variety of competing heretical minorities. Instead, earliest Christianity, as far back as we can trace our sources, could be found in a number of divergent forms, none of which represented the clear and powerful majority of believers against all the others. In some regions of ancient Christendom, what later came to be labeled "heresy" was in fact the earliest and principal form of Christianity. In other regions, views later deemed heretical coexisted with views that came to be embraced by the church as a whole, with most believers not drawing hard and fast lines of demarcation between them. To this extent, "orthodoxy," in the sense of a unified group advocating an apostolic doctrine accepted by the majority of Christians everywhere, simply did not exist in the second and third centuries. Nor was "heresy" secondarily derived from an original teaching through an infusion of Jewish ideas or pagan philosophy. Beliefs that later came to be accepted as orthodox or heretical were competing interpretations of Christianity, and the groups that held them were scattered throughout the empire. Eventually one of these groups established itself as dominant, acquiring more converts than all the others, overpowering its opponents, and declaring itself the true faith. Once its victory was secured, it could call itself "orthodox" and marginalize the opposition parties as heretics. It then rewrote the history of the conflict, making its views and the people who held them appear to have been in the majority from apostolic times onwards.

As should be clear from this thumbnail sketch, Bauer objected to the very terms of the debate between orthodoxy and heresy, which he nonetheless used. For him, historians cannot use the words *orthodoxy* to mean right belief and *heresy* to mean wrong belief. Those are value judgments about theological "truths." But the historian is no more able to pronounce on ultimate "truth" than anyone else. That is to say, historians cannot decide who is right in the question of whether there is one God or two; they can simply show what different people have thought at different times. More than that, however, Bauer objected to the implications of the terms *orthodoxy* as referring to an original and majority position and *heresy* as referring to later corruptions. Much of his book, in fact, is devoted to showing that these implications are completely wrong. Why then continue to use the terms at all? For Bauer they continue to be useful designations not so much for the conflicts of the second and third centuries as for how these conflicts came to be understood in hindsight. Only after Gnostics, Marcionites, Ebionites, and others had been more or less weeded out was there a majority opinion that asserted itself; at that point it makes sense to speak of orthodoxy, that is, a set of beliefs subscribed to by the majority of believers. Speaking about orthodoxy in the earlier period, then, is a kind of intentional anachronism that highlights the problem by using its own terms.

Bauer's views were not established simply by assertion. His book is filled with a detailed analysis of all the relevant sources that were available to him. Seventy years after its publication, it is still essential reading for scholars in the field. Bauer proceeds by looking at certain geographical regions of early Christendom for which we have some evidence—particularly the city of Edessa in eastern Syria, Antioch in western Syria, Egypt, Asia Minor, Macedonia, and Rome. For each place, he considers the available Christian sources and subjects them to the closest scrutiny, demonstrating that contrary to the reports of Eusebius, the earliest and/or predominant forms of Christianity in most of these areas were heretical (i.e., forms subsequently condemned by the victorious party). Christianity in Edessa, for example, a major center for orthodox Christianity in later times, was originally Marcionite; the earliest Christians in Egypt were various kinds of Gnostic, and so on. Later orthodox Christians, after they had secured their victory, tried to obscure the real history of the conflict. But they were not completely successful, leaving traces that can be scrutinized for the truth.

But how did the one form of Christianity, the form at the root of all major branches of the Christian church down to the present day, attain a level of dominance? For Bauer, this was the kind of Christianity that was found predominantly, though not exclusively, in the church of Rome, the capital of the empire, destined to become the center of Christianity. Is it a surprise that it was the *Roman* form of Christianity that became the Christianity of all people in the empire?

Bauer does not simply suggest that Rome was the obvious place from which orthodoxy would move forth and conquer the Christian world; he again provides evidence and makes a case. We have already seen that the earliest noncanonical Christian writing that we have, 1 Clement, is a letter from the Christians in Rome trying to influence the internal workings of the church of Corinth, urging in the strongest terms possible that the Corinthian presbyters be reinstated. But why would Christians in Rome be concerned about the politics of the church in Corinth? Is it because the deposed presbyters, as opposed to the now ruling junta, actually supported the Roman understanding of Christianity? Could they have been proto-orthodox Christians, whereas their opponents were not?

As it turns out, we know of false teachers vying for authority in Corinth from the beginning—the "super apostles" referred to in Paul's letters to Corinth (2 Cor. 11:5), who appear to have thought that there would be no future bodily resurrection of believers. These may well have been forerunners of Gnostic Christians, who devalued fleshly existence. At the time of 1 Clement, some thirty years after Paul's letters, had this group finally won out in a coup? And were the Roman Christians taking action to correct the situation?

It appears, in any event, that the proto-orthodox letter of 1 Clement had its effect. The book itself came to acquire sacred status among the Christians in Corinth and was read as Scripture in their worship services some seventy years later, according to the then proto-orthodox bishop Dionysius. This would scarcely have been likely, had the Gnostic usurpers retained power.

As should be clear, for Bauer, the internal Christian conflicts were struggles over power, not just theology. And the side that knew how to utilize power was the side that won. More specifically, Bauer pointed out that the Christian community in Rome was comparatively large and affluent. Moreover, located in the capital of the empire, it had inherited a tradition of administrative prowess from the state apparatus through a kind of trickle-down effect. Using the administrative skills of its leaders and its vast material resources, the church in Rome managed to exert influence over other Christian communities. Among other things, the Roman Christians promoted a hierarchical structure, insisting that each church should have a single bishop. Given the right bishop, of course, certain theological views could then be preached and enforced. Moreover, the Roman influence, for Bauer, was economic: By paying for the manumission of slaves and purchasing the freedom of prisoners, the Roman church brought large numbers of grateful converts into the fold, while the judicious use of gifts and alms offered to other churches naturally effected a sympathetic hearing of their views. As the Dionysius of Corinth could say to Soter, bishop of Rome:

> From the start it has been your custom to . . . send contributions to many churches in every city, sometimes alleviating the distress of those in need, sometimes providing for your brothers in the [slave] mines by the contributions you have sent. (Eusebius, *Church History* 4.23)

Over time, the proto-orthodox views of the Roman community became increasingly dominant in the cities connected in one way or another to the capital, and since all roads lead to Rome, eventually that meant most of the cities throughout the empire. By the end of the third century, the Roman form of Christianity had established dominance. All it took then was someone like

Eusebius to write the account, and not only the Roman proto-orthodox theology but also the Roman view of the history of the conflict came to be established for ages to come.

Reactions to Bauer

Scholars in Germany immediately recognized the importance of Bauer's radical rewriting of early Christian history. Unfortunately, the book was not translated into English until 1971. Most of the English-speaking world thus knew about it only secondhand and mainly through the refutations of Bauer's opponents. Even so, the impact of the book was enormous.[19]

Specific details of Bauer's demonstration were immediately seen as problematic. Bauer was charged, for good reason, with attacking orthodox sources with inquisitorial zeal and exploiting to a nearly absurd extent the argument from silence.[20] Moreover, in terms of his specific claims, each of the regions that he examined have been subjected to further scrutiny, not always to the advantage of his conclusions.

Probably most scholars today think that Bauer underestimated the extent of proto-orthodoxy throughout the empire and overestimated the influence of the Roman church on the course of the conflicts.[21] Even so, subsequent scholarship has tended to show even more problems with the Eusebian understanding of heresy and orthodoxy and has confirmed that, in their essentials, Bauer's intuitions were right. If anything, early Christianity was even less tidy and more diversified than he realized.[22]

As a result of this ongoing scholarship, it is widely thought today that proto-orthodoxy was simply one of many competing interpretations of Christianity in the early church. It was neither a self-evident interpretation nor an original apostolic view. The apostles, for example, did not teach the Nicene Creed or anything like it. Indeed, as far back as we can trace it, Christianity was remarkably varied in its theological expressions.

In Support of Bauer's Basic Thesis:
A Modern Assessment of Early Christian Diversity

Probably the primary piece of evidence for this widespread variety comes from the proto-orthodox sources themselves, and in a somewhat ironic way. Eusebius and his successors quote these sources at length, including the books of the New Testament, in order to show that at every turn, their proto-orthodox forebears were successful in deposing false teachers and their heretical followers. But what they neglect to point out is that these "successes" presuppose the extensive, even pervasive, influence of false teachers in the early Christian communities.

Take our earliest Christian writings as an example, the letters of the apostle Paul. In nearly all his own churches, the ones he himself founded, there are dangerous "false teachers" propounding an understanding of the gospel that Paul finds reprehensible or even damnable. In many instances, the opposing forces are winning out, so that Paul is compelled to intervene to reverse the trend. In his letter to the Galatians, for example, he contends with "Judaizers," Christian missionaries instructing Paul's converts that to be true members of the people of God they must adopt the ways of Judaism, including circumcision for the men. The success of these missionaries is evident in Paul's angry response; he genuinely fears that the entire community is being led astray (Gal. 1:6–8, 3:1–5).

In his letters to the Corinthians, he is confronted with Christians again, from within his own church, who believe they have already experienced the full benefits of salvation and are already ruling with Christ as superspiritual humans. Some of their beliefs sound almost Gnostic; Paul has confronted some of his opponents face-to-face in Corinth and apparently experienced a public humiliation, suggesting that he may have lost the argument (see 2 Cor. 2:5–11, 13:2). He threatens another visit in which, he promises, things will be different.

His letter to the Romans is to a church that he did not found, and it is written to convince them that his gospel message is legitimate, so they will support him in his missionary endeavors further to the west, in Spain (see Rom. 1:8–15, 15:22–24). But why does he need to convince them? Evidently because they suspected *him* of teaching a false gospel. Someone else must have told them so.[23]

Later letters written in Paul's name presuppose internal tensions in his later churches: some kind of strange Jewish mysticism affecting the Christians of Colossae (Col. 2:8–23), a kind of fervent millenarianism in 2 Thessalonians, where people have quit their jobs expecting the end to come right away (2 Thess. 2:1–12, 3:6–15), some kind of proto-Gnosticism in 1 Timothy (1 Tim. 1:3–7).

Problems with false understandings of the faith appear in non-Pauline books of the New Testament as well. James strongly opposes Christians who have taken Paul's doctrine of justification by faith to mean that good deeds are irrelevant for salvation. Revelation attacks antinomian (lawless) groups for bringing down the faithful. Jude and 2 Peter castigate false teachers who have infiltrated the churches with their foul teachings.

I cannot emphasize enough that all of these opponents in all of these communities identify themselves as followers of Christ. The Judaizers in Galatia, the proto-Gnostics of Corinth, those suspicious of Paul in Rome, the Jewish mystics of Colossae, the millenialists of 2 Thessalonians, the extreme Paulinists of James, the libertines of Revelation, and the vilified nameless of Jude and 2 Peter—what would all these groups of Christians have to say for themselves? We will never know for certain. But we do know that such people existed in the churches, understanding themselves to be Christian, maintaining that their views were not only believable but right. And they were acquiring large numbers of followers. In some cases, possibly most, they may have claimed to represent views held by Jesus' own apostles, the original Christian views. One would think that the Judaizers in Galatia, at least, could make a pretty good case.

Even after the books of the New Testament had been written, the trend continues. There are the churches known to Ignatius in Asia Minor, all of them endangered by false teachers, either Judaizers or docetists or both. There are the heretics known to Irenaeus in Gaul, so numerous that he can't even count all the sects, let alone estimate their numbers, so nefarious that he has to devote five books to refuting their views. There are the heretics known to Tertullian in north Africa, who castigates his fellow proto-orthodox for being "scandalized by the very fact that the heresies prevail to such a degree" (*Prescription* 1), unwittingly admitting, thereby, that heretics could be found virtually everywhere. There are those known to Hippolytus in Rome, so influential that their false views had reached the highest echelons of the church administration, affecting the views of the bishop of Rome himself and threatening therefore to take over the entire church. And so it goes, on and on, for decades to come.

Not only the widespread diversity of early Christianity but also the blurred boundaries between what counted as orthodoxy and heresy—another of Bauer's points—appears to be borne out by the evidence. To be sure, there were certain clear battle lines, especially for the proto-orthodox. Anyone who claimed that there were thirty gods or who denied that Jesus came in the flesh would not escape Irenaeus's plodding attacks or Tertullian's rapier wit. But there were numerous issues that remained vague and unresolved in the second and even third centuries.

Even such basic questions as the nature of Christ's existence were not yet well defined. We have seen how this played out in the patripassianist controversy. But even on more basic issues there was an occasional lack of clarity. Docetic Christologies, of course, were strictly *verboten* among the proto-orthodox. Or were they? Both Origen and his predecessor, Clement of Alexandria, champions of proto-orthodoxy in their own day, expressed some very peculiar ideas about Jesus' body, peculiar at least to later theologians. Both maintained, for example, that Jesus' body could readily change appearance at will (e.g., Origen *Serm. Mount* 100). Clement went even further:

> But in the case of the Savior, it would be ludicrous [to suppose] that the body, as a body, demanded the necessary aids in order for its duration. For he ate, not for the sake of the body, which was kept together by a holy energy, but in order that it might not enter into the minds of those who were with Him to entertain a different opinion of him; in a manner as certainly some afterwards supposed that He appeared in a phantasmal shape. But he was entirely impassible; inaccessible to any movement of feeling—either pleasure or pain. (*Miscellanies* 6.71.2)

In other words, Jesus ate simply to keep people from entertaining docetic notions about him, even though in fact he did not need to eat and could not feel pleasure or pain. It is hard to imagine how that is the same thing as having a real body of flesh and blood. And it is even harder to imagine that any such claim would be acceptable to the orthodox of later times. But there it is: Clement, a leading proto-orthodox spokesperson, with a Christology in the shadows but completely acceptable to other proto-orthodox Christians of his day.

One final point needs to be made in support of Bauer's basic thesis about the relationship of orthodoxy and heresy. He was working, of course, only with the materials available to him at the time, in the early 1930s. Since then there have been additional discoveries, including entire documents that brilliantly confirmed aspects of his basic perspective, especially those of the Nag Hammadi library. Here was a collection of texts held dear by at least one group of Christians, possibly more, texts representing a wide sweep of alternative Christianities, by authors who assume, of course, that their views were right and that other views were wrong. Some of these texts attack proto-orthodox Christians for *their* false views.

Christianity was far more diverse, the battle lines were far more blurred, the infighting was far more intense than we could possibly have known depending just on Eusebius and the classical view of the relationship of orthodoxy and heresy.

The Victory of Proto-orthodoxy

We are still left with a question that perplexed Bauer and many others since his day. Granted that earliest Christianity was so widely diverse, how did the side we have identified as the proto-orthodox establish itself as dominant? We have already observed several factors that contributed to this ultimate victory:

(1) The proto-orthodox claimed ancient roots for their religion—unlike, say, the Marcionites—by clinging to the Scriptures of Judaism, which, they insisted, predicted Christ and the religion established in his name.

(2) At the same time they rejected the practices of contemporary Judaism as taught in these Scriptures—unlike, say, the Ebionites—allowing their form of Christianity to be a universal faith attractive to and feasible for the majority of people in the ancient world.

(3) The proto-orthodox stressed a church hierarchy—unlike, say, some Gnostics, who believed that since everyone (in Gnostic communities) had equal access to the secret knowledge that brings salvation, everyone had an equal standing in the faith. The church hierarchy was invested with an authority that was used to determine what was to be believed, how church affairs (including worship and liturgy) were to be conducted, and which books were to be accepted as scriptural authorities.

(4) The proto-orthodox were in constant communication with one another, determined to establish theirs as a worldwide communion. Witness the

allies who met Ignatius on his way to martyrdom and the letters he wrote in return, the letter written by the church in Rome to the church in Corinth, and the accounts of Christian martyrs sent out by the church of Smyrna on the occasion of the death of their beloved pastor, Polycarp. The proto-orthodox were interested not only in what happened locally in their own communities but also in what was happening in other like-minded communities. And they were interested in spreading their understanding of the faith throughout the known world.[24]

There were other factors as well, which we will explore in the chapters that follow; but they relate in one way or another to each of the ones given above. It is striking that each of the four have one thing in common: All of them involve written texts. This may simply be due to an accident of history, that our surviving remains are principally textual. But there may be more to it than that, for it appears that most, possibly all, of the groups of early Christians placed a high premium on texts, making the use of literature a key element in the conflicts that were raging, as members of various groups wrote polemical tractates attacking their opponents, forged documents in the names of apostles to provide authorization for their own points of view, falsified writings that were in circulation in order to make them more acceptable for their own purposes, and collected groups of writings together as sacred authorities in support of their own perspectives. The battle for converts was, in some ways, the battle over texts, and the proto-orthodox party won the former battle by winning the latter. One of the results was the canonization of the twenty-seven books that we now call the New Testament. In the chapters that follow, we will consider various aspects of this literary battle for supremacy, to see further how this one group emerged as victorious and established, then, the character of Christianity as it was to come down to us in the modern age.

Chapter Nine

The Arsenal of the Conflicts: Polemical Treatises and Personal Slurs

Doctrinal disputes in early Christianity were not fought with pickaxes and swords. They were fought with words. The spoken word was critical, we can assume, as daily conversations, catechetical teaching, weekly instruction, sermons, private arguments, and public debates must have swayed opinion one way or the other. Unfortunately, we have no access to what anyone actually said in the heat of battle, unless somebody took the trouble to record it.[1] But the written word itself was also important, as theological opponents metaphorically crossed swords, attacking one another's views, casting aspersions on one another's character, appealing to earlier written authorities in support of their perspectives, forging documents in the names of these authorities when necessary or useful, collecting sacred books into canons and assigning them divine status.

We have known all along about the written attacks of the proto-orthodox on Christians of other persuasions. The writings of such heresiologists as Irenaeus and Tertullian, for example, have long been available, even though others, such as those of the second-century writers Hegessipus and Justin, have, for the most part, been lost. But until recently we have not been well informed about the assaults of others on the proto-orthodox, with just a few scattered indications revealing what must have been lively battles. Because this opposing literature has been almost entirely destroyed or lost, the polemical literature from the period looks completely one-sided—so much so, that many readers have simply accepted the idea that "heretics" had little to say for themselves and were more or less obliged to submit to a literary lashing from which they could never recover. A closer look at the surviving remains, however, including some available only in more recent discoveries, suggests the more realistic view, that those who thought they were "right"—that is, every side in the disputes—stood up and fought for their views so that the war of words was waged heartily all round. Just because one side emerged as triumphant, we should not assume that its victory was assured at the outset or that its opponents were easily defeated. Even if his name, girth, strength, and dexterity are not recorded for posterity, the loser of a heavyweight bout may have been quite a bruiser in his time.

Ebionites against the Proto-orthodox Paul: The Pseudo-Clementine Literature

One of the indications that a healthy literary battle, rather than a one-sided onslaught, raged in the early Christian centuries comes to us in a set of writings known for many years but recognized as embodying polemics *against* proto-orthodox Christianity only in relatively modern times.[2] We have already seen that Christians of the second and third centuries were fond of telling tales of the apostles, accounts of their missionary adventures after the ascension of Jesus, embodied now in such apocryphal accounts as the Acts of John and the Acts of Peter. So too, stories were occasionally circulated about companions of the apostles, such as the Acts of Thecla. Included among this latter kind of tale are legendary stories about Clement, the bishop of Rome and reputed author of 1 Clement. There are, in fact, two collections that survive, along with several other writings. The first is a set of twenty *Homilies* allegedly delivered by Clement, in which he discusses his travels and adventures, including his extensive contacts with the apostle Peter, who had converted him to faith in Christ. The other major collection is an account in ten books of Clement's journeys, framed by his search for lost relatives. The quest ends happily, thus giving the name to the account, the *Recognitions*. The relationship between the *Homilies* and the *Recognitions* is highly complex, one of the thorniest issues that scholars of ancient Christian literature have to deal with. Both accounts appear to go back to some kind of older document that was modified and edited in different ways over time. In any event, some of these writings about Clement embrace Jewish-Christian concerns; moreover, in doing so, they sometimes oppose, quite openly, other forms of Christianity, including proto-orthodoxy.

All together these various works are known as the Pseudo-Clementine literature.[3] The basic story line running through these books involves Clement's search for his family and for the truth. Clement is a member of an aristocratic family in Rome. When he is young, his mother is said to have a mysterious vision that compels her to leave town, taking along her twin sons, Clement's older brothers. Eventually his father leaves to track them down; he, too, never returns. Meanwhile, Clement grows up and devotes himself to a religious quest that takes him through various forms of pagan philosophy, none of which satisfies his intellectual curiosity. But then he hears that the Son of God has appeared in Judea, and he journeys off to find him. But he is too late. By the time Clement arrives, Jesus has already been executed. Clement meets the apostle Peter, converts to faith in Christ, and accompanies Peter on his missionary journeys. These are filled with adventures that include, most notably, a number of confrontations between Peter and the magician Simon Magus, whom Peter betters through the miraculous power of God. In the end, Clement finally becomes reunited with all of his family, and so harmony is restored. He has found the true faith, along with his parents and brothers.

The heretic Simon Magus thus occupies an important place in these accounts. But in places, at least, it appears that the person Peter opposes is not the magician we know about from the Acts of the Apostles and the early heresiological reports.[4] Here he appears to be a cipher for none other than the apostle Paul. That is to say, on some level it is Paul who is portrayed as the enemy attacked in these books. Peter's gospel, which insists on the ongoing validity of the Law of Moses for all Christians, Jew and Gentile, is here set over against the heretical notions of Paul, who is understood to preach a version of the Christian message that is, literally, lawless.

The controversy between Peter and Paul presupposed in these fictional accounts is premised on a real, historical conflict between the two, evidenced in Paul's own writings. In particular, in his letter to the Galatians, Paul speaks of a public encounter with Peter in the city of Antioch over the issue of whether Gentiles who have become Christian need to observe the Jewish Law (Gal. 2:11–14). Paul reports the encounter and states in the strongest terms his own view, that Gentiles are under no circumstances to be required to keep the Law. As scholars have long noted, however, Paul does not indicate the outcome of the public altercation—leading to the widely held suspicion that this was one debate that Paul lost, at least in the eyes of those who observed it.

The Pseudo-Clementines take up the debate to show Peter supporting the ongoing validity of the Law against Paul, thinly disguised as Simon Magus. The books are prefaced by a letter allegedly from Peter to James, the brother of Jesus and head of the church in Jerusalem (one of a number of letters we have that are forged in Peter's name). In it Peter speaks of his "enemy" who teaches the Gentiles not to obey the Law, and he sets out his own authoritative position in contrast:

> For some from among the Gentiles have rejected my lawful preaching and have preferred a lawless and absurd doctrine of the man who is my enemy. And indeed some have attempted, while I am still alive, to distort my words by interpretations of many sorts, as if I taught the dissolution of the Law. . . . But that may God forbid! For to do such a thing means to act contrary to the Law of God which was made to Moses and was confirmed by our Lord in its everlasting continuance. For he said, "The heaven and the earth will pass away, but not one jot or one tittle shall pass away from the Law." (*Letter of Peter to James*, 2.3–5)[5]

The Law of Moses, therefore, is always to be kept by Jew and Gentile. It does not take much to recognize who Peter's "enemy" is here, the one who opposes this view "among the Gentiles." The apostle Paul consistently portrayed himself as the apostle to the Gentiles and insisted that they not keep the

Law (e.g., Gal. 2:15, 5:2–5). As to who may have been responsible for teaching that Peter himself urged "the dissolution of the law," one again does not
need to look far: The New Testament book of Acts, allegedly written by Paul's
own traveling companion Luke, portrays Peter as taking just that position (Acts
10–11, 15). Even though Paul and Acts eventually became part of the proto-
orthodox canon, for this author they are both heretical. This Pseudo-Clementine
writing, then, appears to embody an Ebionite polemic against the view adopted
by proto-orthodox Christianity.

The attacks on Paul and on what he stood for become yet clearer in portions
of the *Homilies*. In one section in particular, Peter is said to have developed the
notion that in the plan of God for humans, the lesser always precedes the greater.
And so, Adam had two sons, the murderer Cain and the righteous Abel; two
also sprang from Abraham, the outcast Ishmael and the chosen one Isaac; and
from Isaac came the godless Esau and the godly Jacob. Bringing matters down
to more recent times, there were two who appeared on the Gentile mission
field, Simon (Paul) and Peter, who was, of course, the greater of the two, "who
appeared later than he did and came in upon him as light upon darkness, as
knowledge upon ignorance, as healing upon sickness." (*Homilies* 2.17)

A final example of this polemic comes in an imaginary scene in which Peter
attacks a thinly disguised Paul for thinking that his brief visionary encounter
with Christ could authorize him to propound a gospel message at variance with
those who had spent considerable time with Jesus while he was still alive and
well among them.

> And if our Jesus appeared to you also and became known in a vision and met you
> as angry with an enemy [recall: Paul had his vision while still persecuting the
> Christians; Acts 9], yet he has spoken only through visions and dreams or through
> external revelations. But can anyone be made competent to teach through a vi-
> sion? And if your opinion is that that is possible, why then did our teacher spend
> a whole year with us who were awake? How can we believe you even if he has
> appeared to you? . . . But if you were visited by him for the space of an hour and
> were instructed by him and thereby have become an apostle, then proclaim his
> words, expound what he has taught, be a friend to his apostles and do not contend
> with me, who am his confidant; for you have in hostility withstood me, who am a
> firm rock, the foundation stone of the Church. (*Homilies* 17.19)

Peter, not Paul, is the true authority for understanding the message of Jesus.
Paul has corrupted the true faith based on a brief vision, which he has doubtless
misconstrued. Paul is thus the enemy of the apostles, not the chief of them. He is
outside the true faith, a heretic to be banned, not an apostle to be followed.

The Pseudo-Clementines, then, especially in their older form, which came
to be modified over time, appear to present a kind of Ebionite polemic against
Pauline Christianity and against the proto-orthodox of the second and third
centuries who continue to follow Paul in rejecting the Law of Moses. For these

Ebionite Christians, the Law was given by God, and, contrary to the claims of Paul and his proto-orthodox successors, it continues to be necessary for salvation in Christ.

Gnostic Assaults on Proto-orthodoxy

Of all the polemical literature that must have been generated against the proto-orthodox by their opponents, we are best informed now of that produced by the Gnostics. This is the direct result of the discovery of the Nag Hammadi library, which contains several treatises that attack proto-orthodox positions. Before this discovery we knew that battles must have been raging, but we heard only the voluminous assaults by Irenaeus, Tertullian, Hippolytus, and their successors—page after page of harsh polemic meant to destroy their Gnostic enemies and obliterate their views. We will examine these proto-orthodox tactics in a moment. For now we should consider what the other side had to say.[6]

The Gnostic polemic is somewhat different from what one might expect. The Gnostics—at least the ones about whom we are best informed—did not maintain that the proto-orthodox views were utterly wrong. Instead, these views were inadequate and superficial—in fact, laughably inadequate and superficial. That is to say, Gnostics did not deny the validity of the proto-orthodox doctrinal claims per se; instead, they reinterpreted them in a way that they considered more spiritual and insightful. Gnostics could confess the proto-orthodox creeds, read the proto-orthodox Scriptures, accept the proto-orthodox sacraments. But all these things were understood differently for Gnostics, based on their fuller insight into their real meaning, a fuller insight available to them because of their superior knowledge (*gnosis*) of divine truth. And so, as the proto-orthodox heresiologists themselves bemoaned, the Gnostics were not the enemies "out there" somewhere. They were the enemy within, worshiping in proto-orthodox churches but understanding themselves to be a spiritually elite, an inner circle who recognized the deeper spiritual meaning of doctrines, Scriptures, rituals that the proto-orthodox took (simply) at face value.

Among the Gnostic attacks on the superficiality of proto-orthodox views, none is more riveting than the Coptic Apocalypse of Peter, discovered at Nag Hammadi. This is not to be confused with the proto-orthodox Apocalypse of Peter in which Peter is given a guided tour of heaven and hell. The Nag Hammadi "apocalypse" or "revelation" portrays the true nature of Christ and castigates the ignorance of the simple minded (the proto-orthodox) who do not recognize it.

The book begins with the teachings of "The Savior," who informs Peter that there are many false teachers who are "blind and deaf," who blaspheme the truth and teach what is evil. Peter, on the other hand, will be given secret knowledge (Apoc. Pet. 73). Jesus goes on to tell Peter that his opponents are "without perception." Why? Because "they hold fast to the name of a dead man."[7] In other words, they think that it is Jesus' *death* that matters for salvation. That, of course, had been the proto-orthodox view from the beginning. But for this author, those who maintain such a thing "blaspheme the truth and proclaim evil teaching" (74).

Indeed, those who confess a dead man cling to death, not to immortal life. These souls are dead and were created for death.

> Not every soul comes from the truth nor from immortality. For every soul of these ages has death assigned to it. Consequently, it is always a slave. It is created for its desires and their eternal destruction, for which they exist and in which they exist. They [the souls] love the material creatures that came forth with them. But the immortal souls are not like these, O Peter. But indeed as long as the hour has not yet come, she [the immortal soul] will indeed resemble a mortal one. (75)

Gnostics in the world may appear to be like other people, but they are different, not clinging to material things or living according to their desires. Their souls are immortal, even though this is not widely known: "Others do not understand mysteries, although they speak of these things which they do not understand. Nevertheless, they will boast that the mystery of the truth is theirs alone" (Apoc. Pet. 76). Who are these who fail to understand, who do not teach the truth? "And there will be others of those who are outside our number who name themselves 'bishop' and also 'deacons,' as if they have received their authority from God. . . . These people are dry canals" (79). This is scarcely complimentary to the leaders of the Christian churches: They are not fountains of knowledge and wisdom but dried up river beds.

But what is this knowledge that is accessible to the immortal souls that are not riveted to material things? It is knowledge about the true nature of Christ himself and his crucifixion, which is only mistakenly thought (by the proto-orthodox) to refer to the death of Christ for sins. In fact, the true Christ cannot be touched by pain, suffering, and death but is well beyond them all. What was crucified was not the divine Christ but his physical shell.

In a captivating scene, Peter is said to witness the crucifixion, and he admits to being confused by what he sees:

> When he had said those things, I saw him apparently being seized by them. And I said, "What am I seeing, O Lord? Is it you yourself whom they take? . . . Who is this one above the cross, who is glad and laughing? And is it another person whose feet and hands they are hammering?"

Jesus then gives the stunning reply, which shows the true meaning of the crucifixion:

> The Savior said to me, "He whom you see above the cross, glad and laughing, is the living Jesus. But he into whose hands and feet they are driving the nails is

his physical part, which is the substitute. They are putting to shame that which is in his likeness. But look at him and me." (Apoc. Pet. 81)

Only Christ's physical likeness is put to death. The living Christ transcends death, literally transcends the cross. For there he is, above it, laughing at those who think they can hurt him, at those who think the divine spirit within him can suffer and die. But the spirit of Christ is beyond pain and death, as are the spirits of those who understand who he really is, who know the truth of who they really are—spirits embodied in a physical likeness who cannot suffer or die. The vision continues:

> And I saw someone about to approach us who looked like him, even him who was laughing above the cross, and he was filled with a pure spirit, and he was the Savior. . . . And he said to me, "Be strong! For you are the one to whom these mysteries have been given, to know through revelation that he whom they cru-cified is the first-born, and the home of demons, and the clay vessel in which they dwell, belonging to Elohim [i.e., the God of this world], and belonging to the cross that is under the law. But he who stands near him is the living Savior, the primal part in him whom they seized. And he has been released. He stands joyfully looking at those who persecuted him. . . . Therefore he laughs at their lack of perception. Indeed, therefore, the suffering one must remain, since the body is the substitute. But that which was released was my incorporeal body." (Apoc. Pet. 82)

The body is just a shell, belonging to the creator of this world [*Elohim*, the Hebrew word for God in the Old Testament]. The true self is within and cannot be touched by physical pain. Those without this true knowledge think they can kill Jesus. But the living Jesus rises above it all and laughs them to scorn. And who is really the object of his derision? The proto-orthodox, who think that the death of Jesus is the key to salvation. For this author, this is a laughable view. Salvation does not come *in* the body; it comes by *escaping* the body. It is not the dead Jesus who saves but the living Jesus. So-called believers who don't understand are not the beneficiaries of Jesus' death; they are mocked by it.

A closely related attack on the proto-orthodox may be found in another Nag Hammadi tractate, the Second Treatise of the Great Seth, which, like the Coptic Apocalypse of Peter, ridicules those who have a superficial, literalistic under-standing of Jesus' death:

> For my death, which they think happened, happened [instead] to them in their error and blindness. They nailed their man up to their [own] death. For their minds did not see me, for they were deaf and blind. . . . As for me, on the one hand they saw me; they punished me. Another, their father, was the one who drank the gall and the vinegar; it was not I. They were hitting me with the reed; another was the one who lifted up the cross on his shoulder, who was Simon. Another was the one on whom they put the crown of thorns. But I was rejoicing

in the height over all the riches of the archons . . . laughing at their ignorance. . . .
For I kept changing my forms above, transforming from appearance to appearance. (Second Treatise of the Great Seth 55–56)[8]

This notion of Jesus changing forms calls to mind one of the most disturbing versions of the crucifixion to be propounded by a Gnostic teacher, one not
found among the Nag Hammadi tractates but in the now lost writings of
Basilides, as retold by Irenaeus. The New Testament accounts indicate that on
the road to crucifixion, Simon of Cyrene was compelled to carry Jesus' cross
(see Mark 14:21). According to Basilides, Jesus used the opportunity to pull a
supernatural switch, transforming himself to look like Simon and Simon to
look like himself. The Romans then proceeded to crucify the wrong man, while
Jesus stood to the side, laughing at his subterfuge (*Against Heresies* 1.24.3).
Simon, presumably, did not find it so funny.

But Jesus' laughter is not simply about the tricks he can pull. In these accounts
the laughter is directed against those who do not have eyes to see, who do not
understand Jesus' true nature or the significance of his alleged death on the cross.
The true "Gnostics," on the other hand, do understand: knowing where they have
come from, how they got here, and how they will return. After the death of this
mortal shell, they will return to their heavenly home, having found salvation not
in this body or in this world but salvation from this body and from this world.
Anyone who fails to understand the nature of that salvation, who looks only to
the surface of things, only to the outward, material side of reality, is rightly subject to ridicule, both by Jesus and by those who have received his truth.

The Proto-orthodox on the Attack

In another sense, however, it was the proto-orthodox who had the last laugh.
Through their polemical attacks the proto-orthodox managed to weed Gnostics
out of their churches, destroy their special Scriptures, and annihilate their following. So effective was the destruction that it was not until recent times that
we had any clear idea just how significant Gnostics were in the early centuries
of Christianity and how they tried to fight back. For the most part, our only
evidence of the confrontation was the virulent opposition written by the Gnostics'
proto-orthodox opponents. To be sure, this opposition, carried out in the literary realm, was enough to make us suspect that the proto-orthodox were up
against something they genuinely feared; and we had good reason to think that
the fears were grounded in a substantial social reality. But before the discovery
of the Nag Hammadi library, we were more or less at a loss concerning the
counterstrategies of the Gnostic opponents.

The strategies of the proto-orthodox heresiologists, on the other hand, were
all too clear. They were repeated time and again throughout the literature until
they became virtually stereotyped.

Unity and Diversity

Part of the proto-orthodox strategy involved stressing the notion of "unity" on all levels. The proto-orthodox stressed the unity of God with his creation: There is one God, and he created the world. They stressed the unity of God and Jesus: Jesus is the one son of the one God. They stressed the unity of Jesus and Christ: He is "one and the same." They stressed the unity of the church: Divisions are caused by heretics. And they stressed the unity of truth: Truth is not contradictory or at odds with itself.

Moreover, as we have seen, proto-orthodox authors insisted that their views were handed down from the very beginning: There was thus a continuity in the history of their belief, rooted in the unity of Jesus with his apostles and the apostles with their successors, the bishops of the churches. Wherever, then, there was disunity, there was a problem. And the problem was not simply on the social level of community; it was a problem that went deep, as deep as the truth of the gospel. Disunity shows division and division is not of God.

This understanding came to be applied early on to "heresies," in that heresies were claimed to bring not unity but division. They divided God from his creation, the creator from Jesus, Jesus from the Christ. They divided the church, and they divided the truth. Moreover, the fact that heretics were divided among themselves provided clear evidence that their views could not be from God. At one point Irenaeus laments his own inability to grapple with the internal sects of Valentinian Gnostics: "Since they differ so widely among themselves, both as respects doctrine and tradition, and since those of them who are recognized as being most modern make it their effort daily to invent some new opinion and to bring out what no one ever before thought of, it is a difficult matter to describe all their opinions" (*Against Heresies* 1.21.5).[9]

Not only was it difficult to describe all their opinions, but the widespread diversity among the Valentinian Gnostics showed Ireneaus that the whole system contained nothing but lies: "The very fathers of this fable [the Gnostic myth] differ among themselves, as if they were inspired by different spirits of error. This very fact forms an a priori proof that the truth proclaimed by the Church is immovable and that the theories of these men are but a tissue of falsehoods" (*Against Heresies* 1.9.5). Or, as Tertullian somewhat more succinctly put it, "Where diversity of doctrine is found, there, then, must the corruption both of the Scriptures and the expositions thereof be regarded as existing" (*Prescription* 38).[10]

Sense and Nonsense

It was not simply the heretics' internal contradictions that were attacked, however; it was also their contradictions to what the proto-orthodox considered to be good sense and logic. Many of these contradictions involved the complicated myths underlying the views of different Gnostic groups. Before detailing some of these proto-orthodox objections, I should point out that some scholars have come to suspect that Gnostic Christians did not, in fact, treat their myths as literal descriptions of the past, in the way modern fundamentalist Christians might treat the opening chapters of Genesis. In the modern world, most *nonfundamentalist* Christian churches agree that Genesis contains mythical and legendary accounts; one scarcely has to believe in a literal six-day creation or in the existence of Adam and Eve as historical persons in order to belong to one of these communities. Gnostic Christians evidently took a similar approach to their own myths. Proto-orthodox heresiologists, however, interpreted the myths in a literalistic way, treating them as propositional statements about the past and then showing how ridiculous they are. This may have been a case where an attack was both completely off the mark and rhetorically convincing to an outside audience.

Simply recounting the myths at length, one after the other, can have the effect of making them appear absurd, and Irenaeus and his followers appear to have known it. How could such complex and involved descriptions of creation *possibly* be right? Moreover, as pointed out, one set of myths cannot be reconciled with another—assuming both contain "propositional" statements about what happened in the past. But the heresiologists did not stop with providing all the details, page after page. Instead they went on to pick the myths apart to show they could not be true. For example, in discussing the Valentinian Gnostic theogony (the account of how the divine realm came into being), Irenaeus observes that in one of the prominent myths, among the first group of aeons to emerge from the one true God were both Silence (Sige) and Word (Logos); but this doesn't make any sense, since once there is a word, there can be no more silence (*Against Heresies* 2.12.5). Or a second example, drawn from a multitude: In the account of how the cosmic disaster took place leading to the creation of the world, the twelfth aeon, Sophia (Wisdom), frustrated by her ignorance, attempts to understand the Father of All, overreaches herself, and falls. But this is nonsense, argues Irenaeus, since Wisdom, by its very nature, cannot be ignorant (*Against Heresies* 2.18.1).[11]

Some of the proto-orthodox objections to the logic of the heretical systems did not involve such minor details, but strove to get to the heart of the matter. Tertullian's five-volume attack against Marcion, for example, starts off by dealing directly with the question of whether it is logically possible to have two gods. Tertullian states the principle he will stand by: "God is not, if he is not one" (*Against Marcion* 3). Tertullian's logic is that for any theological discussion to take place, one must have an agreed upon definition of "God." Moreover, he indicates, everyone of conscience will acknowledge what that definition is: "God is the great Supreme existing in eternity, unbegotten, unmade, without beginning and without end." But once that is conceded (and Tertullian assumes, of course, that everyone will concede it, since otherwise they are not "of conscience"), there is an insurmountable difficulty with having more than one God. It is impossible to have *two* beings who are "Supreme" because if two of them exist, neither one is supreme. And if one of them is greater than the other, then that other one cannot be God, since it is not supreme. Tertullian goes on to argue that it will not do to argue that two gods could each be supreme in his own sphere (e.g., one be supreme in goodness and the other in justice), because that would mean that in the *overall* scheme of things, each god is only partially supreme; but God, to be God, must be completely supreme.

The failure or refusal of their heretical opponents to see logic occasionally drives the proto-orthodox heresiologists to sarcasm and mockery. Tertullian's quips in particular make for a lively read. Marcion's two gods, he indicates, come from his seeing double: "to men of diseased vision even one lamp looks like many" (*Against Marcion* 1.2). Physical realities disprove (the now dead) Marcion's views about being saved from the creator god: "In what respect do you suppose yourself liberated from his kingdom when his flies are still creeping upon your face?" (1.24). Marcion's phantom Christ is like Marcion's phantom intelligence: "You may, I assure you, more easily find a man born without a heart or without brains, like Marcion himself, than without a body, like Marcion's Christ" (4.1).

Truth and Error

A somewhat more substantial argument comes in the proto-orthodox claim that truth always precedes error. This argument comes in several guises. On the most basic level, the heresiologists point out that the distinctive viewpoints of each heresy were created by their founders: for example, Marcion, the founder of the Marcionites, Valentinus, the founder of the Valentinians, and for Tertullian, at least, Ebion, the founder of the Ebionites. But if these teachers were the first to propound the proper understanding of the truth of the gospel, what of all the Christians who lived before? Were they simply *wrong?* This makes no sense to the proto-orthodox. For them "truth precedes its copy, the likeness succeeds the reality" (Tertullian, *Prescription* 29).

Another way the argument was used involved a kind of "contamination" theory, sounded repeatedly throughout the proto-orthodox writings. In this view, the original truth of the Christian message came to be corrupted by foreign elements, which were secondarily added into it so as to alter it, sometimes beyond recognition. In particular, these authors were incensed by heretics who utilize Greek philosophy in order to explicate the true faith. Tertullian was especially aggravated:

> Indeed heresies are themselves instigated by philosophy. From this source come the [Gnostic] aeons, and I know not what infinite forms and the trinity of man [i.e., the tripartite division of humans as flesh, soul, and spirit, corresponding to people who are animal, "psychic," and spiritual] in the system of Valentinus, who was of Plato's school. From the same source came Marcion's better god, with all his tranquility; he came of the Stoics. (*Prescription*, 7)

Tertullian completely rejects the infusion of philosophy into the truth of the Christian gospel; as he famously asks, "What indeed has Athens to do with Jerusalem? What concord is there between the Academy and the Church? What between heretics and Christians?" (*Prescription*, 7).

Irenaeus too finds the use of philosophical notions reprehensible, and likens those who take "the things which have been said by all those who were ignorant of God, and who are termed philosophers," to those who "sew together a motley garment out of a heap of miserable rags," thereby "furnishing themselves a cloak that is really not their own" which in reality is "old and useless." If philosophy could reveal the truth about God, asks Irenaeus, what was the point of sending Christ into the world? (*Against Heresies* 2.14.6–7).

No one objected more strenuously to the "philosophical" element of heresy than Hippolytus of Rome, whose ten-volume *Refutation of All Heresies* is entirely devoted to showing that heresy derives from Greek philosophical traditions. The first four volumes of the book, in fact, discuss Greek philosophers on their own terms; the final six show how each and every known heresy borrows its leading ideas from them. To some readers this has seemed to be a bit of overkill, especially since Hippolytus (sticking with the metaphor of Irenaeus, above) had to tailor a number of the heresies to make them fit their reputed philosophical pattern.

The proto-orthodox heresiologists used one other aspect of contamination theory: the notion that, as time goes on, one heretic corrupts the already corrupted work of his predecessor, so that in heretical circles, the variations become wilder and the truth becomes more remote with the passing of time. This view of the progressive perversion of truth explains why the heresiologists are so invested in the genealogical roots of heresy. For Irenaeus and his successors, Simon Magus was the father of all heretics,[12] Simon was succeeded by Menander, who was followed by Saturninus and Basilides, and so on (see Irenaeus, *Against Heresies* 1.23ff.). According to this view, so creative are the heretics that none of them could be content simply with taking over the false system of his teacher; each has to corrupt the truth yet more in line with his own imagination. And so heresies begin popping up in wild and uncontrolled reproductions and permutations, many-headed hydra who sprout additional heads faster than they can be cut off.

This multiplicity of heretical views appears to have been frustrating for the heresiologists. On the other hand, they could rest in the assurance that they stood for the truth, once and for all delivered to the saints, the orthodoxy taught by Jesus to his disciples and passed along unchanged and unsullied to their own day.

The Apostolic Succession

As we have seen time and again, the claim for apostolic connections to the truth played a central role in the debates over heresy. The proto-orthodox had a variety of strategies for linking their views to those of the apostles. The most basic argument involved the "apostolic succession," seen already in a quite early form in 1 Clement. There the Roman church insisted that the Corinthians reinstate their deposed presbyters because the leaders of the churches (including these presbyters) had been appointed by bishops who had been handpicked by apostles who had been chosen by Christ who had been sent from God. To oppose the leaders of the churches, therefore, meant to oppose God (1 Clement 42–44).

In the hands of Tertullian, the notion of apostolic succession was developed in a somewhat different way, so that it referred not simply to the authorization of church offices but also to the authorization of church *teaching*. As Tertullian works it out, Christ commanded the apostles after the resurrection to preach his gospel to all the nations; they did so, establishing major churches throughout the world based on the same preaching of the same gospel in every place. These churches that the apostles established then sent forth missionaries to found yet other churches. "Therefore the churches, although they are so many and so great, comprise but the one primitive church, founded by the apostles, from which they all spring. In this way all are primitive, and all are apostolic" (*Prescription* 20). Tertullian's conclusion, then:

> From this, therefore, do we draw up our rule. Since the Lord Jesus Christ sent the apostles to preach, our rule is that no others ought to be received as preachers than those whom Christ appointed. . . . If, then, these things are so, it is in the same degree manifest that all doctrine which agrees with the apostolic churches . . . must be reckoned for truth, as undoubtedly containing that which the said churches received from the apostles, the apostles from Christ, Christ from God. (*Prescription* 21)

He goes on to name churches that can trace their direct lineage to apostles, although it is perhaps surprising and possibly telling that he names only two: Smyrna (whose bishop Polycarp was appointed by the apostle John) and Rome (whose bishop Clement was appointed by Peter). Still, he challenges the "heretics" to come up with *any* of their churches about which this could be said, and appears to be confident that none will be able to take up his challenge (ch. 32).

It seems like an effective argument. But it is worth noting that *other* groups besides the proto-orthodox could claim a direct lineage of their teaching straight back to the apostles. We know from Clement of Alexandria, for example, that Valentinus was a disciple of Theudas, who was allegedly a follower of Paul; and the Gnostic Basilides studied under Glaukia, a supposed disciple of Peter (*Miscellanies* 7,17,106). For the most part, these connections were simply discounted by the proto-orthodox.

The Rule of Faith and the Creeds

The proto-orthodox claim to represent the apostolic teaching eventuated in a set of doctrinal affirmations that expressed for them the true nature of the religion.

By the second century, before there were universal creeds to be said by all Christians everywhere, this body of belief came to be known as the *"regula fidei,"* literally, "the rule of faith." The regula included the basic and fundamental beliefs that, according to the proto-orthodox, all Christians were to subscribe to, as these had been taught by the apostles themselves. There are various proto-orthodox authors who propound the *regula fidei,* including Irenaeus and Tertullian, and it never achieved any kind of set form. But it was clearly directed in every case against those who opposed one or another aspect of it. Typically included in the various formulations of the regula was belief in only one God, the creator of the world, who created everything out of nothing; belief in his Son, Jesus Christ, predicted by the prophets and born of the Virgin Mary; belief in his miraculous life, death, resurrection, and ascension; and belief in the Holy Spirit, who is present on earth until the end, when there will be a final judgment in which the righteous will be rewarded and the unrighteous condemned to eternal torment (thus, e.g., Tertullian, *Prescription* 13).

Eventually, in addition to the *regula fidei* there developed Christian creeds to be recited, possibly, at the outset, by converts who had undergone a program in Christian education (catechesis), at the time of their baptism. The creeds may well have begun as a series of questions delivered and answered in three parts, in conformity with the threefold immersion under the water as suggested by Matthew 28:19–20: "Make disciples of all the nations, teaching all that I have commanded you and baptizing them in the name of the Father, the Son, and the Holy Spirit." The creeds then became tripartite, stressing proper doctrines about Father, Son, and Spirit. Like the *regula fidei,* they were directed against the improper doctrines espoused by other groups.

Eventually, by the fourth century, the creeds familiar to Christians still today had been developed in rudimentary form, most notably the Apostles' and Nicene Creeds. It is worth emphasizing that these are formulated against specific heretical views. Take the opening of the Nicene Creed, "We believe in one God, the Father, the Almighty, maker of heaven and earth, of all that is, seen and unseen. We believe in one Lord, Jesus Christ, the only Son of God." Throughout the history of Christian thought, such words have been not just meaningful but also deeply generative of serious theological reflection. At the same time we should recognize that they represent reactions against doctrinal claims made by groups of Christians who disagreed with them, Christians, for example, who believed there was more than one God, or that the true God was not the creator, or that Jesus was not the creator's son, or that Jesus Christ was not one being but two. It is especially worth noting that, as a result of the context of their formulation, many of the views espoused in these creeds are profoundly paradoxical. Is Christ God or Man? He is both. If he is both, is he two persons? No, he is the "one" Lord Jesus Christ. If Christ is God and his Father is God, are there two Gods? No. "We believe in *one* God."

The reason for the paradoxes should be clear from what we have seen. Proto-orthodox Christians were compelled to fight adoptionists on one side and docetists on the other, Marcion on one side and various kinds of Gnostics on the other. When one affirms that Jesus is divine, against the adoptionists, there is the problem of appearing to be a docetist. And so one must affirm that Jesus is human, against the docetists. But that could make one appear to be an adoptionist. The only solution, then, is to affirm both views at once: Jesus is divine and Jesus is human. And one must also deny the potentially heretical implications of both affirmations: Jesus is divine, but that does not mean he is not also human; Jesus is human, but that does not mean he is not also divine. And so he is divine and human, at one and the same time.

And thus the proto-orthodox paradoxical affirmations embodied in the creeds, about God who is the creator of all things, but not of the evil and suffering found in his creation; about Jesus who is both completely human and completely divine and not half of one or the other but both at once, who is nonetheless one being not two; about the Father, the Son, and the Spirit as three separate persons and yet comprising only one God.

The Interpretation of Scripture

A significant aspect of the proto-orthodox polemic against various heretics involved not just stressing the doctrines that were to be affirmed, but the interpretation of sacred texts on which these doctrines were based. There were, to be sure, disagreements over which books should be accepted as sacred, an issue we will be addressing in another chapter. But there was also the matter of how to interpret texts that had been accepted. This had been an issue from the beginning of Christianity, since Jesus and his followers, like Paul, quoted the Scriptures extensively and interpreted them in their teachings.

In the ancient world there was no more unanimity about how to interpret a text than there is today. Indeed, if the meaning of texts were self-evident, we would have no need of commentators, legal experts, literary critics, or theories of interpretation. We could all just read and understand. People may *think* that there is a commonsensical way to construe a text. But put a dozen people in a room with a text of Scripture, or of Shakespeare, or of the American Constitution, and see how many interpretations they produce.

It was no different in antiquity. Early on in the controversies over heresy and orthodoxy, people realized that having a sacred text is not the same thing as interpreting it. In order to reach unanimity about what a text meant, there needed to be certain textual constraints imposed from the outside, rules for reading, accepted practices of interpretation, modes of legitimation, and the like. The matter became increasingly important as different teachers from different theological persuasions interpreted the same texts in different ways, and then appealed to these texts in support of their points of view.

Marcion, to take a prominent example, insisted on a literal interpretation of the Old Testament, which led him to conclude that the God of the Old Testament was inferior to the true God. The Old Testament God, Marcion pointed out, did not know where to find Adam in the Garden of Eden, he was talked out of destroying Sodom and Gomorrah for a time, he ordered the destruction of all the innocent men, women, and children in Jericho, and he promised harsh measures against anyone who breaks his law. In other words, simply reading the Jewish Scriptures literally, the Jewish God was occasionally ignorant, indecisive, wrathful, and vengeful. For Marcion, this did not sound like the God of Jesus, and he could make the point simply by taking the text "at face value."

Marcion's proto-orthodox opponent, Tertullian, however, insisted that passages that speak of God's ignorance and emotions were not to be taken literally but figuratively. Since God could not *really* be ignorant or indecisive or mean-spirited, these passages needed to be interpreted in light of the full knowledge of what God really is like. Tertullian, in fact, interpreted a large number of passages in a figurative way, in order to illustrate his own understanding about God and Christ. To take just one example: There is an important passage in Leviticus 16 that describes two goats that are presented by the Jewish priests on the Day of Atonement. According to the text, one of these goats is to be driven out into the wilderness and the other is to be offered up as a sacrifice. The two goats, Tertullian tells us, refer to the two advents (i.e., appearances on earth) of Christ—the first time coming as one who is cursed (cast off into the wilderness), the next time (in his "second coming") providing salvation to those who belong to his spiritual temple (*Against Marcion* 3.7).

Or consider Irenaeus, who interprets the "clean and unclean" foods of the Law of Moses. The children of Israel are allowed to eat animals that have cloven hooves *and* that chew the cud, but not animals without cloven hooves or that do not chew the cud (Lev. 11:2; Deut. 14:3; etc.). What does this mean? For Irenaeus the passage indicates the kinds of people Christians are to associate with. Animals with cloven hooves are clean because they represent people who steadily advance toward God and his Son through faith (God + Son = cloven hoof). Animals who chew the cud but do not have cloven hoofs are unclean, representing the Jews who have the words of Scripture in their mouths but do not move steadily toward the knowledge of God (*Against Heresies* 5.8.4).

By preferring a figurative interpretation in places, Tertullian and Irenaeus were following solid precedent among their proto-orthodox forebears. You may recall Barnabas's extensive use of figurative interpretations in order to attack Jews for keeping the literal meaning of their laws.

On other occasions, however, when proto-orthodox writers faced opponents like certain Gnostics, who interpreted Scripture figuratively, they vehemently insisted that only a literal interpretation of the text would do. Irenaeus in particular objects to Gnostic modes of figurative interpretation used to support their points of view, and gives specific instances. For example, Gnostics who believed in thirty divine aeons appealed to the claim of the Gospel of Luke that Jesus started his ministry when he was thirty years of age, and to the parable of the vineyard, where the owner hired workers at the first, third, sixth, ninth, and eleventh hour (which add up to thirty). They also maintained that these thirty aeons were divided into three groups, the final one consisting of twelve aeons, the twelfth of which was Sophia, the aeon who fell from the divine realm, leading to the creation of the universe. This notion of Sophia (Greek for Wisdom), the twelfth aeon, is evidenced in Jesus' appearance in the Temple as a twelve-year-old confronting the teachers of the law (showing forth his "wisdom"), and by the fact that Judas Iscariot, the twelfth of the disciples, fell away to become a betrayer (see *Against Heresies* 2,20–26).

Irenaeus considered these interpretations ludicrous. In his view, Gnostics were simply making texts mean what they wanted them to mean, and ignoring the "clear and plain" teachings of the text, which, for Irenaeus, included the view that there is only one God, who is the good creator of a good creation, which has been marred not by the fall of a divine aeon but by the sin of a human. In a harsh but effective image, Irenaeus likened the capricious use of Scripture among the Gnostics to a person who, observing a beautiful mosaic of a king, decides to dismantle the precious stones and reassemble them in the likeness of a mongrel dog, claiming that this was what the artist intended all along (*Against Heresies* 1.8).

To modern observers of these ancient debates, it may seem to be a problem that the proto-orthodox insisted on literal interpretations of the text, while appealing to figurative interpretations when it suited their own purposes. Still, it is probably fair to say that for these proto-orthodox authors, *literal* interpretations of the text were to be primary, and that figurative interpretations were to be used only to support views established on literal grounds. This was true even of the most famous proto-orthodox allegorist of them all, Origen of Alexandria, who was remarkably adept at supplying deep and rich figurative interpretations of Scripture, but who insisted that the methods were to be applied only when the literal meanings of the text appeared hopelessly contradictory or absurd (Origen, *On First Principles,* bk. 4).

In any event, whether or not the insistence on the primacy of a literal interpretation struck Gnostics as convincing, they did carry a kind of probative force for others in the debates, especially proto-orthodox sympathizers. For them, Scripture was to be interpreted following literal methods of interpretation, that is to say, letting the words say what they normally mean, and following widely accepted practices of grammatical construction. When they are so interpreted, the words yield the meaning of the author. And since these authors were all thought to be apostles, this kind of interpretive practice can reveal the apostolic teaching delivered once and for all to the churches that stand within the orthodox tradition of Jesus.

Charges of Reprobate Activity

Of all the weapons in the proto-orthodox literary arsenal, one was particularly barbed. The heretics, we are constantly told, not only corrupt the truth and the Scripture but they also corrupt other people and are themselves corrupt. The heresiologists insist that their opponents are morally reprehensible and sexually perverse. And their foul practices threaten the church, as they take the innocent and defile them.

Eusebius's claim, seen already, that Simon Magus and his followers engaged in activities "more disgusting than the foulest crime known" is typical of these charges. Irenaeus, for example, says that the Gnostic followers of Valentinus instruct those who possess the divine seed (i.e., Gnostics with a spark of the divine within) to give their spirit to spiritual things and their flesh to fleshly things, making indiscriminate copulation not only permissible but a *desideratum* for those who are truly spiritual (*Against Heresies* 1,6,3–4); that the Carpocratians—whom we met in conjunction with Secret Mark[13]—practice indiscriminate sex, indeed, that their theology compels them to violate every conceivable moral law and ethical norm so as to avoid being reincarnated time and again (since they must experience all things before attaining salvation; 1,25,4); and that the heretic Marcus excites attractive women by inspiring them to speak prophecies, after which they become putty in his lascivious hands (1,13,3).

In making such charges Irenaeus appears to be applying heresiological techniques already found as early as the writings of the New Testament. Consider, for example, the small epistle of Jude, which opposes deviant Christians (we are never told what these people actually believed or taught—just that they are reprehensible) by indicating that they are licentious (v. 4), indulge in unnatural lust (v. 7), corrupt the flesh (v. 8), carouse together (v. 12), and follow ungodly passions (v. 18). As one commentator has pointed out, it seems hard to imagine that such wild folk could catch a congregation unawares (v. 4), making it appear that the author of this letter is himself falling back on traditional rhetoric to attack his unnamed opponents.[14]

Lying behind such slurs is the notion that those who side with God will lead moral, upright lives and be unwilling to do anything to defile themselves or others. The champions of the proto-orthodox cause are the martyrs, willing to bear the tortures of the flesh rather than do anything in violation of God's holy laws. How stark a contrast to the reprobates found among the heretics, especially the Gnostics who come in for the lion's share of the polemic—probably unfairly, given the ascetic lifestyles that they themselves appear to have endorsed.

And yet the charges of immorality continued for as long as there were orthodox polemicists to make them. They continue today, among Christian groups inclined to accuse others of heresy. Often their false teachings are said to be matched by their promiscuous lives.

Possibly the most shocking instance from the ancient world occurs near the end of the fourth century in the writings of Epiphanius, in his discussion of a group of Gnostics called (among other things) the Phibionites. It is an intriguing account in no small measure because Epiphanius claims to have known members of the group and to have read their writings. In Book 26 of his *Panarion* (Medicine Chest), Epiphanius outlines the beliefs of this group and, in shocking detail, describes their orgiastic and cannibalistic practices. The stunning detail has made scholars wonder: Could this account possibly be true? It may be worth our while to consider Epiphanius's polemic in detail, as an extreme instance of the orthodox penchant for maligning the character of their heretical opponents.[15]

Epiphanius claims that the Phibionites indulge in sumptuous feasts that begin with a special greeting: The men shake hands with the women, secretly tickling or stroking their palms underneath (*Pan.* 26.4.2). His description of this entrance ritual may be deliberately ambiguous: It has been read both as an erotic gesture and as a code designed to alert members to the presence of outsiders. But it is only after the company is sated with food and drink that the real festivities begin. Married couples separate to engage in a liturgy of sexual intercourse, each with another member of the community (*Pan.* 26.4.4). The union is not meant to be consummated, however, for the man withdraws before climax. The couple then collects his semen in their hands and ingests it together while proclaiming, "This is the body of Christ." When possible, the couple also collects and consumes the woman's menstrual blood, saying "This is the blood of Christ" (*Pan.* 26.4.5–8). If for some reason the woman becomes pregnant, the fetus is allowed to develop until it can be manually aborted. Then, claims Epiphanius, it is dismembered, covered with honey and spices, and devoured by the community as a special Eucharistic meal (*Pan.* 26.5.4–6).

The leaders of the group who have already attained perfection no longer require women for these festive occasions. They indulge in homosexual relations with one another (*Pan.* 26.11. 8). Furthermore, Epiphanius informs us, members of the group engage in sacred masturbation. They can then consume the body of Christ in the privacy of their own room (26.11.1). This practice is reportedly justified by an appeal to Scripture: "Working with your own hands, that you may have something to give also to those in need" (cf. Eph. 4:28).

It is clear from Epiphanius's account that these proceedings are not at all unrelated to the Phibionites' understanding of the cosmos and their liberation from it. They are said to subscribe to the notion, found among other Gnostic groups as well, that this world is separated from the divine realm by 365 heavens, each with its own ruling archon. Just as the divine redeemer who brought the secret knowledge of salvation into the world descended through all 365 heavens and then reascended, so too the redeemed must pass by all the archons, twice. The journey is foreshadowed here on earth through a kind of empathy, as the man, during the course of the sex liturgy, calls out the secret name of one of the ruling archons, effecting a kind of identification with him that allows for safe passage through his realm. Since each archon must be passed by twice, as Epiphanius is quick to point out, each of the Phibionite men can expect to seduce female devotees on at least 730 occasions.

The connections between these alleged practices and the Phibionites' theology are not restricted to the notion of an ascent through the heavenly realms.

As Epiphanius himself suggests, they relate equally to the basic Gnostic notion that the divine seed has been implanted in humans and needs to be liberated from this material world. The goal of human existence is to return to the divine realm, a return made possible only by the reunification of the divine seeds that are currently scattered throughout the world. Since the seed is passed on through the bodily fluids, that is, the man's semen and the woman's blood, these are to be collected and consumed, effecting the requisite reunification. When, however, the seed is left inside the woman, it develops into another human being, who represents then yet another entrapped particle of the divine. While procreation therefore defeats the goal of existence and leads to further entrapment and bondage, the ritualistic ingestion of semen and menses, or of fetuses, provides liberation.

Can this tale of unbridled lust and ritual cannibalism be true? As a rule, in most of his polemical attacks on heretics, Ephiphanius has to be treated with a healthy dose of skepticism. He constantly exaggerates, he invents connections between historical events that we otherwise know are unrelated, and he explicitly claims that his horrific accounts (there are others) are designed to repulse his readers from the heresies he describes (*Pan.* Proem 1.2). But a number of scholars have believed his account of the Phibionites, in part because he claims to have been personally acquainted with the sect. As a young man in Egypt he encountered two Phibionite women who tried to convert him to their group. His description of this encounter—written long after the fact—is intriguing, in no small measure because it is couched in sexual terms. The women were attractive and attempted to seduce him. After learning something of their beliefs, however, Epiphanius successfully repelled their advances (*Pan.* 26,17). He also indicates, as we have seen, that he then acquired and read a number of their writings, so that he could discuss their teachings from their own Scriptures.

Aside from any general skepticism on our part, are there any particular reasons to question the reliability of Epiphanius's account of the Phibionites' sacred festivities?

The place to begin is with Epiphanius's sources. I don't think anyone doubts that as a young man Epiphanius had personal contacts with members of the group. He explicitly recounts the advances of his two "seductresses," and there seems to be little reason to think that he made up the story, so far as it goes. On the other hand, this surely cannot be taken as some kind of warrant for the accuracy of his report concerning the group's private sex rituals. Epiphanius never says that he actually participated in or even witnessed any of the group's activities as a young man. Quite the contrary, he explicitly states that he spurned these women *before* they had enticed him into joining the sect. Among other things, this must mean that he was never admitted to the festivities. And it goes without saying that ceremonies of this kind would not have been open to the public.

Nor can we think that the women had actually divulged to him what the group was doing behind closed doors. Epiphanius does say that they told him about their group (*Pan.* 26,18,2). But he is remarkably vague concerning *what* they told him, and he does *not* indicate that they revealed to him their secret rituals. And it seems implausible that these illicit proceedings would have been explained to potential converts during the preliminary stages of their acquaintance with the group. Even if the group did engage in such activities, they must have been kept secret to all but the initiates. And Epiphanius tells us in unequivocal terms that he spurned the group long before he would have been admitted as an initiate (26.17.5–7).

Is it possible then that Epiphanius had uncovered descriptions of the Phibionite rituals in the group's sacred books? He clearly had read a good deal of their literature. He discusses several of their works throughout his treatment and quotes a number of their teachings.[16] But he never claims that he found the group's orgiastic and cannibalistic practices described in them. And it stretches all credulity to think that they could have been: These books could hardly have been "how-to manuals." Nor would such literature have been publicly available at the local bookstall.

Given the problems posed by Epiphanius's alleged sources, we do well to consider why he names them in the first place. In fact, as should be self-evident, his encounter with members of the group and his ability to refer to some of their writings serve to authenticate his description—not only of their beliefs but also of their bizarre practices. This authentication has proved remarkably successful. Even down to our own day his readers have accepted the report as trustworthy—disregarding the fact that he never says that he actually saw any of these things take place or even found them prescribed in the Phibionites' own books. But it appears that Epiphanius made up his accounts of the lascivious Phibionites, possibly creating bizarre ritual activities based on what he knew of their theological beliefs.

In this connection I should perhaps stress once again that since the discovery of the Nag Hammadi library we have been able to study the actual writings of a bewildering variety of Gnostic Christians. And far from condoning, let alone promoting, such outlandish moral behavior, these writings urge and assume just the contrary social and personal ethics. One of the few constants among all the Nag Hammadi tractates is their ascetic orientation. Gnostic Christians appear to have believed, as a rule, in punishing the body, not indulging it. Apparently then, Gnostics were consistently attacked by orthodox Christians as sexually perverse, not because they actually were perverse but because they were the enemy.

And so the struggles for dominance in early Christianity were in no small measure carried out on literary battlefields. We have seen some of the important ploys used in the directly polemical literature of the period, most of it surviving from the proto-orthodox camp, although some remnants of the opposing forces are still, now, in clear evidence.

Literature was used for more than direct assault, however. There were also indirect polemics, seen for example, in the forgery of apostolic authorities to support one point of view over another, in the falsification of existing texts in order to make them more clearly attest a cherished perspective or to prevent their "misuse" by those taking alternative sides, and in the collection of sacred texts into an authoritative canon of Scripture to be revered and followed by all those who subscribe to the true faith. It is these other less directly polemical ploys that we will consider in the chapters that follow.

Chapter Ten

Additional Weapons in the Polemical Arsenal: Forgeries and Falsifications

One of the distinctive features of early Christianity, in all its guises, was its literary character. Literature served to provide sacred authority for Christian belief and practice, to defend the religion against its cultured despisers, to unite local communities of believers into a worldwide church, to encourage the faithful in their time of suffering, to instruct them how to live, to entertain them with accounts of heroes of the faith, and to warn them against enemies within, promoting some forms of the faith and denouncing others. With the partial exception of Judaism, no other religion of the Roman Empire was so rooted in literary texts.

This is not to say that Christians were necessarily more literate than other people. It is extremely difficult to gauge levels of literacy in antiquity, but the most persuasive estimates for the Greco-Roman world put the rates at around 10 to 15 percent of the populace in the best of times and places (e.g., in fifth-century BCE Athens).[1] The rates may well have been toward the lower or middle end of that range during the second and third Christian centuries. Moreover, if the pagan authors who attacked Christianity can be believed (their Christian respondents conceded the point), the majority of Christians came from the lower uneducated classes. So possibly the literacy rates among Christians were even lower than in the wider population. That, however, has little bearing on the question of the importance of literature for the movement, since in the ancient world, literature was meant to be read aloud, and "reading" a book most often meant "hearing" the book read by someone else who was literate. For Christians this would have happened all the time and in all sorts of social settings: church worship services, education "classes," social gatherings, and in the home.[2]

Given the literary nature of the religion, it is no surprise that a good deal of the conflict among competing understandings of the faith occurred in writing, with polemical treatises, sacred texts, legendary tales, forged documents, and

fabricated accounts all having their role to play. We have seen already the polemical arguments back and forth, with remnants of what must have once been
substantial Jewish-Christian and Gnostic attacks on proto-orthodox Christians,
and still more substantial attacks from the winning side, the proto-orthodox, on
heretical opponents of various kinds. To some extent we have also seen how
forgeries were important in the back and forth. But to this point we have focused principally on "heretical" forgeries, for example, in the Gospels of Thomas, Peter, Philip, and Mary, the Coptic Apocalypse of Peter, the letter of Peter
to James, and the Pseudo-Clementine literature.

Proto-orthodox Christians commonly charged heretical groups with forging just such writings in the names of apostles and companions of the apostles.
Representatives of these other groups no doubt returned the compliment, charg-
ing the proto-orthodox with creating forged documents of their own. Unfortunately, as we have noted time and again, most of the polemical claims of these
other groups have been lost. But there certainly would have been grounds for
the charge, as the practice of forgery was widespread on all sides, and not least
the proto-orthodox.

It should be stressed at the outset, however, that proto-orthodox forgeries
(or heretical forgeries, for that matter) were not produced only for theological
reasons, pure and simple. Early Christians, of every stripe, were interested in
far more than doctrine. Some of the surviving forged documents betray these
other interests. Occasionally this makes it difficult to determine the identity
and theological affiliation of the forger. This is true for some of the most intriguing forgeries we have.

Forgeries with Nontheological Agenda

As an example, we may consider a noncanonical Gospel that deals with a period in Jesus' existence passed over, for the most part, by the canonical texts.
The New Testament Gospels present only a few stories relating to Jesus' young
life, for example, Matthew's account of the worship of the magi and the flight
to Egypt and Luke's story of Jesus' visit to the Temple as a twelve-year-old.
After the New Testament Gospels were written, however—and possibly earlier, although we have no hard evidence—Christians began telling stories about
Jesus as a child. We are fortunate that later authors collected some of these
stories into written texts, the so-called Infancy Gospels, which began to appear
in the first half of the second century.[3] For the most part, the legendary character of these fictions is easily detected.

One of the earliest is called the Infancy Gospel of Thomas (not to be confused
with the Coptic Gospel of Thomas discovered near Nag Hammadi),[4] an entertaining account of Jesus' activities starting at the tender age of five. Behind the
narrative lies a question that intrigues some Christians even today: "If Jesus was
a miracle-working Son of God as an adult, what was he like as a child?"

The narrative opens with the young Jesus playing by the ford of a stream. Taking some clay, he models twelve sparrows. But, we are told, it was a Sabbath when he did this. A Jewish man passing by sees what Jesus has done and hurries off to tell his father, Joseph, that his son has profaned the Sabbath (by "making" things). Joseph comes and upbraids Jesus for violating the Law. Instead of apologizing or repenting for a sin, Jesus claps his hands and cries to the sparrows, "Be gone!" They immediately come to life and fly off chirping.

This opening story is indicative of much to come in the narrative: Jesus cannot be faulted for breaking the Sabbath (he has effectively destroyed all evidence of malfeasance!), and already as a young child he is seen as the author of life, not bound to human rules and regulations.

One might have expected that with such supernatural powers, Jesus would have been a useful and entertaining playmate for the other kids in town. As it turns out, however, the boy has a temper and is not to be crossed. When another child accidentally runs into him on the street, Jesus turns in anger and declares, "You shall go no further on your way." The child falls down dead. (Jesus later raises him from the dead, along with others that he curses on one occasion or another.) And Jesus' wrath is not reserved for other children. Joseph sends him to school to learn to read, but Jesus refuses to recite the (Greek) alphabet. His teacher pleads with him to cooperate, until Jesus replies with a scornful challenge, "If you really are a teacher and know the letters well, tell me the power of Alpha and I'll tell you the power of Beta." More than a little perturbed, the teacher cuffs the boy on the head, the single largest mistake of an illustrious teaching career. Jesus withers him on the spot. Joseph is stricken with grief and gives an urgent order to his mother: "Do not let him go outside. Anyone who makes him angry dies."

As time goes on, however, Jesus begins using his powers for good—saving his brother from a deadly snake bite, healing the sick, and proving remarkably handy around the house: When Joseph miscuts a board and is in danger of losing an important customer, Jesus performs a miracle to correct the mistake. The account concludes with Jesus as a twelve-year-old in the Temple, surrounded by scribes and Pharisees who hear him teach and who bless Mary for the wonderful child she has brought into the world.

The proto-orthodox church father Irenaeus claimed that this Infancy Gospel of Thomas was forged by a group of Gnostics he calls Marcosians, who, he says, "adduce an unspeakable number of apocryphal and spurious writings, which they themselves have forged, to bewilder the minds of foolish people" (*Against Heresies* 1,20,1). He goes on to relate "that false and wicked story" in which the young Jesus confounds his teacher about the nature of the Alpha and the Beta. For Irenaeus, the account ties into the Marcosians' love of numbers and letters, which they adduced in order to support their heretical understandings of the divine realm. In support of this view, one might argue that since Jesus shows up his learned teachers (on two additional occasions to the one I've summarized), the book is portraying him as one with superior "gnosis."

On the other hand, there is nothing particularly Gnostic about this text: Jesus is a real child here, who feels pain, for example, when his father yanks his ear in anger. Indeed, the text as a whole does not appear to promote a theological agenda of any particular branch of Christianity—Gnostic, proto-orthodox, or otherwise. It is probably better to think of it as a forgery in the name of Jesus' reputed brother, Thomas, derived simply from Christian imagination, a set of entertaining episodes that explore what the miracle-working Son of God may have been like as a child growing up in the household of Joseph and Mary.

A second example of a "nontheological" forgery involves a set of letters allegedly written to and from the apostle Paul, letters that became quite famous in the Middle Ages. Paul's alleged correspondent in these letters was none other than the great Roman philosopher, Seneca. The historical Paul, of course, did not know Seneca, who ran in much higher circles: He was tutor and then political advisor to the emperor Nero and the highly prolific author of moral essays, philosophical tractates, poetical works, and scientific treatises.

At a later time (possibly the fourth century) Christians were puzzled that the important figures in their religion, especially Jesus and Paul, were completely unknown to the major political and intellectual leaders of their day (as it turns out, neither of them is ever mentioned by any Roman author of the first century). The forged correspondence between Paul and Seneca works to redress this situation.

Fourteen letters survive, eight allegedly from Seneca to Paul and six from Paul to Seneca. In them, Seneca and Paul are portrayed as close companions, with Seneca expressing admiration and astonishment at Paul's brilliance and learning. In return, Paul is depicted as a teacher who has convinced Seneca of the truth of the Christian message. Early on in the correspondence Seneca praises the superiority of Paul's thoughts: "They are so lofty and so brilliant with noble sentiments that in my opinion generations of men could hardly be enough to become established and perfected in them" (Letter 1).[5] High praise from the greatest philosopher of Paul's day. More than that, Seneca indicates that he has read Paul's writings to the emperor Nero himself, who is astounded and moved by Paul's understanding of the truth: "[The emperor] was affected by your sentiments. . . . He was amazed that one whose education had not been normal [i.e., who was not highly trained] could have such ideas" (Letter 7).

Several references in these letters provide verisimilitude for their claims to authenticity—a common ploy among forgers. In particular, Seneca refers to the fire in Rome which, according to the Roman historian Tacitus, Nero himself had started in order to destroy part of the city so as to allow him to implement his own architectural plans, blaming the Christians, then, to avoid suspicion: "That ruffian, whoever he is [this is an attempt at tact], whose pleasure is murdering and whose refuge is lying is destined for his day of reckoning, and just as the best is sacrificed as one life for many, so he shall be sacrificed for all and burned by fire" (Letter 11).

The overarching points of these forged letters, however, are to show that Paul was known and acknowledged by one of the greatest and most influential thinkers of his day, that his views in fact were superior to the pagan philosophical traditions, and that his influence reached to the upper echelons of Roman power and authority. As they appear to have been forged sometime during the fourth century, their real author obviously did not adhere to any of the forms of lost Christianity we have been discussing, but just as obviously, his forgery is not designed to win a theological argument. Sometimes forgers had other incentives.

Forgeries Against the Heretics

There are numerous other instances of proto-orthodox forgery, however, in which the deceit served clear polemical purposes, in opposing "false" understandings of the religion and promoting the cause of proto-orthodoxy. To take an example drawn from the noncanonical Gospels, we might consider a book that was arguably as important to the piety and art of the Middle Ages as anything that became part of the canon, the Proto-Gospel of James.[6] The book is called a "proto-Gospel" because it narrates events prior to and leading up to Jesus' birth and infancy. In fact, it is for the most part an account of the birth, upbringing, and young adulthood of Jesus' mother, Mary, designed to show how she was chosen by God as a worthy vessel to bear his Son.[7]

According to this account, Mary herself was born supernaturally, in a way very similar to and modeled on the account of the birth of the prophet Samuel in the Hebrew Bible (1 Samuel 1–2). In the opening story of the narrative, her mother, Anna (cf. Samuel's mother, Hannah), cannot bear a child. But after she and her husband, Joachim, mourn and pray to the Lord, he answers their prayer and allows her to conceive. Overjoyed by the good news, Anna gives birth to a girl, names her Mary, and dedicates her to a life of service to God. As an infant, Mary is kept from any corrupting influences of daily life, as Anna builds a kind of sanctuary for her in her bedroom, and there she stays. Then, when Mary turns three, in fulfillment of Anna's vow of dedication, she is taken to live in the Temple in Jerusalem. There Mary grows up, raised in absolute purity, fed every day by the hand of an angel.

When she turns twelve, the priests are concerned that she might defile the Temple, presumably by beginning her menstruation cycle. They decide to give her in marriage to a widower in the land of Israel. At the bidding of the high priest, every prospective man comes to a specially called meeting, and God reveals that Mary is to be given to Joseph, an elderly widower who has grown children and who is reluctant to accept the assignment.[8]

Joseph is meant to keep Mary chaste, and so he does. As soon as they arrive home, he immediately leaves for an extended trip to tend to some building projects. In his absence, Mary conceives by the Holy Spirit, much to Joseph's

The Birth of Mary, as described in the Proto-Gospel of James, by Giotto di Bondone
(1266–1336). Scrovegni Chapel, Padua, Italy.

shock and horror when he returns. Still, God convinces both him and the Jewish priests (who understandably suspect that one of them has engaged in illicit
activities) that Mary is still a virgin.

The story continues with the account of Joseph and Mary making a trip to
Bethlehem to register for a census. But en route, Mary's birth pangs come
upon her, and she is forced to come off the donkey and give birth. Joseph
quickly finds a grotto outside of town, leaves her in the care of his sons, and
goes off to try to find a midwife to deliver the child.

Then comes a remarkable scene, narrated in the first person, of how time
stood still when the Son of God appeared in the world:

> But I, Joseph, was walking, and I was not walking. I looked up into the air, and
> I saw the air greatly disturbed. I looked up to the vault of the sky, and I saw it
> standing still; and the birds of the sky were at rest. I looked back to the earth and
> saw a bowl laid out for some workers who were reclining to eat. Their hands
> were in the bowl, but those who were chewing were not chewing; and those

who were taking something from the bowl were not lifting it up; and those who were bringing their hands to their mouths were not bringing them to their mouths. And everyone was looking up. And behold, a flock of sheep was being herded; yet they did not move forward but were standing still; and the shepherd raised his hand to strike them with his staff, but his hand remained in the air. I looked down at the torrential stream, and I saw some goats whose mouths were over it, but they were not drinking. Then suddenly everything returned to its normal course. (Proto-Gospel of James 18)

An even more remarkable scene follows. Joseph locates a midwife, who comes to the cave and sees a bright cloud overshadowing it and then a child appear. Realizing that this has been a miraculous "birth," the midwife rushes out and finds a companion, another midwife, named Salome, and informs her: "Salome, Salome, I can describe a new wonder to you. A virgin has given birth, contrary to her natural condition." Salome, however, refuses to take her friend's word for it. The only way to know for certain—this is a very peculiar moment— is to give Mary a postpartum inspection. And so Salome says: "As the Lord my God lives, if I do not insert my finger and examine her condition, I will not believe that a virgin has given birth."

Salome has committed a serious error in judgment; one should never distrust miracles of the Lord. As soon as she inserts her finger to see if Mary is still intact, her hand begins to burn as if it had caught fire. She kneels before the infant Jesus and prays, "O God of my fathers, remember that I am a descendant of Abraham, Isaac, and Jacob. Do not make me up an example to the sons of Israel, but deliver me over to the poor. For you know, O Master, that I have performed my services in your name and have received my wages from you" (Proto-Gospel of James, 20). An angel appears and tells Salome to pick up the child; she does so, and her hand is healed.

The account continues by describing the visit of the wise men; the destruction of all the babies of Bethlehem by Herod the Great; the miraculous escape by Jesus' cousin, the infant John (the Baptist), and his mother, Elizabeth, who are both swallowed up by a mountain to keep them from the soldiers' grasp; and the murder of John's father, Zacharias, in the Temple. It ends with a comment by the alleged author, who claims to be "James."

And who is James? It is the brother of Jesus himself (see Gal. 1:19). Who would know better about Jesus' family history and birth than his (step) brother? The real author, however, was probably living in the second half of the second century. Clearly he had theological concerns, compatible with a proto-orthodox agenda. Jesus here is portrayed as the Son of God at birth—in contrast, say, to the views of the Marcionite Christians, who claimed that Jesus descended from heaven as a full-grown but phantasmal adult at the start of his ministry. And here Jesus is born of a virgin, in contrast, say, to the views of the Ebionite Christians, who believed he was the natural son of Joseph and Mary. In fact, in this text, Mary not only conceives as a virgin; she remains a virgin (i.e., physically intact) even after giving birth, as Salome learns in such unambiguous terms. The perpetual virginity of Mary became an important doctrine in later Christianity, intimately related to the doctrine of her own "assumption," that is, her ascent into heaven without dying, made possible by the circumstance that she had never sinned—for example, by having sex.

Moreover, as a result of her perpetual virginity, the "brothers" of Jesus, who are also mentioned in the New Testament Gospels (e.g., Mark 6, John 7), are portrayed here not as his actual brothers, born of Joseph and Mary. They are Joseph's children from a previous marriage. This view created problems for the reception of the Proto-Gospel of James in the fourth century, as the greatest Christian scholar of the period, Jerome, insisted that James, Jude, and the others were not in fact Jesus' stepbrothers but his cousins. Jerome's opposition to this Gospel account was enough to limit its influence on Western, Latin-speaking Christianity.[9] But it continued to enjoy popularity in eastern Christendom, as evidenced by the abundant number of Greek manuscripts that preserve it (there are over a hundred) and by its influence on Christian art.

A second example of a proto-orthodox forgery produced in order to counter heretical views may be found in another letter allegedly from Paul, but this one (unlike the correspondence with Seneca) focused on doctrinal concerns. The letter is embedded in the Acts of Paul as a response to questions that the Christians of Corinth allegedly raised, in a letter also forged for the occasion. Paul's reply is commonly known as 3 Corinthians.[10]

Readers of the New Testament are familiar with 1 and 2 Corinthians, but most people have never heard of 3 Corinthians. The book is nonetheless preserved in a number of ancient manuscripts of the New Testament and was eventually accepted as part of the canon by Armenian and some early Syrian Christians. In some ways, 3 Corinthians continues the conversation between Paul and the Corinthians found in the canonical letters. As we have seen, the church in Corinth had encountered some severe difficulties soon after Paul had founded it, and Paul's authentic letters reflect these problems. The community was experiencing serious disunity among its members, to the extent that some were taking others to court over their differences. There was chaos in the worship services, including their periodic communal meals, at which some members were gorging themselves and getting drunk while others had almost nothing to eat and drink. There were instances of gross immorality, including some men in the church visiting prostitutes and bragging about it in church and one other man living with his stepmother. And several genuine questions had arisen concerning proper behavior in this world: Is it right, for example, to eat meat that had already been sacrificed to pagan idols? And if bodily pleasure is to be restricted, is it permissible to have sex with your spouse? Presumably the latter question was not being asked by the men who were consorting with prostitutes.[11]

The biggest problem in Corinth, however, was one that Paul chose to deal with at the end of his first letter: There were people in the congregation who did not understand, accept, or believe that there was to be a future resurrection of the fleshly body. According to them, the resurrection was a spiritual event that had already occurred for believers, presumably at their baptism. These believers, therefore, claimed already to be living a spiritual existence, transcending the needs and restrictions placed on their bodies. This was the major problem in the community, and it lay at the root of all the others. It explains why they were disunified (different Christians were trying to show their spiritual superiority) and how they could justify their immoral behavior (if the body doesn't matter, then it doesn't matter what you do with your body). In 1 Corinthians, however, Paul stresses that salvation is not yet complete but is still future. Salvation will come when Jesus returns to redeem this body by raising it from mortality to immortality (1 Corinthians 15). Eternal life, therefore, will be a bodily, not just a spiritual, existence. As a result, it *does* matter what one does with the body, both the individual body of the believer and the collective body of the church.[12]

Some of these same problems are evident in the later forged correspondence of 3 Corinthians as well. As I indicated, the letter is introduced in the Acts of Paul by a letter allegedly from the Corinthians to Paul. The Corinthians write that they have been disturbed by the teachings of two teachers, Simon and Cleobius, who maintain that the Old Testament prophets are not valid, that the God of this world is not the true God, that the true God did not create humans, that there is no future resurrection of the flesh, that Jesus was not really flesh and blood, and that he was not really born of Mary. In other words, these alleged opponents are some kind of docetist, like Marcion or possibly some kind of Gnostic.

But for early proto-orthodox Christians, including the forger of 3 Corinthians, it was important to think not only that God created this material world but also that he would redeem it, along with everything in it, including the human body. The body would therefore be raised from the dead, not left to corrupt. 3 Corinthians deals with the heretical claims of Simon and Cleobius one by one. "Paul" here insists that Jesus really was born of Mary, that he was truly a flesh and blood human, and that God was the creator of all there is, who sent the Jewish prophets and then Jesus in order to overcome the devil, who had corrupted the flesh.

For I delivered to you first of all what I received from the apostles before me who were always with Jesus Christ, that our Lord Jesus Christ was born of Mary of the seed of David, the Father having sent the Spirit from heaven into her that he might come into this world and save all flesh by his own flesh and that he might raise us in the flesh from the dead. . . . For the almighty God, maker of heaven and earth, sent the prophets first to the Jews to deliver them from their sins. . . . [Those] who assert that heaven and earth and all that is in them are not a work of God . . . have the accursed belief of the serpent. . . . And those who say that there is no resurrection of the flesh shall have no resurrection. Whoever deviates from this rule, fire shall be for him and for those who preceded him, since they are Godless people, a generation of vipers." (3 Cor. 4–9, 24–25, 37–38)[13]

Here then, we have a proto-orthodox forgery created precisely in order to counter the views of "heretical" teachers of the second century.

More Subtle Proto-orthodox Forgeries

Other proto-orthodox forgeries served a similar end, but they achieved it by more subtle means.

It is probably safe to say that most of the Apocryphal Acts were written not to advance any particular theological agenda but for other reasons, for example, to provide entertaining tales of the heroes of the faith for some Christian light reading, or to promote a certain view of asceticism (e.g., the Acts of Thomas), especially among Christian women (e.g., the Acts of Thecla). But some of these tales do function to support a proto-orthodox doctrinal position, none more clearly than the episodic record of the adventures of Jesus' chief disciple in the Acts of Peter.

These tales, like those of the other Apocryphal Acts, may have originated as oral traditions about Jesus' disciples; possibly they were written down near the end of the second century or the beginning of the third. In them we find a plotline similar to that already encountered in the Pseudo-Clementine literature, for here, too, there is an ongoing set of confrontations between Peter, head of the apostolic band and faithful representative of the Lord Christ, and that nefarious father of heretics, Simon Magus. In this instance, however, Simon does not appear to be some kind of cipher for the apostle Paul; here he is the man of evil himself, the original Gnostic, from whom, according to this author, flowed villainy of every kind. The doctrinal function of these confrontations is clear: The representative of proto-orthodoxy, Peter, eventually bishop of the church of Rome, is shown to be superior in every way to Simon, father of the Gnostics. This superiority is demonstrated in numerous miracle-working contests throughout the narrative. In these tales, the good guys always win, and the truth is vindicated by their acts of power.

A good portion of the text, then, narrates a series of miraculous one-upmanship, sometimes as the apostle and the heretic go head to head. And the stakes are rather high. At one point the entire Roman Senate gathers in the arena, with Peter and Simon placed as combatants in the ring. The challenge goes forth from Peter to Simon to do his worst, so to speak, to support his views. Peter's own views are clear: "I believe in the living God, through whom I shall destroy your magic arts."[14] Simon, who has already taken a beating hither and yon by the apostle, nonetheless opts to take up the challenge, first by declaring the folly of Peter's proclamation: "You have the impudence," says Simon, "to speak of Jesus the Nazarene, the son of a carpenter, himself a carpenter, whose family is from Judea. Listen, Peter. The Romans have understanding. They are no fools." Then, addressing the crowd he says, "Men of Rome, is a God born? Is he crucified? Whoever has a Lord is no God" (Acts of

Peter 23). Here, then is a Gnostic proclamation against a proto-orthodox theology of the real incarnation and death of Jesus.

But the matter comes down to proof, and the proof comes in miraculous power. The Roman prefect challenges the adversaries to prove who is superior. Sending a favored slave into the arena, he instructs Simon to kill him and Peter to raise him from the dead. Obviously it is easier to kill than to raise, but Simon performs his act with panache, simply speaking a word in the servant's ear. With yet greater flair, however, Peter raises him from the dead through the power of God. The God of Peter is the God of life. And to cap off his demonstration, he also raises the dead son of a lonely widow, brought into the arena for just the occasion. The people standing by realize the implication and make the appropriate proclamation: "There is only one God, the God of Peter." (Acts of Peter 26)

Other miraculous demonstrations are a bit more humorous, involving bizarre animal tricks, as in Peter's use of a talking dog to castigate the chief of all heretics in front of the crowds, and his demonstration of power by bringing a smoked tuna back to life:

> But Peter turned round and saw a smoked tuna fish hanging in a window; and he took it and said to the people, "If you now see this swimming in the water like a fish, will you be able to believe in him whom I preach?" And they all said with one accord, "Indeed we will believe you!" Now there was a fish pond near by; so he said, "In your name, Jesus Christ, in which they still fail to believe" (he said to the tuna) "in the presence of all these be alive and swim like a fish!" And he threw the tuna into the pond, and it came alive and began to swim. And the people saw the fish swimming; and he made it do so not merely for that hour, or it might have been called a delusion, but he made it go on swimming, so that it attracted crowds from all sides and showed that the tuna had become a live fish; so much so that some of the people threw in bread for it, and it ate it all up. And when they saw this, a great number followed him and believed in the Lord." (Acts of Peter 5)[15]

In the ultimate showdown between the heretical sorcerer and the man of God, Simon the magician announces that he will use his powers to leap into the air and fly like a bird over the temples and hills of Rome. But once the impressive aerial show begins, Peter is not to be outdone. He calls upon God to smite Simon in midair. God complies, much to the magician's dismay. Unprepared for a crash landing, Simon plunges to earth and breaks his leg in three places. Seeing what has happened, the crowds rush to stone him as an evildoer. He eventually dies of his injuries.

A yet more subtle and certainly less entertaining use of forgery may be found in a proto-orthodox composition known as Paul's Letter to the Laodiceans. We have seen that it was a popular exercise to forge letters in Paul's name. This was happening already by the time of 2 Thessalonians, as the author there mentions a letter "reputedly" from Paul (2:2). Moreover, it appears that the

Pastoral epistles of the New Testament were written by someone other than Paul, as were the correspondence with Seneca and 3 Corinthians. The Letter to the Laodiceans, however, is a peculiar case. In most of the other instances, there are reasonably clear and obvious reasons for the forgeries, as the letters convey a decided point of view, for example, against apocalyptic enthusiasm in 2 Thessalonians or against docetic Christologies in 3 Corinthians. But the Letter to the Laodiceans appears banal and harmless; it has no real ax to grind, no major points to stress. In fact, it appears to be little more than a simple pastiche of Pauline phrases thrown together one after the other. Fairly typical is the following:

> For my life is in Christ and to die is joy. And his mercy will work in you, that you may have the same love and be of one mind. Therefore, beloved, as you have heard in my presence, so hold fast and work in the fear of God, and eternal life will be yours. For it is God who works in you. And do without hesitation what you do. (vv. 8–12)[16]

Most of this is reminiscent of Philippians, but it scarcely drives home a hard lesson. At an earlier point the author does say: "And may you not be deceived by the vain talk of some people who tell tales that they may lead you away from the truth of the gospel which is proclaimed by me" (v. 4). This sounds more promising from a heresiological perspective, but the author never indicates what these vain talkers say in their various tales.

Why would an author forge a letter that does not appear to advance any kind of agenda? Scholars have long recognized one piece to this puzzle, but have not considered another which, I think, can provide the answer. The widely recognized motivation for the letter involves its concluding request: "See that this epistle is read to the Colossians and that of the Colossians to you" (v. 20). This is an important line, because it mirrors the advice found in the New Testament letter of Colossians (which, ironically enough, is also suspected by critical scholars to be non-Pauline): "And when this letter is read by you, have it read as well to the church in Laodicea, and be sure that you read the letter to the Laodiceans" (Col. 4:16). It may be that someone, knowing that Paul had allegedly written a letter to the Laodiceans, forged one to fill the void created by its known absence.

But there may be another motivation for the letter, one that is slightly more subtle, making this seemingly harmless forgery full of proto-orthodox intent. As we will see in a later chapter, the earliest surviving "canon list" to come down to us from early Christianity—that is, a list of books that an author considered to be canonical Scripture—is called the Muratorian Canon, named after the eighteenth-century scholar who discovered it, L. Muratori. In addition to listing books that were thought to belong to the Scriptures, the anonymous author of this fragment also cites a number of writings to be excluded, some of them as heretical forgeries. Among these he numbers a Letter to the Laodiceans, which he claims was a "Marcionite forgery."[17]

Some scholars have argued that the surviving Letter to the Laodiceans is just this forgery. Not many people have been convinced, however, since there is nothing particularly Marcionite about the letter, nothing that intimates a Marcionite understanding of God, Christ, or Scripture, for example. Yet if it is not the Marcionite forgery mentioned in the Muratorian canon, how *does* one explain the creation of this pastiche of Pauline catchphrases? One solution is that it is an *anti-Marcionite* production—not in the sense that it attacks Marcionite views head on, but in the sense that it was produced by a proto-orthodox author as *the* letter of Paul to the Laodiceans, so as to show that the Marcionite forgery, which was in circulation, but which no longer survives for us today, was *not* that letter. A simple pasting together of Pauline-sounding ideas would suit the purpose perfectly. Once this document was produced, the other could be discounted as a forgery, and the proto-orthodox agenda was thereby fulfilled.

The Falsification of Sacred Texts

We have seen a number of weapons used in the literary battles for Christian supremacy: the construction of polemical refutations, the publication of character slurs, the creation of forged documents in the names of the apostles. These did not exhaust the arsenals of the various combatants, however. In the next chapter we will see how the formation of a canon of sacred authorities proved to be a particularly valuable instrument in battle. Here we will consider one other. This involved not the creation of "new" (i.e., forged) documents in the names of the apostles but the *falsification* of writings that had already been produced, that is, the alteration of the wording of documents held to be sacred, in order to make them more clearly oppose "false" teachings and more clearly support "correct" ones. Once again, this was a strategy available to all sides of the conflict, and there is good evidence to suggest that all sides did in fact make use of it. It is certainly clear that all sides were *accused* of tampering with their texts to make them say what they wanted them to mean.

We have already seen some of these accusations. Most (in)famous, of course, was Marcion and his followers, who not only rejected the entire Old Testament but also claimed that the writings of Paul and the Gospel (of Luke) had been altered by Christians with Jewish sympathies, so that references to God as creator, quotations of the Old Testament, and affirmations of the goodness of creation had been *inserted* into these texts, which originally lacked them. Their solution was to remove these false insertions so as to return the texts to their pristine state. The proto-orthodox, of course, saw this attempt at restoration to be nothing short of mutilation, and argued that the Marcionites were falsifying their texts simply by removing from them anything that did not coincide with their own theological agenda.

Marcion was not the only one susceptible to the charge. Near the opposite end of the theological spectrum from Marcion were the Theodotians, the second-century Christians in Rome who followed Theodotus the Cobbler in claiming that Jesus was a human being, pure and simple (as opposed to the Marcionites, who thought he was divine). According to an anonymous tractate quoted by Eusebius, the Theodotians, like the Marcionites, intentionally corrupted their texts of Scripture, altering its sacred words in light of their own adoptionistic views. The evidence for the charge was the discrepant copies of Scripture produced by the leaders of the group:

> If anyone will take the trouble to collect their several copies and compare them, he will discover frequent divergences; for example, Asclepiades' copies do not agree with Theodotus's . . . nor do these agree with Hermophilus's copies. As for Appoloniades, his cannot even be harmonized with each other; it is possible to collate the ones which his disciples made first with those that have undergone further manipulation, and to find endless discrepancies. (Eusebius *Church History* 5.28)

Thus Theodotians are accused of altering their sacred texts in different ways, but always to the same end of serving their own purposes. So, too, the Ebionites, Jewish-Christian counterparts of our Roman adoptionists, were accused of excising the first two chapters of the Gospel according to Matthew to accommodate their rejection of the doctrine of Jesus' virginal conception.

Various groups of Gnostics proved susceptible to the charge as well, even though in their case one might expect to find it with less frequency, given their uncanny ability (at least in the eyes of their proto-orthodox opponents) to discover their views in virtually any text, regardless of its wording. Nonetheless, they occasionally stood condemned on precisely such ground, as when Tertullian argued that the Valentinians had altered the verbal form of John 1:13 from the singular to the plural. Originally, claimed Tertullian, the verse referred to the miraculous birth of Jesus ("who was born not from blood nor from the will of the flesh nor from the will of man, but from God"); the Valentinians, however, had modified the text to make it refer to their *own* supernatural generation through gnosis ("who were born not from blood . . .").

What is revealing about this particular instance is that Tertullian was clearly in the wrong: It is he who preserves the corruption. Of all our surviving Greek manuscripts of the Gospel of John, none gives the verse in the form cited by Tertullian, and of all the surviving Latin manuscripts, only one does. This leads to the striking observation that despite the fact that "heretics" were commonly charged with altering their texts of Scripture, there are almost no traces in our surviving manuscripts of their having done so.

This does not mean that the alternative forms of Christianity were guiltless in the matter. The winners not only write the history; they also reproduce the texts. Even if there were instances in which manuscripts of the books that came to be included in the New Testament had been altered to support one heretical view or the other, as surely there were, these particular manuscripts would not have been preserved or recopied for posterity. Burning heretical books did not only mean destroying books created by heretics; it also meant destroying (or not reproducing) books altered by heretics.

If "heretically altered" texts of Scripture do not survive, what about texts altered by the proto-orthodox? Did scribes standing in the tradition that eventually claimed victory ever falsify their texts in order to make them more serviceable for the proto-orthodox cause, making them *say* what they were already thought to *mean?* In fact, this did happen, as is abundantly evident throughout our manuscript tradition of the New Testament. I will give a few examples in a moment. First I need to give some background information to help make sense of the discussion.[18]

Some Background Information

We do not have the "originals" of any of the books that came to be included in the New Testament, or indeed of any Christian book from antiquity. What we have are copies of the originals or, to be more accurate, copies made from copies of the copies of the copies of the originals. Most of these surviving copies are hundreds of years removed from the originals themselves.

I can explain the situation by giving a solitary example of how things worked.[19] When the Thessalonians received Paul's first letter, someone in the community must have copied it by hand, one word at a time. The copy itself was then copied, possibly in Thessalonica, possibly in another community to which a copy was taken or sent. This copy of the copy was also copied, as later was this copy of the copy of the copy. Before long, there were a number of copies of the letter circulating in communities throughout the Mediterranean, or rather a number of copies of copies, all made by hand at a pace that would seem outrageously slow to those of us accustomed to the world of word processors, photocopiers, desktop publishing, and electronic mail.

In this process of recopying the document by hand, what happened to the original of 1 Thessalonians? For some unknown reason, it was eventually thrown away or burned or otherwise destroyed. Possibly it was read so much that it simply wore out. The early Christians saw no need to preserve it as the "original" text. They had copies of the letter. Why keep the original?

They might have realized why, had they more fully appreciated what happens to a text that is copied and recopied by hand—especially by scribes who are not trained professionals but simply literate persons with the time and money to do the job. Copyists, even if they are skilled specialists, inevitably make mistakes. (Anyone who doubts this should copy a long document by hand and see how well he or she does.) Moreover, whenever a copyist makes a copy from a copy that has already been copied, the mistakes that have accrued with

The first chapter of the book of Hebrews in one of the oldest and best surviving manuscripts of the New Testament, Codex Vaticanus (Vatican). Notice the marginal note between the first and second columns. A corrector to the text had erased a word in verse 3 and substituted another word in its place; a second corrector came along, erased the correction, reinserted the original word, and wrote a note in the margin to castigate the first corrector. The note reads, "Fool and knave, leave the old reading, don't change it!"

each reproduction multiply; scribes not only introduce their own mistakes but also, necessarily, reproduce mistakes found in the copy being copied—unless they try to "correct" the mistake, which more often than not leads to an "incorrect" correction.

We do not have the original of 1 Thessalonians (i.e., the text that Paul actually wrote) or of any other New Testament book. Nor do we have copies made directly from the originals, nor copies made from the copies of the originals, nor copies made from the copies of the copies. Our earliest "manuscripts" (handwritten copies) of Paul's letters date from around 200 CE, that is, nearly 150 years after he wrote them. The earliest full manuscripts of the Gospels come from about the same time, although we have some fragments of manuscripts that date earlier, including P^{52}, a credit card-sized fragment, usually dated to the first part of the second century, of verses from John 18, discovered in a trash heap in Egypt. But even our relatively full manuscripts from around the year 200 are not preserved intact. Pages and entire books were lost. Indeed, it is not until the fourth century, nearly three hundred years after the New Testament was written, that we begin to get complete manuscripts of all of its books.

After the fourth or fifth century, copies of the New Testament become far more common. Indeed, if we count up all of the New Testament manuscripts that have been discovered, it is an impressive number overall. We currently know of nearly 5,400 Greek copies of all or part of the New Testament, ranging from tiny scraps of a verse or two that could sit in the palm of your hand to massive tomes containing all twenty-seven books bound together. These copies range in date from the second century down to, and beyond, the invention of the printing press in the fifteenth century. As a result, the New Testament is preserved in far more manuscripts than any other book from antiquity. There are, for example, fewer than 700 copies of Homer's *Iliad*, fewer than 350 copies of the plays of Euripides, and only one copy of the first six books of the *Annals* of Tacitus.

What is unsettling for those who want to know what the original text said is not the number of New Testament manuscripts but the dates of these manuscripts and the differences among them. Of course, we would expect the New Testament to be copied in the Middle Ages more frequently than Homer or Euripides or Tacitus; the trained copyists throughout the western world at the time were Christian scribes, frequently monks, who for the most part were preparing copies of texts for religious purposes. But the fact that we have thousands of New Testament manuscripts does not in itself mean that we can rest assured that we know what the original text said. If we have very few early copies—in fact, scarcely any—how can we know that the text was not changed significantly *before* the New Testament began to be reproduced in such large quantities? Most surviving copies were made during the Middle Ages, many of them a thousand years after Paul and his companions had died.

I should emphasize that it is not simply a matter of scholarly speculation to say that the words of the New Testament were changed in the process of copying. We know that they were changed, because we can compare these 5,400 copies with one another. What is striking is that when we do so, we find that no two copies (except the smallest fragments) agree in all of their wording. There can be only one reason for this. The scribes who copied the texts changed them. Nobody knows for certain how often they changed them, because no one has been able yet to count all of the differences among the manuscripts. Some estimates put the number at around 200,000, others at around 300,000 or more. Perhaps it is simplest to express the figure in comparative terms: There are more differences among our manuscripts than there are words in the New Testament.

Most changes are careless errors that are easily recognized and corrected. Christian scribes often made mistakes simply because they were tired or inattentive or, sometimes, inept. Indeed, the single most common mistake in our manuscripts involves "orthography," significant for little more than showing that scribes in antiquity could spell no better than most of us can today. In addition, we have numerous manuscripts in which scribes have left out entire words, verses, or even pages of a book, presumably by accident. Sometimes scribes rearranged the words on the page, for example, by leaving out a word and then reinserting it later in the sentence. And sometimes they found a marginal note scribbled by an earlier scribe and thought that it was to be included in the text, and so inserted it as an additional verse. These kinds of accidental changes were facilitated, in part, by the fact that ancient scribes did not use punctuation and paragraph divisions, and did not in fact separate the words on the page butprintedthemalltogethermakingmistakesinreadingfairlycommon.

Other kinds of changes are both more important and harder for modern scholars to detect. These are changes that scribes appear to have made in their texts intentionally. I say that they "appear" to have made such changes intentionally simply because the scribes are no longer around for us to interview about their intentions. But some of the changes in our manuscripts can scarcely be attributed to fatigue, carelessness, or ineptitude; instead, they suggest intention and forethought.

It is sometimes difficult to know what might have motivated a scribe to change his text, but it often appears to have been some kind of problem in the text itself that he found disturbing. Sometimes, for example, scribes ran across a statement that appeared to be mistaken. This happens, for instance, in Mark 1:2, where a citation from the book of Malachi is quoted as coming from Isaiah. At other times, scribes thought that a passage they were copying contradicted another one. For example, Mark 2:25 indicates that Abiathar was the high priest when David entered the Temple to eat the showbread, whereas the story in the Hebrew Bible itself (1 Sam. 21:1–7) indicates that it was not Abiathar but his father, Ahimelech. In all such cases, scribes appear to have had little compunction about changing their texts so as to "correct" them: Both Mark 1:2 and 2:25 were commonly altered.

And so a verse found in some manuscripts will appear to embody a mistake, a contradiction, or an awkward construction, but in others it will be worded differently in such a way as to avoid the problem. Scholars have to decide then which form of the verse was probably original and which represents the change made by a scribe.

Some textual changes can be important for interpretation. For example, the earliest manuscripts of the Gospel of Mark end at 16:8 with the report that the women fled Jesus' empty tomb in fear and told no one what they had seen or heard. But later manuscripts append an additional twelve verses in which the resurrected Jesus appears before his disciples and delivers a remarkable speech in which he says, among other things, that those who believe in him will be able to handle venomous snakes and drink deadly poison without suffering harm. Are these verses original, or did scribes add them to a text that otherwise seemed to end too abruptly? It is important to remember that this is not a question of whether scribes changed the text. Some of them must have changed it, because the manuscripts differ from one another. The only question is whether a scribe omitted the twelve verses or whether a different scribe added them. Most scholars think the Gospel originally ended at 16:8.

Did the author of the Fourth Gospel write the famous story of the woman taken in adultery, or was this a later addition to the Gospel by a well-meaning scribe? The story is found in many of our later manuscripts between chapters 7 and 8 but not in the earliest ones; moreover, the writing style is significantly different from the rest of the Gospel. Almost all scholars acknowledge that the story was added to manuscripts of John's Gospel many years after it had first been circulated.

In spite of the remarkable differences among our manuscripts, scholars are convinced that we can reconstruct the oldest form of the words of the New Testament with reasonable (though not 100 percent) accuracy. Scholars tend to look to see which textual readings are supported (a) by the oldest manuscripts, on the assumption that the older the manuscript, the fewer the scribal hands between it and the original, and so the fewer opportunities for changing the text; (b) by the manuscripts that are most geographically diverse, so that a text is not just some kind of localized variant; and (c) by the manuscripts, that tend to preserve the superior reading whenever the judgment is obvious, on the assumption that manuscripts that are *known* to contain lots of mistakes cannot be trusted as much as those known not to contain so many mistakes. Moreover, scholars take into account such issues as whether a form of the text coincides with an author's literary style, vocabulary, and theology (that would speak in its favor) and whether readings coincide with the agenda of scribes (that might suggest the scribes created the readings). Making these decisions is obviously a complicated business; as a result, there are numerous places of textual variation where scholars continue to disagree concerning the "original" form of the text.

We may now return to our original question: Given the enormous number of changes in our manuscripts of the New Testament, is there any evidence that the surviving texts were ever modified in light of the doctrinal controversies of the second and third centuries? Yes, there is abundant evidence, sometimes in just the places you might look for it. As I have indicated, almost all of this evidence involves proto-orthodox changes of the text.

Possibly the easiest way to illustrate the point is by giving several examples, classifying them according to the heretical views that appear to have motivated the change.[20]

Antiadoptionistic Alterations

I'll begin with textual alterations that appear to have been motivated by an opposition to adoptionistic Christologies, for example, those of the Ebionites or the Roman Theodotians, which maintained that Jesus was completely human, not divine, born of the sexual union of Joseph and Mary.

After Jesus is born in Luke's Gospel, his parents take him to the Temple "to present him to the Lord" (Luke 2:22). They are met there by a prophet, Simeon, who recognizes Jesus as "the Lord's Christ," and praises Jesus as the one who will be "a light for revelation to the Gentiles, and for glory to your people Israel" (2:32). This high praise elicits the expected response: "And his father and his mother marveled at what was said about him" (Luke 2:33). But the response caused some consternation among proto-orthodox scribes, because it appears to assume that Joseph was the *father* of Jesus. That, of course, is exactly what adoptionists said about him—Joseph and Mary were Jesus' actual parents. Recognizing the problem, some scribes changed the text. In these altered manuscripts we are told that "Joseph and his mother marveled at what was said about him." Now there is no problem: Joseph is not called Jesus' father. And no one who thinks he was can use the text to prove the point. This, then, is a proto-orthodox "correction" that involved a textual alteration.

So, too, in the account of Jesus as a twelve-year-old in the Temple. Jesus has gone to Jerusalem with his parents to celebrate the Passover feast. When it is over, they all return home; but Jesus, unbeknownst to them, remains behind. When they realize he is not with them, they return to Jerusalem and, after three days, find him in the Temple, discussing matters of the Law with the Jewish teachers there. His mother is miffed with her precocious child and says, "Son, why have you treated us like this? See, your father and I have been anxiously looking for you!" (Luke 2:48). Your father and I? Once again there is a problem. And once again, some scribes changed the text, this time to read "*We* have been anxiously looking for you!"

Take a different kind of alteration, although similarly motivated. Adoptionists, of course, believed that Jesus was divine not by nature but by adoption. Many of them believed that this happened at his baptism, that it was at this point that God made him his son. As it turns out, there is an interesting textual variant in Luke's account of Jesus' baptism. In all three Gospels of Matthew, Mark, and Luke, there is a similar sequence of events: The heavens open up, the Holy Spirit descends upon Jesus in the form of a dove, and a voice speaks from heaven. But what does the voice say? In both Mark and Matthew it appears to allude to Isaiah 42. In Mark it says, "You are my beloved Son, in whom I am well pleased," and in Matthew, where the voice speaks to the crowds rather than directly to Jesus, it says, "This is my beloved Son, in whom I am well pleased." In the oldest surviving witnesses to Luke's Gospel, however, the voice instead quotes the words of Psalm 2:7 "You are my Son, today I have begotten you" (Luke 3:22).

For our purposes here, I am interested not in the question of what the voice *really* said (as if we could ever decide that on historical grounds), but in what it is reported to have said in Luke. "Today I have begotten you"? That is exactly what the adoptionists were saying, that it was at the baptism of Jesus that God made Jesus his son. No surprise then that the text came to be widely changed in the manuscripts of the New Testament. It would have been difficult for scribes to change the text into the form found in Matthew, since there the voice speaks to the crowds rather than to Jesus. The easier way to prevent the text from being (mis)used by adoptionists was to harmonize it with the text found in Mark. And so most of our manuscripts of Luke also now read, "You are my beloved Son, in whom I am well pleased." This is one proto-orthodox alteration that proved remarkably successful. Even though the potentially dangerous ("heretical") form of the text is found in virtually all our oldest witnesses and is less easy to explain as a scribal alteration, it is the *altered* form of the text that is found in the majority of surviving manuscripts and reproduced in most of our English translations.

As we have seen, the key debate between the proto-orthodox and Ebionites, Theodotians, and the like was over the nature of Christ, whether he was divine or simply a man adopted, as an adult, to be in a special relationship with God. The proto-orthodox insisted that he was himself God. The original writings of the New Testament, though, rarely come out with anything so bold as a statement, "Jesus is God."[21] And so proto-orthodox scribes copying their manuscripts occasionally modified them to clarify Jesus' divine character. A striking instance occurs in the opening lines of the Gospel of John, which speak of the "Word" of God which was in the beginning, was with God, and was itself God (1:1–2). This Word, through whom God created all things (1:3), became a human being (1:14), and was, then, of course, Jesus Christ himself, God's Word become flesh. This open hymn of praise to Christ concludes with the familiar words, "No one has seen God at any time; but the only Son, who is in the bosom of the Father, that one has made him known" (John 1:18).

Quite an exalted view of Christ. He, the only Son of God, is the one who resides in God the Father's own bosom and is the one who explains God. But as exalted as the view was, it was not exalted enough for some scribes, who made a remarkable alteration of the text, so that now it says, "No one has seen God at any time; but the only God, who is in the bosom of the Father, that one has made him known." In the manuscripts that embody this change, Jesus is not simply the unique Son of God. He himself is the unique God. No ambiguity here about Jesus' divine character. This appears to be a proto-orthodox change directed against a "low" adoptionistic Christology that was not sufficiently impressed with his status as God.

Antiseparationist Alterations

A second kind of proto-orthodox alteration of the texts they considered Scripture is directed not against adoptionists but against Gnostics who differentiated between the man Jesus and the divine Christ. This kind of Christology could be called "separationist," in that it saw two clear and separate persons, the human being Jesus and the divine aeon Christ who temporarily dwelled in him. According to some forms of these Gnostic views, the Christ descended into Jesus at his baptism, empowering him for his ministry, and then left him prior to his death. Thus it was that the divine Christ escaped suffering. Jesus, in this view, suffered alone.

This Gnostic understanding appears to have affected proto-orthodox scribes who occasionally altered their texts in light of the controversy. One rather peculiar example occurs in the letter of 1 John, where the author is attacking some false teachers of his own day: "Every spirit that confesses that Jesus Christ has come in the flesh is from God; and every spirit that does not confess Jesus is not from God; this is the spirit of the Antichrist" (1 John 4:3–4). It may be that the author of this letter was himself counteracting some kind of "docetic" Christology, in which Jesus was understood to be so *much* divine that he was not at all human, that he did not really have a flesh-and-blood body ("come in the flesh"). But there is an interesting textual variant for the verse, rarely attested but evidently dating back to the second century. In this altered form of the text, we are told, "Every spirit that confesses that Jesus Christ has come in the flesh is from God; and every spirit that looses Jesus is not from God; this is the spirit of the Antichrist." Every spirit that *looses* Jesus? What does *that* mean? In fact, it is a bit hard to know what it means, outside of the Gnostic controversies raging when the text first came to be altered. But within those controversies the change makes good sense. Those who "loose" Jesus are those who separate him from the Christ, claiming that there were in fact two distinct beings instead of the "one Lord Jesus Christ." The change, then, appears to be a falsification designed to attack a Gnostic kind of Christology.

Another example of this kind of alteration occurs exactly where one might expect it, in the crucifixion scene of Mark's Gospel. We are told by Irenaeus that Mark was the Gospel of choice for those who "separate Jesus from the Christ" (*Against Heresies* 3.11.7). This comes as no wonder to those who know Mark's Gospel well, for in this account, at the baptism scene, the Spirit (the divine element) is actually said to enter "into" Jesus (in the Greek; Mark 1:10); and at the end of his life, on the cross, Jesus is said to cry out, "My God, my God, why have you forsaken me?"—or more literally, "Why have you left me behind?" (Mark 15:34). We know that some Gnostics interpreted the verse to indicate that the Christ had abandoned Jesus to face his death alone. The Gnostic Gospel of Philip, for example, interprets the words as follows: "It was on the cross that he said these words, for it was there that he was divided" (v. 68). Recognizing the Gnostic interpretation of the verse can help explain why it came to be changed in some manuscripts, where instead of crying out, "Why have you forsaken me?" Jesus cries, "My God, my God, why have you mocked me?"

It is a fascinating change, in part because it fits so well with what has happened in Mark's passage otherwise, in that everyone *else* has mocked Jesus: the soldiers, the two criminals being crucified with him, those passing by. And here at the end, even God has mocked him. Still, that is not what the original text said. Almost all our manuscripts preserve the more familiar text, which is, by the way, the correct translation of the Aramaic words that are quoted in the preceding verse: "Eloi, Eloi, lema sebachthani?" Why, then, was the verse changed? Evidently because the original form of the text had proved so useful for the Gnostic interpretation of the crucifixion. And so the textual variant may have been a proto-orthodox falsification of the text.

The change of Mark 15:34 did not make a huge impact on the manuscript tradition, since, as I have indicated, most witnesses retain the original reading. The same cannot be said of the final example I will cite, which comes not from the Gospels but from Hebrews. In a very interesting passage in this letter, the author indicates that Jesus died for all people "by the grace of God" (Heb. 2:9). Or *is* that what the author said? In several manuscripts, the text instead says that Jesus died "apart from God." But what would it mean to say that Jesus died "apart from God"? In Hebrews, in fact, the statement makes perfect sense, since elsewhere as well it emphasizes that Jesus experienced his suffering as a full human being without any divine succor that might have been his as God's son. He suffered just like the rest of us, apart from any divine intervention or supernatural painkiller (cf. Heb. 5:7, 12:2–3).

But at a later time, in the second and third centuries, this kind of statement could be highly problematic, since Gnostics were saying that Jesus literally died "apart from God," in that the divine element within him had left him. Evidently, for that reason, scribes in the period modified the text to the more familiar phrase, which is common in the writings of Paul but not in this particular letter, that Jesus died by the "grace of God." Their change in this instance was remarkably successful; it is the wording you will find still in most English translations.

Antidocetic Alterations

Finally we might consider changes that appear to combat docetic interpretations of Jesus, such as those advocated by Marcion and some Gnostics, which stressed that Jesus was so completely divine he was not at all human. Proto-orthodox alterations of their sacred texts, as you might expect, would emphasize just the opposite, that Jesus really was a human, that he really did suffer, bleed, and die, that he really was a man of the flesh. There are a number of changes in our manuscripts of this kind. Here I'll cite just two that are particularly interesting.

One of the most famous passages of the Gospel of Luke comes in the scene immediately before Jesus' arrest, where he is praying and begins to "sweat blood" (this is where the phrase comes from): "And an angel appeared to him from heaven, giving him strength; being in great agony, he began to pray more fervently, and his sweat became like great drops of blood falling to the ground"

(Luke 22:43–44). Here is a gripping scene of Jesus in agony, very human, terrified of his coming death. The problem, however, is that these verses are not found in our oldest and best witnesses to the Gospel of Luke (and they occur in no other Gospel). Did scribes take the verses out of the text because they found them strange, or did they add them because they found them necessary? There are good reasons for thinking that scribes added them, including the one I mentioned, that they are not found in our oldest and best manuscripts. It is particularly worth noting in this case how the verses were used in the earliest authors who cite them. In every instance, they occur in proto-orthodox heresiologists (Justin, Irenaeus, and Hippolytus) who quote the verses to show that contrary to some heretical teachers, Jesus really was a flesh-and-blood human being, who suffered very real human emotions, sweating blood in agony while waiting for his arrest. It appears then that Luke's betrayal-and-arrest scene was altered by proto-orthodox scribes wanting to stress Jesus' humanity in the face of docetic Christians who denied it.

The second example comes two chapters later, when Jesus has been raised from the dead. The women who go to the tomb learn the wonderful news. When they report it to the disciples, however, they are ridiculed for telling silly tales. But their report is confirmed by the head apostle Peter, who runs to the tomb and sees for himself that it is empty of all but the linen burial cloths (Luke 24:12). Jesus then appears to the two people on the road to Emmaus and soon to all the disciples. But what about this business of Peter himself finding the empty tomb?

In fact, the verse that reports it is not found in some of our important textual witnesses. And when one looks at the verse carefully, it contains a disproportionate number of words and grammatical characteristics not otherwise found in Luke's Gospel (or in Acts). Moreover, it looks very similar to an account found in John 20:3–10, almost like a summary or synopsis of that story. How does one account for all this? Probably the easiest explanation is that the verse was an addition to Luke's original account. In considering reasons for a scribe to have added it, we should not overlook how the verse could serve the proto-orthodox cause. Here Jesus is raised bodily from the dead; this is not some kind of spiritualized resurrection as some docetists would have it. The proof is in the linen cloths, hard evidence of the tangible nature of the resurrection. And who sees them? Not just women telling a silly tale, but Peter, the chief of the apostles, eventually the bishop of Rome, the head of the proto-orthodox church. This appears, then, to be a proto-orthodox change of the text, made to counter a docetic understanding of Jesus.

We have seen a wide range of strategies used by the various combatants in the literary battles for dominance in early Christianity: polemical treatises with stereotyped but harsh attacks on the views of others, forged documents in the names of apostolic authorities heartily advocating one form of the religion or maligning another, and now falsification of literature already accepted as sacred by one or the other side in the disputes. There was, however, one more strategy that was used with particular effect by the winning side of these altercations. This was the collection of a group of texts into a canon of Scripture, which was invested, then, with sacred authority as having come from God. This final strategy had significant long-term effects, greater than any of the others we have considered to this point. For it gave us our New Testament, the twenty-seven books accepted by Christians since the fourth century down to the present day as canonical Scripture. The battle for this collection of writings, however, was long and hard. We will consider key aspects of this battle in the chapter that follows.

Chapter Eleven

The Invention of Scripture: The Formation of the Proto-orthodox New Testament

The victory of proto-orthodox Christianity in its quest for dominance left a number of indelible marks on the history of Western civilization. Of these, none has proved more significant than the formation of the New Testament as a canon of Scripture.

To be sure, the development of a church hierarchy was important, but there are numerous denominations today, with a range of church structures. The formulation of the orthodox creeds was significant as well, but in some churches new creeds have replaced the old, and almost no one has weekly Creedal Studies to discuss how the Nicene affirmations can make a difference in their lives. The New Testament is another matter: It is accepted and read by millions of people around the world and is understood by most Christians to be the word of God, the inspired Scripture, the ultimate basis for faith and practice—even for Christians who stress "tradition" as well. In common Christian understanding, these are twenty-seven books given by God to his people to guide them in their lives and understanding.

It comes as a bit of a shock to most people to realize that the Church has not always had the New Testament. But the Christian Scriptures did not descend from heaven a few years after Jesus died. The books that eventually came to be collected into the sacred canon were written by a variety of authors over a period of sixty or seventy years, in different places for different audiences. Other books were written in the same period, some of them by the same authors. Soon thereafter the Church saw a flood of books also allegedly written by the earliest followers of Jesus, forgeries in the names of the apostles, produced for decades, centuries even, after the apostles themselves were long dead and buried. Virtually all of this other literature has been destroyed, forgotten, lost. Only a fraction of the early Christian writings came to be immortalized by inclusion in the sacred canon.

But why were these twenty-seven books included, and not any others? Who decided which books to include? On what basis? And when? It is one thing for believers to affirm, on theological grounds, that the decisions about the canon, like the books themselves, were divinely inspired, but it is another thing to look at the actual history of the process and to ponder the long, drawn-out arguments over which books to include and which to reject. The process did not take a few months or years. It took centuries. And even then there was no unanimity.

Starting at the End:
The Canon after Three Hundred Years

To begin our reflections on the formation of the New Testament canon, perhaps we would do well to set the context and then start at the end.[1] Most of the books of the New Testament were written in the first century of the common era, from the earliest letters of Paul, written about 50 CE, some twenty years after Jesus' death,[2] to 2 Peter, widely thought to be the final New Testament book to be written, around 120 CE. The controversies we have been examining date, for the most part, to the two hundred years that followed. But even at the end of this two-hundred-year period there was no fixed New Testament canon.

The first Christian author of any kind to advocate a New Testament canon of our twenty-seven books and no others was Athanasius, the fourth-century bishop of Alexandria. This comes in a letter that Athanasius wrote in 367 CE— over three centuries after the writings of Paul, our earliest Christian author. As the Alexandrian bishop, Athanasius sent an annual letter to the churches in Egypt under his jurisdiction. The purpose of these letters was to set the date of Easter, which was not established well in advance, as in our modern calendars, but was announced each year by the church authorities. Athanasius used these annual "Festal" letters to provide pastoral advice and counsel to his churches. In his famous thirty-ninth Festal letter of 367 CE he indicates, as part of his advice, the books that his churches were to accept as canonical Scripture. He first lists the books of the "Old Testament," including the Old Testament Apocrypha (which were to be read only as devotional literature, not as canonical authorities). Then he names exactly the twenty-seven books that we now have as the New Testament, indicating that "in these alone the teaching of godliness is proclaimed. Let no one add to these; let nothing be taken away from them."[3]

Numerous scholars have unreflectively claimed that this letter of Athanasius represents the "closing" of the canon, that from then on there were no disputes about which books to include. But there continued to be debates and differences of opinion, even in Athanasius's home church. For example, the famous teacher of the late-fourth-century Alexandria, Didymus the Blind,[4] claimed that

2 Peter was a "forgery" that was not to be included in the canon. Moreover, Didymus quoted other books, including the *Shepherd* of Hermas and the Epistle of Barnabas, as scriptural authorities.[5]

Going somewhat further afield, in the early fifth century, the church in Syria finalized its New Testament canon and excluded from it 2 Peter, 2 and 3 John, Jude, and Revelation, making a canon of twenty-two books rather than twenty-seven. The church in Ethiopia eventually accepted the twenty-seven books named by Athanasius but added four others not otherwise widely known—Sinodos, the Book of Clement (which is not 1 or 2 Clement), the Book of the Covenant, and the Didascalia—for a thirty-one book canon. Other churches had yet other canons. And so, when we talk about the "final" version of the New Testament, we are doing so in (mental) quotation marks, for there never has been complete agreement on the canon throughout the Christian world.

There has been agreement, however, throughout most of the Roman Catholic, Eastern Orthodox, and Protestant traditions. The twenty-seven books named by Athanasius are "the" New Testament. Even so, the process did not come to a definitive conclusion through an official ratification of Athanasius's canon, say, at a church council called for the purpose.[6] There was no official, churchwide pronouncement on the matter until the Council of Trent in the mid-sixteenth century (which, as a Roman Catholic council, was binding only on Roman Catholics). But by then, the twenty-seven books were already "set" as Scripture.

Thus, the canon of the New Testament was ratified by widespread consensus rather than by official proclamation. Still, by the beginning of the fifth century, most churches in the Christian world agreed on its contours.

The Beginning of the Process

How did the process begin? Why did it take so long to get resolved (if, in fact, we can consider it resolved)? How did Christian leaders decide which books to include? What were the motivating factors, the impetus?

We have already seen something of what motivated the formation of the canon, at least in part. Given the nature of Christianity from the outset, as a religion that stressed proper belief and that required authorities on which to base that belief, literary texts very soon took on unusual importance for this religion. The apostles of Jesus, of course, were seen as authoritative sources of knowledge about what Jesus himself said and did. But apostles could not be present everywhere at once in the churches scattered throughout the empire. Apostolic writings therefore had to take the place of an apostolic presence, and so the written word became a matter of real importance.

There was another motivation behind the formation of a sacred canon of Scripture, and it starts long before the Christian mission to establish churches. In some sense, the Christian movement had a canon of Scripture at its very beginning, prior even to the writing of any apostolic texts. Jesus and his earthly followers themselves had a collection of sacred writings. They were all Jews, and they fully accepted the authority of books that came to be included in what later Christians would call the "Old Testament."

There is no doubt that during his public ministry Jesus accepted, followed, interpreted, and taught the Hebrew Scriptures to his disciples. This is not to say that the Hebrew canon of Scripture had already reached its final form in Jesus' day. It appears, on the contrary, that the twenty-two book canon now accepted by Jews was itself in the process of development, not to be completed until the early third century of the common era.[7] Even so, virtually all Jews of Jesus' day accepted the sacred authority of the first five books of what is now the Hebrew Bible, known as the Torah or the Law of Moses and sometimes called the Pentateuch (which means "five scrolls"). Many Jews, Jesus included, also accepted the sacred authority of the Hebrew prophets (Isaiah, Jeremiah, and the others) along with some of the other writings, such as the Psalms.

Jesus was well versed in these books of Scripture, and his teachings are, in large measure, an interpretation of them. In early traditions he is called a "rabbi" (meaning "teacher" of Scripture). He enters into disputes with his opponents, the Pharisees, over the proper interpretation of the laws of Scripture, such as what it means to honor the sabbath.[8] When someone asks him how to have eternal life, he replies that he must keep the commandments—and then lists some of the Ten Commandments to illustrate the point (see Matt. 19:17–19). When asked about the key commandments of the Law, he responds by quoting Deuteronomy 6:4, that "you should love the Lord your God with all your heart, soul, and strength," and Leviticus 19:18, that "you should love your neighbor as yourself" (see Matt. 22:34–40). These are not commandments that Jesus himself invented; he was quoting Scripture. Even when he appears to abrogate the Law of Moses in some of the so-called Antitheses of the Sermon on the Mount, he does so in order to bring out what is, in his judgment, their true meaning and intent: The Law says not to murder, Jesus says not to be angry; the Law says not to commit adultery, Jesus says not to lust; the Law says take an eye for an eye, Jesus says turn the other cheek (Matt 5:21–48). The deep intentions of these laws, for Jesus, are to be followed, not simply their surface meaning. Jesus saw the Law as a direction from God about how to live and worship.

His earliest followers did as well. Like him they were law-observant Jews, already possessing a collection of Scripture at the beginning. This is also true of later Christian authors whose books eventually came to be included in the New Testament: Paul, Matthew, Luke, the author of Hebrews, and most of the rest quote the Jewish Scriptures as authoritative texts for the life and worship of the Christian communities they were addressing. These authors quote the Scriptures in their Greek translation (called the Septuagint) because their readers spoke Greek. For most early Christians this translation had as much authority as the original Hebrew.[9] Moreover, these Christians saw Jesus not as the founder of a *new* religion that cast aside the old, but as the fulfillment of the old, who brought something new to an understanding of God that was already anticipated in the Hebrew Bible.

Most Jews, of course, rejected the notion that Jesus was the fulfillment of ancient prophecies concerning the Messiah, and so they rejected the Christian message. This itself provided some motivation for early Christians to devise their own sacred authorities: to separate themselves from Jews, who refused to accept the "authoritative" interpretations of Jewish Scripture pronounced by Christians.[10]

The movement toward establishing a distinctively Christian set of authorities can be seen already in the writings of the New Testament. Jesus himself, of course, presented his *interpretations* of Scripture as authoritative, meaning that they were to be accepted as normative for his followers, who thought of them not only as right and true but as divinely inspired. After Jesus' death, his teachings—not just his interpretations of Scripture per se, but everything he taught—were granted sacred authority by his followers. In fact, it was not long at all before Jesus' teachings were widely thought to be as authoritative as the Jewish Scriptures themselves. We see this movement already in the writings of Paul, who on several (though rare) occasions quotes Jesus' teachings to resolve ethical issues in his churches:

> To those who are married I give charge, not I but the Lord, that the wife should not separate from her husband . . . and that the husband should not divorce his wife. (1 Cor. 7:10–11)

Jesus taught that married couples should not divorce, despite the fact that the Law of Moses allowed for it. But Jesus maintained that Moses had made this allowance because of "the hardness of your heart" (Mark 10:2–11). For the Christians, Jesus' teaching could trump the provisions of the Law.

Even more, by the end of the first century, Jesus' words were being construed by Christian authors as "Scripture." In a striking passage in 1 Tim. 5:18, the author (claiming to be Paul) urges his readers to pay double honor to the presbyters in the church, and he quotes two passages of "Scripture" to support his view. The first is Deut. 25:4 ("Do not muzzle an ox that is treading the grain"), but the other is a saying of Jesus, now found in Matt. 10:10 ("The worker is worthy of his hire"). Here Jesus' own words are equated with Scripture.

In some circles, the teachings of Jesus were not simply on a par with Scripture; they far surpassed it. We have seen this already in the Coptic Gospel of Thomas, a collection of 114 sayings of Jesus, the correct interpretation of which is said to bring eternal life. In proto-orthodox circles, however, it was not Jesus' secret teachings but those found in apostolic authorities that were seen as authoritative. And just as important as his teachings were the events of his life. Accounts of Jesus' life—his words and deeds, his death and resurrection—were eventually placed in circulation and accepted as sacred Scripture, at least as authoritative for most proto-orthodox Christians as the texts of the Jewish Bible.

Along with these authoritative accounts of Jesus' life were the authoritative writings of his apostles, which were being granted sacred status before the end of the New Testament period. The final book of the New Testament to be written was probably 2 Peter, a book almost universally recognized by critical scholars to be pseudonymous, not actually written by Simon Peter but one of many Petrine forgeries from the second century (cf. the Gospel of Peter, the Apocalypse of Peter, the letter from Peter to James, etc.). One of the striking features of this letter is that it discusses the writings of the apostle Paul and considers them, already, as scriptural authorities. In attacking those who misconstrue Paul's writings, twisting their meaning for their own purposes (some kinds of proto-Gnostics?), the author says:

> Our beloved brother Paul wrote to you according to the wisdom given to him, saying such things as he does in all his letters. Some things in them are hard to understand, which the foolish and unstable pervert, leading to their own destruction, as they do with the rest of the Scriptures. (2 Pet. 3:16)

By grouping Paul's writings with "the rest of the Scriptures," this author has made a significant move. Apostolic writings are already being revered and placed into a collection as books of Scripture.

And so, by the end of the New Testament period, we have a movement toward a bipartite New Testament canon, consisting of the words (or accounts) of Jesus and the writings of the apostles. In speaking of this as a "movement" we should guard against being overly anachronistic. It is not that Christians at this time were all in agreement on the matter, as we have seen time and again, and it is not that anyone thought they were in a "movement" that was heading somewhere else. These authors understood that there were certain authorities that were of equal weight to the teachings of (Jewish) Scripture. They had no idea that there would eventually be a twenty-seven book canon. But looking back on the matter from the distance afforded by the passage of time, we can see that their claims had a profound effect on the development of proto-orthodox Christianity, as eventually some of these written authorities came to be included in a canon of Scripture.

Authors and Authorities

Probably every Christian group of the second and third centuries ascribed authority to written texts, and each group came to locate that "authority" in the status of the "author" of the text. These authors were thought to be closely connected to the ultimate authority, Jesus himself, who was understood to represent God. Different groups tied their views to apostolic authorities in different ways: The Ebionites, for example, claimed to present the views advocated by Peter, Jesus' closest disciple, and by James, his brother; the Marcionites claimed to present the views of Paul, which he received via special revelation from Jesus; the Valentinian Gnostics also claimed to represent Paul's teachings, as handed down to his disciple Theudas, the teacher of Valentinus.

The proto-orthodox claimed all of these apostles as authorities—Peter, James, Paul, and many others. But not all of the books used by the proto-orthodox churches were written by apostles—or in some cases even claimed to be. The four Gospels that eventually made it into the New Testament, for example, are all anonymous, written in the third person *about* Jesus and his companions. None of them contains a first-person narrative ("One day, when Jesus and I went into Capernaum . . ."), or claims to be written by an eyewitness or companion of an eyewitness. Why then do we call them Matthew, Mark, Luke, and John? Because sometime in the second century, when proto-orthodox Christians recognized the need for *apostolic* authorities, they attributed these books to apostles (Matthew and John) and close companions of apostles (Mark, the secretary of Peter; and Luke, the traveling companion of Paul). Most scholars today have abandoned these identifications,[11] and recognize that the books were written by otherwise unknown but relatively well-educated Greek-speaking (and writing) Christians during the second half of the first century.

Other books that came to be accepted as authoritative were not anonymous but homonymous, that is, written by someone who had the same name as a person well known in Christian circles. Whoever wrote the New Testament book of James, for example, gives no indication that he is James, the brother of Jesus. Quite the contrary, he says nothing at all about a personal tie to Jesus. Moreover, the name James was very common in the first century—as many as seven men named James are found just within the New Testament.[12] In any event, the book of James was later accepted as apostolic on the grounds that the author *was* the brother of Jesus, although he never claimed to be.

The name John was common as well. Even though the Gospel and Epistles of John do not claim to be written by someone of that name, the book of Revelation does (see Rev. 1:9) . But the author does not claim to be John the son of Zebedee, one of Jesus' apostles. In fact, in one scene "John" has a vision of the throne of God surrounded by twenty-four elders who worship him forever (Rev. 4:4, 9–10). These twenty-four elders are usually taken to refer to the twelve patriarchs of Israel and the twelve apostles. But the author gives no indication that he is seeing himself. Probably, then, this was not the apostle. And so, the book is homonymous, later accepted by Christians as canonical because they believed the author was, in fact, Jesus' earthly disciple.

Yet other books are pseudonymous—forgeries by people who explicitly claim to be someone else. Included in this group is almost certainly 2 Peter, probably the pastoral Epistles of 1 and 2 Timothy and Titus, quite likely the deutero-Pauline Epistles of 2 Thessalonians, Colossians, and Ephesians, and possibly 1 Peter and Jude. But why would someone claim to be a famous person from the past? As we have seen, it was principally in order to get a hearing for his views.

And these authors' views were not merely heard; they were accepted, respected, granted authority, and included in sacred Scripture.

Were any of the books that made it into the New Testament actually written by apostles of Jesus? As we have seen, critical scholars are fairly unified today in thinking that Matthew did not write the First Gospel or John the Fourth, that Peter did not write 2 Peter and possibly not 1 Peter. No other book of the New Testament claims to be written by one of Jesus' earthly disciples. There are books by the apostle Paul, of course. Thirteen go by his name in the New Testament, at least seven of which are accepted by nearly all scholars as authentic.[13] If, then, by "apostolic" book we mean "book actually written by an apostle," most of the books that came to be included in the New Testament are not apostolic. But if the term is taken in a broader sense to mean "book that contains apostolic teaching as defined by the emerging proto-orthodox church," then all twenty-seven pass muster.

Uncertain Steps Toward a Canon

We return now to the question of how, when, and why the twenty-seven books of our New Testament became part of the canon. As we have seen, the process was already in motion by the end of the New Testament period, but it did not come to any kind of closure until the final part of the fourth century, nearly three hundred years later, at the earliest. Why did it take so long, and what drove the process?

It may seem odd that Christians of earlier times, while recognizing the need for authoritative texts to provide guidance for what to believe and how to live, did not see the need to have a fixed number of apostolic writings, a closed canon. But there is no evidence of any concerted effort anywhere in proto-orthodox Christianity (or anywhere else, for that matter) to fix a canon of Scripture in the early second century, when Christian texts were being circulated and ascribed authority. In fact, there was a range of attitudes toward sacred texts among the proto-orthodox Christians of this early period.

I can illustrate the point by considering views found in three proto-orthodox authors from about the second quarter of the second century.[14] It is difficult to assign dates to these writings with any precision, but it appears that the Letter of Polycarp to the Philippians was written by 130 CE, the *Shepherd* of Hermas between 110 and 140 CE, and the sermon known as 2 Clement sometime around 150 CE.[15] All three are proto-orthodox productions. The latter two, in fact, were occasionally accepted as canonical Scripture by orthodox Christians of later times (both are included in early manuscripts of the New Testament). But they represent widely disparate understandings of sacred textual authorities.

Polycarp's letter is a virtual pastiche of citations and allusions drawn from the writings that eventually came to be included in the New Testament: nearly a hundred such quotations in a letter of fourteen relatively brief chapters, in contrast to only about a dozen from the Old Testament. On one occasion Polycarp may actually refer to the book of Ephesians as "Scripture," but the interpretation of the passage is debated. And sometimes he will refer to an explicit authority (e.g. "Remember what the Lord taught . . ."). In most instances, however, Polycarp simply uses lines and phrases familiar from New Testament writings without attribution, especially from the works of Paul, Hebrews, 1 Peter, and the Synoptic Gospels. Were his letter the only proto-orthodox text available to us from the period, we might think that here we could detect the steady movement toward ascribing authority to earlier writings—those that came to be included in the New Testament.

But that there was not a steady movement in this direction is suggested by the *Shepherd* of Hermas, which probably reached its final form *after* Polycarp's letter. This is a much larger book, longer than any book that made it into the New Testament. And so one might expect a correspondingly greater number of quotations and allusions. On the contrary, even though the book is filled with authoritative teachings and ethical exhortations, there is only one explicit quotation of any textual authority to be found. And that, as it turns out, is of a now-lost and unknown Jewish apocalypse called the Book of Eldad and Modat. Some readers have suspected that Hermas knew and was influenced by the book of James, and possibly by Matthew and Ephesians, but the arguments are rather tenuous. In contrast to Polycarp, Hermas does not appear to have any investment at all in sacred textual authorities or an emerging canon of Scripture.[16]

With the third example we find yet another situation, neither Polycarp's feast nor Hermas's famine. The mid-second-century sermon known as 2 Clement makes several statements that have verbal similarities to some of the New Testament Epistles (e.g., 1 Corinthians and Ephesians), but it does not quote these books as authorities. With relatively greater frequency it quotes the words of Jesus ("the Lord said"), but it does so without attributing these words to any of our written Gospels. What is possibly most remarkable is that of the eleven quotations of Jesus' teachings, five do not occur in the canonical Gospels. One of the most interesting we have already considered:

> For the Lord said, "You will be like sheep in the midst of wolves." But Peter replied to him, "What if the wolves rip apart the sheep?" Jesus said to Peter, "After they are dead, the sheep should fear the wolves no longer. So too you: do not fear those who kill you and then can do nothing more to you; but fear the one who, after you die, has the power to cast your body and soul into the hell of fire." (2 Clem. 5:2–4)

The source for this odd dialogue is unknown, although it may derive from the Gospel of Peter. Even more noteworthy for our purposes is the saying found in 2 Clement 12:2:

> For when the Lord himself was asked by someone when his kingdom would come, he said, "When the two are one, and the outside like the inside, and the male with the female is neither male nor female."

This is very much like a saying found not in a canonical Gospel but in the Coptic Gospel of Thomas (Saying 22):

> They said to him, "Shall we then, as children, enter the kingdom?" Jesus said to them, "When you make the two one, and when you make the inside like the outside and the outside like the inside, and the above like the below, and when you make the male and the female one and the same, so that the male not be male nor the female . . . then will you enter the kingdom."[17]

Far from supporting Polycarp in showing a reliance exclusively on books that were to become part of the canon, then, and from supporting Hermas in overlooking earlier textual authorities, 2 Clement appears to accept a wide range of authorities, especially sayings of Jesus—even some that were not finally sanctioned by being included within the canon of Scripture.

And so, by the mid-second century, the questions of the canon were still unresolved in proto-orthodox circles. This conclusion coincides nicely with other findings of our study: Christians in Rhossus accept the Gospel of Peter, as does at first their bishop Serapion, only to reject it later;[18] some Christians accept the Apocalypse of Peter or Paul's letter of 3 Corinthians as Scripture, others do not;[19] some see the Epistle of Barnabas or of 1 Clement as canonical, others do not; Revelation and the Epistle to the Hebrews are matters of constant debate.

Motivations for Establishing the Canon

There can be little doubt that events of the second half of the second century created a demand for a proto-orthodox canon of Scripture. Chief among the motivating factors were prophetic movements such as Montanism from *within* proto-orthodox circles and opposition to heretical forces *outside* these circles.

The effect of Montanism we have already seen. So long as proto-orthodox Christians like Montanus and his two female companions could claim to have direct revelations from God, there were no visible constraints to prevent heretical Christians from making comparable claims. Thus, even though the Montanists— Tertullian chief among them—were orthodox in their theology, their activities had to be proscribed. And so, the recognition of possible abuses (exacerbated, no doubt, by the failure of the Montanist prophecies of an imminent end of all things) led Christian leaders to more certain authorities. These were written authorities, solid and fixed, rather than inspired prophecies in the Spirit, fluctuating and impermanent. They were authorities grounded in the truth, transmitted from Jesus to his own apostles, and they were writings with permanent validity, not just for the moment.

More than anything, however, the interactions with heretical forms of Christianity forced the issue of canon. In this, no one was more important than Marcion, to our knowledge the first Christian of any kind to promote a fixed canon of Scripture, in his publication of modified versions of Luke and ten Pauline Epistles. It is possible to evaluate Marcion's effect by considering the views of two of his proto-orthodox opponents, one writing just as he was beginning to make a large impact and one writing soon afterwards.

Justin Martyr was one of the most productive proto-orthodox authors of the second century. Still preserved are two "apologies" that he wrote, intellectual defenses of the faith against its pagan detractors, and a work called the "Dialogue with Trypho," in which he tries to show the superiority of Christianity over Judaism, largely by appealing to a Christian interpretation of the Jewish Scriptures. His other writings were lost, however, including an attack on heresies of his day that was later used as a source by Irenaeus.

Despite his frequent appeals to authoritative texts, Justin shows no inclination toward a fixed canon of New Testament Scripture in his surviving writings.[20] He does quote the Gospels over a dozen times, but he typically refers to them as "Memoirs of the Apostles." He does not name the *authors* of these books as authorities; the books appear to derive their authority from the fact— to Justin it is a fact—that they accurately recall the words and deeds of Jesus. Moreover, it is not altogether clear whether these quotations derive from the separate Gospels as we have them or from some kind of Gospel harmony that Justin, or someone else in Rome, had created by splicing the available Gospels together into one long narrative.[21] His quotations often use a phrase from Matthew and a phrase from Luke, combining them in a way not found in any surviving Gospel manuscript.[22]

Even more noteworthy than his loose use of the Gospels as authorities is the circumstance that Justin never quotes the apostle Paul. Is it because Marcion, who was active in Rome while Justin was there, used Paul almost exclusively, so that Justin associated him with the heretic?

Even though Justin speaks of Marcion's influence already extending throughout the world (*Apology* 1.26), his real impact did not come until later. And so it is interesting to contrast Justin's relatively casual use of written authorities with what one finds in Irenaeus, another well known proto-orthodox author who also opposed heresies by quoting authoritative texts. But now some thirty years after Justin there is a clear notion of a canon, at least so far as a canon of sacred Gospels is concerned. In a famous passage, Irenaeus laments the fact that heretics not only fabricate their own Gospels but rely on just one or the other of those in the canon to justify their aberrant views. Thus, he says, the Ebionites use only the Gospel of Matthew, those who "separate Jesus from the Christ" (i.e., most Gnostics) use only Mark, the Marcionites use only Luke, and the Valentinian Gnostics use only John. For Irenaeus, however, this curtailment of the Gospel is as bad as the forgery of false texts:

> It is not possible that the Gospels can be either more or fewer in number than they are. For, since there are four zones of the world in which we live, and four principal winds, while the Church is scattered throughout all the world, and the

pillar and ground of the Church is the Gospel and the spirit of life; it is fitting
that she should have four pillars, breathing out immortality on every side. (*Against Heresies* 3.11.7)

And so, just as there are four corners of earth and four winds, there must be
four Gospels, neither more nor fewer.

What is worth observing here is that whereas Justin had a very loose notion
of sacred authority, rooted in unnamed, unspecified, and unenumerated "Memoirs" produced by Jesus' apostles, in Irenaeus, writing thirty years later, we
have a fixed set of named, specified, and enumerated Gospels. What separates
Irenaeus and Justin? One thing that separates them is thirty years of Marcionite
Christianity, thirty years of a brand of Christianity proposing a canon of just
eleven edited books.[23]

It is also worth noting that whereas Justin never quotes Paul, Irenaeus does
so extensively. Some scholars have thought that this was an attempt on Irenaeus's
part to reclaim Paul from the heretics, as he was a favorite not only of Marcion
but also of Gnostics.[24] If this view is right, it might make sense that the proto-
orthodox canon included 1 and 2 Timothy and Titus along with the ten letters
known to Marcion, for nowhere in the New Testament is there a more proto-
orthodox Paul than in these Pastoral Epistles, with their stress on the election
of worthy men as bishops and deacons and their opposition to false "gnosis"
and baseless "mythological speculation" (cf. 1 Tim. 1:4, 6:20). Here is a forged
Paul for a proto-orthodoxy forging ahead, seeking to overcome all heretical
opposition.[25]

The Muratorian Canon and the Criteria of Canonicity

Given these motivations for forming a set canon of Scripture, how did proto-
orthodox Christians go about deciding which books to include and which to
exclude? One of the best ways to follow their line of reasoning is to consider
the earliest surviving canonical list, the Muratorian canon, a fragmentary text
that has been subject to considerable debate in recent years.[26]

This "canon" is a list of books that its anonymous author considered to be
part of the New Testament Scriptures. It is named for the eighteenth-century
scholar L. A. Muratori, who discovered it in a library in Milan. In 1740 Muratori
published the manuscript that contained the list, not so much to provide access
to the various documents that it contains—which are principally treatises of
several fourth-century and fifth-century church fathers—but in order to show
how sloppy copyists in the Middle Ages could be. In a treatise of Ambrose, for
example, the scribe inadvertently copied the same thirty lines *twice*. What is
worse, the second copy of these lines differs from the first in about thirty places—
at least one mistake per line. Who knows how poorly the scribe worked when
we don't have his own copy with which to correct him?

In any event, the Muratorian canon is part of this poorly transcribed manuscript. Most scholars date the manuscript and its ill-suited scribe to the eighth century. The text is in Latin, truly awful Latin, but is a translation of a Greek original. The debates of recent years concern the date and location of the original. The common view of the matter since the days of Muratori has been that it was written somewhere in the vicinity of Rome in the second half of the second century, possibly during the time of Hippolytus. Recent scholars have tried to argue that the text is better located in the fourth century, somewhere in the eastern part of the empire. But the arguments have not proved altogether compelling.[27] The beginning of the text is lost. There can be little doubt, however, about the books it initially described, given the way the fragment itself starts:

> . . . at which nevertheless he was present, and so he placed [them in his narrative]. The third book of the Gospel is that according to Luke.[28]

The author goes on to describe who Luke was, and then to speak of the "fourth of the Gospels," which "is that of John." This list, in other words, begins by discussing the four Gospels, the third and fourth of which are Luke and John. It is fairly clear that it began by mentioning Matthew and Mark, the latter of which is only allusively referred to in the partial sentence that begins the fragment.

Thus the Muratorian canon includes the four Gospels that eventually made it into the New Testament, and no others. After discussing John, the canon names the Acts of the Apostles and then the Epistles of Paul, mentioning seven to seven churches (Corinthians, Ephesians, Philippians, Colossians, Galatians, Thessalonians and Romans), two of which (Corinthians and Thessalonians), the author tells us, Paul wrote twice, and then four to individuals (Philemon, Titus, and two to Timothy). This canon, in other words, includes all thirteen Pauline epistles. It explicitly rejects, however, the epistle "to the Laodiceans" and the one "to the Alexandrians," both of which, it claims, were "forged in Paul's name to further the heresy of Marcion." These, it indicates in a memorable image, "cannot be received into the catholic church, for it is not fitting that gall be mixed with honey."

The list proceeds to list as acceptable the epistle of Jude, two epistles of John, the Wisdom of Solomon (a book that obviously did not make it into the New Testament),[29] the Apocalypse of John, and the Apocalypse of Peter, indicating that some Christians are not willing to have the latter read in church. It maintains that the *Shepherd* of Hermas should be read, but not in church as Scripture, since

> Hermas wrote [it] very recently, in our times, in the city of Rome, while bishop Pius, his brother, was occupying the [episcopal] chair of the church of the city of Rome. (lines 73–76)

In other words, the Shepherd is a recent production (near to "our times") and is not by an apostle (but the brother of a recent bishop). Hence it cannot be included in the canon.

The list concludes by mentioning other rejected books:

> We accept nothing whatever of Arsinous or Valentinus or Miltiades, who also composed a new book of psalms for Marcion, together with Basilides, the Asian founder of the Cataphrygians (i.e., Montanus)—

There the list ends as it began, in midsentence.

When the totals are added up, this proto-orthodox author accepted twenty-two of the twenty-seven books that eventually made it into the New Testament. Not included are Hebrews, James, 1 and 2 Peter, and one of the Johannine Epistles (he accepts two of the three that we have, but does not indicate which two). In addition, he accepts the Wisdom of Solomon and, provisionally, the Apocalypse of Peter. Finally, he rejects some books, either because they are heretical—the Marcionite forgeries of Paul's letters to the Alexandrians and the Laodiceans and other forgeries attributed to Gnostics and Montanists—or because they do not pass his criteria for canonicity.

What are those criteria? As it turns out, they are the same four criteria used across a broad spectrum of proto-orthodox authors of the second and third centuries. For these authors, a book was to be admitted into the proto-orthodox canon of Scripture only if it was:

(a) Ancient: Proto-orthodox authors maintained that a canonical authority had to have been written near the time of Jesus. Part of the reasoning is that which we have seen throughout our study: the suspicion of anything new and recent in ancient religion, where antiquity rather than novelty was respected. To be sure, Jesus himself was not "ancient," even from the perspective of the second or third centuries. But part of the value of antiquity is that it took one back to the point of origins, and since this religion originated with Jesus, for a sacred text to be accepted as authoritative it had to date close to his day. And so the *Shepherd* of Hermas could not pass muster in the Muratorian canon because it was, relatively speaking, a recent production.

(b) Apostolic: An authority had to be written by an apostle or at least by a companion of the apostles. And so the Muratorian canon accepts the Gospels of Luke (written by Paul's companion) and John, along with the writings of Paul. But it rejects the forgeries in Paul's name by the Marcionites. We saw a similar criterion in the case of the Gospel of Peter: Initially it was accepted by the Christians of Rhossus because of its apostolic pedigree. Once it was decided Peter could not have written it, however, it was ruled out of court. Similar arguments transpired over books that *did* make it into the New Testament. The Apocalypse (or Revelation) of John, for example, was widely rejected by proto-orthodox Christians in the eastern part of the empire during the first four centuries, who argued that it was not written by the apostle. The book of Hebrews, on the other hand, was not accepted by most western churches because they did not think it was written by Paul.[30] Eventually each side persuaded the other that the books were written by apostles (in both cases, it turns out, the skeptics were right), and both books came to be included.

(c) Catholic: Books had to enjoy widespread usage among "established" churches to be accepted into the proto-orthodox canon. In other words, canonical books needed to be catholic, the Greek term for "universal." Hence the waffling in the Muratorian canon over the status of the Apocalypse of Peter. This author appears to favor the book, but he recognizes that others in the proto-orthodox community do not accept it for "reading in the church" (i.e., as a scriptural authority, as opposed to devotional material). One of the reasons that some of the shorter "catholic" epistles had such difficulty making it into the New Testament—2 and 3 John, 2 Peter, Jude—is simply because they were not widely used. But eventually they were judged to have been written by apostles and the difficulty caused by their relative disuse was overcome.

(d) Orthodox: The most important criterion for proto-orthodox Christians deciding on the canon had to do with a book's theological character. To some extent, in fact, the other criteria were handmaidens to this one. If a book was not orthodox, it obviously was not apostolic ("obviously," that is, to the one making the judgment) or ancient (it must have been forged recently) or catholic (in that most of the other "orthodox" churches would have had nothing to do with it). To return to Serapion's evaluation of the Gospel of Peter: How did he know that Peter had not written it? It was because the book contained something that looked like a docetic Christology, and obviously Peter could not have written such a thing. This may not be how issues of authorship are decided by historical scholars today, but it proved to be a significant factor among the proto-orthodox. And so, the criterion of orthodoxy is clearly in the foreground in the Muratorian canon, where Gnostic and Montanist forgeries are excluded, as are Marcionite forgeries in the name of Paul, since one cannot "mix gall with honey."

Eusebius and the Canon in the Early Fourth Century

The debates over the contour of the canon raged long after the creation of the Muratorian list in the late second century. Almost all the proto-orthodox eventually agreed that the four Gospels, Acts, the thirteen Pauline Epistles, 1 Peter, and 1 John should be included. But there were extensive disagreements about other books. For some of the books (the shorter catholic epistles) the debates were relatively muted, as not many people were concerned. But other books, such as the Letter to the Hebrews and the Revelation of John, generated considerable disagreement; these were large books, and it mattered whether they were to be considered canonical or not. Was Hebrews' apparent claim that those who had fallen from grace had no chance of restitution to be accepted as a divinely inspired teaching (Heb. 6:1–6)? Was Revelation's teaching that Christ reign here on earth for one thousand years (Rev. 20:1–3) to be taken seriously? The public debates over these books tended to focus on authorship: Did Paul write Hebrews? Did John the son of Zebedee write Revelation? But the *substance* of the debates was over doctrine: Can we accept such a stringent ethical view as Hebrews' or such a potentially crass millenarian view as Revelation's? And what about the Apocalypse of Peter or the Epistle of Barnabas?

That the issues were not quickly resolved is evidenced by later writers standing in the proto-orthodox tradition. Writing a century and a half after the Muratorian canon, for example, Eusebius shows how debates over canon were still very much alive.[31] At one point of his ten-volume work, Eusebius states his intention is "to summarize the writings of the New Testament" (*Church History* 3.25.1). To do so, he sets forth four categories of books. The first he calls "acknowledged" books, meaning those books accepted by all sides within the orthodox tradition (the only one he is concerned with at this point): the Four Gospels, Acts, the (fourteen) Epistles of Paul (he includes Hebrews), 1 John, 1 Peter, and "if it really seems right," he says, the Apocalypse of John. Here, some scholars have noted, Eusebius undercuts his own categories, since the Apocalypse, one of his "acknowledged" books, is not universally acknowledged; Eusebius goes on to say that "we shall give the different opinions [about the Apocalypse of John] at the proper time."

His second category involves books that are "disputed," meaning writings that may well be considered canonical but whose status is debated. He includes in this group James, Jude, 2 Peter, and 2 and 3 John.

Eusebius then names books he considers "spurious," a word that typically means "forged," but that in this context appears to mean "inauthentic, although sometimes considered canonical." These include the Acts of Paul (recall what Tertullian said about Paul and Thecla), the *Shepherd* of Hermas, the Apocalypse of Peter, the Epistle of Barnabas, the Didache of the Apostles, and the Gospel according to the Hebrews. Somewhat oddly, Eusebius also includes in this group, "if it seems right," the Apocalypse of John—odd because one might expect it to be listed as "disputed" rather than "spurious."

Finally, Eusebius provides a list of books that are heretical: the Gospels of Peter, Thomas, and Matthias, the Acts of Andrew and John. With regard to the books of this category, Eusebius comments,

> To none of these has any who belonged to the succession of ecclesiastical writers ever thought it right to refer in his writings. Moreover, the character of the style also is far removed from apostolic usage, and the thought and purport of their contents are completely out of harmony with true orthodoxy and clearly show themselves that they are the forgeries of heretics.[32]

These books are not, in other words, catholic, apostolic, or orthodox.

The Canon at the End of the Fourth Century

It was another sixty years—years of back and forth, hard-fought debates *within* the orthodox camp—before anyone came up with a definitive list of books to be included in the canon that matched our list today, in the famous Athanasian letter of 367 CE. Even the powerful Athanasius could not settle the issue once and for all, as we have seen. But his list corresponded well enough with what most other orthodox Christians of his day were saying that it eventually triumphed. The greatest orthodox theologian of antiquity, Augustine of Hippo, threw his weight behind the list and pushed its acceptance at the Synod of Hippo in 393 CE. We no longer have the text of the proceedings of the conference, but we do have

Codex Sinaiticus, the oldest surviving manuscript of the entire New Testament. This fourth-century manuscript includes The *Shepherd* of Hermas and the Epistle of Barnabas (the first page of which is pictured here), books that were considered part of the New Testament by some Christians for several centuries.

that of the Third Synod of Carthage, held four years later, which summarized
the earlier proceedings:

> The canonical Scriptures are these [there follows a list of the books of the Old
> Testament]. Of the New Testament: the Gospels, four books; the Acts of the
> Apostles, one book; the Epistles of Paul, thirteen; of the same to the Hebrews,
> one Epistle; of Peter, two; of John, apostle, three; of James, one; of Jude, one;
> the Revelation of John. Concerning the confirmation of this canon, the church
> across the sea shall be consulted.[33]

And so the canon appears to be settled in North Africa, but the church in
Rome still needs to be consulted on the matter. In some parts of the Church, it
was settled somewhat differently. But for those within the orthodox tradition,
the tradition that stands at the root of most forms of Christianity familiar to us
today—Roman Catholic, Eastern Orthodox, Protestant—the matter was for all
practical purposes resolved. Proto-orthodoxy had triumphed and was simply
working out some of the issues at the margins.

To be sure, the theological debates of later centuries were at least as heated
and, in the eyes of their participants, as monumental as anything that went
before, even if to our eyes the issues became increasingly circumscribed and
the differences between combatants increasingly minute. But these later debates could all presuppose and build on the outcome of the disputes of the
earlier Christian centuries, as proto-orthodoxy became orthodoxy, and theologians moved forward to refine their views.

Chapter Twelve

Winners, Losers, and the Question of Tolerance

The historical significance of the victory of proto-orthodox Christianity can scarcely be overstated. The form of Christianity that emerged from the conflicts of the second and third centuries was destined to became the religion of the Roman Empire. From there it developed into the dominant religious, political, economic, social, and cultural institution of the West for centuries—down to the present. Christians living in the midst of these conflicts could not have imagined how important their outcome would be for the shape of western civilization. The repercussions are still felt today, in ways that even we may have difficulty understanding.

The Significance of Victory

Throughout this study I have tried to hypothesize what it may have been like if some other side had "won." If the Marcionite Christians had gained ascendancy, would people still ask, "Do you believe in God?" Or would they ask, "Do you believe in the two Gods?" Would anyone except scholars of antiquity have *heard* of the Gospels of Matthew, Mark, and John? Would we have an "Old" Testament? How would the social and political relations of Jews and Christians over the centuries have been affected? Would Christians who rejected the Jewish God and all things Jewish feel a need to polemicize against and attack Jews? Or would they simply ignore Jews as not presenting any real competition to their own claims of the knowledge of the other God, who saved them from the creator? Would anti-Semitism be worse, or would it be nonexistent?

If, on the other hand, Ebionite Christians had gained ascendancy, would Christianity have remained a sect within Judaism? Would Christians today worship on Saturdays instead of Sundays? Would they keep kosher? Would these Jewish-Christians have wanted or been able to convert masses of people to their message of salvation, when conversion would have required men to undergo the operation of circumcision? Would Christianity have been anything but a footnote in the history of world religions?

We can probably say with some certainty that if some other side had won—Marcionite, Ebionite, some form of Gnostic—there would have been no doctrine of Christ as both fully divine and human. As a consequence, there would have been no doctrine of the Trinity. How would that have affected the intellectual life of the Middle Ages, the development of scholastic modes of argumentation, the modern Christian debates over the relationship between divine revelation (say, of religious mystery) and human reason (which cannot comprehend the depths of mystery)?

These questions affect everyone, not merely those who call themselves Christian. The beliefs, practices, and institutions of Christianity have played an enormous role in western civilization as a whole, not just for members of the Church. Take the New Testament itself, for example, considered by most people throughout the course of its history to be a single book, with a unified message that serves as the ultimate basis for this religion's faith and practice. The New Testament has been and continues to be the most widely read and revered book in the history of the West. It continues to inspire belief, to stimulate reflection, and to provide hope to millions. It is preached from the pulpit; it is studied in the university; it is attacked by skeptics; it is revered by believers. In the United States it is widely considered to have been a foundational document for the founders; it is quoted on the floor of the Senate to justify acts of war and at peace rallies to oppose the use of military force; its authority is cited by both opponents and proponents of the right of a woman to have an abortion, by both opponents and proponents of the death penalty, by both opponents and proponents of gay rights. It was used to justify slavery and to abolish slavery. It has been used to justify capitalism and socialism. It has been used for good and for evil.

But where did this book come from? It came from the victory of the proto-orthodox. What if another group had won? What if the New Testament contained not Jesus' Sermon on the Mount but the Gnostic teachings Jesus delivered to his disciples after his resurrection? What if it contained not the letters of Paul and Peter but the letters of Ptolemy and Barnabas? What if it contained not the Gospels of Matthew, Mark, Luke, and John but the Gospels of Thomas, Philip, Mary, and Nicodemus? Or what if it did not exist at all?

On an even more fundamental level: If some group other than the proto-orthodox had won, how would our approaches to reading texts and our "natural" ways of thinking differ? Most people, for example, take a commonsensical approach to the task of reading. We know what words mean, we see how words are used in a text, we notice the grammatical connections of the words, and by reading them in sequence in view of our knowledge of the language we reconstruct what an author meant. But what if this "literal" way of reading a text had been marginalized as an inadequate mode of interpretation? What if the religious and intellectual traditions passed down through the centuries, traditions that determine how we read and make sense of texts, indeed, of our world, what if these traditions supported the primacy not of literal readings but of figurative ones, where the assumption is that the real meaning of a text is not the literal one, that words have secret meanings available only to those who have special insights, for example, as given from above? Would we be able to read a newspaper the way we do today?

In considering the importance of the victory of proto-orthodox Christianity, we should also reflect on broader historical implications. A case can be made that this victory was one of the most significant events in the social and political history of western civilization. Had it not happened, one could argue, the vast majority of people in the world who adhere to Christianity—some two billion by some recent estimates, the largest religion on the planet—would still be pagans, adhering to one or another polytheistic religion. The history of western civilization as we know it, from late antiquity through the Middle Ages, to the Renaissance, the Reformation, and into modernity, would never have occurred.

The grounds for this argument have to do with the conversion of the Roman Empire. Probably no ten-year period was more important for the fortunes of Christianity than 303–13 CE, well after the conflicts we have been discussing had been resolved and proto-orthodoxy had established itself as the dominant form of Christian faith. That decade near the beginning of the fourth century saw a shift in Roman imperial policy away from a massive proscription and persecution of Christians to the conversion of the Roman emperor himself and the beginnings of an enormous bestowal of imperial favors on the Christians, which ultimately led to large-scale conversions and to the declaration of Christianity as the official state religion some decades later.

The political history of the period, including church-state relations, is complicated, but for our purposes a brief sketch will suffice, starting with a word of background.[1] Christians of all sorts had been subject to local persecution from the beginning of the religion (2 Cor. 11:23–25); but it was not until the mid-third century that there was any official, empire-wide attempt to eliminate the religion. From about 249 CE onwards, starting with the brief reign of the emperor Decius (249–51), there were periods of persecution, sporadically and inconsistently enforced, along with times of peace. For the most part, these persecutions, like the local ones in earlier periods, were occasioned not by *antireligious* sentiment but precisely by religious sentiment. Many pagans took their religions seriously. It was widely believed that the gods were kind and gracious, but when offended they could become angry and would need to be appeased. And nothing angered them more than the failure of people to worship them by performing the prescribed acts of sacrifice. Christians, of course, refused to sacrifice to the pagan gods, even the gods of the state. They were sometimes blamed, then, for disasters that occurred—famine, drought, disease, earthquake, political setbacks, economic difficulties—and the persecutions were designed to force them to recant and show due reverence to the gods who had long been honored by the state.

In 303 CE, the pagan emperor of the eastern part of the empire, Diocletian, ordered a persecution of Christians, matched to some degree by a persecution in the western part of the empire by his colleague, the emperor Maximian. Several imperial edicts were issued that called for the burning of Christian books, the demolition of Christian churches, the removal of class privileges for Christians, and eventually the imprisonment of high-ranking Christian clergy. In 304, a further edict required all Roman subjects to perform sacrifices to the gods; noncompliance meant death or forced labor. This "Great Persecution," as it is called, lasted on and off for nearly a decade, well beyond the retirement of Diocletian and Maximian in 305 CE. But the persecution failed to force the majority of Christians to recant. For a variety of reasons, official toleration for Christians was pronounced in both the western and eastern parts of the empire by 313. Throughout the empire people were granted freedom of religious choice, and the property of the Christians was restored.

The senior emperor at that time was Constantine. In 312 Constantine had begun to attribute his military and political ascendancy to the God of the Christians and to identify himself, as a result, as a Christian.[2] Once his base of power was secure, Constantine became quite active in church affairs, dealing with various controversies in an attempt to keep the Church united. Some historians think that Constantine saw in the Christian church a way of bringing unity to the empire itself. In 325 CE Constantine called the Council of Nicaea, the first so-called Ecumenical Council of the church, that is, the first council at which bishops from around the world were brought together in order to establish a consensus on major points of faith and practice. All of these bishops agreed with the major theological positions hammered out by their proto-orthodox forebears; as I have noted, the forms of "lost Christianity" we have been discussing had by this time already been displaced, suppressed, reformed, or destroyed. Thus it was the surviving form of Christianity—by now we might call it orthodoxy—that Constantine knew and supported.

As a result of the favors Constantine poured out upon the church, conversion to the Christian faith soon became "popular." At the beginning of the fourth century, Christians may have comprised something like 5 to 7 percent of the population; but with the conversion of Constantine the church grew in leaps and bounds. By the end of the century it appears to have been the religion of choice of fully *half* the empire. After Constantine, every emperor except one was Christian.[3] Theodosius I (emperor 379–95 CE) made Christianity (specifically *Roman* Christianity, with the bishop of Rome having ultimate religious authority) the official religion of the state. He opposed the surviving pagan religions and eventually banned pagan sacrificial practices. More conversions naturally followed, until Christianity became *the* religion to be handed down to the Middle Ages and onwards.

None of this would have happened without Constantine's "conversion." And now the question of relevance to our study. If any other form of early Christianity had established itself as dominant within the religion, would Constantine have embraced it? Would he have been willing to adopt a Jewish form of Christianity, which would have required him and his fellow converts to become Jewish, undergo circumcision, keep kosher food laws, and observe other traditions of the Jewish Law? Or would he have been inclined to accept a Marcionite form of Christianity, which could claim no "ancient" roots, since it abandoned the ancient traditions of Judaism? Would he have been likely to adopt any of the Gnostic forms of Christianity, which maintained that only a spiritual elite could truly understand the revelation of God, that the majority of believers misunderstood the true teachings of Jesus?

It is difficult to see how any of these alternatives could have been attractive to the emperor or would have served to unite the empire. If one of them had become dominant, would Constantine have converted to this faith and promoted it throughout his domain? If he had not, would Christianity have become the "official" religion of the empire some decades later under the emperor Theodosius? If not, would it ever have been anything but another minor religion in an empire filled with religions? To put the question bluntly: Would Christianity have become the religion of the empire? Of the Middle Ages? Of the modern West? And if not, wouldn't those who eventually confessed Christianity—the vast majority of people around the northern and southern Mediterranean, medieval Europe, and on into the new world—wouldn't they, or rather we, have remained pagan? Wouldn't most people today still worship many gods through periodic offerings of animal sacrifice?

All things considered, it is difficult to imagine a more significant event than the victory of proto-orthodox Christianity.

Remnants of What Was Lost

This is not to say, however, that proto-orthodox Christians were absolutely successful in producing a consensus on every important point of faith and practice. Indeed, as soon as the major theological issues of the second and third centuries were more or less resolved, others appeared to take their place. The battles fought in later centuries were no less harsh, and the polemic against "false teachers" was no less vitriolic. Quite the contrary, as the options narrowed, the debates intensified.

To take one example: Once proto-orthodoxy had established that Christ was both human and divine, the relationship between his humanity and divinity still needed to be resolved. How could Christ be both a man and God? Was it that Christ had a human body but that his human soul was replaced by a soul that was divine? If so, then how was he "fully" human? Or was it that the incarnate Christ was two separate persons, one divine and one human? If that were the case, would that not mean he was *half* divine and *half* human, rather than fully both? Or was it that he was one solitary person, but that within that person he had two natures, one fully divine and one fully human? Or does he have just one nature, that is at one and the same time both fully divine and fully human? All of these options were proposed and hotly debated over the course of the fourth and fifth centuries.[4]

The intensity of the disputes, if nothing else, shows that there will always be diverse beliefs so long as there are diverse believers. This diversity shows itself as well in the circumstance that the proto-orthodox victory never did stamp out heretical perspectives completely, despite their every attempt to do so. Heretical views continued to live on, even if only in small pockets of believers in out-of-the-way places. Some of the beliefs and practices that I have described as "lost," in fact, have recurred in modern Christianity where, for instance, there are various groups of "messianic Jews" who insist, somewhat like their Ebionite forebears, on maintaining Jewish customs such as keeping the sabbath, following kosher food laws, and observing Passover, while believing in the death of Jesus for salvation. So, too, there are a number of "Gnostic" churches still (or rather, again) in the world today, especially in California.

What is less obvious but possibly more historically significant is that views of the various proscribed and lost groups of Christians lived on even within orthodox Christianity. In some instances these are views that were "common ground" among various Christian communities; in other instances, however, they are views that the orthodox Christianity took over from "aberrant" groups that had been otherwise reformed or suppressed. Sometimes it is not possible to know which is which, that is, whether a view was "shared" or "borrowed." In either event, the survival of these views shows, to some extent, the capacity of proto-orthodox Christianity not only to attack but also to incorporate disparate understandings of the faith.

Thus, for example, orthodox Christianity shared with (or borrowed from) the Ebionites a profound reverence for the traditions of Israel; they accepted the sacred texts of the Hebrew Bible, emphasized the oneness of God, and stressed the humanity of Jesus. All of these continue to be features of Christianity today. On the other hand, orthodox Christianity shared with (or borrowed from) the Marcionites the sense of the *newness* of God's revelation in Christ; they accepted the idea of a closed canon of Scripture, the primacy of the literal interpretation of the text, and an emphasis on Jesus' divinity. At the same time, they shared with (or inherited from) the Marcionites a disdain for and distrust of all things Jewish, along with the notion, still found among Christians today, that the Old Testament God is a God of wrath, whereas the New Testament God is a God of love and mercy. So, too, orthodox Christianity agreed with (or borrowed from) some groups of Gnostics the idea that there is a spiritual elite within the Christian church at large, who have special insights into the nature of God; possibly they also inherited the stress on figurative ways of interpreting texts, and a sense that the material world is to be rejected in favor of the spiritual, leading to a concomitant rationale for ascetic behavior that punishes the material self by depriving the body of its desires and even needs.

Some of these "common grounds" or "borrowings," whichever they were, obviously stood in tension with one another, and several unique aspects of proto-orthodoxy were the result. For example, while affirming the authority of the Jewish Scriptures (with the Ebionites but against the Marcionites), the proto-orthodox rejected historical Judaism (with the Marcionites against the Ebionites); while affirming the divinity of Jesus (with the Marcionites against the Ebionites), they also affirmed his humanity (with the Ebionites against the Marcionites). While insisting that the one true God is the creator of this world (against Marcion and Gnostics) they often denigrated this world and strove to escape its material trappings through ascetic practices (with Marcion and Gnostics).

The Winners as Losers

And so, as a result of these common grounds or borrowings, not to mention the persistence of various "alternative" forms of Christianity through the years, the proto-orthodox victory cannot be seen as complete. In another sense, however, from a strictly proto-orthodox point of view, the victory was altogether too complete. For as it happened, the victors themselves came to be vanquished when the exclusivistic rhetoric they used in countering the views of their opponents was eventually turned on themselves. That is to say, as orthodox Christianity moved on to refine its theological views to a level unanticipated by its forebears, the views of proto-orthodoxy became not just surpassed but proscribed. In one sense, proto-orthodoxy itself became a lost Christianity.

We have seen this several times throughout the study. From a historical point of view, it appears that the Ebionites did indeed teach an understanding of the faith that would have been close to that of Jesus' original disciples— Aramaic-speaking Jews who remained faithful to the Jewish Law and who kept Jewish customs even after coming to believe that Jesus was the Messiah. But the Ebionites came to be declared heretical by the proto-orthodox. So, too, the Roman adoptionists, followers of Theodotus the Cobbler, may well have proclaimed a christological view similar to that of Jesus' earthly followers, that he was completely human (and not divine) but was adopted by God to fulfill his mission of dying for the sake of others. They, too, were branded as heretics and excommunicated.

As time went on and proto-orthodox Christians came to believe that Christ was both divine and human, they needed to explain how that was possible. Near the end of the second century, one of the common solutions was that Christ was himself God the Father, come to earth in human form. This view was widespread among the proto-orthodox in Rome, and it was the view advocated by the Roman bishop himself at the beginning of the third century. But it came to be mocked as "patripassianist" (a view that made the "Father suffer"), castigated as false, and deemed heretical.

Tertullian was one of the chief opponents of the patripassianists and one of the leading spokespersons of proto-orthodoxy in his day. But since he joined the prophetic movement of the Montanists, in later times his own reputation came to be sullied by association, as the idea that direct revelation from God could take precedence over the written Scriptures led to the condemnation of the Montanist movement.

A worse fate lay in store for the greatest proto-orthodox thinker of the first three Christian centuries, Origen, whose creative attempts to explore the relationship of God and Christ based on a full understanding of scriptural revelation led him to conclude that Christ was a created being who was ultimately subordinate to God the Father, even if in substance he *was* the Word and Wisdom of God because of his intimate connection with and infusion by the Father in eternity past. But Origen's subordinationist Christology, along with his notion of the preexistence of human souls and of the ultimate salvation of all beings, including the devil, led eventually to his condemnation as a heretic.

Other examples could well be chosen, in which the early proponents of the faith, attempting to uncover its mysteries in ways that laid the foundation for later reflection, were themselves condemned by their own successors, who refined their understanding to such a point that the partially developed, imprecise, or allegedly wrongheaded claims of their predecessors were necessarily seen not simply as inadequate but as heretical and so not to be tolerated. Even though proto-orthodoxy led to orthodoxy, it did not simply become orthodoxy without remainder. In some senses, the intolerance that brought about the victory of proto-orthodoxy led to its own demise.

Tolerance and Intolerance
in the Struggles for Dominance

This intolerance was not something proto-orthodox Christianity derived from its broader Roman milieu. In point of fact, the polytheistic religions of the Roman Empire were famously tolerant of one another. None of these religions insisted that if it was right, the others must all be wrong. These religions affirmed the existence of numerous gods and acknowledged the importance of worshiping the gods. For pagans in the empire, since there were so many gods in the world, and these gods deserved worship, it was perfectly legitimate—and even common sense—that they *should* be worshiped.[5]

Some people today may think that the Romans must have been intolerant of other religions, since they are known to have persecuted the Christians. As we have seen, however, the problem posed by the Christians was not that they worshiped their own God, or that they considered Jesus a god, or that they had their own prescribed rituals and practices. The problem was that the Christians refused to worship the other gods, especially the gods of the state. If the state gods had made the state great, then surely they deserved to be acknowledged through acts of worship. Why would anyone refuse? Moreover, since the gods sometimes punished individuals or communities that failed to acknowledge them, Christians could be seen as being at fault when disasters struck. As Tertullian famously exclaimed:

> They [the pagans] think the Christians the cause of every public disaster, of every affliction with which the people are visited. If the Tiber rises as high as the city walls, if the Nile does not send its waters up over the fields, if the heavens give no rain, if there is an earthquake, if there is famine or pestilence, straightway the cry is, "Away with the Christians to the lion!" (*Apology* 40)

Jews were not blamed for such disasters, even though they, too, did not worship the gods, because Jews were following ancestral traditions that forbade them to engage in such worship. Since the *antiquity* of religious tradition was so important in the ancient world, and since Jews could justify their practices through ancient tradition, they were normally not compelled to abandon their religious commitments to participate in civic cult.[6] Christians were a different matter altogether. They also believed that the Jewish God was the only true God. But they did not follow the ancestral customs of the Jews, and so they were not regarded as having a legitimate excuse for failing to worship the state gods—leading to their occasional persecution.

Even so, as I have pointed out, these persecutions were sporadic and isolated, and almost always local affairs, until the persecutions in the second half of the third century. For most of the second and third centuries, in most places throughout the empire, even Christians were left to themselves, tolerated by the state apparatus and by the majority of people at large.

This attitude of tolerance, however, was not shared by the proto-orthodox—at least not by the proto-orthodox authors who have left us any writings. For one thing, these Christians were exclusivistic in their views. They believed that the one and only true God had given one way of salvation, and that the only way to be right with this God was through this way he had provided—the death and resurrection of Jesus. This exclusivity, as we have seen, bred an intolerance toward religious diversity. Since there was only one way of salvation, all other religions were in error. And being in error carried eternal consequences. Those who did not accept the one true God by believing in the death and resurrection of his Son for salvation would be condemned to the flames of hell for all eternity.

It is very hard to know whether other Christian groups were more tolerant than the proto-orthodox, given the sparse writings surviving from their pens. They certainly opposed the proto-orthodox themselves on a number of issues. But there is little to indicate just how strenuously they argued their views or how convinced they were that the differences between themselves and others were of some kind of ultimate, eternal significance. It is not difficult, however, to gauge the tolerance levels of the proto-orthodox. As a group, they were not tolerant at all.

They were certainly not tolerant toward pagans. On this, the narratives of proto-orthodox apostolic heroes and the stories of proto-orthodox martyrs are quite unambiguous: Worshipers of other gods needed to convert to the belief in Jesus as the Son of God or else be subject to eternal torment. Nor were they tolerant toward Jews. Here, too, proto-orthodox writings were unambiguous: Jews who rejected Jesus as the messiah had rejected their own God; he in turn had rejected them.[7]

Of yet greater relevance for our study, they were not tolerant toward heretics. Proto-orthodox Christians insisted that salvation was dependent on faith and that faith was not simply a vague sense of the goodness of God or a general dependence on God's mercy. Faith was *in* something; it had *content*. The content therefore mattered. The *regula fidei* and then the creeds that developed were ways to indicate what it was that people had to believe. Those who rejected the true beliefs adhered, necessarily, to false ones. But since only right belief can bring salvation, wrong belief can do nothing but bring damnation. As a result, heretics would pay for their false teachings with eternal torment.

Discovering What Was Lost

This kind of religious intolerance might itself seem intolerable to us today. Even though we are heirs of the proto-orthodox victory, times have changed, and changed with them has been a sense of what is acceptable and unacceptable in religious dialogue.

To be sure, for many people in the world today—millions of people—the religious views inherited from the early Christian tradition are truths to be cherished. Christian theologians continue to plumb the mysterious depths that these truths affirm; Christian lay people continue to recite the creeds, to read the Scriptures, to listen to the proclamation, to follow the teachings. These teachings stimulate thought and reflection; they guide action and influence behavior; they provide hope and comfort. And yet many Christians people today are less inclined than their proto-orthodox forebears to condemn those who disagree with these teachings. For good or ill, there is a greater sense—though obviously not a universal sense—of the need for tolerance.

The broader interest in and heightened appreciation for diverse manifestations of religious experience, belief, and practice today has contributed to a greater fascination with the diverse expressions of Christianity in various periods of its history, perhaps especially in its earliest period. This fascination is not simply a matter of antiquarian interest. There is instead a sense that alternative understandings of Christianity from the past can be cherished yet today, that they can provide insights even now for those of us who are concerned about the world and our place in it. Those captivated with this fascination commonly feel a sense of loss upon realizing just how many perspectives once endorsed by well-meaning, intelligent, and sincere believers came to be abandoned, destroyed, and forgotten—as were the texts that these believers produced, read, and revered. But with that feeling of loss comes the joy of discovery when some of these texts, and the lost Christianities they embody, are recovered and restored to us. For our own religious histories encompass not only the forms of belief and practice that emerged as victorious from the conflicts of the past but also those that were overcome, suppressed, and eventually lost.

Notes

Introduction

1. The term *canon* comes from a Greek word that means "measuring rod" or "straight edge." It came refer to a "standard" and then to a "standard collection of writings."
2. On Jesus having a twin brother, see below 39–40. For extensive discussions of the Gospel of Peter and the Gospel of Thomas, see chapters 1 and 3.
3. For a collection of the "lost" Christian texts that have now been found, in readable English translations, see the companion volume to this study, Ehrman, *Lost Scriptures.*
4. Of course, on one level it is impossible to know how a different outcome might have affected history, just as it is impossible to know what would have happened had Caesar not crossed the Rubicon or Hitler not lost the war. But it is always possible to *imagine* what might have been different.

Part 1

1. I am not including false ascriptions of books as forgeries, that is, the later attribution of an anonymous book to a famous person (e.g., as when the New Testament book of Hebrews was attributed to the apostle Paul, or as when the first Gospel was attributed to Matthew the tax collector). In these cases we are dealing not with the claims of an author but with those of later readers, a different matter altogether. Nor would the term *forgery* apply, as we will see below, to the use of simple pen names. For further reflections on ancient forgery, see 30–31.

2. For the authorship of the New Testament letter of Titus, see Ehrman, *New Testament,* 389–94 and the bibliography cited on 395.

3. For a fuller discussion of Konrad Kujau and his forged Hitler Diaries, see 66–67.

4. See Ehrman, *New Testament,* 377–79.

5. For discussion of the basic issues that have led scholars to these judgments, see Ehrman, *New Testament,* 389–94.

Chapter 1

1. For example, both the Apostles' Creed and the Nicene Creed, still recited in churches today, descend from creeds developed in the fourth century.

2. Origen: *Homilies on Luke; Fragments on Luke,* 5–6.

3. On early Christian Gnostics, see chap. 6.

4. Translation of J. K. Elliott, *Apocryphal New Testament,* 20.

5. For a translation of the Gospel of Thomas, see Lambdin, in Ehrman, *Lost Scriptures,* 19–28.

6. An accessible translation of Eusebius is provided by G. A. Williamson, *Eusebius: The History of the Church from Christ to Constantine;* the story of Serapion and the Gospel of Peter is found in *Church History* 6.12.

7. See, e.g., Mark 1:10. In the Greek, the verse literally says that the Spirit descended "into" Jesus.

8. This understanding of the relation of Jesus and Christ was dominant in Gnostic circles, which we will be discussing in chap. 6.

9. Good discussions of the discovery and the manuscript itself can be found in John Dominic Crossan, *Four Other Gospels,* 125–30, and Paul Mirecki, "Peter, Gospel of," in the *Anchor Bible Dictionary,* 5:278–81. Mirecki also provides an important bibliography.

10. For a new and readable English translation of the Gospel of Peter, see Ehrman, *Lost Scriptures,* 31–34.

11. The fullest account of all the manuscripts of the Gospel of Peter is, regrettably, not available in English: Schlarb and Lührmann, eds., *Fragmente Apokryph gewordener Evangelien in griechischer und lateinischer Sprache,* 72–95.

12. In Mark's Gospel, both criminals abuse Jesus, but in Luke, only one of them does. See Mark 15:32 and Luke 23:39–43.

13. When the legs were broken, a person being crucified could not push up to relieve the pressure on his chest and so continue to breathe. To prolong the agony, the soldiers here refuse to break the criminal's legs.

14. This tradition is repeated, for example, in the writings of the church father Origen, in his defense of Christianity called *Against Celsus* (4.22). The roots of this charge may be found, however, already in the New Testament; see Matt. 21:33–41, 22:1–7.

15. The earliest version of this letter is anachronistically addressed to Claudius, who did not become emperor for another eleven years after Jesus' death.

16. I have used the translation of J. K. Elliott, *Apocryphal New Testament*, 209.

17. There is no way to make such judgments for certain, of course. Our information about early Christianity comes from the surviving writings from Christians of the period and archaeological discoveries of manuscripts and material objects. Both kinds of sources are problematic in their own ways. The Christian writings that happen to survive are almost entirely those of the proto-orthodox. Their opponents surely wrote as much as they themselves did. But these works "of the enemy" were almost never copied through the Middle Ages, and so they have been largely lost to posterity. And so, for example, we can do little more than wish that we had a copy of the letter that the pastor of the church of Rhossus may have sent back to Serapion, telling him—we might imagine—that the Gospel of Peter actually was written by Peter, that it was not heretical, that it was sacred Scripture, Serapion's suspicions notwithstanding. But no such letter, or anything like it, survives.

18. For a new translation of 2 Clement, see Ehrman, *Lost Scriptures*, 185–90.

19. On 2 Clement, see 237–38.

20. For a readable translation of the Apocalypse of Peter by J. K. Elliott, see Ehrman, *Lost Scriptures*, 280–88.

Chapter 2

1. Thecla remains popular in some parts of the Christian world today, especially Eastern Europe. For a full discussion of her veneration, see Davis, *The Cult of Saint Thecla*.

2. Unfortunately, there are not very many good, full studies of the phenomenon in Christian antiquity that are available in English. A solid and interesting overview can be found in. Metzger, "Literary Forgeries and Canonical Pseudepigrapha." The best thorough treatment is in German: Speyer, *Die literarische Fälschung im heidnischen und christlichen Altertum*. The classic study of the entire phenomenon up to the modern period in English is Farrer, *Literary Forgeries*. Among the many recent books, one of the most fascinating is Grafton, *Forgers and Critics*.

3. On these, see Metzger, "Literary Forgeries," 5–12.

4. The story is recounted by the ancient historian Pausanius in *History of Greece*, 6.18, 2ff.

5. For a readable translation of 3 Corinthians, see Ehrman, *Lost Scriptures*, 157–59.

6. On the pseudo-Pauline letters of 3 Corinthians, to and from Seneca, and Laodiceans, see 206–07, 210–12, and 213–15. For translations, see Ehrman, *Lost Scriptures,* 157–66.

7. Tertullian is sometimes suspected, however, of having made up the story of the presbyter forger precisely in order to counteract the popularity of the stories of Thecla.

8. On the background to the stories found in the Acts of Thecla, see the intriguing studies of Virginia Burrus, *Chastity as Autonomy: Women in the Stories of the Apocryphal Acts;* Davies, *The Revolt of the Widows;* and MacDonald, *The Legend and the Apostle.* For a more recent statement, see Davis, *Cult of St. Thecla,* 13–18.

9. There may have been more writings (e.g., letters) penned in Paul's name in the fuller narrative; unfortunately, we do not appear to have the entire Acts of Paul in any of our surviving manuscripts.

10. For a new translation of the Acts of Thecla, see Ehrman, *Lost Scriptures.*

11. We are not told why Thecla cross-dresses. Is it in order to make it easier to travel? Is it because, as we will see in the Gospel of Thomas (Saying 114) in the next chapter, "every woman who makes herself male will enter the Kingdom of Heaven"?

12. See Davis, *Cult of St. Thecla.*

13. For translations of key excerpts of these Apocryphal Acts, see Ehrman, *Lost Scriptures,* 91–154.

14. The Greek novels are all collected together into a handy volume by Reardon, *Collected Ancient Greek Novels.* For an analysis of their significance, see especially his Introduction.

15. In which the churches are run by ordained ministers, rather than by the Spirit who works through all individuals in the church equally through the distribution of gifts. For church structure of Paul's own communities, see, e.g., 1 Corinthians 12.

16. See Ehrman, *New Testament,* 389–94.

17. For a full discussion of the issues, see the commentary on the passage by Fee, *The First Epistle to the Corinthians.*

18. For a brief discussion of Paul's view of women and their role in his churches, see Ehrman, *New Testament,* chap. 24. Among the many excellent fuller studies, see Kraemer, *Her Share of the Blessings,* and Torjesen, *When Women Were Priests.*

19. For excerpts of the Acts of Thomas in a readable English translation, see Ehrman, *Lost Scriptures,* 122–34 (translation of J. K. Elliott).

20. For a humorous retelling of the tale, see the Roman comic playwright Plautus, *Amphitryon.*

21. Following Elliott's translation in *Apocryphal New Testament.*

22. Elliott's translation in *Apocryphal New Testament.*

23. It is widely recognized that the surviving Acts of John derives from several sources; most scholars recognize that a large portion of the text (chaps.

87–105, or just 94–102) as we now have it was interpolated at a later time into the narrative. See the discussion in Elliott, *Apocryphal New Testament,* 303–4. For a translation of some of the more intriguing accounts of the Acts of John, see the excerpts from Elliott in Ehrman, *Lost Scriptures,* 93–108; that is the translation I am following here.

24. See the discussion in Elliott, *Apocryphal New Testament,* 303–7.
25. For a superb overview of the abundant recent scholarship on the rise of Christian asceticism, see Clark, *Reading Renunciation,* 14–42.
26. See Ehrman, *Jesus: Apocalyptic Prophet of the New Millennium.*
27. See Ehrman, *New Testament,* chap. 24.

Chapter 3

1. For the best discussion of the discovery from an archaeological perspective, dealing as well with the vexed question of the identity of the Dead Sea Scrolls community with the Essenes, see Jodi Magness, *The Archaeology of Qumran and the Dead Sea Scrolls.*
2. Among the many introductions to the Dead Sea Scrolls, two of the best are J. Fitzmyer, *Responses to 101 Questions on the Dead Sea Scrolls,* and James VanderKam, *The Dead Sea Scrolls Today.* For a full discussion of every aspect of the Scrolls, see Shiffman and VanderKam, eds., *Encyclopedia of the Dead Sea Scrolls.*
3. For an introduction to the *Didache,* a translation, and an important bibliography, see Ehrman, *Apostolic Fathers,* vol. 1.
4. For a thorough and authoritative account of the early Christian manuscripts and their relationship to the "original" text, see Metzger, *The Text of the New Testament: Its Transmission, Corruption, and Restoration.* For an intriguing and readable discussion designed for those new to the field, see Parker, *The Living Text of the Gospels.*
5. This shows that it comes from a codex, i.e., what we think of as a regular book, with pages that are bound together, rather than a scroll.
6. Palaeographers can usually date a manuscript within about fifty years of its production. Greater accuracy generally is not possible, based on handwriting alone, since some scribes produced manuscripts over the course of a fifty-year professional life—writing in the same way at the end of their careers as at the beginning. On this manuscript in particular, see Metzger, *Text of the New Testament,* 38–39.
7. For a new translation of the text, see Ehrman, *Lost Scriptures,* 29–30.
8. Hedrick and Mirecki, *Gospel of the Savior.* A more accurate reconstruction of the text and a readable translation can be found in Stephen Emmel, "The Recently Published *Gospel of the Savior.*" This translation is followed in Ehrman, *Lost Scriptures,* 52–56.

9.   For an intriguing account by a principal player in the story, see Robinson's introduction to *The Nag Hammadi Library in English*. See also the entertaining and readable discussion of Dart and Riegert, *Unearthing the Lost Words of Jesus*, 1–35.

10. This information about the skeleton is not generally found in the published reports. I rely here on a private conversation that I had at the Scriptorium Conference, Hereford, England, with Bastiaan van Elderen (May 1998), who was the head of the archaeological team later responsible for exploring the site near Nag Hammadi.

11. The best and most authoritative translation, with brief introductions, is still Robinson, *Nag Hammadi Library in English*.

12. Among the many studies of these writings, probably the most popular and influential has been Pagels, *Gnostic Gospels*.

13. In this case, scholars had not realized that these isolated Greek fragments of the sayings of Jesus, discovered some fifty years earlier, had come from the Gospel of Thomas, until the entire text was uncovered near Nag Hammadi.

14. See the discussion and bibliography in Elliott, *Apocryphal New Testament*, 123–47, and the controversial but significant studies of Crossan, *Four Other Gospels*, 15–62, and Koester, *Ancient Christian Gospels*.

15. I am following the translation of Thomas Lambdin, found in Robinson, *Nag Hammadi Library in English*.

16. For a recent, forceful statement of this view, see Meier, *A Marginal Jew*, 1:130–39.

17. For a fuller explanation of the Synoptic Problem and the evidence for the existence of Q, see Ehrman, *New Testament*, 83–91.

18. See the bibliography and discussion of Fallon and Cameron, "The Gospel of Thomas: A Forschungsberichte and Analysis"; the essays in Uro, ed., *Thomas at the Crossroads;* Valantasis, *The Gospel of Thomas;* and most recently Pagels, *Beyond Belief.*

19. I should stress that the question is not whether meaning is to be imported into or taken out of this or any other text. Everyone, of course, wants to know what a text itself means, not just what an interpreter wants it to mean. But there are some assumptions about a particular text that can make better sense of it than others. And it is never simply a case of "letting the text speak for itself," a common plea of those who want to propose a new interpretation for a text. But as literary theorists have long known, texts don't speak. They are written and read. And they are written and read by people who have thoughts, opinions, perspectives, beliefs, worldviews, values, priorities, likes, dislikes—living, breathing people who have to make sense of the world, including all the texts in it, and can make sense of the world only in light of who they already are and what they already think. It is naive to maintain that we can interpret a text in a vacuum. And if you ever read anyone's attempt to interpret a

text simply by "letting it speak for itself," you'll see that not even wanting to do so can make it possible.

20. So much so that some recent scholars have argued that we should stop using the category "Gnosticism" altogether. See especially the impressive and influential study of Williams, *Rethinking Gnosticism: An Argument for Dismantling a Dubious Category*. Not everyone has been convinced, however, as there are a number of religious movements that are extremely diverse but that are usefully designated by means of an umbrella term: *Christianity*, for example! One of the best overviews of the various Gnostic religions from an older perspective is Rudolph, *Gnosis;* see also the insightful introduction and translations of Layton, *The Gnostic Scriptures*.

21. Consider the words of the first-century Jewish philosopher Philo: "For progress is indeed nothing else than the giving up of the female gender by changing into the male, since the female gender is material, passive, corporeal, and sense-perceptible, while the male is active, rational, incorporeal, and more akin to mind and thought" (*Questions in Exodus* 1.8). See also Martin, *The Corinthian Body*, 33.

Chapter 4

1. There were, of course, numerous newspaper accounts at the time; for an overview see Ian Haywood, *Faking It: Art and the Politics of Forgery*, 1–5. A fuller account can be found in Konrad Kujau's obituary in the *London Times*, September 14, 2000.

2. Such as "The Unknown Life of Jesus Christ," "The Aquarian Gospel," and "The Crucifixion of Jesus, by an Eyewitness," all summarized and discussed in Goodspeed's terrific little book, *Strange New Gospels*. See also the more recent discussions of Beskow, *Strange Tales about Jesus*.

3. See Metzger, "Literary Forgeries," 4.

4. For a full accounting of agrapha, see Stroker, *Extracanonical Sayings of Jesus*.

5. In addition to the work mentioned in note 3, see the fuller account in Metzger's autobiography, *Reminiscences of an Octogenarian*, 136–39.

6. The popular account: *The Secret Gospel: The Discovery and Interpretation of the Secret Gospel according to Mark;* the more learned volume: *Clement of Alexandria and a Secret Gospel of Mark*.

7. Published in the Journal of Biblical Literature Monograph Series, vol. 6 (Philadelphia: Society of Biblical Literature, 1951).

8. That is to say, a fifteenth-century copy of a play written by Sophocles (who lived in the fifth century BCE) was seen as no longer having any inherent value except as paper, and so it was used three hundred years later to strengthen the binding of another book. For modern scholars of

Sophocles, however, the scrap of this otherwise lost play is obviously of real importance.

9. Palaeographers—experts in ancient handwriting—are usually able to date handwriting to within about fifty years. Smith was not an expert in this field, but he had a rough idea concerning the dating of the hand.

10. Clement *Miscellanies* 3.1–2; Irenaeus *Against Heresies* 1.25; Hippolytus *Refutation* 7.20.

11. For a fuller and more scholarly discussion of these seventeenth-century debates, see Lightfoot, *The Apostolic Fathers: Clement, Ignatius, and Polycarp*, pt. 2, *Ignatius and Polycarp*, 1:237ff.

12. Voss's edition did not include Ignatius's letter to the Romans, which was first discovered and published in an uninterpolated Greek text two years later.

13. Smith, *Secret Gospel*, 61.

14. Most people I've met are confused by the passage or have heard a solution that makes so much sense that they're not interested in hearing any of the others.

15. John's text says that Jesus did baptize, but then corrects itself to say that Jesus himself did not actually do any baptizing. It may be that the earlier statement is the (historically) correct one, and the later "correction" is in fact incorrect.

16. Smith, *Secret Gospel*, 113 n. 12.

17. See for example, the review of Quentin Quesnell cited in note 19.

18. This view can be found in the sober analysis—somewhat unusual for this particular controversy—of Brown, "The Relation of 'The Secret Gospel of Mark' to the Fourth Gospel."

19. One of the few to take Smith on directly, not explicitly claiming that he forged the document, but unabashedly stating that the whole affair was highly suspicious, was Quentin Quesnell, "The Mar Saba Clementine: A Question of Evidence," *Catholic Biblical Quarterly* 37 (1975): 48–67. This led to a heated back and forth between the two, as presented in the next issue: *Catholic Biblical Quarterly* 38 (1976): 196–203. A similar approach, in which suspicions are raised but no explicit charge is made, can be found in Metzger, *Reminiscences*, 128–32 (where the *implicit* suggestion that Smith forged it is at least made: The account is found in a chapter that deals with modern "literary forgeries"). Among those who have argued that the letter is forged (without claiming that Smith himself did it) are Eric F. Osborn in "Clement of Alexandria: A Review of Research, 1958–1982," who thinks that it was done by a "pious forger," and A. H. Criddle, "On the Mar Saba Letter Attributed to Clement of Alexandria."

Among those who are now explicitly claiming that Smith forged the document are his own student, Jacob Neusner, with whom he had a famous falling out over another matter (*Are There Really Tannaitic Parallels to the Gospels? A Refutation of Morton Smith*, 27–31), who calls it "the forgery of the century" (28) and, most recently and stridently, Donald Harman Akenson (*Saint Saul: A Skeleton Key to the Historical Jesus*, 83–89), who sees the whole business—including Smith's two books—as nothing but a "nice ironic gay joke at the expense of all of the self-important scholars who not only miss the irony, but believe that this alleged piece of gospel comes to us in the first-known letter of the great Clement of Alexandria" (88). Akenson appears to be building his case on the circumstance that Smith was gay.

For an earlier assessment of scholarly reactions to his work, which were by and large accepting of it, see Morton Smith, "Clement of Alexandria and Secret Mark: The Score at the End of the First Decade," *Harvard Theological Review* 74 (1982): 449–61.

20. See Elliott, *Codex Sinaiticus and the Simonides Affair.*
21. One rather amusing instance was an "ancient" Greek manuscript forged by two seminary students in the 1930s who managed to fool one of the great experts on ancient Greek uncial manuscripts. See Metzger, *Reminiscences of an Octogenarian*, chap. 11.
22. This is the point made by Osborn, one of the leading authorities on Clement, in his article "Clement of Alexandria." He concludes, "There is nothing in Clement that could allow this to be a secret Gospel, or to be something that Clement might write. . . . Clement's style added to a failure to comprehend Clement's ideas implies a forgery" (224).
23. For example, *Miscellanies* 7.16.105, speaking to Christians: "We must never adulterate the truth."
24. Criddle, "On the Mar Saba Letter."
25. See, e.g., Quesnell, "The Mar Saba Clementine.
26. Quesnell, "The Mar Saba Clementine," 65.
27. Murgia, "Secret Mark: Real or Fake?"
28. He was called this because he turned his back on the strict ethical teachings of the Stoic school, which he had earlier embraced, and became a rather infamous profligate.
29. This account comes from a third-century set of biographies by Diogenes Laertius, *Lives of the Philosophers*, 5.92–93. See Grafton, *Forgers and Critics*, 3–4.

Part 2

1. This is true even though the fundamental nature of religion was the same everywhere, consisting of prayers and cultic acts of sacrifice to the gods. For overviews of religions in the Greco-Roman world, see Beard, North, and Price, *Religions of Rome;* Lane Fox, *Pagans and Christians;* and MacMullen, *Paganism in the Roman Empire.*

2. For example, because of his death and resurrection, as in Paul, or through his secret teachings, as in the Coptic Gospel of Thomas.

Chapter 5

1. For scholars who represent these various positions, see Ehrman, *Jesus: Apocalpytic Prophet,* 21–22 n. 1.
2. Even Acts is written from this perspective by one of Paul's own followers and so is usually recognized as not providing a historically accurate account of Peter's view. See further Ehrman, *New Testament,* 289–92.
3. Including Irenaeus, *Against Heresies* 1.26.2; 3.21.1; and 5.1.3; Tertullian, *Prescription* 33; Hippolytus, *Refutation* 7.34 and 9.13–17; Eusebius, *Church History* 3.27; and Epiphanius, *Panarion* 30. For a full summary and listing of all the discussions in the church fathers, see A. F. J. Klijn and G. J. Reinink, *Patristic Evidence,* 19–43.
4. Origen, *On First Principles* 4.3.8.
5. See references in note 3.
6. Irenaeus, *Against Heresies* 3.11.7.
7. See Klijn and Reinink, *Patristic Evidence,* 44–52. For the complications involved in deciding which Jewish-Christian groups used which Gospels, see Klijn, *Jewish-Christian Gospel Tradition,* 27–41.
8. Epiphanius *Panarion* 30. See Klijn and Reinink, *Patristic Evidence,* 154–96.
9. For a translation of these quotations, see Ehrman, *Lost Scriptures,* 12–14.
10. See, e.g., Irenaeus, *Against Heresies* 1.27.2–3, and Epiphanius, *Panarion* 42. Our principal source of information, however, is Tertullian's five-volume work, *Against Marcion,* which still survives intact. The classic, and in many ways still best, study of Marcion is Adolf von Harnack, *Marcion: The Gospel of the Alien God.* See also the influential older studies of Blackman, *Marcion and His Influence,* and Knox, *Marcion and the New Testament.* For a more recent appraisal, see Peter Lampe, *From Paul to Valentinus.*
11. See the works cited in note 10.
12. It is very hard to express ancient currency in modern terms, since valuations changed all the time then and still do now. There is at least one way to put this amount in perspective, however: For a member of the Roman upper-class aristocracy to become an "equestrian," which ranked right below a senator, a man needed to demonstrate that he was worth 400,000 sesterces. Marcion gave *away* half that amount upon entering the Roman church.
13. Most scholars today think that Paul did not write them, that they were forged at a later time, although probably before Marcion's day. See Ehrman, *New Testament,* 389–94.

14. This option would make sense, but Marcion never called this book "Luke" or showed any knowledge, so far as we can tell, that it was thought to have been written by Luke.

15. For references to Marcion's success, see R. Joseph Hoffman, *Marcion: On the Restitution of Christianity,* 33.

16. This was a common argument among the Christian "apologists," that is, the intellectual defenders of the faith starting at least with Justin, who was Marcion's proto-orthodox contemporary in Rome. For a full discussion, see Droge, *Homer or Moses?*

Chapter 6

1. For a selection of some of the most interesting of these documents from Nag Hammadi, see my companion volume, Ehrman, *Lost Scriptures.* Complete translations are available in Robinson, *Nag Hammadi Library in English.*

2. As I will emphasize throughout this chapter, it is important to realize that these documents are widely diverse among themselves. Even though they were presumably all used by a community who interpreted them in a Christian way, the texts were produced in a range of circumstances by authors of varying philosophical and theological persuasion. Some of these authors, for example, were not Christian in any sense. It is interesting to note that some of the non-Christian texts give evidence of having been "Christianized" by later editors. In any event, the books of this collection are no monolith. They represent a wide range of religious beliefs and practices Gnostic and otherwise.

3. Theodotus, according to Clement of Alexandria's *Excerpts from Theodotus,* 78.2.

4. See especially the trenchant study of Williams, *Rethinking "Gnosticism."*

5. Probably the best statement of a traditional view of the various Gnostic religions is Rudolph, *Gnosis.* A nice, succinct overview from the same author, with a basic bibliography, can be found in the *Anchor Bible Dictionary,* 2:1033–40. Among the more recent treatments, especially good for newcomers to the field, is Roukema, *Gnosis and Faith in Early Christianity.* A harder hitting, scholarly treatment, which calls into question the very term "Gnosticism," is Williams, *Rethinking "Gnosticism."* For shorter treatments, see the introductions in Layton, *Gnostic Scriptures,* and Robinson, *Nag Hammadi Library in English.* These volumes also provide expert and accessible translation of the principal texts.

6. For brief overviews, see Rudolph, *Gnosis,* 275–94 and Roukema, *Gnosis and Faith,* 55–101.

7. For a fascinating exploration of some of these materials, see Pagels, *Adam, Eve, and the Serpent.*

8. For a fuller overview of apocalypticism, see the articles and bibliographies by Paul Hanson et al., "Apocalypses and Apocalypticism," in *The Anchor Bible Dictionary* vol. 1, 279–92.

9. The historical events are recounted in the Old Testament Apocryphal books of 1 and 2 Maccabees.

10. For a statement of the importance of Middle Platonism for the development of Gnosticism, see Roukema, *Gnosis and Faith*, 75–92, and the more demanding but intriguing article by Luttikhuizen, "The Thought Pattern of Gnostic Mythologizers and Their Use of Biblical Traditions."

11. See Williams, *Rethinking "Gnosticism,"* who thinks, however, that we should simply discard the term altogether.

12. Translation by John D. Turner, in Robinson, *Nag Hammadi Library in English.*

13. Translation from Rudolph, *Gnosis,* 152–53.

14. Translation from Layton, *Gnostic Scriptures,* slightly modified.

15. All translations of the Gospel of Truth are those of Harold W. Attridge, in Robinson, *The Nag Hammadi Library in English,* reprinted in Ehrman, *Lost Scriptures,* 45–51.

16. See Layton, *Gnostic Scriptures,* 250–52.

17. Translations of Ptolemy's Letter to Flora are those of Bentley Layton, *Gnostic Scriptures,* reprinted in Ehrman, *Lost Scriptures,* 201–06.

18. Translations of the Treatise on the Resurrection are those of Harold W. Attridge, in Robinson, *Nag Hammadi Library in English,* reprinted in Ehrman, *Lost Scriptures,* 207–10.

Chapter 7

1. See the introduction and bibliography for the Letters of Ignatius in Ehrman, *Apostolic Fathers.*

2. See the interesting observations of Pagels, "The Passion of Christ and the Persecution of Christians," in *The Gnostic Gospels,* 70–101.

3. See the introduction and bibliography for the Martyrdom of Polycarp in Ehrman, *Apostolic Fathers.*

4. Unfortunately, Ussher suffered subsequent ignominy for being the one who determined that the earth was created in 4004 BCE, a date still held by some Christians and found in the margins of some versions of the King James Bible. For an interesting account of his chronology of the world, see Gould, *Questioning the Millennium,* chap. 1.

5. See note 1.

6. On the pseudonymous authorship of the pastoral Epistles, see Ehrman, *New Testament,* 389–94.

7. See the introduction and bibliography for the First Letter of Clement to the Corinthians in Ehrman, *Apostolic Fathers.*

8. I should emphasize that other groups had their own versions of the argument for apostolic succession. The Valentinian Gnostics, for example, maintained that their views came from Valentinus, the disciple of Theudas, who was the disciple of Paul the apostle; the Ebionite Christians maintained that their views were handed down to them by James, the brother of Jesus.

9. See 97–98.

10. So named because it was "discovered" in St. Catherine's monastery on Mount Sinai in the mid-nineteenth century by a famous biblical scholar named Constantine von Tischendorf, who claimed that he came away with it as a gift; to this day the monks there maintain that he absconded with it. For the intriguing story, see Metzger, *Text of the New Testament,* 42–46.

11. See the introduction and bibliography for the Epistle of Barnabas in Ehrman, *Apostolic Fathers.*

12. This was a point of some importance not so long ago, when we arrived at the year 2000. Fundamentalists who thought that the world was created around 4000 BCE (based on the calculations of James Ussher) thought that we were now at the End. Of course, Ussher had actually determined that the world was created in 4004 BCE, in fact, on October 23 at noon. And so, on these grounds, the world should have ended well before the reputed turn of the millennium, in fact, near the end of October in 1997.

13. As it turns out, there is no such command in Scripture, making one increasingly suspicious that there is more than a little of the voyeur in this whole business with Barnabas.

14. See the excellent translation of Gerald Hawthorne, reprinted in Ehrman, *After the New Testament,* 115–28.

15. See the introduction and bibliography for the *Shepherd* of Hermas in Ehrman, *Apostolic Fathers.*

16. The group's self-designations were the "New Prophecy" or just "The Prophecy." For a nice overview of Montanism, with bibliography, see Ronald Heine's article on "Montanus and Montanism" in the *Anchor Bible Dictionary,* 4:898–902.

17. Tertullian, "To His Wife." For a translation, see Ehrman, *After the New Testament,* 399–404.

18. On the importance of Montanism for the development of the canon of Scripture, see especially the erudite and now classic study of Hans von Campenhausen, *The Formation of the Christian Bible.*

19. See Pagels, *Gnostic Gospels,* chap. 4.

20. For instance, an anonymous author quoted at length by Eusebius *Church History* 5.28; see also Epiphanius *Panarion* 54.

21. See Tertullian's characteristically witty essay, *Against Praxeas,* and Hippolytus's polemical tractate, *Against Noetus.*

22. There is a massive literature on Origen. The best introductions are probably Crouzel, *Origen,* and Trigg, *Origen: The Bible and Philosophy in the Third-Century Church.*

23. For a full study of the later controversies surrounding Origen's teachings, see Clark, *The Origenist Controversy.*

24. For important texts and overviews of these debates, see Norris, *The Christological Controversy,* and Rusch, *The Trinitarian Controversy.*

25. Later in the early fourth century, the theologian Arius's views on this issue came to be debated at the Council of Nicaea. The Council ended up favoring the view that Christ was of the same "substance" as the Father, and that he had always existed, rather than being a secondarily created, yet divine, being.

Part 3

1. For an excellent overview of the history, theology, and practices of the Pharisees, see Sanders, *Judaism: Practice and Belief,* 380–451.

2. For a fuller discussion of the background to Galatians, see Ehrman, *New Testament,* 332–37.

Chapter 8

1. This form of the Nicene Creed is from the 1979 (Episcopal) Book of Common Prayer.

2. For useful studies, see Grant, *Eusebius as Church Historian,* Chesnut, *The First Christian Historians,* and the essays in Attridge and Hata, *Eusebius, Judaism, and Christianity.*

3. This is comparable to Tertullian's claim that "the blood of the Christians is seed." See Tertullian, *Apology* 50.

4. For the author of Acts, Philip was not one of the original twelve apostles. See Acts 6:1–6.

5. See Grant, *Greek Apologists of the Second Century,* 46–48.

6. See Irenaeus, *Against Heresies* 1,23.

7. Quotations from Eusebius are those of Williamson, *Eusebius.*

8. As in the Jerusalem Conference, called to determine whether Gentiles need to become Jews in order to be Christians. See Acts 15:1–29.

9. For an overview of Reimarus's life and thought, see Talbert's introduction to *Reimarus: Fragments.*

10. English translation by Ralph Fraser, in *Reimarus: Fragments.*

11. But for a peculiar book that sensationalizes a similar view, see Schonfield, *The Passover Plot.*

12. See *Quest of the Historical Jesus,* chap. 2.

13. For further discussion, see Ehrman, *Jesus,* 21–40.

14. For an overview of Baur's life and thought, see Peter Hodgson, *The Formation of Historical Theology.*

15. These two, along with 1 and 2 Corinthians, were the only books that Baur accepted as authentically Pauline; the other nine were all later forgeries.

16. For further discussion of the reliability of Acts, see Ehrman, *New Testament,* 289–92.

17. Already, prominently, in Edward Gibbon's 1776–88 classic, *The Decline and Fall of the Roman Empire.* See, e.g., his discussion of Eusebius's gullible acceptance of Constantine's version of his victory over Maxentius, effected by the words "By This Conquer" placed on his standards because of a dream, an account that Gibbon calls "the Christian fable of Eusebius" (vol. 2, chap. 20).

18. For some of the earlier reactions to Bauer, see appendix 2 in the English translation, "The Reception of the Book," written by Georg Strecker and revised and updated by Robert Kraft. Additional bibliography can be found in Ehrman, *The Orthodox Corruption of Scripture,* chap. 1.

19. See, e.g., the supplementary essay by George Strecker (trans. Robert Kraft), "The Reception of the Book," in the English translations of *Orthodoxy and Heresy,* 286–316. In addition, see Harrington, "The Reception of Walter Bauer's *Orthodoxy and Heresy in Earliest Christianity* during the Last Decade."

20. As an example: Why did neither Ignatius nor Polycarp write a letter to the Christians of Thessalonica? Bauer's answer: Because the Thessalonians must have been Gnostics! But how can we know they never sent letters there?

21. It can be pointed out, for example, that neither Paul's letter written to Rome nor the letter of 1 Clement written from Rome explicitly deals with heresy. And the *Shepherd* of Hermas, also written from Rome, but in the middle of the second century, is focused not on a proto-orthodox theology but on ethical concerns involving those who lapse into sin after being baptized. Moreover, there does not seem to be a proto-orthodox hierarchy in Rome until later: Ignatius pushes for the monepiscopacy, but in his letter to the Romans he does not assume that they have a single bishop. Neither does 1 Clement or Hermas.

    Still, in Bauer's defense, "correct" (proto-orthodox) theology *does* become important in Roman circles in the mid-second century: Marcion, for example, was excommunicated from the church around 144 CE, as were the Theodotians a few decades later. And Hippolytus set himself up as an antipope precisely because the bishop Callistus held to a patripassianist Christology.

22. See, e.g., the learned and compelling essays of Drijvers, *East of Antioch.*

23. For further discussion, see Ehrman, *New Testament,* 350–52.

24. In this they were not alone. The Marcionites also used this strategy, but, evidently, much less effectively.

Chapter 9

1. This does happen on occasion. Cf. Origen's *Dialogue with Heraclides,* a public debate that was recorded for posterity, available in English translation in Daly, *Treatise on the Passover.*
2. These texts were important for F. C. Baur and the Tübingen School he founded, in showing a primitive stage of Jewish Christianity.
3. For an introduction and readable translation, see Johannes Irmscher and Georg Strecker, "The Pseudo-Clementines," in Schneemelcher, *New Testament Apocrypha,* 2:483–541; for some of the important extracts, see Ehrman, *Lost Scriptures,* 191–200.
4. See 165–67.
5. Translations are those of Irmscher and Strecker, "Pseudo-Clementines." For the full translation of the letter from Peter to James, see Ehrman, *Lost Scriptures,* 191–94.
6. I should emphasize here, once again, that Gnosticism itself was a widely diverse phenomenon; when I speak of "Gnostic" views in this chapter, I am again referring to that kind of Gnostic thought and belief that I sketched in chapter 3, without assuming that these particular thoughts and beliefs were those of all Gnostic groups.
7. Translations of the Coptic Apocalypse of Peter are those of Birger Pearson, in *Nag Hammadi Codex VII.* See Ehrman, *Lost Scriptures,* 78–81.
8. Translations of The Second Treatise of the Great Seth are those of Birger Pearson, in *Nag Hammadi Codex VII.* See Ehrman, *Lost Scriptures,* 82–86.
9. I am following the old, but still usable, translation of Irenaeus, *Against Heresies,* in the reprinted vol. 1 of *The Ante-Nicene Fathers,* ed. Roberts and Donaldson.
10. This is an interesting point and has proved compelling to many readers. All the same, one wonders how it might be turned against the proto-orthodox themselves, who also had a wide range of opinions on numerous topics. Or better yet, if Ebionite Christians were to consider all Marcionites, Gnostics, and proto-orthodox together and declare that none of them could be right because they all disagreed with one another, where might that leave us? The translation of Tertullian's works comes from the reprinted vol. 3 of *The Ante-Nicene Fathers,* ed. Roberts and Donaldson.
11. As I have suggested, once these myths are understood as metaphorical descriptions of the world and our place in it, this kind of objection may seem irrelevant. It is a bit like objecting to the truth claims of the morn-

ing paper when it indicates that "sunrise" is at 6:36 A.M., since any reasonably intelligent person knows that the sun never rises at all, or like claiming that "Jabberwocky" can't be an English poem because *brillig* isn't an English word.

12. See 165–67.
13. See 67–89.
14. See Wisse, "The Epistle of Jude in the History of Heresiology," 133–43.
15. A good translation of the *Panarion* is in Frank Williams, *The Panarion of Epiphanius of Salamis.*
16. Books that he mentions by name include "Noria," "The Gospel of Perfection," "The Gospel of Eve," "The Greater Questions of Mary," "The Lesser Questions of Mary," the "Books of Seth," the "Gospel of Philip," and the "Birth of Mary."

Chapter 10

1. See the now-classic study of William Harris, *Ancient Literacy.* On literacy in Jewish circles during our period, see Catherine Hezser, *Jewish Literacy in Roman Palestine,* who argues that Jewish literacy, at least in the Jewish homeland, was—contrary to what one might think—actually lower than in Greco-Roman society at large.
2. For a full discussions of literacy, uses of literature, the nature of available libraries, and related issues in early Christianity, see Gamble, *Books and Readers in Early Christianity.*
3. Much of the following has been borrowed from my discussion of the Infancy Gospels in Ehrman, *New Testament,* 207–08.
4. For a new translation of the Infancy Gospel of Thomas, see Ehrman, *Lost Scriptures,* 57–62.
5. Translation by Elliott, *Apocryphal New Testament;* reprinted in Ehrman, *Lost Scriptures,* 160–64.
6. See, most recently, Cartlidge and Elliott, *Art and the Christian Apocrypha,* chap. 2.
7. For a new translation of the Proto-Gospel of James, see Ehrman, *Lost Scriptures,* 63–72.
8. The traditional depiction of Joseph as an old man at the time of their betrothal can be traced back to this account.
9. See Elliott, *Apocryphal New Testament,* 48–52.
10. For a translation of 3 Corinthians, see Ehrman, *Lost Scriptures,* 157–59.
11. For more on the situation in Corinth and Paul's response, see Ehrman, *New Testament,* 317–27.
12. See the discussion of Martin, *The Corinthian Body.*
13. Translation of Elliott, *Apocryphal New Testament.*

14. Translations of the Acts of Peter are those of Elliott, *Apocryphal New Testament*. For a translation of important excerpts of the Acts of Peter, see Ehrman, *Lost Scriptures*, 135–54.

15. Translation of William Schneemelcher, in Hennecke and Schneemelcher, *New Testament Apocrypha*, tr. R. M. Wilson, vol. 2, modified slightly.

16. The translation is that of Elliott, *Apocryphal New Testament*. See Ehrman, *Lost Scriptures*, 165–66.

17. For a translation, see Bruce Metzger, in Ehrman, *Lost Scriptures*, 331–33.

18. For a full study of the phenomenon, see Ehrman, *Orthodox Corruption of Scripture*.

19. For a somewhat fuller statement, see Ehrman, *New Testament*, chap. 29. For an interesting book-length treatment, focused on the Gospels, see Parker, *Living Text;* for a full and authoritative account, see Metzger, *Text of the New Testament*.

20. It appears that all the changes I will mention here go back to the second and third centuries. For fuller documentation and numerous other examples, see Ehrman, *Orthodox Corruption of Scripture*.

21. There are some passages that come close to this (e.g., John 8:58, 10:30, 14:9)—which is one of the reasons the proto-orthodox liked these passages—but none of them makes an explicit equation of Jesus as God.

Chapter 11

1. An accessible discussion of the formation of the Christian canon can be found in Gamble, *The New Testament Canon*. A full, authoritative account is provided by Metzger, *The Canon of the New Testament*.

2. As already noted, Paul's letters were produced before the New Testament Gospels, which date from 65–70 CE (Mark) to 90–95 CE (John).

3. Translation from Metzger, *Canon*, 212.

4. He became blind at the age of four, but developed an uncanny memory and passion for Scripture, much of which he memorized.

5. See Metzger, *Canon*, 213–14.

6. The twenty-seven book canon *was* occasionally sanctioned at this or that synod or council meeting. But such church councils were understood to be local affairs, and their proceedings were not binding on the whole church. The first synod to ratify Athanasius's canon was in Hippo Regius, North Africa, in 393 CE. See Ehrman, *Lost Scriptures*, 341–42.

7. The twenty-two books of the Hebrew Bible are the same as the thirty-nine books of the Christian Old Testament, but they are numbered and ordered differently. The twelve "minor prophets" in most English translations, for example, form one book, "The Twelve," in the Hebrew Bible. On the formation of the Hebrew Bible canon, see Sanders, "Canon."

8. It should be noted that Jesus and the Pharisees agreed the sabbath was to be honored; the difference involved *how* it was to be honored.

9. Except, of course, those like the Marcionites, who denied the Old Testament any authority at all.

10. Scholars have long noted that Christians preferred to use codexes for their books (i.e., sheets written on both sides, sewn together, like our books today) rather than scrolls. Before Christianity, virtually all literary texts were written on scrolls. Is it possible that Christians began using the codex form in order to differentiate their sacred texts from the sacred writings of the Jews, revered precisely as scrolls? On codexes and scrolls, see Gamble, *Books and Readers*, 42–66.

11. See Ehrman, *New Testament*, 58–59.

12. Two of them were disciples: James the son of Alphaeus and James the son of Zebedee.

13. See Ehrman, *New Testament*, 287–89.

14. For fuller discussions of these authors, see Metzger, *Canon*, chap. 3.

15. For the dating of these works and related issues, see my two-volume edition of the *Apostolic Fathers*.

16. One might be tempted to attribute the lack of references to authoritative texts in the *Shepherd* to the circumstance that it is an apocalypse, that is, a revelation given directly from God to a prophet. Why quote Scripture when the vision itself is authoritative? There is some truth to this counterclaim, but it should also be noted that other apocalyptic texts do make extensive allusions to scriptural texts. The book of Revelation, for example, even though it does not directly quote the Old Testament, alludes to it extensively; and the Apocalypse of Peter shows the clear influence of earlier Christian texts, such as the Gospels. Given the inordinate length of the *Shepherd* and the numerous occasions Hermas had to quote Scripture (e.g., when giving the "commandments"), it may seem peculiar that he never does so.

17. Translation of T. Lambdin in Robinson, *Nag Hammadi Library in English.*

18. See 14–16.

19. See 24–27 and 210–12.

20. See the discussion in Metzger, *Canon*, 143–48.

21. A Gospel harmony of this sort *was* created by Justin's student from Syria, Tatian. It was called the Diatesseron, meaning "through the four," because it was made by combining and interweaving the accounts of the four Gospels that were eventually canonized into one long narrative. The Diatesseron was *the* Gospel used in Syria for several centuries (rather than the "separate" Gospels of Matthew, Mark, Luke, and John). Whether Tatian's teacher, Justin, also produced or used a Gospel harmony has been a matter of intense debate among scholars.

22. There is one passage that sounds like a quotation from John ("Christ also said, 'Unless you are born again you will not enter into the kingdom of heaven,'" 1 Apol. 61:4), but Justin does not attribute it to a written Gospel.

23. They are also separated by thirty years of other heretical movements, including the growth of various Gnostic religions. But since these did not appear to stress the importance of a closed canon, they may not have been as influential on Irenaeus's views that there were four and only four Gospels.

24. See Pagels, *Gnostic Paul.*

25. See also MacDonald, *The Legend and the Apostle.*

26. See the discussion in Metzger, *Canon,* 191–201.

27. The fullest presentation of this position is by Hahneman, *The Muratorian Fragment and the Development of the Canon.* The difficulties that it poses are convincingly shown by several scholars who have written reviews of his work, especially Ferguson, Holmes, and Metzger.

28. Translation by Metzger, *Canon,* 305.

29. It is one of the Deutero-Canonical books of the Old Testament in Roman Catholic and Eastern Orthodox traditions.

30. It should be noted that Hebrews is not accepted in the Muratorian canon, whereas the Apocalypse is. This is one of the indications that this list came from the West, as traditionally thought, not from the East.

31. Eusebius is famously confusing, or confused, in the way he delineates the categories of (potentially) sacred books in this discussion. See Metzger, *Canon,* 201–07.

32. Translation in Metzger, *Canon,* 310.

33. Translation in Metzger, *Canon,* 315.

Chapter 12

1. Numerous scholarly treatments are available. For one that is introductory but detailed and authoritative, see Frend, *The Rise of Christianity,* chaps. 13 and 14, along with the bibliography he cites. On persecutions in particular, see Frend's classic study, *Martyrdom and Persecution in the Early Church,* and Lane Fox, *Pagans and Christians,* 419–92. For studies of the "Christianization" of the Roman Empire, see Lane Fox, *Pagans and Christians;* MacMullen, *Christianizing the Roman Empire;* and Rodney Stark, *The Rise of Christianity.*

2. Scholars have long debated whether Constantine fully converted to Christianity, as he continued to show devotion to pagan deities and did not receive baptism until his death bed. For our purposes, the semantics of conversion do not matter as much as Constantine's commitment to bestowing favors on the Christian church and to seeking its internal unity.

3. The exception was Constantine's nephew, Julian "the apostate," emperor from 361 to 363 CE, who was raised Christian but later embraced paganism and unsuccessfully attempted to enforce it on his subjects.

4. For an overview of these debates, the various positions proposed, and a nice translation of the primary texts, see Norris, *The Christological Controversy;* for the related debates over the nature of the Trinity, see Rusch, *The Trinitarian Controversy.*

5. For useful overviews of pagan "religiosity," see Lane Fox, *Pagans and Christians,* and MacMullen, *Paganism in the Roman Empire.*

6. It is also worth noting that Jews for the most part were not "monotheists" in the way we might think of today, insisting that since their views of God were right, everyone else needed to accept their views and worship their God, or else be "wrong" and pay the consequences. Jews were not for the most part interested in converting others to their religion. It was *their* religion, for *them,* the Jews; other people had other religions. The Jewish God was the only God to be worshiped *by Jews.*

7. A compelling argument can be made that this virtually unheard of religious intolerance played a significant role in the missionary success of Christianity. Unlike other religions, when people accepted this one, they were compelled to give up their previous religious practices. As a result, Christianity destroyed competing religions as it built up its own. See MacMullen, *Christianizing the Roman Empire.*

Bibliography

Akenson, Donald Harman. *Saint Saul: A Skeleton Key to the Historical Jesus.* New York: Oxford University Press, 2000.

Attridge, Harold, and Gohei Hata, eds. *Eusebius, Judaism, and Christianity.* Detroit: Wayne State University Press, 1992.

Bauer, Walter. *Orthodoxy and Heresy in Earliest Christianity.* English translation eds. Robert A. Kraft and Gerhard Krodel. Philadelphia: Fortress, 1971; German original, 1934.

Beard, Mary, John North, and Simon Price. *Religions of Rome.* Cambridge: Cambridge University Press, 1998.

Beskow, Per. *Strange Tales about Jesus: A Survey of Unfamiliar Gospels.* Philadelphia: Fortress, 1983. Rev. translation of *Fynd och fusk i Bibelns värld: om vår tids Jesus-Apokryfer.* Stockholm: Proprius, 1979.

Blackman, E. C. *Marcion and His Influence.* London: SPCK, 1948.

Brown, Raymond E. "The Relation of 'The Secret Gospel of Mark' to the Fourth Gospel." *Catholic Bible Quarterly* 36 (1974): 466–85.

Burrus, Virginia. *Chastity as Autonomy: Women in the Stories of the Apocryphal Acts.* Lewiston, N.Y.: E. Mellen Press, 1978.

Campenhausen, Hans von. *The Formation of the Christian Bible.* Translated by J. A. Baker. Philadelphia: Fortress, 1972; German original, 1968.

Cartlidge, David R., and J. Keith Elliott. *Art and Christian Apocrypha.* London: Routledge, 2001.

Chesnut, Glenn. *The First Christian Historians: Eusebius, Socrates, Sozomen, Theodoret, and Evagrius.* 2d ed. Macon, Ga.: Mercer University Press, 1986.

Clark, Elizabeth A. *The Origenist Controversy: The Cultural Construction of an Early Christian Debate.* Princeton: Princeton University Press, 1992.

———. *Reading Renunciation: Asceticism and Scripture in Early Christianity.* Princeton: Princeton University Press, 1999.

Criddle, A. H. "On the Mar Saba Letter Attributed to Clement of Alexandria." *Journal of Early Christian Studies* 3 (1995): 215–20.

Crossan, John Dominic. *Four Other Gospels: Shadows on the Contours of Canon.* Minneapolis: Winston Press, 1985.

Crouzel, Henri. *Origen.* Translated by A. S. Worrall. San Francisco: Harper and Row, 1989. French original, 1985.

Daly, Robert J. *Treatise on the Passover; and, Dialogue of Origen with Heraclides and His Fellow Bishops on the Father, the Son, and the Soul.* New York: Paulist, 1992.

Dart, John, and Ray Riegert. *Unearthing the Lost Words of Jesus: The Discovery and Text of the Gospel of Thomas.* Berkeley, Calif.: Seastone, 1998.

Davies, Stevan L. *The Revolt of the Widows: The Social World of the Apocryphal Acts.* Carbondale: Southern Illinois University Press, 1980.

Davis, Stephen J. *The Cult of Saint Thecla: A Tradition of Women's Piety in Late Antiquity.* New York: Oxford University Press, 2001.

Drijvers, Han. *East of Antioch: Studies in Early Syriac Christianity.* London: Variorum Reprints, 1984.

Droge, Arthur J. *Homer or Moses? Early Christian Interpretations of the History of Culture.* Tübingen: Mohr, 1989.

Ehrman, Bart D. *After the New Testament: A Reader in Early Christianity.* New York: Oxford University Press, 1999.

———. *The Apostolic Fathers.* 2 vols. Loeb Classical Library. Cambridge: Harvard University Press, 2003.

———. *Jesus: Apocalyptic Prophet of the New Millennium.* New York: Oxford University Press, 2000.

———. *Lost Scriptures: Books That Did Not Make It into the New Testament.* New York: Oxford, 2003.

———. *The New Testament: A Historical Introduction to the Early Christian Writings.* 3d ed. New York: Oxford University Press, 2004.

———. *The Orthodox Corruption of Scripture: The Effect of Early Christological Controversies on the Text of the New Testament.* New York: Oxford University Press, 1993.

Elliott, J. K. *The Apocryphal New Testament.* Oxford: Clarendon Press, 1993.

———. *Codex Sinaiticus and the Simonides Affair: An Examination of the Nineteenth-Century Claim That Codex Sinaiticus Was Not an Ancient Manuscript.* Analekta Vlatadon, 33. Thessalonike: Patriarchikon Idryma Paterikon Meleton, 1982.

Emmel, Stephen. "The Recently Published *Gospel of the Savior*" ("Unbekanntes Berliner Evangelium"): Righting the Order of Pages and Events." *Harvard Theological Review* 95 (2002): 45–72.

Fallon, T., and R. Cameron. "The Gospel of Thomas: A *Forschungsberichte* and Analysis." In *Aufstieg und Niedergang der römischen Welt.* Principat 2.25.6. Berlin: de Gruyter, 1988, 4195–4251.

Falls, Thomas B. *Saint Justin Martyr.* Washington, D. C.: Catholic University of America Press, 1948.

Farrer, James Anson. *Literary Forgeries.* London: Longmans, Green, 1907.

Fee, Gordon D. *The First Epistle to the Corinthians.* New International Commentary on the New Testament. Grand Rapids: Eerdmans, 1987.

Ferguson, Everett. Review of Geoffrey Mark Hahneman, *The Muratorian Fragment and the Development of the Canon. Journal of Theological Studies* 44 (1993): 691–97.

Fitzmyer, Joseph A. *Responses to 101 Questions on the Dead Sea Scrolls.* New York: Paulist, 1992.

Frend, W.H.C. *Martyrdom and Persecution in the Early Church: A Study of a Conflict from the Maccabees to Donatus.* Oxford: Blackwell, 1965.

————. *The Rise of Christianity.* Philadelphia: Fortress, 1984.

Gamble, Harry. *Books and Readers in Early Christianity: A History of Early Christian Texts.* New Haven: Yale University Press, 1995.

————. *The New Testament Canon: Its Making and Meaning.* Philadelphia: Fortress, 1985.

Goodspeed, Edgar J. *Strange New Gospels.* Chicago: University of Chicago Press, 1931.

Gould, Stephen Jay. *Questioning the Millennium: A Rationalist's Guide to a Precisely Arbitrary Countdown.* New York: Harmony Books, 1997.

Grafton, Anthony. *Forgers and Critics: Creativity and Duplicity in Western Scholarship.* Princeton: Princeton University Press, 1990.

Grant, Robert M. *Eusebius as Church Historian.* Oxford: Clarendon, 1980.

————. *Greek Apologists of the Second Century.* Philadelphia: Westminster, 1988.

Hahneman, Geoffrey Mark. *The Muratorian Fragment and the Development of the Canon.* Oxford: Clarendon Press, 1992.

Hanson, Paul, A. Kirk Grayson, John Collins, and Adela Yarbro Collins. "Apocalypses and Apocalypticism." In *Anchor Bible Dictionary,* ed. David Noel Freedman, 1:279–92. New York: Doubleday, 1992.

Harnack, Adolf von. *Marcion: The Gospel of the Alien God.* Translated by John E. Steely and Lyle D. Bierma. Durham, N.C.: Labyrinth Press, 1990 (2d ed. of the 1924 German original, only partially given in this English translation).

Harrington, Daniel. "The Reception of Walter Bauer's *Orthodoxy and Heresy in Earliest Christianity* during the Last Decade." *Harvard Theological Review* 73 (1980): 289–98.

Harris, William V. *Ancient Literacy.* Cambridge: Harvard University Press, 1989.

Haywood, Ian. *Faking It: Art and the Politics of Forgery.* New York: St. Martin's Press, 1987.

Hedrick, Charles W., and Paul Mirecki. *Gospel of the Savior: A New Ancient Gospel.* California Classical Library. Santa Rosa, Calif.: Polebridge Press, 1999.

Heine, Ronald. "Montanus and Montanism." In *Anchor Bible Dictionary*, ed. David Noel Freedman, 4:898–902. New York: Doubleday, 1992.

Hezser, Catherine. *Jewish Literacy in Roman Palestine*. Texts and Studies in Ancient Judaism, 81. Tübingen: Mohr Siebeck, 2001.

Hodgson, Peter. *The Formation of Historical Theology: A Study of Ferdinand Christian Baur.* New York: Harper and Row, 1966.

Hoffman, R. Joseph. *Marcion: On the Restitution of Christianity*. Chico, Calif.: Scholars Press, 1984.

Holmes, Michael W. Review of Geoffrey Mark Hahneman, *The Muratorian Fragment and the Development of the Canon*. *Catholic Bible Quarterly* 56 (1994): 594–95.

Irmscher, Johannes, and Georg Strecker. "The Pseudo-Clementines." In *New Testament Apocrypha*, ed. W. Schneemelcher, 2:483–541. Philadelphia: Westminster Press, 1991.

Klijn, A.F.J. *Jewish-Christian Gospel Tradition*. Supplements to Vigiliae Christianae, 17. Leiden: Brill, 1992.

Klijn, A.F.J., and G. J. Reinink. *Patristic Evidence for Jewish-Christian Sects*. Supplements to Novum Testamentum, 36. Leiden: Brill, 1973.

Knox, John. *Marcion and the New Testament*. Chicago: University of Chicago Press, 1942.

Koester, Helmut. *Ancient Christian Gospels: Their History and Development*. Philadelphia and London: Trinity Press International and SCM Press, 1990.

Kraemer, Ross. *Her Share of the Blessings: Women's Religions among Pagans, Jews, and Christians in the Greco-Roman World*. New York: Oxford University Press, 1992.

Laertius, Diogenes. *Lives of Eminent Philosophers*. 2 vols. Loeb Classical Library. Translated by R. D. Hicks. Cambridge: Harvard University Press, 1925.

Lampe, Peter. *From Paul to Valentinus: Christians at Rome in the First Two Centuries*. Philadelphia: Fortress, 2003. German original, 1987.

Lane Fox, Robin. *Pagans and Christians*. New York: Knopf, 1987.

Layton, Bentley. *The Gnostic Scriptures*. New York: Doubleday, 1987.

Lightfoot, J. B. *The Apostolic Fathers*. 5 vols. London: Macmillan, 1885–90. Reprinted Peabody, Mass.: Hendrickson, 1989.

Luttikuizen, Gerard P. "The Thought Pattern of Gnostic Mythologizers and Their Use of Biblical Traditions." In *The Nag Hammadi Library after Fifty Years: Proceedings of the 1995 Society of Biblical Literature Commemoration*, ed. John D. Turner and Anne McGuire, 89–101. Nag Hammadi and Manichaean Studies, 44. Leiden: Brill, 1997.

MacDonald, Dennis R. *The Legend and the Apostle: The Battle for Paul in Story and Canon*. Philadelphia: Westminster, 1983.

MacMullen, Ramsay. *Christianizing the Roman Empire, A.D. 100–400*. New Haven: Yale University Press, 1984.

———. *Paganism in the Roman Empire*. New Haven: Yale University Press, 1981.

Magness, Jodi. *The Archaeology of Qumran and the Dead Sea Scrolls.* Grand
    Rapids: Eerdmans, 2003.
Martin, Dale B. *The Corinthian Body.* New Haven: Yale University Press, 1995.
Meier, John P. *A Marginal Jew: Rethinking the Historical Jesus.* Vol. 1. New
    York: Doubleday, 1991.
Metzger, Bruce M. *The Canon of the New Testament: Its Origin, Development,
    and Significance.* Oxford: Clarendon, 1987.
———. "Literary Forgeries and Canonical Pseudepigrapha." *Journal of Bibli-
    cal Literature* 91 (1972): 3–24.
———. *Reminiscences of an Octogenarian.* Peabody, Mass.: Hendrickson,
    1997.
———. Review of Geoffrey Mark Hahneman, *The Muratorian Fragment and
    the Development of the Canon. Critical Review of Books in Religion* 7 (1994):
    192–94.
———. *The Text of the New Testament: Its Transmission, Corruption, and
    Restoration.* 3d ed. New York: Oxford University Press, 1992.
Mirecki, Paul. "Gospel of Peter." In *Anchor Bible Dictionary,* ed. David Noel
    Freedman, 4:278–81. New York: Doubleday, 1992.
Murgia, Charles. "Secret Mark: Real or Fake?" In *Longer Mark: Forgery, In-
    terpolation, or Old Tradition,* ed. Reginald Fuller, 35–40. Berkeley, Calif.:
    Center for Hermeneutical Studies, 1976.
Neusner, Jacob. *Are There Really Tannaitic Parallels to the Gospels? A Refu-
    tation of Morton Smith.* Atlanta: Scholars Press, 1993.
Norris, Richard A. *The Christological Controversy.* Philadelphia: Fortress, 1980.
Origen. *Homilies on Luke: Fragments on Luke.* Fathers of the Church, 94.
    Translated by Joseph T. Lienhard. Washington, D.C.: Catholic University
    of America Press, 1996.
Osborn, Eric F. "Clement of Alexandria: A Review of Research, 1958–1982."
    Second Century 3 (1983): 223–25.
Pagels, Elaine. *Adam, Eve, and the Serpent.* New York: Random House, 1988.
———. *Beyond Belief: The Secret Gospel of Thomas.* New York: Random
    House, 2003.
———. *The Gnostic Gospels.* New York: Random House, 1979.
———. *The Gnostic Paul: Gnostic Exegesis of the Pauline Letters.* Philadel-
    phia: Fortress, 1975.
Parker, David C. *The Living Text of the Gospels.* Cambridge: Cambridge Uni-
    versity Press, 1997.
Pearson, Birger, ed. and trans. *Nag Hammadi Codex VII.* Nag Hammadi Stud-
    ies, 30. Leiden: Brill, 1996.
Plautus, "Amphitryon," in *Plautus: The Comedies,* ed. David R. Slavitt and
    Palmer Bavie. Baltimore: Johns Hopkins Press, 1995.
Quesnell, Quentin. "Mar Saba Clementine: A Question of Evidence." *Catholic
    Biblical Quarterly* 37 (1975): 48-67.
———. "Reply to Morton Smith." *Catholic Biblical Quarterly* 38 (1976): 200–
    203.

Reardon, B. P., ed. *Collected Ancient Greek Novels.* Berkeley: University of California Press, 1989.

Roberts, Alexander, and James Donaldson, eds. *The Ante-Nicene Fathers.* 10 vols. Grand Rapids: Eerdmans, 1987.

Robinson, James M., ed. *The Nag Hammadi Library in English.* 4th rev. ed. Leiden: Brill, 1996.

Roukema, Riemer. *Gnosis and Faith in Early Christianity: An Introduction to Gnosticism.* Harrisburg, Pa.: Trinity Press International, 1999. Dutch original, 1998.

Rudolph, Kurt. *Gnosis: The Nature and History of Gnosticism.* Translated by Robert McLachlan Wilson. San Francisco: Harper and Row, 1987. German original, 1977.

———. "Gnosticism." In *Anchor Bible Dictionary,* ed. David Noel Freedman, 2:1033–40. New York: Doubleday, 1992.

Rusch, William. *The Trinitarian Controversy.* Philadelphia: Fortress, 1980.

Sanders, E. P. *Judaism: Practice and Belief, 63 BCE–66 CE.* Philadelphia: Trinity Press International, 1992.

Sanders, James. "Canon." In *Anchor Bible Dictionary,* ed. David Noel Freedman, 1:837–52. New York: Doubleday, 1992.

Schlarb, Egbert, and Dieter Lührmann. *Fragmente apokryph gewordener Evangelien in griechischer und lateinischer Sprache.* Marburger theologische Studien, 59. Marburg: N. G. Elwert, 2000.

Schneemelcher, Wilhelm. *New Testament Apocrypha.* 2 vols. Edited by R. McL. Wilson. Philadelphia: Westminster Press, 1991.

Schonfield, Hugh J. *The Passover Plot: New Light on the History of Jesus.* London: Hutchinson, 1965.

Schweitzer, Albert. *The Quest of the Historical Jesus.* Translated by W. Montgomery, J. R. Coates, Susan Cupitt, and John Bowden. Minneapolis: Fortress, 2001. German original, 1906.

Shiffman, Lawrence, and James C. VanderKam, eds. *Encyclopedia of the Dead Sea Scrolls.* New York: Oxford University Press, 2000.

Smith, Morton. *Clement of Alexandria and a Secret Gospel of Mark.* Cambridge: Harvard University Press, 1973.

———. "Clement of Alexandria and Secret Mark: The Score at the End of the First Decade." *Harvard Theological Review* 74 (1982): 449–61.

———. *Jesus the Magician.* San Francisco: Harper and Row, 1978.

———. "On the Authenticity of the Mar Saba Letter of Clement: Reply to Q. Quesnell." *Catholic Biblical Quarterly* 38 (1976): 196–200.

———. *The Secret Gospel: The Discovery and Interpretation of the Secret Gospel according to Mark.* New York: Harper and Row, 1973.

———. *Tannaitic Parallels to the Gospels.* Journal of Biblical Literature Monograph Series, 6. Philadelphia: Society of Biblical Literature, 1951.

Speyer, Wolfgang. *Die literarische Fälschung im heidnischen und christlichen Altertum. Ein Versuch ihrer Deutung.* Handbuch der Altertumswissenschaft, 1. München: Beck, 1971.

Stählin, Otto. *Clemens Alexandrinus.* 4 vols. Leipzig: J. C. Hinrichs, 1905–36.

Stark, Rodney. *The Rise of Christianity: A Sociologist Reconsiders History.* Princeton: Princeton University Press, 1996.

Stroker, William D. *Extracanonical Sayings of Jesus.* Atlanta: Scholars Press, 1989.

Talbert, Charles H., ed. *Reimarus: Fragments.* Philadelphia: Fortress, 1970.

Torjesen, Karen Jo. *When Women Were Priests: Women's Leadership in the Early Church and the Scandal of Their Subordination in the Rise of Christianity.* San Francisco: HarperCollins, 1993.

Trigg, Joseph W. *Origen: The Bible and Philosophy in the Third-Century Church.* Atlanta: John Knox Press, 1983.

Uro, Risto, ed. *Thomas at the Crossroads: Essays on the Gospel of Thomas.* Edinburgh: T & T Clark, 1998.

Valantasis, Richard. *The Gospel of Thomas.* New York: Routledge, 1997.

VanderKam, James C. *The Dead Sea Scrolls Today.* Grand Rapids: Eerdmans, 1994.

Williams, Frank. *The Panarion of Epiphanius of Salamis.* Leiden: Brill, 1987.

Williams, Michael A. *Rethinking Gnosticism: An Argument for Dismantling a Dubious Category.* Princeton: Princeton University Press, 1996.

Williamson, G. A. *Eusebius: The History of the Church from Christ to Constantine.* Rev. ed. by Andrew Louth. London: Penguin, 1989.

Wisse, Frederik. "The Epistle of Jude in the History of Heresiology." In *Essays on the Nag Hammadi Texts in Honour of Alexander Böhlig,* ed. Martin Krause, 133–43. Nag Hammadi Studies, 3. Leiden: Brill, 1972.

Index

Abraham, 147
Acts, apocryphal, 3, 36, 39, 41, 44, 46, 212
Acts of the Apostles, 42, 165, 167–68, 170–72, 183–84, 246
Adoptionists, 15, 101, 153–54, 194–95, 216, 221–23
Agraphon, 69
Alexandrians, epistle to the, 241–42
Ambrose, 240
Anaximenes, 31
Andrew, Acts of, 244
Anti-Judaism, 18, 20–22, 111, 117, 145–48
Anti-Semitism. *See* Anti-Judaism
Apocalypse, as genre, 26
Apocalypse, of John. *See* Revelation of John
Apocalypticism, 44–46, 117–20
Apocrypha, Christian. *See* Pseudepigrapha
Apostles' Creed, 194
Apostolic constitutions, 10
Apostolic succession: Ebionite view of, 271n.8; Proto-orthodox view of, 142–143, 192–93; Valentinian view of, 193, 235, 271n.8
Aristotle, 30, 112, 134
Arius, 272n.25
Asceticism, 44–46, 126, 201, 212. *See also* Sexual Renunciation

Athanasius, 54, 230–31, 245, 276n.6
Augustine, 245

Baptism, 32, 35, 37, 48, 80–81, 102, 126, 149, 194, 211
Barnabas, epistle of, 3, 6, 87, 145–49, 231, 238, 244–45
Basilides, 188, 192–93, 242; gospel of, 13, 28
Baur, F. C., 170–72
Bauer, Walter, 172–79, 273n.21

Canon: definition of, 259n.1; New Testament, 4–6, 11, 54, 107, 180, 227, 229–46, 276n.6; Old Testament, 232, 276n.7
Carpocratians, 72–73, 85–86, 198
Carthage, Third Synod of, 246
Christianity, varieties of ancient, 2–5, 91–94, 135–36, 172–73, 176–79, 251–53
Circumcision, 96–98, 100, 103, 135, 144–45, 147, 160–61, 251. *See also* Law, Jewish
Clark, Elizabeth, 83
Clement (bishop of Rome), 182, 193. *See also* First Clement
Clement, (Armenian) Book of, 231
Clement, First, 141–42, 174–75, 182, 193, 238

289